HISPANIC CHRISTIAN THOUGHT AT THE DAWN OF THE 21ST CENTURY

D1411831

HISPANIC CHRISTIAN THOUGHT

AT THE DAWN OF THE 21ST CENTURY

APUNTES IN HONOR OF
Justo L. González

EDITED BY

ALVIN PADILLA

ROBERTO GOIZUETA

ELDIN VILLAFAÑE

Abingdon Press
Nashville

HISPANIC CHRISTIAN THOUGHT AT THE DAWN OF THE 21ST CENTURY
APUNTES IN HONOR OF JUSTO L. GONZÁLEZ

Copyright © 2005 by Abingdon Press

All rights reserved.
No part of this work may be reproduced or transmitted in any form or by any means, electronic or mechanical, including photocopying and recording, or by any information storage or retrieval system, except as may be expressly permitted by the 1976 Copyright Act or in writing from the publisher. Requests for permission can be addressed to Abingdon Press, P.O. Box 801, 201 Eighth Avenue South, Nashville, TN 37202-0801, or e-mailed to permissions@abingdonpress.com.

This book is printed on acid-free paper.

Library of Congress Cataloging-in-Publication Data

Hispanic Christian thought at the dawn of the 21st century : apuntes in honor of Justo L. Gonzalez / edited by Alvin Padilla, Roberto Goizueta, Eldin Villafañe.
    p. cm.
    Includes bibliographical references.
    ISBN 0-687-09813-0 (binding: pbk.: alk. paper)
    1. Hispanic American theology.   I. Gonzalez, Justo L.   II. Padilla, Alvin.
III. Goizueta, Roberto S.   IV. Villafañe, Eldin, 1940–

BT83.575.H56 2005
230.089'68073—dc22

2005026450

All scripture quotations unless noted otherwise are taken from the *New Revised Standard Version of the Bible*, copyright 1989, Division of Christian Education of the National Council of the Churches of Christ in the United States of America. Used by permission. All rights reserved.

Orlando Espín, "The State of U.S. Latino/a Theology: An Understanding," published in *Perspectivas*, Fall, 2000.

Daisy Machado, "Latino Church History: A Haunting Memory," published in *Perspectivas*, Fall 1998.

Fernando F. Segovia, "Toward a Hermeneutics of the Diaspora." Reprinted by permission from *Reading from This Place* Vol. 1 by Fernando F. Segovia and Mary Ann Tolbert, copyright © 1995 Augsburg Fortress.

Roberto S. Goizueta, "Beyond the Frontier Myth," from *The Church as Counterculture*, edited by Michael Budde and Robert Brimlow. Copyright © 2000 by SUNY Press. Used by permission.

Excerpts from *Santa Biblia* by Justo González © 1996 by Abingdon Press. Used by permission.

Excerpts from *Mañana* by Justo González © 1990 by Abingdon Press. Used by permission.

"Hispanic Creed" from *Mil Voces para Celebrar* © 1996 by Abingdon Press. Used by permission.

The Graeca® fonts used to print this work are available from Linguist's Software, Inc., PO Box 580, Edmonds, WA 98020-0580 tel (206) 775-1130.

Luis N. Rivera-Pagán, "Justo Luis González: Scholar, Man of His Community, Friend," *Apuntes* 20, no. 1 (Spring 2000): 29-35. Reprinted with permission of *Apuntes: Reflexiones teologicas desde el contexto Hispano-Latino*. For subscription information, contact the Mexican American Program, Perkins School of Theology, Dallas, Texas.

Eldin Villafañe, "Spirit without Borders," *Apuntes* 22, no. 4 (Winter 2002): 124-39. Reprinted with permission of *Apuntes: Reflexiones teologicas desde el contexto Hispano-Latino*. For subscription information, contact the Mexican American Program, Perkins School of Theology, Dallas, Texas.

Excerpts from Mark G. Brett, *Genesis: Procreation and the Politics of Identity*, copyright © 2000 by Routledge Press.

05 06 07 08 09 10 11 12 13 14—10 9 8 7 6 5 4 3 2 1

MANUFACTURED IN THE UNITED STATES OF AMERICA

For Justo Luis González

on the occasion of his sixty-seventh birthday,

presented by his colleagues

in Hispanic theological education

CONTENTS

Contents

PREFACE

This *Festschrift* intends to honor our esteemed colleague Justo Luis González by examining the state of Latina/o Christian thought as this marginalized community continues its numerical growth and expanding influence in the North American cultural landscape. It is our aim to approach Latina/o Christian thought by way of the four primary sources of Christian theology, the so-called formula of authority advocated by John Wesley and the Methodist tradition, the quadrilateral of Scripture, tradition, reason, and experience. This paradigm serves as the prism by which the authors address their particular discipline.

By employing the phrase *Christian thought* we are intentionally expanding the boundaries of rational discourse about God (i.e., theology proper) to include the various academic, ministerial, and ecumenical interests that Justo has so expertly championed over the years. However, the breadth and depth of his many soundings might impose a sense of disjointedness on our collection of essays. In other words, we are in need of a unifying thesis for our collection, otherwise readers might be led to believe that the unifying theme of the book is simply that all the writers share a common Latin American background.

In order to avoid a disjointed collection of diverse academic essays on various topics of interest to Justo and academia, it is our aim, first of all, to approach Christian thought from the sociohistorical location and theological tradition of Latina/o Christianity. Second, this "ideological" perspective will be informed and guided by the so-called basic sources of Christian theology: Scripture, tradition, experience, and reason. This quadrilateral of authority will serve as the undergirding criterion of validity on our particular essays.

The individuals selected to contribute to this collection have more than just academic expertise and reputations to bring to the table. They all share the experience of being an oppressed ethnic-minority Christian. Each has devoted his or her life to ministry in this sociohistorical reality and have—each in his or her unique way—suffered for it. "Theologizing" from this reality, we are convinced, is rewarded by insights and perspectives not easily available to our brothers and sisters from the dominant culture. Examples of this, and we have dozens from which to choose, are Justo's own *Mañana* and *Santa Biblia*. However, while engaging in this "ideological" reading of the discipline/theme, the contributors go beyond the understanding and significance for Latina/o people onto a global perspective. It is our conviction that the insights gained by our theologizing as Hispanics are of tremendous benefit to our church and society as a whole. Reading *Santa Biblia*, to continue with one of Justo's own contributions, from a Hispanic American perspective not only blesses us as Latina/o Christians but also challenges and blesses our brothers and sisters from all other sociohistorical traditions.

The contributors will filter the focus of Latina/o Christian thought to this quadrilateral in a way that dominant Western traditions may not have had in mind. If these widely accepted criteria are to be pertinent to our sociohistorical reality, we need to engage them in a new global perspective that will push us beyond the boundaries imagined by its originators. These criteria will offer us guidelines that demonstrate to us when we are most likely within the ballpark and when we are wandering among the maze of our own imaginations. Let us look briefly at each criterion.

Of these, the primary source is, of course, *Scripture*, the Hebrew and Christian documents that together make up the Bible. In Scripture we find the faithful record of God's saving deeds in ancient Israel and the early Christian community. It testifies to God's self-disclosure as witnessed to and interpreted by the people of God through its multiple documents. As moderns, we read these Scriptures and feel the need to interpret; we are unable simply to turn to any book at will and read directly God's thoughts. This hermeneutical process is, as all are aware, a rather complex one that divides the Christian world into various theological camps. As Latina/o Christians we need to engage Scripture from our own socioreligious perspective and ask ourselves which things in Scripture function in our own context in such a way that they point toward the dismantling of evil, toward the life of reconciliation, forgiveness, justice, and peace for which we struggle daily. Socioscientific and postcolonial criticisms are but two recent examples wherein our Latina/o heritage greatly enhances our ability to interpret Scripture. Reading Scripture from the margins and looking at it through the paradigmatic quadrilateral will, we trust, enable us to offer a new reading that will effectively meet the challenges of the new millennium.

Tradition is the process through which the Christian community transmits its legacy of faith to a new generation. For most people tradition promotes only conservatism—harking us back to the church fathers, the Reformation, the Enlightenment, and so on—seemingly benefiting only the current status quo. This view assumes a pristine purity of the past that often neglects the sociohistorical realities of the originators of the revered tradition.

Tradition has to be more than just a process of transmission and preservation of the church's faith. We must also see tradition as the process that reformulates and reconstructs the church's mission. From this perspective tradition is not static but dynamic, becoming part of the life and thought of many peoples. Through the prism of tradition we filter what we receive and seek new insights concerning God's mighty acts in history. These new insights must not, however, contradict the explicit teaching of Scripture. Instead, they clarify, expand, and deepen the explicit teaching of Scripture.

Had we been there when the tradition originated, and had we at our disposal the knowledge, options, and sensibilities of that age, with whom would and should we have sided? This is the question that should be kept at the forefront of our thoughts as we review tradition. This question should tamper our assurance that our own Latina/o perspective should not, necessarily, be right just because it is new. Emphasis will be given to reading anew from the Christian past and present those symbols of resistance, survival, and hope—the subversive and liberating memory that has informed Latina/o Christian experience and promises to contribute to the vitality of the church universal.

Reason is both a source for theological inquiry and a means by which we process the content of our theologizing. That is, since the claims of faith and of conviction have to make sense across numerous boundaries (confessional, cultural, sexual, racial, linguistic, and ideological), reason is the tool by which we process our particular views and present them as "universal." If we grant that culture shapes the articulation of theology ("theologizing"), can we still assert that the truths we believe are absolute or objective in any significant sense? If truth can be known, and we the contributors to this volume would answer in the affirmative, then there must be some mechanism to explain why everyone does not agree with the "truth." The philosophical principles (themselves assumptions) of realism and bias serve us in providing an answer. "Right" reason ought to be cognizant of both the realism principle and the bias principle. The abandonment of either one of these principles invites distortion. "Right" reason will enable us to assess the validity of our Latin Christian thought without denying our particular bias(es). "Right" reason makes theological discourse possible and enables us to speak of theological matters in ways that are coherent, consistent, and compelling to the multicultural (multibiased?) dimensions of our society. As we communicate our particular Christian thought, are we free from our cultural bias? How are we to reasonably convince others of the legitimacy of our views?

Experience/culture is the learning process that occurs through direct contact with persons, things, and thoughts. It is knowledge gained through praxis (action/reflection). Christian experience is the process by which each of us encounters God in Christ. We assimilate that encounter into our being with the resulting life journey and begin the exploration into the meaning and implications of that encounter for ourselves and our culture. For our purposes it is understood to be the peculiar manner that we as Latina/o Christians enter into contact with the faith and interpret and incorporate it into our own history and culture. The experiences of oppression, injustice, and hate shared by many of us are touchstones of authority as we develop Christian thought for the larger Christian community. However, the experience of creativity, and construction and the overcoming of the negative experience are vitally important for the Christian church to incorporate into its theologizing.

We have asked the contributors to write on a theme within the categories of Christian thought and within the parameters outlined above. The themes will address, first and foremost, Latina/o understanding/knowledge of the discipline as it contributes to the broader understanding of the discipline and to the church universal (i.e., global perspective). The collection comprises four distinct sections integrating the theological disciplines with Hispanic American reality as follows.

In part 1, "Scripture and Marginalization," the essayists have been asked to present a reading of the biblical text that incorporates into its interpretative methodology the experience of alienation and marginalization that is our socio-historical reality.

The chapters in "Subversive and Liberating Memories" constitute part 2. Here the authors have been asked to offer readings of church history/tradition that have given expression to the subversive and liberating reality of Christians throughout the ages and how those memories "liberate" Latinas/os and others from contemporary oppressive experiences.

Part 3 consists of "Liberating Truth" wherein the authors have been asked to offer fresh perspective on theological truth, incorporating the distinctive Latina/o sources, loci, and expressions.

Finally in part 4, "Liberating Praxis," the authors have been asked to reflect on current Latina/o religious experience (i.e., religiosity, church life, and ministry) and to reflect on the way this experience is changing or will change the landscape of Western Christianity in the twenty-first century.

Alvin Padilla
Roberto Goizueta
Eldin Villafañe

JUSTO LUIS GONZÁLEZ: SCHOLAR, MAN OF HIS COMMUNITY, FRIEND

Luis N. Rivera-Pagán

> *I desire to press in my arms the loveliness which has not yet come into the world.*
>
> James Joyce[1]

When David Maldonado called me several months ago to inquire whether I would be willing to participate in a ceremony honoring Justo Luis González, I immediately answered affirmatively. It is both a pleasure and a privilege to be invited to say at least some of the many good things one could assert about a person I have known, admired, and loved for already thirty-eight years.

But when I received Maldonado's letter clarifying the character of the event, I became concerned. I discovered a distinction between what our good friend, the Roman Catholic Mexican American theologian Virgilio Elizondo, was supposed to do and what I had been requested to do. I was to speak about the person of Justo, and Virgilio was to speak about his work; a classic scholastic distinction between *vita* and *operae*, between the inner essence of Justo and its external manifestations, between Justo's *ousia* and his *personae*, in the classical Greek theatrical sense.

Now, think about it: in our post-Platonic worldview, for which *being* is composed of a process of acts, how can one speak meaningfully about a person, a *vita*, without entering into the realm of his or her works, his or her *operae*? It is an arbitrary distinction, impossible to respect, if, at least, I want to assert something significant about Justo, apart, certainly, from saying that he is tall, well-built, and handsome, especially now that the graying of his hair gives him an additional appearance of academic aristocratic elegance. In our postmodern environment, in which the classic Cartesian notion of a substantive subject has been exiled to the atavistic quarters of Dante's inferno, how can I even try to say

1

something worthwhile about the subject, the ego, of Justo, if I have to abstain from mentioning his actions, his work?

In theology, Karl Rahner's principle has the day: there is such a coherence and correspondence between the divine immanent and economic trinity that it is inadequate, from the human perspective, to talk about God's being without proceeding from God's acts in history. To distinguish therefore between the person of Justo and his work is thus quite a philosophical and theological bewildering quandary.

I must confess that this dilemma, this aporia, worried me deeply until I realized that the real problem, for two reasons, is Virgilio's, not mine. One: since I was to speak first, I felt free to infringe and violate Maldonado's distinction and let Virgilio face the fact that he might be forced to allude to some of the things that I have already mentioned. As my good friends, I have never felt much guilt or contrition for transgressing social norms or rules. There is a second reason for transferring my concern to Virgilio, the mention of which I will postpone for now in this essay.

Here, I will limit myself to mention briefly three of Justo González's many qualities.

First, Justo González is a scholar of first order. He got his PhD from Yale University, in historical theology, when he was not yet twenty-four years old. He has written or edited tens of books (my bibliography indicates sixty-seven, it might not be complete, and he is still going on) some of which are used as textbooks in theological seminaries and institutions in many parts of the world. Truly a book-of-the-month club just by himself! Written in Spanish or English, many of them have been translated into Portuguese, German, or Korean, and are in the process of being translated into Chinese. Just to pick an arbitrary date, in 1997, five books by him were published, not including his edition of the works of John Wesley in Spanish.

His *History of Christian Thought*—in Spanish, English, and Korean—has served for many years as both an enticing introduction and a constant source of reference in the Christian theological traditions for thousands of students all over the world. The first edition of the first volume of that book was published in Spanish in 1965. In my personal library, that work belongs to a special category. With the first volume of Jaroslav Pelikan's *Christian Tradition,* a nice bound translation of Aristotle's *Politics,* and several others, it constitutes a distinguished never-to-be-forgotten-or-forgiven section; namely, it is one of those books that should be there, but is not. It is one of those books that I know I have not lent, and yet I do not have. Which means that its absence is due to the self-serving generosity of some good friends who seem to consider that this is what friends are for, to borrow books without asking for them and even less giving them back. As you all know, there are friends and friends. Because many of these so-called friends are, unfortunately, Protestants, they do not seem to be intimidated by a sign I have in my library that threatens with perpetual excommunication, *sub excomunicationis late sententiae pena,* as the traditional anathema formula used to read, anybody that dares to do what these theologically minded friends of mine have done: steal books from my library. So Justo's 1965 *Historia del pensamiento cristiano* belongs to the section entitled *libri absconditi,* in analogy to Pascal's *Deus absconditus.* There have been certainly, I know, further editions of it; but, you see, I considered that specific volume as a kind of *incunabulum;* I had been one of the first not only to acquire and read it but also to witness its process of creation as a student in Justo's courses in history of Christian theology between 1963 and 1965 at the Evangelical Seminary of Puerto Rico.

This might be the proper occasion to spell out the second reason it is Virgilio and not I who should be deeply concerned about the tenuous distinction that the organizers of the act made between Justo's *vita, ousia,* and his *operae, personae.* Permit me to relay to you a brief interchange between Justo and Virgilio at the aforementioned honoring ceremony. Justo asked Virgilio, "Hey, have you read my last book?" The answer came back immediately: "I hope I did Justo, I sure hope I have read your last book." Only after most cordially accepting Maldonado's request to say a few words about Justo's *operae,* as always in a splendid way, did Virgilio realize that for the next five months he would be doing nothing else but reading Justo Luis González. Which, as I assure you, and Virgilio certainly will affirm, can be very instructive. But I have also the certainty that Virgilio is by now ready for another, less prolific author.

Second, Justo Luis González is a man of his community. Scholars can be lonely and solitary. Not Justo. Many of his intellectual works have been conceived as contributions for the enrichment of a community—the Hispanic/Latina/o community. Most of his books do not only reveal his immense erudition and scholarship but also manifest his vision and passion for the development of a Hispanic/Latina/o community that might be able to intertwine profound religious commitment with solid academic excellence. Many of his writings are tools for the betterment of his community; they are meant to be part of an intellectual process to reconstruct the memory, the grammar, and the culture of Christian faith from the perspective of the Hispanic/Latina/o diasporic community. His book *Mañana: Christian Theology from a Hispanic Perspective,* published in 1990, is one of the foundational texts in the construction and development of a theology with a Hispanic twist (or better: with a Latin rhythm, a Hispanic salsa) in North America.

People in diaspora, or in exile, as González has been for most of his life, are often driven by a desire to forge an imagined new community for oneself and others in the same predicament. That urge might lead to frustration and desperation; it might also, as in the case of González, lead to a life of transnational solidarity. When homecoming is out of the question, danger of paralysis always lurks behind the charms of nostalgia. Indeed, but there is also the promise to recreate a new homeland, the *patria* of faith and reason in the diaspora.

As a creative member of his community, Justo has been able to gather the resources of many men and women of faith and intellect, many of whom are contributors to this volume, in order to imagine first and forge then structures and institutions that might construct a network of solidarity. Let me briefly mention four of them: *Apuntes*, "notations" or "marginal notes," a journal that he founded and has edited for almost two decades as a vehicle for intellectual discourse and dialogue regarding Hispanic/Latina/o religiosity; the Association for the Hispanic Theological Education, which he founded at the beginning of the 1990s and has chaired for several years; the Hispanic Theological Initiative,which was begun only a few years ago with Justo as its first executive director, is the product of Justo's inspiration; and finally the Hispanic Summer Program, which each summer brings together Hispanic students and scholars in the theological fields and whose immensely fruitful existence during the past decade we celebrate today.

Third and finally, Justo is a friend, a friend who knows that above and beyond the academic quest for knowledge, the search for *aletheia*, for *veritas*, there is love, in all its manifold expressions: *éros, filía,* and *ágape*. For, as Paul writes to the Corinthians, there are many virtues, but "the greatest of these is love" (1 Corinthians 13:13).

Do not get excited, by the way, at the mention of *éros*. In Justo's case, at least, the love that I want to underline is the spiritual affection that shapes and forges true friendship. Justo is a friend in all the manifold nuances of that highly charged word. This I can say as a privileged witness, for if I chose historical theology as my academic field, if I went to Yale to do my doctoral studies, and if I am here at Princeton Theological Seminary as a professor, a lot of that has to do with the friendship and mentoring that I have received and enjoyed during the last four decades from Justo Luis González. And I know that I am only one in a "cloud of witnesses."

I can mention many expressions of Justo's friendship, but let me limit myself to two that have been of value for many here present. I do not know whether you have perused the millennium edition of the *Guinness Book of World Records*. It includes several new entries, categories, and names. I examined it this week and, eureka!, there I found Justo González honored as the holder of two world records. First, as the main worldwide author of prefaces, forewords, introductions, and commendations of books written by Hispanic/Latina/o friends and colleagues. There it is, you can check it, in page 364 of the 2000 Guinness edition. Many Hispanic colleagues in theological education have had Justo as a kind of intellectual godfather and have shared a portion of his generosity by means of such a baptism: a preface, a foreword, a commendation of some writing, some text, that we have been developing for several years and that we present to the critical academic community with fear and trembling, but with Justo's benediction. That benediction might serve as a kind of exorcist formula, as a *vade retro, Satanas*, against possible demonic criticisms. And second, as the writer of letters of references on behalf and benefit of many Hispanic/Latina/o students and colleagues applying for divinity schools, graduate schools, and theological seminaries. There it you can check it, in page 478 of the 2000 Guinness edition. I myself have benefited from both these two expressions of Justo's friendship and solidarity. Sometime by the end of 1965 Justo wrote a letter of reference to Yale University, and I was admitted to its PhD program. In 1992, he wrote the preface to the English translation of *Evangelización y violencia: La conquista de América*. And that book has sold well.

The second dimension of Justo's friendship that I want to stress is his humor. There are jokes that demean and degrade. There are jokes that blemish human dignity. We all know the many subspecies of that category: ethnic jokes, sexist jokes, linguistic tricks that transform a human being into an object of laughter. There are malicious ways of ridiculing human flaws and disabilities. And then, there is also a type of witty, enlightening, light humor that overcomes hostility and creates smiling bridges of human understanding and compassion. Justo could write an encyclopedia of jokes that could be included in this second uplifting category. All of Justo's friends must now confess that we are thieves; for years we have been repeating here and there jokes that we first heard from Justo. I am the first to confess *mea culpa, mea culpa*. Even in this article, by the way, I have repeated and plagiarized one of his witty jokes.

We can be certain that Justo shares the many turmoils of the soul that haunt our nights, when in solitude and stillness we face our frailty and mortality. In that moment of anxiety and anguish, which we all know, there is also what Milan Kundera once referred to as the laughter of God that refreshes and renews human existence and delivers our existence from its nightmarish specters. Allow me this theological heterodox statement: Justo's humor is an expression of God's laughter.

The grace of Justo González might be the clue for one of his most important assets: his bewildering and bewitching ability to be a human vehicle of communion and collaboration between people so diverse in theological ideas, religious experiences, and national identities, as we in this group are. In this community there are Catholics, like Virgilio Elizondo, Roberto Goizueta, Otto Maduro, Ada María Isasi-Díaz, and many others; there are Pentecostals, like Samuel Soliván, Eldin Villafañe, and Lucy Rivera de Alvarado; and there is a legion of many different mainline Protestants, like Edwin Aponte, Luis Pedraja, and David Maldonado. And there are the North Americans, Anglos, and African Americans who have accepted Justo's call to widen their horizon and ours by allowing their cultural identities creatively to face ours. The most creative and extraordinary Anglo near Justo González is his wife, Catherine, the person most responsible for the fact that Justo looks today amazingly more handsome than when I met him first in 1961.

All of us are of different "colores, olores y sabores," but are, I am sure, unanimous in one statement about Justo: he is our friend. In this case it is not a cliché, not a worn-out word. I must confess, however, that I almost ruined my friendship with Justo some years ago, in 1995 to be exact. I had written a collection of essays to be printed in book form in Quito, Ecuador, by the Latin American Council of Churches (CLAI) under the title *Los sueños del ciervo* (The Dreams of the Deer). It began with a dedication of the work to George Pixley and Justo González. In the preface I alluded to both of them as my dear former teachers and now friends. The person in CLAI's office in charge of converting the files from Microsoft Word to PageMaker and proofreading them had just read in a newsletter that Justo González had recently passed away; he thus took the liberty to make a slight but significant change in my preface making clear the recent death of Justo González. The guy did not know that there were two Justo Gonzálezes—Justo and Justo's father, who was the one who had recently died. In my first reading of the galley proofs I did not notice that change, and only some minutes before giving the green light to print the book did the confusion come to my attention. I almost achieved two original things at the same time: dedicate a book to Justo and prematurely announce his death.

I had the privilege of meeting and getting acquainted with three human beings who were extremely significant in Justo's life and who, I am sure, are deeply inscribed in his memory: Justo's father, don Justo, his mother, doña Luisa, and his brother, Jorge. It was a family that was able to harmonize nature and grace, a home environment that made possible the intertwining of intellectual enhancement and profound religiosity, the happy union of faith and wisdom, of *fides* and *ratio*.

The loss of a dear one, of a person near to one's heart and mind, is always a painful event, but it is a sorrow that is part and parcel of human existence; it is an unavoidable dimension of this vale of tears that we have inherited as our universal human and historical context. Allow me, in this celebration of Justo as God's gift to us, to briefly bring to our memory Jorge, a brother and a friend whose presence is among us, in spirit, in the remembrance and the love of a brother, a widow, Ondina, a niece, Juana Luisa, and a sister-in-law, Catherine. On Tuesday, April 9, 2000, Justo sent the following e-mail to many of us:

> Friends:
> My brother Jorge, who was not only my only brother, but also my best friend, passed away rather unexpectedly last night. I cannot tell you how I feel. Please forgive this general notice, rather than personal calls or contacts. Catherine and I crave your prayers, and are counting on your love and support. Thanks.
> Justo

Several hours before that general message, Lizzie Oquendo had called me and reported the sad news. It had only been a few weeks since I had the shattering experience of watching, in deep sorrow and loneliness, my mother's death. All of us here who have gone through the *via crucis* of utter solitude while a most dear person dies know that we will always carry, deep in our souls, a severe scar that will never totally heal. The good news, however, is that we develop a special sensibility toward other people's similar experiences. Thus, some hours before Justo's announcement, I e-mailed him the following message:

Justo:

Lamento profundamente la muerte de Jorge. Aunque no hay nada más inevitable que la finitud y mortalidad, cuando nos toca de cerca en la persona de alguien que amamos y con quien nuestra vida se ha ligado por mucho tiempo, nos duele intensamente.

Lo lindo es poder recordar a esa persona fallecida, cercana al alma propia, como un ser amable, cordial, inteligente, laborioso y noble, que por mucho tiempo compartió nuestra aventura de vida y fe. Puedes disfrutar de ese recuerdo y celebrar la vida compartida de tu hermano. Nunca olvidaré lo mucho que él disfrutaba de tus ocurrencias y de tu gracia. Dale por favor mis condolencias a su familia.

Un abrazo de amigo y hermano,

Luis

In many instances, Isabel Allende's terse and tragic dictum, included in her exquisite book *The Stories of Eva Luna,* might be true—"sometimes death is more powerful than love"—but not in the case and the person of Jorge González.[2] In our stubborn and rebel memory, the love of and for Jorge González overcomes even the apparent finality of death.

In the name of all your friends and colleagues, I express to you Justo, Ondina, Catherine, and Juana Luisa—the family of Jorge González—our deepest solidarity and our profound understanding of the sorrow that is still there, at the skin's level. You can be proud of Jorge, for he was a wonderful human being, an excellent teacher, a graceful friend, and a magnificent brother and husband. He was also a man of God. We miss him. A lot.

Don Justo, doña Luisa, Jorge. The first to depart from this earthly dimension of existence was doña Luisa, then don Justo, and finally, Jorge. They all can rest in peace for many reasons, one of which is their contribution to the formation of Justo as the extraordinary human being, splendid Christian, and excellent scholar he is. Wherever and whenever there is fertile ground, prime seed, and substantial spiritual nourishment, we might expect a wonderful tree. Many of us here have been able to rest and refresh ourselves in the shadows of Justo's magnificent tree.

Thanks Justo, for your excellent scholarly production, for offering your time and immense talents to our community, and for being the friend you have been, you are, and you will continue to be. You have enriched our existence as individual human beings, as a historical community, and as a people of God.

May God bless you now and always!

I

SCRIPTURE AND MARGINALIZATION

MARGINALITY AND SOLIDARITY IN 1 CORINTHIANS

Efrain Agosto

Justo González has taught us that biblical hermeneutics through Hispanic eyes includes the paradigms of marginality, poverty, *mestizaje* and *mulatez*, exile and alienness, and solidarity.[1] This essay, written in his honor and with appreciation for his contributions to theological education and scholarship, will use several of these motifs, in particular marginality and solidarity, to analyze the Apostle Paul's First Letter to the Corinthians, particularly 1 Corinthians 1–4, from the perspective of the marginalized. The marginalized in Corinth become models for the solidarity Paul seeks for this community.

First Corinthians 1–4 has traditionally been understood as the place in this letter where Paul addresses the issue of division in the Corinthian church community. However, community conflict permeates the entire letter. In 1 Corinthians 1–4, Paul sets the tone for addressing subsequent issues. Early in the section, Paul notes the vital presence of marginalized persons in the community (1:26) and ends the section with a word of warning to those in power (1 Cor 4:18-21). In between, Paul seeks solidarity in this divided community by identifying his ministry with the socially powerless of the church.

A WORD ABOUT THE GONZÁLEZ PARADIGMS

Before applying the paradigms of solidarity and marginality to 1 Corinthians 1–4, I will briefly define all the González paradigms. By marginality, González posits that those on the margins of society can often see things in the biblical text that those in power, or at the center of a society, cannot. For example, in the Gospels and Acts we read stories about Jesus, the Apostles, and those who opposed them, oftentimes referred to in the text as "the Jews." Those who stand outside the center of power today can understand how such references do not somehow indict a whole race, but rather really refer to the problems people on the margins of a society (Jesus and the peasant population he served; the earliest Christians) often face with those who hold power, such as the Jewish and

Roman leadership in Jerusalem.[2] Similarly, the Apostle Paul in 1 Corinthians wants to alert the powerful social elite in the Corinthian church that those whom their society in Corinth normally marginalized can in fact exercise some measure of leadership within their own community of faith.

With regard to poverty, González emphasizes that a Latina/o reading of the Bible, given the economic status of so many Hispanics in the United States, is not just about what the Bible says about the poor, but more about what the poor have to say about the Bible. Because recent studies in biblical hermeneutics agree that "what one finds in the Bible depends to a large degree on one's perspective from which one reads the Bible," then the question is, "what does the Bible say when read from the perspective of the poor?" Put another way: "what do the poor find in the Bible that the nonpoor easily miss?"[3] Ultimately, it is not just a question of helping the poor by telling them what the Bible says about them, but realizing that the reading of the Bible by the poor can contribute to the whole church.

Similarly, Paul acknowledges that division in the Corinthian church community may be due in part to class and economic division between rich and poor. Economic division is also a form of marginalization.

González also explores *mestizaje* and *mulatez*. These key terms in Latina/o theology refer to the status of many Hispanic groups as mixed races. For example, Mexicans and Mexican Americans are considered *mestizos* because of their miscegenation with native peoples and the conquering Spaniards, and later with the North American populations of the United States.[4] In addition, particularly in the Caribbean Latin American culture, we have the phenomenon of *mulatez*, which represents the miscegenation of African black and European white races. González further points out that while these were initially pejorative terms, both have become points of pride and contribution to the larger, dominant cultures with the notion of "la raza cósmica," the cosmic race. With increasing *mestizajes* all over the world, including the United States, the Mexican American and Caribbean experience can be models to lead the way toward mutual understanding and just, joint living.

Nonetheless, living as a *mestizo* or *mulatto* is not easy. Struggles with identity abound. With what group does one most identify, especially in light of the pressures of the dominant cultures in which one finds oneself, which may be of one or the other group, or maybe of neither? Thus, these terms speak to the problem "of belonging and yet not belonging, of being both fish and fowl, and therefore fowl to the fish, and fish to the fowl." One also understands "the fish as no fowl can, and the fowl as no fish can."[5]

González cites the example of the Apostle Paul as depicted in the book of Acts. He calls Paul a "cultural mestizo," because of his two names, one, "Saul," reflecting his Jewish heritage, the other, "Paul," the name he used when relating to Roman and Greek culture. In the book of Acts, when the Pauline mission turns to the Gentiles, "Saul" becomes "Paul" (almost obliquely in Acts 13:9).[6]

We will not have occasion below to develop further the notions of *mestizaje* and *mulatez* with regard to 1 Corinthians, nor how these play out in Paul's Letters. In fact, Paul never refers to the name "Saul" in his letters, although he does emphasize at several key junctures his Jewish heritage (Gal 1:13-14; Phil 3:4-6; cf. Rom 9:1-5). Of course, with regard to Paul's Letters, one must note his "literary mestizaje," with the complex admixture of Jewish midrashic and Hellenistic rhetorical literary styles, to cite two main examples. These issues, however, which González's paradigms can also help us to develop, are beyond the scope of this current essay.

"Exile and alienness," González's fourth set of motifs, also need further development and application to a variety of New Testament documents, including Paul's Letters. Often cited with regard to Israel's Babylonian exile, these terms speak to the fact and feeling of leaving one's center to enter somebody else's center. Thus, closely related to marginality, exile and alienness represent "a strange sort of marginalization" precisely because one leaves a center to enter the periphery. However, González reminds us that, among Latinas/os, that move often implies that one's beloved center, a homeland, has deteriorated due to "outside invasion or intervention, civil strife, economic disorder and decline, or economic and political oppression." Thus "the land that our eyes first saw can no longer sustain the life of peace and joy that God intends."[7] We must leave it for somebody's center.

Exile and *alienness* imply, therefore, that difficult experiences await those in this state, as expressed in the psalmist's lament over the Babylonian exile: "By the rivers of Babylon—/ there we sat down and there we wept" (Ps 137:1). Yet, the Bible also emphasizes several positive aspects and challenges. First, the notion of caring for the "stranger" is important in the Bible, especially because, in a sense, we are all "exiles and aliens" in one form or another. Israel, formed out of a band of nomads, needed to constantly remember that history by just treatment of the immigrant, the "stranger."[8]

Second, the Bible encourages the exile to make the best of his or her new situation. González cites Jeremiah's challenge to the exiles in Babylon: "Build houses and live in them; plant gardens and eat what they produce. . . . But seek the welfare of the city where I have sent you into exile, and pray to the LORD on its behalf, for in its welfare you will find your welfare" (Jer 29:5, 7). This is a challenge to Latina/o immigrants as well to make their new home a safe and just one, confronting those in power to make the changes necessary to ensure the well-being of the new immigrant.

Third, the Bible teaches that the center must understand the opportunity it now has with the new influx of new peoples who can help bless the land and improve on it, rather than consider these outsiders a burden. González recounts the story of Ruth and Naomi, "the story of a woman who becomes an alien for the sake of her husband, and another woman who becomes an alien for the sake of her mother-in-law." Further, "the alien who followed Naomi to Bethlehem became the great-grandmother of the great king of Israel!" Thus it is of utmost importance, given such a reading of the biblical text, for "the powerful—particularly if they seek to do the will of God—[to] seek the alien, discover their gifts, and seek whatever wisdom and guidance those gifts might offer." The immigrant today is also a "giver," who can "bring enhanced meaning to freedom," and can "also contribute significantly to the economic well-being of the whole."[9]

With regard to 1 Corinthians, in this essay I will not address the motifs of exile and alienness. However, we know that many in the city of Corinth at the time of Paul's ministry there in the mid-first century were immigrants. One could explore how such status might have affected the problems that developed in Corinth. Perhaps these could be traced to the conflict between longtime residents of Corinth and new arrivals worshiping together one God in one community.

Solidarity is the last of González's hermeneutical paradigms for reading the Bible through Hispanic eyes. It is one that has particular application to the Corinthian situation. Unlike the other terms, which reflect in many ways the negative experiences of Hispanics in the United States, solidarity is at the heart of the good news of Jesus Christ. The companion terms of *family* and *community* constitute ways in which both the Bible and the Hispanic also express solidarity. *Unity* is another related term. Certainly, if nothing else, the Apostle Paul seeks solidarity and unity for his congregates in Corinth.

Many communities in the Bible seek solidarity. González cites the community to which the author of 1 Peter writes, an exile community for whom the Christian assembly provides "a 'spiritual house' for the homeless (1 Pet 2:5); a 'chosen race' for those with no family; a 'holy nation' for those with no country (1 Pet 2:9)."[10] Thus the church becomes "a home for the homeless."[11]

In addition to the notion of a "home," the theme of family is prevalent throughout the Scriptures. It is an important theme for Hispanics as well, especially for many who have immigrated from abroad and lost the sense of *extended* family, which is so important to us. For many Latinas/os, the church becomes the extended family that we have lost by coming to the United States, with its focus on the nuclear family.

Citizenship is another related theme. González reminds us that in the Roman world of the early Christians, citizenship was no easy matter. It required not only legal residence but also a certain amount of social and economic status. Not many, therefore, were citizens of a local city, or Roman citizens empire-wide. Most depended on slave or client relations with citizens in order to acquire some sense of belonging in a particular social setting. Those who were "strangers" (*xenoi*), with no such ties, were worse off than any other noncitizens.[12]

Clearly, the Apostle Paul's citizenship status, according to the book of Acts, gave him an enormous amount of freedom to carry out his gospel mission across the Greco-Roman world. However, not everyone in his churches, no doubt, had this status. In Corinth, conflict between persons of different citizenship status may have caused divisiveness as well as an elite, patronal attitude of some over against others.

Yet, the Christian assembly should be a home and a family for many who otherwise do not have a place that gives them a measure of status and community. It is this sense of community solidarity that Paul tries to build in Corinth but experiences all kinds of trouble doing so, according to both 1 and 2 Corinthians. González describes the church as an integral part of the gospel; it is not a mere "instrument" or "vehicle" or an add-on. For the Hispanic, in particular, it is the "extended family" that we miss so much as a result of our immigrant status, as "aliens" in a new land.[13]

Indeed, González adds that the Bible is "the story of our family, the people of God." In it we find out who we are.[14] We also find out what we are supposed to do. Solidarity creates a sense of community, family, and belonging, a "home." Therefore, we become more capable to return to our people like Moses after the experience of the burning bush, and the Samaritan woman after the encounter with Jesus at the well, "to do the work of God with and among them."[15] Solidarity creates mission.

González concludes his chapter on solidarity quoting one of his sermons, which includes the following: "By means of solidarity between those who have and those who have not, between those who can and those who cannot, a new people shall be born, a new holy nation unto the Lord our God."[16] Bringing together the haves and the have nots is precisely what Paul attempts throughout his First Letter to the Corinthians (cf. 1 Cor 11:22, where the language of have and have not appears specifically). Let us see an example of this in the section of 1 Corinthians 1–4.

1 CORINTHIANS 1–4

The language of marginality and solidarity permeates the arguments against division in 1 Corinthians 1–4. First, Paul pursues solidarity from the outset of this letter: "I appeal to you, brothers and sisters, by the name of our Lord Jesus Christ, that all of you be in agreement and that there be no divisions [*schismata*] among you, but that you be united in the same mind and the same purpose" (1:10). Paul fills his appeal with the language of political concord ("be in agreement," "that there be no" *schismata*, "be united in the same mind and the same purpose") to combat discord.[17] What precipitated the discord?

If Paul had followed this "thesis statement" in 1:10,[18] with the problem detailed in 11:17-34, the abuse of the Lord's Supper, we would have less trouble assigning some social or economic cause to the problem of division. In the latter passage, the hosts for the community meal in Corinth were apparently having their own, class-specific feasts prior to the rest of the community, most likely the least well-off, arriving. The latter only partook of the bread and wine of the communion meal, rather than a more substantial meal like the higher status members of the community had enjoyed.[19] Thus Paul, like he has earlier in the letter with regard to taking fellow believers to court (1 Cor 6:1-11) and eating meals in pagan temple districts (8-10), strongly challenges the action of the socially elite members of the community:

> When you come together, it is not really to eat the Lord's supper. For when the time comes to eat, each of you goes ahead with your own supper, and one goes hungry and another becomes drunk. What! Do you not have homes to eat and drink in? Or do you show contempt for the church of God and humiliate those who have nothing? What should I say to you? Should I commend you? In this matter I do not commend you!
>
> (1 Cor 11:20-22)

To echo González, to go hungry in light of others being well fed, to have nothing when others have abundance, is not an experience remote from many in our day and age, including far too many Hispanics. Thus, many of us can readily identify with those who seemed to have been marginalized, even from the "*agape* meals," as we have learned to call them, of the early Christian communities. Who is to say that this social division at the meal does not reflect the divisions discussed in other parts of this First Letter to the Corinthians, including chapters 1–4?

Certainly, there are indications of social division between those in power and the marginalized in the language throughout 1 Corinthians 1–4. First, Paul talks about the gifts with which the Corinthians have been "enriched" (*eploutisthēte*) (1:4). Later, he will complain about the Corinthians' attitude about their spiritual accomplishments: "Already you have all you want! Already you have become rich [*eploutēsate*]!" (1 Cor 4:8). In the thanksgiving, Paul begins to slow down the "over-realized eschatology" exhibited in 4:8 by reminding the Corinthians of the Parousia: "So that you are not lacking in any spiritual gift as you wait for the revealing of our Lord Jesus Christ" (1:7).

Nonetheless, Paul often uses the language of "being rich" in both spiritual and concrete terms. When he wants to remind the Corinthians of their obligations with the Jerusalem collection, he reminds them that "our Lord Jesus Christ . . . though he was rich [*plousios*], yet for your sakes he became poor, so that by his poverty you might become rich [*ploutēsēte*]" (2 Cor 8:9). Paul wants all the Corinthians, including the financially "rich," to give to the collection for the poor in the Jerusalem church and thereby follow the example of the spiritually "rich" Jesus Christ. Jesus the Christ was a poor carpenter's son, who enriched us all, spiritually, with his death on the cross, the death of a poor man at the hands of the powerful Romans.

When one reads Paul's efforts at collecting an offering from the Corinthians

(1 Cor 16:1-4; 2 Cor 8–9), one is reminded that oftentimes it is harder to raise money from those who have an abundance of it than those who have little. Paul makes this precise point in comparing the giving of the Macedonian Christians to that of the Corinthians (2 Cor 8:1-5). Indeed, as he did in the thanksgiving of 1 Corinthians, he reminds the Corinthians of their exalted giftedness, which they should now turn into a more concrete, monetary gift on behalf of the struggling Jerusalem church (2 Cor 8:6-7).[20]

Thus Paul's figurative use of the language of "riches" in 1 Corinthians 1:5 and 4:8 must have its background in the actual status of at least some among the Corinthian believers. In the same way, when Paul describes the status of the Corinthian believers in 1 Corinthians 1:26, he may have this dual meaning in mind, the figurative in terms of their spiritual status, but also the concrete reality of their social status.

These two meanings are intertwined in other ways. With the discussion of division over leaders in 1:10-17, it may well be a division about the beliefs of these leaders (particularly Paul and Apollos, see 1 Cor 3:5-9, 22; 4:6), but ultimately it is a power struggle, concretely speaking, about which leaders to follow. "The terms with which σχίσμα [division] is associated to make it clear that it is neither a religious heresy nor a harmless clique that the author has in mind, but factions engaged in a struggle for power."[21] These terms include political terms such as *erides* ("quarrels") in 1:11 and a form of *meris* ("party" or "faction") in 1:13 ("Is Christ divided?" or "Is Christ factioned among you").[22] According to Paul, the parties pledged their allegiance to a particular figure: "I belong to Paul," "I belong to Apollos," "I belong to Cephas," "I belong to Christ" (1:12, albeit the "Cephas" and "Christ" parties are probably rhetorical devices used by Paul[23]). These phrases also exhibit the language with which ancient politics referred to party affiliations (i.e., belonging to some named individual).[24]

Thus, in Corinth, at least, the presence of social division may have been more important to Paul than abstract theological division. "What threatened the survival of the community of chosen people was not seductive gnostic theology or infectious Judaistic propaganda, but the possibility that its adherents might 'behave like ordinary men' (3:3)."[25] As Paul writes, "For when one says, 'I belong to Paul,' and another, 'I belong to Apollos,' are you not merely human?" It is the normal, social relations and divisions of society that have infiltrated the Corinthian community that worry Paul and for which he seeks solidarity.

What is at the heart of that search for solidarity? The Corinthians must realize the diversity that is present in the Christian community, even in such a social-status-conscious city like Corinth. Part of that search for social status was appropriating the right kind of *sophia* or "wisdom." Thus Paul spends a good deal of this section in 1–4, dealing with the Corinthian enamorment with *sophia*. His own preaching has not had the appropriate level of *sophia* to satisfy the Corinthian elite (2:1-5). Scholars have noted the social status implications of exhibiting "lofty words or wisdom" (2:1).[26] For Paul, ornamental speech was secondary to a "demonstration of the Spirit and of power" (2:4).

Further, the idea that the founder of their movement was actually someone who was crucified on a Roman cross and who identified with the most marginalized segments of society must have greatly disturbed the most elite members of the Corinthian community, who sought honor by appropriate social connections. Certainly, an eloquent speaker, like perhaps Apollos, for example, or even Paul if he could accept their patronage, could help enhance their reputations by their association with him.[27] However, for Paul the ultimate association of the believer was with the crucified Lord. Thus, "the message about the cross is foolishness to those who are perishing, but to us who are being saved it is the power of God" (1 Cor 1:18).

Paul identifies those "who are being saved" with marginal groups of Corinthian society. Those who could "perish" he identifies with any who insist on applying the normal expectations of status to life and relations in the Christian community:

> Where is the one who is wise? Where is the scribe? Where is the debater of this age? Has not God made foolish the wisdom of the world? For since, in the wisdom of God, the world did not know God through wisdom, God decided, through the foolishness of our proclamation, to save those who believe. For Jews demand signs and Greeks desire wisdom, but we proclaim Christ crucified, a stumbling block to Jews and foolishness to Gentiles, but to those who are the called, both Jews and Greeks, Christ the power of God and the wisdom of God. For God's foolishness is wiser than human wisdom, and God's weakness is stronger than human strength. (1 Cor 1:20-25)

With the dichotomy between *wise* and *foolish,* and between *strong* and *weak,* Paul intends to identify the marginalized of Corinth ("the foolish" and "weak") with those who have accepted the crucified Christ as their Lord. Those within the Corinthian church who continue to maintain these dichotomies between the center and the margins are in danger of *not* standing outside "those who believe" and "are being saved."

Paul drives the dichotomy home with the crucial next passage:

> Consider your own call, brothers and sisters: not many of you were wise by human standards, not many were powerful, not many were of noble birth. But God chose what is foolish in the world to shame the wise; God chose what is weak in the world to shame the strong; God chose what is low and despised in the world, things that are not, to reduce to nothing things that are, so that no one might boast in the presence of God. (1 Cor 1:26-29)

Some scholars interpret the "wise," "powerful," and "noble" as those with "claims to exalted spiritual status," whether rich or poor.[28] However, the terms are most clearly identified with those who already had a certain semblance of power and status in the outside world, and are now trying to add to that status with some additional spiritual status in this new phenomenon, the Christian community.[29]

Paul rejects their search for social status through their newfound spiritual status. In his estimation, Christian status, given its identification with a crucified Lord, will never achieve the worldly status of other Hellenistic philosophies or religions. It is too much a countercultural phenomenon. Its members, for the most part, are those "low and despised in the world, things that are not." Further, God reduces "to nothing things that are," including social status in this world. So even if "the wise, the powerful and the noble" have achieved newfound spiritual status with their own understanding of *wisdom,* it would do them no good out in the world, Paul believes. So why bother? Jesus Christ is the true "source of your life," the one "who became for us wisdom from God."

Thus Paul, with these striking images in 1 Corinthians 1:26-31, identifies the Christian status with the marginalized of society in Corinth. The status of a marginal slave, freed person, woman, laborer becomes the model for Christian status in the world, whether the Corinthian believer was rich or poor.[30]

In addition, Paul must ground Christian leadership with this approach from the underside of society. He does so in this letter, first with a discussion of his leadership and that of Apollos:

> What then is Apollos? What is Paul? Servants through whom you came to believe, as the Lord assigned to each. I planted, Apollos watered, but God gave the growth. So neither the one who plants nor the one who waters is anything, but only God who gives the growth. The one who plants and the one who waters have a common purpose, and each will receive wages according to the labor of each. For we are God's servants, working together; you are God's field, God's building. (1 Cor 3:5-9).

Thus servant leadership becomes the hallmark of what is needed in Corinth, over against the search for status through the exercise of leadership, which seems to have been the case among some in Corinth. Apparently, with his great oratory (if we are to follow Acts 18:24-28), Apollos impressed the leadership in Corinth, perhaps even to the detriment of Paul in their eyes, a source of the division over leaders in the community. Paul thus must put the leadership of himself and Apollos in the appropriate light, that is, servanthood, not status enhancement.[31]

Similarly when talking about his own ministry, Paul cites the hardships of apostleship over against any attending glory (1 Cor 4:9-13). Social status enhancement is the last thing one achieves from Christian leadership, if ever at all. The Corinthian leadership seeks the wrong kind of status and thereby causes division in the community. To achieve solidarity they must be willing to identify with the marginalized in society, the "hungry and thirsty . . . poorly clothed and beaten and homeless" (v. 11). Paul writes that apostles like himself "grow weary from the work of our own hands" and "have become like the rubbish of the world, the dregs of all things, to this very day" (vv. 12-13). This must have been strong medicine for his readers, especially the elite among them.[32]

Indeed, Paul addresses them directly at the close of this section in 1 Cor 4:14-21. He will visit the community; unlike some "arrogant" ones (*ephusiuthēsan*) among them believe. Already Paul has referred to those who are "puffed up *[phusiosthe]* in favor of one against another" (4:6) and thus cause divisions over which leader to follow, especially whether Paul or Apollos.[33] Now clearly there are some, also "puffed up," who challenge Paul's loyalty to the community because of prolonged absence (the implication of 4:18). Further, immediately in the next section in 5:2, the "arrogant" (*pephusiōmenoi*) have allowed a fellow church member to engage in incestuous relations with his father's wife (presumably the individual's stepmother). Paul challenges them harshly on their negligence in that incident (5:1-13).

All of these references point to a socially elite ("puffed up"[34]) group of leaders within the Corinthian community who have rejected the leadership of Paul, perhaps in favor of Apollos or some other visiting preacher, thereby causing discord within the community. These leaders may also be the same persons allowing immorality among one of their own social peers (5:1-13), taking other, presumably less affluent, fellow believers to court (1 Cor 6:1-11) and partaking of pagan meals with social equals in ways that further divide the community and again marginalize less affluent brothers and sisters (1 Cor 8–10). Finally, quite likely these are the same "puffed up" individuals hosting class-specific meals when they should be receiving the entire community—rich and poor—for worship, Communion, and joint meals (11:17-34).

Thus a direct link can be made from 1 Corinthians 1–4 to 1 Corinthians 11:17-34. Division caused by social status practices are at the heart of the matter.[35] Solidarity must be achieved by accepting the socially marginalized as integral members of the Christian community, not an easy task given the status- and power-conscious cities of the Roman Empire, including Corinth. Nonetheless, the nature of the gospel, with its crucified Lord, called for such cohesion within the gospel community. Those accustomed to being in the center of power, or looking to enhance the centrality of their power by leadership in the Christian community of Corinth, must accept the diversity of this community, including eating at the table and sharing leadership with those at the margins of the outside world. For me, this makes the best and most consistent sense and order out of the various trajectories and problems that Paul addresses in this First Letter to the Corinthians. The search for solidarity through the acceptance of the marginal and the marginalized lies at the heart of the letter's intentions.

CONCLUSION

This then is a reading of 1 Corinthians through Latino eyes, with the aid of the hermeneutical rubrics of Justo González. Such a reading understands the interplay of solidarity and marginality and sees it clearly depicted in Paul's dealings with the Corinthians. The other hermeneutical tools that González offers—including poverty, *mestizaje* and *mulatez,* and alienness and exile—could also be helpful in reading 1 Corinthians. Indeed, the Pauline corpus as a whole could benefit from a fresh reading through Hispanic eyes, like those that Justo González has provided for so many years.

GENESIS 1:1–2:4

APUNTES FOR A HISPANIC/LATINA/O READING

Francisco O. Garcia-Treto

I

The seminal work of Russian literary critic Mikhail M. Bakhtin (1895–1975) has already had a significant impact in biblical studies and will foreseeably continue to do so as more biblical scholars become acquainted with his legacy.[1] In a recent study of the book of Genesis, Mark Brett[2] makes use of the Bakhtinian concept of hybridity to argue that the final editors of the Pentateuch—and of Genesis in particular—did in fact produce a text marked by their critical stance toward ideological constructs (the "holy seed," the prohibition of intermarriage with the "people of the land," e.g.) of Judean colonial rulers during the Persian period. Brett begins by stating that "the presumption of [his] study . . . will be that the activity of the final editors [of the Pentateuch] can be characterised as 'intentional hybridity.' "[3] Bakhtin himself, in a discussion of the characteristics of the novel, defined *hybridization* in these terms: "What is a hybridization? It is a mixture of two social languages within the limits of a single utterance, an encounter, within the arena of an utterance, between two different linguistic consciousnesses, separated from one another by an epoch, by social differentiation or by some other factor."[4]

One of the characteristics of Bakhtin's legacy has been the extensibility of his concepts, or as Barbara Green puts it, "the most fruitful use of Bakhtin involves not simply exegeting and explicating his work but developing it while simultaneously appropriating it—a project both compatible with all that Bakhtin represents and also undertaken by most Bakhtin scholars."[5]

Brett is, of course, appropriating and extending Bakhtin's observation on the modern novel, a genre quite remote from Genesis. Bakhtin introduced hybridization in his discussion of "devices in the novel for creating the image of a language," which for heuristic purposes he classified into three groups: "(1) hybridizations, (2) the dialogized interrelation of languages and (3) pure dialogues."[6] While in the novel such devices may be seen as intentional authorial productions, Bakhtin also recognized that "unintentional, unconscious hybridization is one of the most important modes in the historical life and evolution of all languages. We may even say that language and languages change historically primarily by means of hybridization."[7]

In fact, one of his most often-cited images in this respect is his reference to "the mythical Adam, who approached a virginal and as yet verbally unqualified world with the first word,"[8] as the only human capable of language not marked by hybridization, heteroglossia, or "dialogic inter-orientation."

Brett locates the "intentional hybridity" of the text of Genesis, in his judgment both "subversive and artful," in the subjectivity of Judean editors of the Persian period, opposed to the centers of power in Jerusalem society who, like Ezra and Nehemiah, derived their power from the Persian Empire and whose rule expressed the interests of the colonial power through political and religious legislation. Brett proposes that there are in the text of Genesis certain "patterns of incongruity" that "point to an ancient editorial agency which is contesting the privileged grasp of colonial power in the Persian period." Far from being "the product of a pure, egalitarian and consistent consciousness" or, for that matter, of the artful labor of an anachronistic Dostoyevskian author, for Brett "the text of Genesis seems to reveal a hybrid inter-subjectivity, not necessarily perspicuous to itself, incorporating diverse cultural elements both from within Israelite tradition and from outside it. Older literary sources may well have been used without any knowledge of the origins of such sources."[9]

Before continuing to see how, precisely, Brett casts light on the text of Genesis 1:1 to 2:3 and how, in my judgment, his analysis may be extended to ground Hispanic/Latina/o readings of that text, it will be necessary to bring in one more basic Bakhtinian concept: the chronotope. In his classic definition of the term, Bakhtin said,

> We will give the name *chronotope* (literally, "time space") to the intrinsic connectedness of temporal and spatial relationships that are artistically expressed in literature. . . . What counts for us [about this term] is the fact that it expresses the inseparability of space and time. . . . We understand the chronotope as a formally constitutive category of literature. . . .
>
> In the literary artistic chronotope, spatial and temporal indicators are fused into one carefully thought-out, concrete whole. Time, as it were, thickens, takes on flesh, becomes artistically visible; likewise, space becomes charged and responsive to the movements of time, plot and history. This intersection of axes and fusion of indicators characterizes the artistic chronotope.[10]

Barbara Green helpfully defines "Bakhtin's chronotope" as "the particularity of the time-space that anchors the productions, settings, narration, and reading of texts," adding that "to ask about time/space forces specificity."[11] Green also goes on to point to an essential insight that could be derived from Bakhtin, and that is that the interaction between the author's and the readers' chronotopes ever continues to expand and discover new meaning in a strong text. She quotes

Gary Saul Morson and Caryl Emerson's clear-cut statement of the importance of this insight: "Readers may make the differences an occasion for exploring the potentials of the work in a way not available to its original authors and readers, and so become enriched by something truly in the work but needing their own special experience to provoke."[12]

What Green has seen clearly is that Bakhtin has much to say to readers of the Bible who want to understand the text shaped by the ancient authors' chronotopes in relation to their own, whether postmodern, feminist, postcolonial, Hispanic/Latina/o, and so on.

For the purposes of the rest of this essay, I want to propose an experiment in "simultaneous translation" in which, first, the terms *hybridity* and *hybridization* will become transparent and equivalent to the term *mestizaje*, by now a commonplace of Hispanic/Latina/o theological discourse. Second, I want to specify the chronotope, which may be identified as mine: Hispanic/Latino, more precisely as that of a Cuban exile who is now a U.S. citizen long-settled in the United States. This chronotope will interact with the one that Brett identifies as that of the final editors of Genesis, not only in terms of my own experience and perceptions but also by drawing upon two literary products of authors who also in general terms may be said to share it: a theological essay by Roberto Goizueta,[13] and a poem in which Richard Blanco rereads Genesis 1 *a lo cubano*.[14]

II

The chapter in which Brett presents his reading of Genesis 1–11 clearly announces its thematic intent in the subtitle "Creation and dominance." The title of the section which concerns me here reiterates this: "Dominance in Genesis 1–3."[15] In Brett's reading, issues of religiopolitical dominance are foregrounded by the editors of Genesis 1. The first of these is the issue of the names and number of God. One of the cornerstones of the classic historical-critical source theory in the Pentateuch, this issue is posed by Brett as a series of questions that the text raises and deliberately leaves unanswered: "Is God one, or is God many? Is there differentiation in the heavens? How is God named, and what implications does this naming have for human beings? The book of Genesis resists a clear answer to such questions."[16]

Brett sees an intentional ambiguity in the decision to preserve the variety of divine names (Elohim, Yahweh, El Elyon, El Roi, El Shaddai, and so on) as well as in the retention in the text of instances of plural grammatical agreement for Elohim. Moreover, says Brett, in the Genesis creation stories "there is no focus on the author's own people or temple. Nor is there an account of the creation of the gods themselves, a common feature of the mythological literature of the time."[17] In fact, in spite of the well-known correspondence of the *Tehom* ("deep") of Genesis 1 and *Tiamat* ("the goddess of salt water") slain by Marduk in the battle that makes creation possible in the Babylonian creation account, Brett points out that this only serves to underscore the fact that "by comparison, Genesis 1 is extraordinarily peaceful in its representation of creation and extraordinarily reserved about the nature of divinity."[18]

Brett raises the chronotope-specific question—"what can be said about the significance of these verses as the beginning to a book which was finally edited in Israel during the Persian period of colonial administration?"[19]—and points, in beginning to sketch an answer, to the "remarkable lack of the agonistic creation motifs which can be found both elsewhere in the Bible and elsewhere all over the ancient Near East" as well as to the "pronounced reticence in speaking about the divine, . . . reflected also in the use of a generic term, Elohim, rather than the proper name Yahweh—the God clearly associated with Israel."[20] The editors could hardly be seen, as some scholars have recently suggested, as promoting "an exclusivist religion, and a sharply defined ethnic identity" but rather to stand for what Brett terms "eirenic inclusivism" so that "in the primordial creativity of Elohim, the identity of Israel is not a matter of contestation."[21]

In similar fashion, Brett looks at the issue of the importance of the concept of separation or division in the text of Genesis 1, present not only in the recurrence of forms of the verb *hibdil* but also in "the idea that the plants and animals were created 'according to their kinds' "[22] Scholars have seen in these elements of the text coded references to an ideological defense of "social separation" and a coded allusion to "an Israelite exclusiveness" . . . "being secretly legitimised by the cosmic ordering." For Brett, on the contrary, the text precisely contests that reading. So, "the use of *hibdil* refers not to the order of living creatures but exclusively to the cosmic ordering" and "the vocabulary of separation is simply a small part of the dialectical oscillation between divine exhortations and the celebratory refrain." Even in the case of humans, created "in the image of God," there is an element of continuity—the commandment to procreate, already given to animals—with nonhuman life, which undermines the idea of a total "distinctiveness of the human species"—it "has to share the divine vocation of co-creation with the earth and with other creatures"—Brett sees "no licence for Israelite separatism."[23] The "Image of God" concept, Brett says, is used in Genesis 1 in a way that subverts the "standard" Near Eastern discourse present in the ideological pronouncements of all the imperial courts, *mutatis mutandis*, that exalts the monarchy to absolute dominion over the nations and elevates the monarch to divine status or to special and unique association with the divine. In Genesis 1, the important fact is not that recognizable elements of this discourse are present, but that they are "democratized."[24] Which is to say that the text of Genesis 1 is a deliberately subversive text in which power and dominion language, usually associated with Mesopotamian kings, Egyptian pharaohs, or their Persian successors, devolves not on a monarch, whether human or divine, and not even on any particular nation—not even Israel—but on all humankind, male and female. The radical message encoded by the editors in Genesis 1, says Brett, is that "in Genesis 1.28, it is humankind as such who are to rule 'over all the earth', but there is no expectation that this rule will entail the subjugation of distant enemies and nations, as Psalm 72.9-11 suggests. In Genesis 1, the vision of human expansion over all the earth does not envisage social conflict."[25] Penultimately, Brett observes that the dominion to be exercised by humans over the earth according to Genesis 1 defines a utopian condition, intertextually defined on one side by prophetic texts such as Hosea 2:18, where "the security of a new covenant with Yahweh envisages not only the end of war but a covenant with 'the beasts of the field, the birds of the heavens, and the creatures that move on the earth'. . . . Hosea's vision of peace in human society," says Brett, "is integrally linked with a return to ecological utopia, and this is characteristic of prophetic hope."[26] On the other hand, this hope is placed in tension by the actual reality of the world of the editors, in which wild animals do indeed become a threat for human beings.

I have left for last Brett's observation that the absence of "the language of holiness" in Genesis speaks for its final editors' rejection of Ezra's notion of Israel as a "holy seed." Certainly, he notes, "if Israelite seed is in any sense sacred, it is not Elohim's reproductive blessing that makes it holy."[27] That blessing, as Genesis 1 makes clear, is not only shared by all humankind but also by the animals as well. Only here and in passing, Brett speaks briefly about the seventh day's rest in Genesis 2:2-3, the only instance in Genesis of something being pronounced holy, and "as the polemical Isa. 56.6-7 makes clear anyone can participate in Sabbath worship, not just native-born Israelites."

Brett's reading of Genesis 1 convincingly postulates a chronotope for the final editors of Genesis, which places them on the margins of power in postexilic Judea, subverting many of the ideological positions taken by the center, where the interests of the temple hierarchy and of Persian power came together. Such a reading is indeed sympathetic to Brett's contemporary postcolonial chronotope and, as I have indicated, resonates well with my own.

III

Any careful reader of Genesis 1:1–2:4 will be struck by the obvious and consistent structure that shapes it. Commentators may differ about the way in which the details of one or another day are to be seen in relation to the others, but there is no question that the story progresses from "day one" to a seventh day, and that as has been said above, the seventh day is the culmination of the narrative, marked by God's rest and by God's blessing, and thus made holy. That obvious structure leads also to an apparent consensus among interpreters that the passage is at least in some sense "about" the Sabbath. A perusal of commentaries on this passage shows that particularly modern Christian authors appear either to be significantly more interested in the details of the first six days than in the significance of the seventh, or extend the significance of the seventh day's rest and blessing well beyond the establishment of the Jewish Sabbath.

As an example of the first kind of interpretation, I take Hermann Gunkel's commentary, undoubtedly one of the great classics in this category. Gunkel remarks on the style of "P" that "one must read the whole source in sequence in order to perceive the sobriety and monotony of this remarkable book. The author is apparently painfully precise and exemplarily orderly, but he, like many other scholars, was not gifted with a feeling for poetry."[28]

To be sure, he grants that "especially in Gen[esis] 1" P achieves "a degree of solemn dignity."[29] Genesis 1, for Gunkel, shows traces of polytheistic roots as well as evidence of the presence of a myth of "primordial peace." The Priestly writer took this ancient material and "cast over it a new structure which explained the Sabbath and, through an energetically engaged redaction, stamped it with strict supernaturalistic Judaism and the priestly spirit."[30] In spite of this judgment and of the importance that the Sabbath has in the Priestly ideological scheme as Gunkel reconstructs it, it is somewhat surprising that his commentary has very little to say about Genesis 2:1-3. Claus Westermann identifies and rejects among his predecessors "two explanations which are sharply opposed to each other. The first refers the blessing and sanctification of the seventh day to God alone and to his work as creator; so W. H. Schmidt and many other exegetes: 'The rest, like the whole of creation, remains simply a work of God.' "[31]

That is to say that the rest of the seventh day would remain remote from humankind with no implications for cult or religious practice. Rejecting that as inadequate, Westermann presents an alternative associated with Gerhard von Rad and his influential Genesis commentary. Von Rad understands the sanctification of the seventh day in Genesis to mean

> that P does not consider it as something for God alone but as a concern of the world, almost as a third something that exists between God and the world. The way is being prepared, therefore, for an exalted, saving good. Nothing of that is apparent to man. . . . Thus Gen. 2.1 ff. speaks about the preparation of an exalted saving good for the world and man, of a rest "before which millennia pass away as a thunderstorm" (Novalis). It is as tangibly "existent" protologically as it is expected eschatologically in Hebrews (Heb., ch. 4).[32]

Westermann ultimately rejects von Rad's view as one that, albeit "protologically and eschatologically," in effect shuts humankind out of the blessing of the seventh day as completely as the first. "I do not think that this explanation takes sufficient account of the human orientation of creation. When P says that God blesses and sanctifies the seventh day, then first that must have something to do with humankind; only then can 2:3 really be the goal of the creation account of P."[33]

Westermann comes, in my opinion, close to expressing what I would like to propose below as a reading of the blessing of the seventh day of creation when he identifies it as determining that "the time which begins with creation [is] structured time, . . . within which one day is not just the same as another"[34] and when he specifies that "there is here much more than a mere reference to the Sabbath in later Israel. The sanctification of the Sabbath institutes an order for humankind according to which time is divided into time and holy time, time for work and time for rest."[35] And, Westermann concludes, "The blessing gives the day, which is a day of rest, the power to stimulate, animate, enrich and give fullness to life. It is not the day in itself that is blessed, but rather the day in its significance for the community. In the context of creation it is for the world and humankind."[36]

I want here to suggest that "the day blessed in its significance for the community" can be given a fuller explanation, one that also brings it into full relation to Brett's reading of Genesis 1, if we translate *rest* as "fiesta" in the theological sense in which Roberto Goizueta defines the term.[37]

Goizueta, it must be said, is not writing specifically about Genesis 1 or even doing biblical exegesis in his essay. His clearly-stated thesis is that

> the fiesta, as a central element of Latino culture, reflects and expresses a theological anthropology fundamentally different from the modern notion of the autonomous subject-as-agent and that, as such, the fiesta is a principal form of cultural resistance. That is, the understanding of human life underlying and expressed through the fiesta is one in which the attitude of agency (doing, making) is grounded in an attitude of receptivity and response; more specifically, the former mediates the latter. In turn, it is precisely in his or her character as receiver and respondent that the human person is *capable* of celebrating. Thus, what lies at the heart of the Latino affinity for festive celebration is . . . a fundamentally different *understanding* of the human and, specifically, of the nature of human activity in the world.[38]

Understood in this sense, *fiesta* is prophetic and political, indeed subversive; it is a strategy of resistance.[39] *Fiesta* is not at all, in this sense, to be equated with *party*, but is rather an act of commemoration or celebration, which of course may include elements of fun. *Fiesta* is play, but it is also work and typically "blurs the distinction between religious and civil celebrations."[40] *Fiesta* is grounded on receptivity, and is therefore liberating and subversive since

> for the Latino community receptivity is the most fundamental form of human praxis, through which one is freed and empowered to act, to think "subjunctively," to celebrate *communitas*. . . .
> The fiesta represents precisely that attitude of trust in the ultimate goodness of life, both as a reality in the present and as an unrealized future that challenges and subverts the status quo. . . . Insofar as the fiesta celebrates the *ultimate* goodness of life (even in the midst of suffering and, indeed, as the "subjunctive" denial of the ultimacy of death), it celebrates life as a gratuitous gift *that cannot be destroyed* by a dominant culture that, objectifying life, would destroy it.[41]

What God blesses and hallows on the seventh day, in Westermann's mode of expression, is a structure of time divided into days of work and days of rest. Keeping in mind that a straightforward translation of that phrase into Spanish would be "dias laborales y dias de fiesta," I propose that we use Goizueta's concept of fiesta to read the Genesis 1:1–2:4 account of creation "subjunctively," that is, prophetically, politically, and as a celebration of the gifts of life and of the Gift of Life in community.

IV

As a coda to this rather sober discussion, I want to look briefly at a contemporary reading of the first creation account, not by a theologian or biblical scholar, but by a poet. Cuban-born Miami poet Richard Blanco tropes on Genesis 1 in his witty "Havanasis,"[42] a short prose poem in which the Cuba/Havana of the exile's memory replaces ancient Semitic cosmology as the object and result of the divine creative act. No mere parody, even though underlaid by Blanco's sly ironic view of his own and his fellow exiles' tendency to embellish and oversimplify a Cuba forever lost, the poem skillfully captures essential elements of the Cuban exile's cultural self-vision. Blanco begins by identifying the chaos of Genesis 1 with lack of musical rhythm: "In the beginning, before God created Cuba, the earth was chaos, empty of form and without music. The spirit of God stirred over the dark tropical waters and God said, 'Let there be music.' And a soft conga began a one-two beat in the background of the chaos."[43]

Music pervades "Havanasis." The opposite of chaos is not a rigid, inflexible order, but a rhythmic dance in which God takes part. God creates the instruments: "He fashioned goats, used their skins for bongos and *batús*[44]; he made *claves* and *maracas* and every kind of percussion instrument known to man."[45] He also creates the authors and composers of music, "*Cachita* the sorceress to strike the rhythm of his music, and a poet to work the verses of their paradise."[46] Most significantly, God is also taken up in the rhythm from beginning to end, from "God saw that this was good, tapping his foot to the conga beat"[47] to "On the seventh day, God rested from the labors of his creation. He smiled upon the celebration and listened to their music."[48] "Havanasis" revels on the hybridity—the *mestizaje/mulatez*—of Cuban ethnicity, religion, and culture; celebrates Cuban food, vegetation, climate, and life—and for anyone who understands what it is to live in exile and to mourn the loss of an ideal country that perhaps never was but that is nevertheless very real, presents a perfect example of what Goizueta has called "life in the subjunctive."

SONGS OF THE
SERVANT OF THE LORD

AN ECCLESIASTICAL READING

Samuel Pagán

> *He was despised and rejected by others;*
> *a man of suffering and acquainted with infirmity.*
> *Isaiah 53:3*

SONGS OF THE SERVANT

A theme of fundamental importance in the study of the book of Isaiah is related with the analysis and understanding of the poems of the Servant of the Lord, also known as the "Songs of the Suffering Servant."[1] In the book Isaiah of Babylonia or Deutero-Isaiah,[2] particularly in its second section known as the "Book of Consolation," the word *servant* (Heb. *ebed*) and related concepts with this term appear very frequently.[3] The idea that is generally manifested in religious circles, and which also is invoked in careful studies of the texts, is the image of a disciple of the Lord whose fundamental mission is to proclaim and affirm the true faith, to support an intense series of sufferings to take away the sins of the people, and to finally be glorified by the Lord.

The Christian church, from its beginnings, has identified these poems with the mission of Jesus of Nazareth and with the proclamation of his redemptive death and also with the glorification of Christ, known, affirmed, and celebrated among believers as the Servant of the Lord par excellence (see Acts 8:30-35).[4] For some studies, inclusive, the title of the Servant of the Lord is in the heart itself of the New Testament Christology, since its origin can be intimately and directly related with the self-understanding that Jesus had of his ministry. Also, the figure of the Servant has been interpreted as the personification of the people of God, to relate it with the "new" Israel, that is, the Christian church.[5]

In the study of the Hebrew word *ebed*, and in reference to the figure of the Servant in Deutero-Isaiah, various peculiarities of great exegetical, theological, and hermeneutical or interpretative importance are discovered. Generally, the word is used in its singular form (see 54:17) to describe some personality of importance; additionally, the term is related, in the majority of the cases, with the people of Israel, also known in those texts as Jacob.

Although this initial evaluation of the Songs could make one think that the Servant is clearly the people as a collective reality, the reality is that in various instances the Servant and the people are in diametrical and evidently opposing positions (see 49:5-6; 53:8). Also, the biblical texts present characteristics of the Servant that are difficult to apply to all the people of Israel; for example, the attributes of patience, fidelity, and innocence. Its essential characteristics are two: obtain the vicarious representation of the community through suffering and restore the covenant or alliance of God with the people.

Studies of the poems of the Servant of the Lord are generally grounded in the analysis of the following four basic passages and their literary and theologically immediate contexts: 42:1-4; 49:1-6; 50:4-9; 52:13–53:12.[6] Based on the analysis of those texts, some medullar subjects referring to the Songs and the Servant have been pondered and extensively discussed: that is, the number of key texts related with the Servant and the extension of each passage;[7] the author of each of the poems; the relationship with the diverse contexts in the book of Isaiah, particularly with the second section of the work (chs. 40–55); and the fundamental subject of the Songs: the identity of the Servant.

In the First Song (42:1-4) it is the Lord who speaks, sustains, and commissions the Servant.[8] Furthermore, God himself, according to the poem, selects and puts the Spirit on the Servant so that the Servant can impart justice to the nations and make known the divine truth to the world. It is in this theological and literary context that the very important phrase is included that affirms, according to the text of the Reina-Valera version, that the soul of God "tiene contentamiento" ("delights") in the Servant (42:1).

The Second Song (49:1-6) indicates that the Lord has chosen the Servant to restore the people of Israel and, furthermore, bring light and salvation to the nations. Here the fundamental missionary work of the Servant who was called by God from the womb of his mother (49:1) is presented: his mission surpasses the territorial and ethnic limits of Israel to contribute to the salvation of humanity in an outstanding manner. The Lukan literature of the New Testament alludes on two occasions to the fact that the Servant—related to Jesus of Nazareth—is light to the nations: the first is in the narratives of his birth, specifically in the mouth of Simeon (Luke 2:30-32; cf. Acts 26:23) and the second, in the synagogue of Antioch, during the ministry of Paul and Barnabas (Acts 13:47).

A new theological and missionary contribution is introduced in the Third Song (50:4-9): the Servant is the one speaking and is presented as a wise and obedient teacher who has encountered opposition while carrying out his mission. Nevertheless, according to the biblical text, his educative and restoring program will have success, since the Lord accompanies and helps him. The poem speaks particularly of the obedience of the Servant and also highlights the abuses and injustices to which he is submitted.

For Christians, the most famous of the Songs is the Fourth (52:13–53:12), since the church has frequently associated it with the evangelical narratives of the life, ministry, death, and resurrection of Jesus of Nazareth. In the specific case of this poem, the person who relates what happens to the Servant is not identified in a precise way. The protagonist is an afflicted and wounded person, who eventually dies. Nevertheless, his death has an expiatory and liberating function for many people, with which the narrator, in effect, identifies himself. And, although the story indicates that he is responsible for his lot, the Servant will, when all is said and done, be vindicated and will see the result of his expiatory death.

In these poems, the Servant has some functions similar to those of the preexilic kings and the prophets. Also, the Songs use a language characterized with that of the literature of the prophets and kings to describe the mission of the Servant.[9] The role of the preexilic servants of the Lord in the Old Testament is of political and religious character, and, in the execution of the divine plan, they persuade the community to also comply with the designs of the Lord.

Of particular importance in the Songs that we find in the book of Isaiah is the call of the Servant that evokes and reminds one of the vocations of Moses and of Jeremiah; the mission of the Servant also is presented in similar terms to that of the famous legislator and biblical liberator. This relation should not surprise the readers and scholars of the Songs since in these texts of the book of Isaiah the return to Palestine from Babylon is presented as a novel liberation, as a new exodus.

An adequate understanding of the Songs requires the study of the world of ideas that surround the writing of that important theological literature. Since the people lived an exiled experience, the theology of the centrality of Zion and the election of David play a prominent role. In view of the destruction of Jerusalem and the exile of the king, this real theology took on proportions of importance. Also, the same experience of exile made the people and their leaders ponder the effects of the crisis of the defeat of Israel before the Babylonian armies. That history provoked theological reflection; the experiences of life generated pertinent theological and social dynamics that permitted the people to surpass the difficulties and overcome the pains of life in Babylon.

The Songs, in effect, have possibly a history of a particular writing and come from different authors. They are included in the book of Isaiah, particularly in the section of Second Isaiah, to affirm the theology of hope and restoration of the people at the same time as it alludes to the historic suffering of Israel. Specifically the Songs reflect on their exilic experience. The Songs also highlight the role of the Servant and the missionary purpose of the community of exiles in the future of the people.[10] The theological unity of the Songs comes from the contribution that they make in the understanding of the mission of the people of Israel in history, particularly in the time of the exile. Nevertheless, the results of extensive and systematic studies of the Songs of the Servant have not resolved all of the difficulties the poems present. The literary and poetic argumentations, the linguistic and semantic evaluations, the theological and historical studies, and the exegetical and contextual analyses have not exhausted the possibilities of interpretation nor have they been able to respond convincingly to all of the questions that those particular Isaianic passages present. Those studies, in effect, have identified, at least, five basic theories for the interpretation of the poems: the collective, the individual, the ideal, the mixed, and the messianic. These interpretations of the Songs are important marks of reference that can support the adequate comprehension of the individual passages, along with contributing significantly to the understanding of the texts as a particular theological block.

COLLECTIVE INTERPRETATIONS

Some interpreters see in the Servant the personification of the people of Israel as a singular entity, that is, collectively: this is perhaps the oldest of the theological understandings of the Songs. It is essentially grounded on a basic and literal reading of the available biblical texts (e.g., 41:8; 44:1, 2, 21; 45:4; 49:3). The Septuagint version of these texts is based possibly on this type of literal understanding and incorporates this theological point of view in the biblical text. For example, in the translation of Isaiah's work, the Septuagint identifies the Servant, in a precise way, as "Israel" and "Jacob" in 42:1.[11]

The major argument to support this interpretation of these texts—and the hermeneutical perspective of the passages—is related with the following fact: in various portions of the book of Isaiah it is indicated in a direct and clear form that the people of Israel are the servant of God; and this important characterization is made more intense in Deutero-Isaiah. According to this interpretation, Israel has the mission to instruct and proclaim justice to the nations (42:1-4); it also should be a light to the people and a vehicle of salvation for humanity (49:6); furthermore, according to the biblical texts, Israel will suffer intensely and vicariously (50:4-9; 53:12).

If we assume that the people of Israel are the Servant who is represented in the Fourth Song, the theme of the death and resurrection present there is much easier to explain. A community like the Israelites, which suffers historical difficulties, social scarcity, spiritual anguish, and, furthermore, the political and military "death" of exile, is resurrected thanks to the marvelous divine intervention that allows them to leave captivity and exile in Babylon and return to Palestine to reconstruct the temple of Jerusalem and renovate worship and sacrifices (cf. Ezek 37:1-14).[12]

This interpretative perspective of the Songs, although at first instance attractive to the reader and to the student of the poems, does not take into consideration various theological, thematic, and textual factors of major importance. The First Song does not present difficulties in establishing that relationship of identity of the Servant with Israel. The serious conflicts of interpretation, according to that hermeneutical theory, began with the calm evaluation of the rest of the passages and Songs to be studied.

In the Second Song, the Servant is alluded to as an important agent in the salvation of Israel, nullifying, or at least putting in question, the real possibility of the relation and identity of the Servant with the people of Israel. In the Third Song, the difficulties increase: the Servant is prophet and teacher at the same time. Identifying the Servant with the people of Israel, therefore, would be theologically and exegetically forceful and inadequate. We should add to these difficulties that if in the Fourth Song the Servant is the people, then the person who relates the passage is a voice of the nations, something that is not present in any other text in Deutero-Isaiah.

The major difficulty of this collective interpretation of the Songs, nevertheless, is that in various texts the Servant and the people are clearly opposed to each other and that the identification to the two personalities makes violent the message of the texts in a global form.[13]

To overcome these difficulties some scholars have indicated that the Servant does not represent all of the people of Israel, only an intimate community of the faithful and pious—a remnant. The image of the Servant alludes, according to this interpretation of the stories, to the faithful remnant of "genuine Israelites" who are prophets and teachers and who also suffer in representation of all of the exiled Jewish community.

Other scholars do not relate the figure of the Servant with historical Israel but with an ideal Israel, as we shall see subsequently. They indicate that the Servant is a people who recognizes its mission and lives to accomplish it. This particular kind of Servant only exists in the eschatological and ideal future, and its mission does not have historically concrete repercussions. Regarding these forms of interpretation we should indicate that these forms of seeing the people are not a prioritized theological pattern in the Hebrew Bible.[14]

INDIVIDUAL AND HISTORICAL INTERPRETATIONS

If the Servant is not the representation of the people of Israel, this important literary figure of the book of Isaiah should relate to a concrete person or a specific individual. The Servant, also from this perspective, can be a fictitious literary figure created by the prophet, or he can be referring to a definite historical personality.

In the case that the figure of the Servant could be a poetical creation, we should not attempt to relate the concept with concrete historical personalities, since what is important is not its precise identification, but its message. If, on the contrary, the Servant alludes to a specific historical personality, then, from the perspective of the Songs, we should precisely note whether the individual existed in the past, is contemporaneous with the author of the text, or will exist sometime in the future.

Regarding the poems of the Servant and his identity, the list of figures and leaders of the people who are related with this important personality is certainly varied and extensive. For some scholars, the Servant is an anonymous prophet and teacher of the law, who ministered in the same exilic period as Deutero-Isaiah and died in a violent way. Other scholars have related the Servant with Moses, Zorobabel, Joaquim, Cyrus, or another historical figure. These interpretations, although interesting and bold, have lacked general support from the church, the synagogue, and academia since they lack a solid theological, hermeneutical, and biblical foundation.

Some scholars have intended to relate the figure of the Servant with various historical personalities. A possibility exists that the Servant is the same anonymous prophet whose work is found in Isaiah 40–55 and who we know under the name of Deutero-Isaiah. According to this interpretation, the suffering of the Servant, described dramatically in the Songs, is part of a biography or an autobiography of the prophet.[15] The primary reason to reject this theological understanding of the Songs is that, according to that second section of Isaiah (chs. 40–55), the mission of the Servant is not synonymous to that of the prophet described in those very chapters of the book of Isaiah.

Another possibility in the process of identification of the figure of the Servant is to indicate that we are speaking of a historical personality of the future. For example, the Servant is the Messiah that is awaited in the theology of the Old Testament. In this theological tradition, the Servant is a monarch that will come to impart justice and restore the people of Israel.

In effect, the New Testament church used this theological perspective to relate and interpret the Songs of the Servant with the life, work, and death of Jesus of Nazareth. This theological interpretation is the one that is presented in the story of Philip the Evangelist and the official of the Queen of Ethiopia (see Acts 8:32-35).[16] From this use onward, this Christian explanation of the Songs of the Servant has played a fundamental role in the history of the church, particularly in moments of greater apologetic importance.

The individual interpretation is based on the descriptions that are made of the Servant in various important passages. The analysis of the characteristics of his personality has led scholars to identify a historical personality who subscribes to these descriptions.[17] Nevertheless, the exegetical, theological, and historical complications that these identifications pose do not appear to be of much help to the interpretative process of the poems. Of particular importance is to determine to whom do the Songs refer specifically, during the historical time frame of the final author of the book of Isaiah. The basic questions for the adequate comprehension of the Songs are the following: who was really the Servant for the exiled Jewish community in Babylon, and what was the specific significance of the mission for the people that was divided between the Babylonian exile and the misery in Judah and Jerusalem?

IDEAL INTERPRETATIONS

Referring to the understanding of the Songs of the Servant, an additional hermeneutical possibility is to indicate that these poems allude to an ideal figure. Based on various parallels with Babylonian literature, this theory indicates that the images of the Suffering Servant arose from the rites and ceremonies of the new year in which the Mesopotamian king actively participated. Essentially these festivities recreated the death and resurrection of the gods of vegetation, since they were part of the agrarian ceremonies in Babylonia. The death of the god, represented by the king, was a return to the initial cosmic disorder; and his resurrection was the symbol of triumph of the order over the hostile forces of the chaos. In these ceremonies, the king lost his throne and his powers—symbolized by his death—which subsequently were returned by the hands of the god Marduk—which represented his resurrection.

Certain scholars have suggested that the images of the Servant, particularly as presented in the Fourth Song, are grounded in this particular and important Babylonian ceremony. This would then be the cultural and religious environment of the images of the vicarious suffering and the death and resurrection of the Servant.[18]

Although this might at first seem rather persuasive, this interpretation of the Songs, grounded in its analogy with traditions, ceremonies, and parallels with the Babylonian culture, is not probable for various reasons. In the first place, the theme of the vicarious suffering of the Servant does not have real parallels in the Old Testament, nor can similar ideas be discovered in extrabiblical documents of old. On the other hand, the relationship of the book of Isaiah with the culture and religion of Babylonia and Mesopotamia is certainly one of hostility.[19]

Another possible interpretation arises if we evaluate even more carefully the perfection of the figure of the Servant. Since the figure of the Servant cannot be related with precision to any historical figure of the past or of his time, nor is it founded in the images and rites of extraction of Babylonia, we should possibly explore the possibility that the Servant is a figure who represents the ideal Israel, the people of God par excellence. That interpretation is based in a very interesting and peculiar characteristic of the biblical literature known as "the cooperative personality" of various personalities of the Scripture. This manner of understanding the Songs can give us new hermeneutical and interpretative clues, which says that they can offer new ways of understanding and explaining the poems of the Servant.[20]

The basic goal of the Deutero-Isaianic message is to affirm and emphasize the word of consolation and hope to the community of Jews exiled in Babylonia. In that historical, theological, and literary environment the Songs of the Servant are included to manifest the mission of the people of Israel, even in the midst of exilic alienation and marginalization.

The Servant, seen from that perspective, is not a historic figure of the past, present, or future, but one who represents the best of the people, symbolizes the way Israel should act in life, and alludes to the fundamental character of the Jewish community. This ideal figure—which, in effect, for the author of the poems and for the theology of the book of Isaiah, does not belong to history, but affirms a value that surpasses the limits of time—manifests the heart of the divine will for the nation: the Servant should be the light to the nations and should also live and act as a person "familiar with suffering"; that is, the Servant should be a person who is an expert in the adequate management of situations of optimal conflict and extreme difficulties.

The patriarchs and kings, in Israel as in Judah, not only are individuals and important leaders in the biblical narratives but also represent the people in a full and extensive way. This perception of leadership is manifested also in other ancient cultures and between the neighbors of Israel.[21]

The particular case of the patriarchs is worth mentioning and explaining. The people received, in effect, by divine revelation, the name of an individual: Israel and Jacob (Gen 32:22-32). That peculiarity is affirmed in a definitive way when studying the patriarchal narratives. There it is discovered that the actions and characteristics of the personality of some patriarch clearly alludes in a concrete way to the being and actions of the people (i.e., the experiences of Abraham in Canaan and the relationships of Jacob and Esau). In this manner it is noted that the narratives of the patriarchs do not refer only and exclusively to the life of individuals, but represent the national history of the people of Israel.

In the same theological tradition of "the cooperative personality," the King-Messiah of Israel is not conceived as a new historic David who would reach the throne, or as the culmination of the Davidic dynasty among the people.[22] According to this hermeneutical concept, the King-Messiah awaited by Israel will fulfill all the political, religious, and social aspirations of the people, besides having all the ideal qualities of the monarchy (i.e., capacity for the implantation of justice and peace). In this way he represents all of the aspirations and most noble desires of the people. The different representatives of the Davidic dynasty reign with the hope that the divine promises are fulfilled in that ideal figure for whom they await in an undetermined future. This ideal King-Messiah of Israel personifies all the kindnesses of the monarchy, without its defects, sins, and errors.

With that framework of the theological reference of the "corporate personality" we can then analyze and understand the figure of the Servant of the Lord in the Songs of Deutero-Isaiah. The Servant is not only an individual who suffered, was persecuted, and was assassinated in the exilic period in Babylonia, but one who represents the people of Israel in this manner.

Nevertheless, this representation does not only allude to the historical Israel of the past, present, or future, but to the people it should be, the one who plainly personifies the divine will in the midst of the realities of life: the Servant is the ideal Israel that precisely fulfills the designs of God.

From this theological point of view the problems of the tension between the presentation of the Servant as an individual in some poems and as a nation in others is resolved. In effect, the Servant is an individual who represents the community and who incorporates in his life the best of the religious, social, political, and missionary life of the people of Israel. Although he is persecuted, hurt, and assassinated, he gains his vindication and triumph without war, which leaves the kings of the period surprised and astonished (52:15). The Servant is the personification of the virtues of Israel and in him the history of the people arrives at its plain and optimal culmination: it incorporates the best of the past of the people, reveals the most noble of the present character of Israel, and personifies the kindness and ethical virtues of the future of the nation.

The Servant of the Lord is also a new Moses, since he is the voice of a divine revelation and carries the people to a renewed liberation (cf. 40:1-12). He also acts as a prophet since he communicates a new divine message: affirms that the future of the people is not to be a captive in the political world and the war, but in the implementation of justice and peace.[23] The Servant is the climactic figure in the history of the prophets and prophetesses of the Old Testament, who announces the promises of salvation and also whose lives are converted into agents and means to obtain those liberating purposes of God (i.e., the prophet Jeremiah lived that experience; see Jer 18–20).

The future of the exiled and postexilic Israel lies not in being another military power in the constellation of nations of the ancient Middle East. The great message of the Songs is that the people should convert into a Servant to live the will of God and overcome the exilic crisis with authority and a sense of mission. Only the Israel-Servant will be capable of overcoming the difficulties of deportation, the anguish of seeing destroyed the national institutions and the temple of Jerusalem, and the marginalization of living away from the promised land.

"Mixed" Interpretation

A variant in the traditional interpretation of the Songs of the Servant is related with this mixed category, which affirms that the poems do not present one Servant alone. Since the poems are a product of diverse authors and are generated in diverse contexts, the Servant is a figure that alludes to more than one image: to Israel (40–48), to the faithful remnant of the people (49:1-6, 7-13; 52:13–53:12), to the prophet (50:4-11), to Cyrus (42:1-9), and inclusively to God, who fulfills certain functions of the Servant (43:23-24).

This "mixed" interpretation does justice to and emphasizes the literary and theological complexities of each of the poems. It presupposes that each poem has an independent theological purpose and that in the final editing of the work the totality of the poems to affirm the central message and the particular contribution of the Songs to the theology of Deutero-Isaiah was not taken into consideration. This interpretation does not recognize that the Songs, as a whole, contribute in an outstanding way to the adequate interpretation of the totality of the book of Isaiah.

Messianic Interpretation

Traditionally Christians have interpreted the Songs of the Servant of the Lord according to the messianic theory. From the New Testament (see especially, Matt 8:17; 12:18-21; Luke 22:37; Acts 8:32-35; 1 Pet 2:22, 24), the church has related the mission of the Isaianic Servant with the ministry of Jesus; that is, believers have interpreted the poems of the Servant as a prophetical anticipation of the person and mission of Christ.

The Songs describe the Servant, according to this form of interpretation, as a prophet commissioned by the Lord who should effectively carry out the mission, benefiting not only Israel but also all of the nations (42:1, 4). To obtain his objective, the Servant should overcome many difficulties and endure sufferings; but the Lord sustains and elevates him to a level that generates admiration from the nations and their leaders (52:12-15).[24]

For Christians, this messianic interpretation is foundational. It is a theological and hermeneutic way to relate the prophet message of the book of Isaiah with the ministry of Christ, and it was a contextual way to understand the mission of the church that exceeds the ethnic limits of the people of Israel. According to the Songs, and according to the message of Jesus and his followers, salvation cannot be held captive by nationalistic or racial considerations, and the Songs of the Servant give to believers the necessary theological and biblical tools to present the evangelistic and educational mission of the incipient primitive Christian community. Additionally, in the synagogue of Nazareth, according to the Gospel of Luke, Jesus read and applied the text of Isaiah 61 to himself, which, in effect, is intimately related with the Songs of the Servant, and he also interpreted it. The Songs, particularly the Fourth (52:13–53:12), have been used frequently in the apologetic task of the believers.

THE SERVANT OF THE LORD AND
THE DAUGHTER OF ZION

A new way of reading the Songs of the Servant is related to the study of various passages in Isaiah that stand out and affirm the feminine figure of the Daughter of Zion. These poems, as well as those of the Servant of the Lord, present a narrative and literary continuity, and they also emphasize a theological perspective and a particular missionary task that compare to the mission of the Servant.[25]

In the entire book of Isaiah there are seven passages that explicitly include the literary image of the "Daughter of Zion" (1:8; 3:16; 10:32; 16:1; 37:22; 52:2; 62:11), although other texts allude to a feminine personality who acquires the leading role and particular prominence in the final section of the work (40–66). Like the Servant, the Daughter of Zion is clearly identified in some biblical portions (such as, 49:14), although in others, the literary and thematic context is what gives us the key to the adequate identification (such as in ch. 54).

From the very beginning of the book of Isaiah it is discovered that the city of Jerusalem is personified as a figure of a woman (1:21-26). And, even though that literary image is repeated in the work (37:22), it acquires optimal dimension in the second and third sections of the book (40–55 and 56–66).

At the very beginning of the second section of Isaiah, or the Book of Consolation (40:1-3), the text indicates that the heart of Jerusalem is spoken to with tenderness, since "her penalty is paid"; and it is added, also, that the herald of Zion brings good news. As in the case of the Servant, the Daughter of Zion is identified in various forms: as Zion or Jerusalem; or, inclusively, at times the identification is not as precise and is not presented with clarity.

In the Songs of the Servant, as in the poems of the Daughter of Zion, particularities that reveal thematic continuity are evident. The stories that include both images have progression and independence: from abandonment to triumph, from the shouts of hurt to victory and joy, from loneliness to companionship, and from weakness to power. Even though the stories, in both cases, are presented in the book of Isaiah in a fragmented way, the analysis of the contents of the passages reveal a sense of direction, continuity, and progression. The final editor of Isaiah not only took into consideration the particularity and the totality of the themes of each poem, but each Song and each poem forms part of a total that is revealed in the reading of the complete work.

Comparing the Songs of the Servant and the poems of the Daughter of Zion, the reader encounters very interesting thematic and literary parallels. Especially between the Song of 52:13–53:12 and the poem of chapter 54: both of the leading personalities—the Servant and the Daughter of Zion—are humiliated and afflicted; however, both are vindicated and liberated afterwards. Also, both will see their descendants, and the nations of the world will feel the effect of

what has happened to them. In both narrative poems the theologically fundamental Hebrew word *shalom* is used, and the important biblical concept of peace
is affirmed, with a particular sense of well-being and reconciliation.

The study of the poems of the Daughter of Zion will surely help us to understand the Songs of the Servant for various reasons. In the first place there are
parallels in the climax of both personalities. In Isaiah 66, the Daughter of Zion
is presented in an experience of extraordinary triumph, following her sufferings,
alongside images of joy associated with childbirth. This final victory of the
Daughter of Zion confirms the definite triumph of the Servant, which surely is
detached from the Songs.

In the Songs of the Servant as in the poems of the Daughter of Zion sarcastic
references to the inadequate behavior of both personalities are included: the
Servant is criticized for having offended the Lord with their sins (43:22-24) and
to the Daughter of Zion her sinful behavior is remembered (57:6-13). It is important to also note that in the identification of the two personalities there are
serious complications: some passages appear to refer to individuals, while in
others they clearly allude to the people (be it Israel or Jerusalem).

With the theory of "the corporative personality" in Israel, nevertheless, both
images can be explained. The two images, however, have played a fundamental
role in the history of the Christian interpretation of the Old Testament: the
Servant is related with the ministry of Jesus (Luke 4:18-20), and in Revelation
12:1-6, the Daughter of Zion is understood to be Mary, the mother of Jesus, and
is related also with the church.

Finally, we must add that these parallels and thematic and literary relationships are not fortuitous. They reveal, in effect, that we should not, nor can we,
fruitfully study the Songs of the Servant away from their particular literary and
theological contexts. These Songs are intimately related with the other
Deutero-Isaiah texts, like the poems of the Daughter of Zion and with the rest
of the book of Isaiah.

The poems of the Daughter of Zion are important for an adequate comprehension of the Songs because they present the necessary evidence to indicate
that the final editing of the extraordinary work of Isaiah was not a product of
chance, but that it is subject to a specific theological purpose: affirm the hope of
a people who had lost its basic institutions in Palestine and who lived as exiled
people in Babylon, dreaming of their return, which, with the passing of time, was
daily becoming more and more difficult to realize.

The contrast between the feminine figure of Zion and the masculine figure of
the Servant should not be ignored, because it manifests a fundamental literary
and theological shift for the book of Isaiah, which frequently uses feminine
images with force. Zion is abandoned and dishonored but will triumph; the
Servant is afflicted and rejected, but he confides in the Lord and his triumph is
definitive. Zion complains and suffers; the Servant consoles or is quiet. The past
of Zion is divine anger; the past of the Servant is intimacy and love. The

important theme of triumph and prosperity is common in both personalities, but the way to get it is different.

The manner in which the Lord directs each personality, according to the Songs and the poems, is worth mentioning. For the Servant, the Lord, although he manifests love (43:4), essentially acts as judge and king who wants to demonstrate his legal power and authority. Toward the Daughter of Zion the Lord reveals his love and his desire to forgive; additionally, he manifests his affection; and, like a husband to his wife, he promises to be faithful (54:10).

In regard to the Daughter of Zion, the poems end with the theme of a new creation, in the image of childbirth. They allude to creation and the development of a new Israel, a new people who will overcome the difficulties related with the exile in Babylon.[26]

The literary and theological role between the Servant of the Lord and the Daughter of Zion, in a moment of exile, is a means of hope and consolation. The Servant, in his redemptive mission, will transform the city so that it can be converted into the cultic and spiritual center of humanity.

INTERPRETATIONS OF THE SERVANT OF THE LORD IN THE OLD AND NEW TESTAMENTS

The images of the Servant of the Lord in Isaiah are so intense, powerful, and influential that they rapidly generated an extensive and continued interpretative task.[27] These continued readings and applications of the images of the Servant reveal the hermeneutic creativity of the readers of the text from Isaiah and also manifests the power of invocation and inspiration of the metaphors of the Servant.

Possibly one of the first interpretations and contextualizations of the Songs of the Servant is found in Isaiah 61, in which a poem is included that describes the anointing of a person—in the tradition of the poems of the Servant—so that the good news is brought to the afflicted and the year of the Lord is announced. Later, Zechariah 12:10, in this same theological tradition, continues the theme of anointing and indicates that the Lord will pour, on the house of David and the inhabitants of Jerusalem, his spirit of compassion and intercession in support of the Servant who had been hurt and in anguish.

The last vision in the book of Daniel alludes to a group of men who impart wisdom to the people and teach how to be faithful to the law. These men are identified with the Hebrew term of *maskilim,* which traditionally has been translated as "wise ones" or "teachers." The fury of the persecution of Antiochus Epiphanes fell on them (see Dan 11:33). The crisis and the affliction were of such magnitude that some deserted the group of the faithful; nevertheless, that same act of desertion affirms and confirms the purification and faithfulness of those who stayed and resisted the hostility and persecution.

Those *maskilim* who showed their faithfulness will shine in the firmament in the age to come of the Resurrection; particularly those who lead "many" to righteousness and justice (Dan 12:3). That reference who "leads" toward righteousness and justice can be an allusion to Isaiah 53:11, which indicates that the Servant has similar responsibilities. The *maskilim* are possibly the "Saints of the Almighty" (Dan 7:21-28), who in a previous vision are indicated as severely suffering under the "small horn," which is a possible reference to Antiochus Epiphanes.

The Qumran community, which was certainly the heir of the traditions of the *maskilim* of the book of Daniel, interpreted the mission according to the theology of the Servant of the Lord. The deprivations and persecutions to which the Qumranites were exposed, on the part of the Wicked Priest and other oppressors, were interpreted as experiences that earned them merits before God for the salvation not only from its community, but from all of Israel.[28] The Qumranites applied to themselves the images of the Servant, since they believed that their way of life and the vicissitudes to which they were subjected were part of the mission of the Servant that they had to live and experience in an age of wickedness and suffering.[29]

The biblical Greek translation, known as the Septuagint (LXX), includes in the First Song a clear and direct reference to Jacob and Israel, since it interprets that the Servant is an image of the people.[30] And the Aramaic Targum of the prophets,[31] in the section of Isaiah, directly relates the Servant to the Messiah. The first reference reveals the interpretation of the Servant with the people, and the second manifests the relation of the Servant with the theology of the Messiah, which certainly is old in the biblical literature and history. This union is important since afterward the Christian church continued that interpretative tradition of the Servant as not only the Christian Messiah but also an image of the church.

The writers of the New Testament regularly used the images of the Songs of the Servant in the educative and evangelistic task of the church. They particularly related the Fourth Song with the mission and vicarious suffering of Jesus of Nazareth. The Gospel of Luke as well as the Acts of the Apostles testify of the important evangelistic use of the poems of the Servant (see, for example, Luke 4:18-20; Acts 13:26-40).

Peter, in his famous discourse in front of the Beautiful Gate of the temple of Jerusalem (Acts 3), announced that the God of Abraham, Isaac, and Jacob, the God of the patriarchs and matriarchs of Israel, had glorified his "servant" Jesus, in a direct reference to the humiliation, suffering, and death of Christ. Later, the Ethiopian eunuch asked Philip, reading the text of Isaiah 53, to whom did the prophet refer (Acts 8:26-40). The answer of the evangelist included an exposition of the scripture, which ended with the affirmation of the good news of Jesus.

The theme of the vicarious suffering of the Servant, to free humanity of their sins, also is regularly manifested in the rest of the New Testament. The Apostle

Paul, in sections that highlight the nature and extent of the apostolic preaching, clearly indicated that the Lord Jesus Christ died and gave himself "for our sins" (Gal 1:3-5) and added that God "gave" Jesus as sin for us (2 Cor 5:21).[32]

Those references that relate the ministry of Jesus with the images of the Servant who suffers for humanity are repeated in the literature of the New Testament (such as, Rom 8:3; Phil 2:5-11; 1 Pet 2:24; Rev 5:5.). That continuous and systematic use reveals the importance of this theological interpretation of the Servant, and also underlines its use in Christian circles from the beginning of the evangelistic mission of the church.

The origin of the relation of the Songs of the Servant with the figure of the preacher of Nazareth should have started with Jesus. Early in the discharge of his mission, Jesus possibly related himself to the themes that are included in the Songs of the Servant and identified himself with them. The continuous reference of the evangelists to the identification and relation of Jesus with the Servant of the Lord can be a clear indicator that the interpretation was born out of his self-perception of the divine will for his life. Jesus, according to the testimony in the synagogue of Nazareth, was anointed by God, in the tradition of Isaiah, to announce the acceptable year of the Lord and to save humanity from their sins.[33]

THE CHURCH AS SERVANT OF THE LORD

For the Christian church, one of most important theological, educative, evangelistic, and apologetic themes of the book of Isaiah is that of the Servant of the Lord, or the Servant. The fundamental mission of this important personality, which is presented in the passages that are studied on the Servant, is to complete the work of redemption to benefit not only the people of Israel but also all nations. The Servant is anointed to face many sufferings and fulfill the salvific purpose of God.

In the Old Testament the title of *servant* is applied to people who carry out tasks of great importance in the service of the Lord (e.g., Moses, Joshua, and David; Josh 1:1-2; 24:29; Ps 89:20; Jer 25:4). According to the book of Isaiah, the title of *servant* is applied in various occasions to the people of Israel (41:8; 44:2, 21; 45:4; 48:20; see especially 49:3). According to that interpretation, Israel, as a suffering people, after experiencing the shortage and anguish of the exile, will resurge not only to serve the Lord but also to be a light to the nations, to take salvation to the ends of the earth (49:6). In the Judaic tradition, identification of the Servant and the people of Israel is very old.

The Christian church, as we have already seen, and from very early in its history, related the poems of the Servant of the Lord with the salvific and expiatory mission of Jesus of Nazareth. That theological perception is revealed in various passages of the New Testament, particularly in the Gospels (Matt 8:17; 12:18-21; Luke 22:37).

Nevertheless, although the messianic interpretation of the Songs of the Servant was transformed, with the passing of time, in the theological posture generally accepted by Christians, this did not impede the manifestations of other understandings and interpretations of the Songs among the primitive believers.

In the poem known as the "Song of Mary" (Luke 1:46-55), in continuity with the Judaic traditional interpretation, the figure of the Servant is related with the people of Israel (Luke 1:54). Afterward, in the book of the Acts of the Apostles, the figure of the Servant, in addition to applying it to Jesus (Acts 8:34-40), is related specifically with the Apostle Paul (26:17-18). That reference to the apostle is very important because it reveals that, although the relation between the figure of the Servant and Jesus was very common and appreciated, this did not impede the image being applied to other believers, particularly to the leaders who fulfilled leading functions in the church.

Another additional reference with regard to the study and the application of the figure of the Servant is necessary. In one of Jesus' most important speeches, known as the Sermon on the Mount (Matt 5:1–7:27), again some images that appear in the Songs of the Servant can be identified, this time applied to the disciples. This scriptural reference is fundamental in this analysis because, according to the evangelistic story, it comes directly from Jesus.

The exhortations to be the "light of the world" and to "turn the other [cheek]" to those who insult and offend (Matt 5:14, 16, 39), can be related with some ideas clearly exposed in the Songs (cf., Isa 49:3, 6; 50:6). In this way, various responsibilities and attributes of the Servant were continually applied to the Christian believers. The use of the image of the Servant of the Lord was not exhausted with the application to Jesus; the believers continued to relate responsibilities of the Servant with the ministry of the church. The hermeneutic possibilities of the images of the Servant did not remain captive in the individual, historic, or messianic interpretations; and they served to describe and affirm the ministry of the church.

That possibility of collective interpretation of the image of the Servant is fundamental for the development of a healthy theology of the Servant today. The church, in its missionary task, is also a servant that suffers the shortages and conflicts of the world. We cannot engage in relevant ministry from afar but rather only as we accompany a world that suffers and groans for redemption. The relevancy in the ministry is attained when there is an incarnation of the believers and the congregations and institutions of the church in the life of the world in which they are to serve and transform. An effective and accepted ministry cannot be done at a "long distance" in contemporary society.

The suffering church is one that is present in the midst of the joys and tribulations of the people. The suffering church is the one that lives in the midst of the dynamics that can generate death and despair. The suffering church is the one that announces life in the midst of the parameters of death. The suffering church is the one that lives "among a people of unclean lips" (Isa 6:5), and to which the Lord again says: "Now that this [tong] has touched your lips, your guilt has departed and you sin is blotted out" (Isa 6:7).

The study of the Songs of the Servant confronts us again with the heart of the message from Isaiah and with the transformational nature of the vocational experiences. The whole book, including the mission of the Servant, is grounded in "the vision" of the will of God that the prophet received. In that vision the basic question is asked: "Whom shall I send, and who will go for us?" (Isa 6:8).

Isaiah and many prophets who have studied and actualized its message have responded with courage and assurance: "Here am I; send me" (Isa 6:8).

CHAPTER 4

"IT IS THESE YOU OUGHT TO HAVE PRACTICED, WITHOUT NEGLECTING THE OTHERS"

LIFE IN A HEALTHY TENSION—AN ALTERNATIVE MODEL TO LIVE IN COMMUNITY

Guillermo Ramírez-Muñoz

INTRODUCTION

I wish to employ Jesus' remark to the Pharisees in Matthew 23:23 and Luke 11:42—"It is these you ought to have practiced, without neglecting the others"—as a basis to reflect upon several matters. First of all, in recognition of Justo L. González, who has challenged us many times with similar comments. Second, and inspired by his example and academic work among our communities, I wish to explore the value and the need to critically and intentionally reevaluate the importance and function of (a) alternative models and (b) certain ritual practices as instruments of resistance and support of our Hispanic/Latina, Caribbean, and Latin American communities.[1]

IN HONOR OF JUSTO

I selected the text as part of the title of this reflection because it evokes the diatribe that on multiple occasions Justo has employed to teach and challenge us to rethink our particular reality. Many of us, like the Scribes and Pharisees, have left aside very important issues to pursue peripheral matters. Justo, with much patience, has demonstrated and insisted on the relevancy of other alternative models, particularly those having to do with our Christian mission and identity; our religious, cultural, and political traditions and how they can be integrated creatively to our academic and pedagogical task; how we should and can create spaces to strengthen them; and of equal importance, what criteria we must employ in order to evaluate ourselves in the light of a biblical and theological interpretation that responds to our reality.[2]

THE BIBLICAL TEXT

Jesus' statement is part of the pericope that appears in the Gospels of Matthew (23:13-33) and Luke (11:42-52). The particular saying we refer to represents, for diverse reasons, an idea that has received relatively little attention in the history of the exegesis of this unit. This thought could reflect the concerns of some groups within the early Christian community striving to integrate certain laws and rituals inherited from the rich Jewish tradition into its new understanding of the world, with the purpose of strengthening and deepening the relationships between social justice and the rich legal traditions in their communities. For reasons that are impossible to clarify after so many centuries of history, this thought has not received due analysis, probably because the main part of the statement was oriented to the topic of justice, and those who suffered the abuses of oppressive ritualisms of the period, for obvious reasons, gave the biggest attention to the last part of the commentary. The truth is that the commentary continues to be pertinent nowadays and may very well serve to make us rethink several matters relative to the employment of alternative models to approach our reality, as well as to reflect on the role of rites in communitarian life.[3]

Let us consider for a moment this commentary attributed to Jesus in two of the Synoptic Gospels: in Luke 11:42 and in Matthew 23:23.[4] Although found in two different places of Jesus' ministry, in both instances it reflects Jesus' serious conflicts with the Pharisees and the Scribes. In both texts Jesus is very forceful in his criticism of the hypocrisy of these groups in employing the legal traditions related to offerings.[5] We should bear in mind that Jesus' addressees are religious and orthodox people who perceived themselves as morally and legally right. Nevertheless, in both texts Jesus is presented as inviting them to explore a different relationship among their valuable traditions. In Matthew, the pericope appears toward the end of Jesus' ministry, and it identifies the audience as Scribes, Pharisees, and hypocrites. In Luke 11:42, this comment appears earlier in his ministry. We find it in the specific context of a dinner where Jesus is with the Pharisees and teachers of the law. What we cannot oversee is the fact that it also implies a certain proximity of Jesus to these groups. In Luke, the expression is part of the defense and reaction of Jesus to a series of insults and accusations that these factions of Jews imputed to him in order to discredit him.[6] From the point of view of its literary genre, the expression appears in the framework of the laments addressed by Jesus to the Pharisees.[7] It is evident that the contexts reveal harsh criticism, hypocrisy, and the misuse of certain laws on offerings by these groups. Notwithstanding, these traditions—the portrayal of Jesus in Matthew and Luke's

Gospels—reflect great respect and appreciation toward the law. There is consensus in associating this expression to the Q source, which supports our thesis that there were groups in the early Christian community who fought to preserve and establish a critical integration between their rich legal traditions associated with the Jewish rites of offerings and the communal social justice. As a good Jew, Jesus does not separate obedience to the legal statutes (the customs and values) and their ultimate purpose, that is, justice, mercy, and strengthening of life in community. Jesus accepted tithe offerings as a devotional expression to God, but he saw these practices as contradictory if the community ultimately ignored its goal: justice and communal love.[8] The well-known expression—"Do not think that I have come to abolish the law or the prophets; I have come not to abolish but to fulfill"—may support this tradition (Matt 5:17). What I wish to highlight is that in this tradition Jesus accepts and presupposes life in community as one in healthy tension. Tension among what they ought to have practiced (the traditional things, the orthodox things, the smallest things that were expected of them) and "the other things" (that which is just and necessary, that which transcends the expectations of orthodoxy, that which goes to the very root of the issues). So I see Jesus here neither rejecting the law nor the rites as such but reproaching the misuse of these laws by Pharisees and Scribes who did not have the capacity nor the sensibility of exploring other models to correlate to. Jesus proposed a creative model to them, a model that was not politically correct for the expectations of these Pharisees, a paradigm that can be an "alternative model" today. A model that explored, challenged, and transcended the conservative paradigms, as well as the liberal paradigms, used to reduce life to mutually exclusive alternatives: white or black, pro or con, mine or yours. Jesus' proposal did not simplify their lives. He offered neither an easy alternative, neutrality, nor a model that did not seek to eliminate the tensions and conflicts through a magical formula. Jesus did not ignore the tension between the "important issues" (justice and mercy) and the "peripheral issues" (ritual traditions) but rather correlated them in a creative way. Jesus' proposal accepted the tension and the conflict as part of life but responded to that tension and conflict in innovative, creative, and radical ways. Jesus invited them to rehearse a model that needed constant attention and care in order to be pertinent. Could this model also be valid for many of the situations that we face now? We are not suggesting that this be the only model or answer to all situations but believe it should be considered among other models to explore, a model that accepts and presupposes a healthy tension in life.

RITES AS INSTRUMENTS OF RESISTANCE

Not only in modern and postmodern times is there resistance and tension when one speaks of the role that rites and ceremonies play, but in the biblical text we also find a great tension when the traditions of the communities that constituted the Old and the New Testament are judged. The history of Latin American and Hispanic interpretation is not exempted from those misunderstandings. Having been influenced, to a great extent, by modern, European, and Euro-American interpretations, we have been very sensitive in noticing an aspect of that tension, that is to say, the misuse and abuse of the rites criticized by the prophets and by Jesus. However, we have denied and ignored other biblical traditions showing a more critical view of the function of rites in the community.[9] In the last decades, critical studies—from the so-called social scientific criticism, cultural anthropology, and rituals studies—have shed new light on how to interpret the value and function of the rites in the diverse biblical and nonbiblical contexts.[10]

RITUAL STUDIES DURING THE LAST DECADES

In recent decades investigations into the purpose and meaning of rites in the life of the biblical communities has experienced a renewed interest.[11] These new studies represent a diversity of perspectives, foci, and anthropological and sociological schools. Until the mid-twentieth century, a considerable number of critical studies manifested the prejudices against the role of most ritual activity in biblical religion. We find few studies that valued ritual activities. For a long time, most types of rituals were considered remains of superstitious practices of the pre-Israelite religion. However, a renovated interest has been spurred in ritual studies from theological, biblical, anthropological, and sociological perspectives emphasizing liberating elements that have hardly been explored.[12]

The understandings and concerns for these practices are no longer reduced, for example, to exploring pathological manifestations associated with old, prescientific, medieval, sanguinary, scandalous rituals and sacrificial offerings and holocausts of savages, magical and superstitious practices that perpetuated the oppression and "status quo" (which we do not deny it still can be true in many cases). Rather, these practices have been recognized to be means of resistance and affirmation of the most treasured cultural traditions of the people and communities. Nowadays it is affirmed that they have the potential of challenging, and in some cases, even defying the established order.[13] These studies have highlighted an array of important subtopics, of which I would like to point out at least two: (a) there is no community, group, or people that does not have a certain "system" of rites incorporated in their collective life. To express it positively, all human groups (consciously or unconsciously) follow a series of practices (rites and ceremonies) through which they manifest and perpetuate their beliefs, traditions, and myths. (b) One of the new questions scholars have explored is to what extent these ritual traditions served as instruments of liberation and means to affirm and to perpetuate their most valued traditions. The questions are no longer limited to exploring the possible negative aspects of the rites and ceremonial practices but rather the liberating effects that these practices could have had in these communities. Most of the studies on rituals concern the value of these practices in times of social crisis, exile, and cultural threat; in particular, those instances when groups or communities do not have the might (political and/or economical) to face changes caused by other more powerful groups (whether they be empires, foreign towns, or even factions in conflict within a group).[14] For example, in New Testament studies, Mark McVann demonstrates that the Gospel of Mark uses baptism, an initiation rite, to direct Jesus' followers to affirm their identity amid the persecution.[15] The list of Old Testament studies is also extensive. Among the most significant examples are the works of Daniel Smith, *The Religion of the Landless*, and Mary Douglas, *In the Wilderness: The Doctrine of Defilement in the Book of Numbers*.[16]

RITES AND CEREMONIES

In our day-to-day experience we do not make a distinction between rites and ceremonies. Anthropologically speaking, there is a distinction between these two practices and concepts. Without trying to offer an exhaustive analysis, we can say briefly that the rituals serve to legitimize status transformation—when people change from one role or status to another—whereas ceremonies affirm the status, values, and structures already institutionalized in the society. The rituals are irregular practices that only happen in certain moments of people's lives, such as baptisms, coronations, marriages, or funerals. Ceremonies are regular and predictable, such as the liturgical Christian year: seasons of Advent, Lent, Easter, Epiphany, and Pentecost; in the Old Testament the festivals of the unleavened bread or Passover (Exod 12:1-13; Lev 23:4-14; Deut 16:1-18); feast of the firstfruits or the weeks (Exod 23:16; Deut 16:9-12); feast of the booth (Exod 23:16; Lev 23:33-36; Deut 16:13-16). Scholars concur that both types of practices help us to understand the boundaries the groups create to make distinctions between role and status in the symbolic world they forge in order to socialize and affirm their identities and to perpetuate their traditions and values. In the Christian community, these rites reaffirm their beliefs and confessions of faith.

THE BABYLONIAN EXILE AS AN EXAMPLE

Another interesting investigation in the Old Testament has been that of Daniel Smith. In his work, Smith analyzes a series of behaviors that minority groups in exile employ in situations of repression in order to create social limits and boundaries to affirm their identity and resist political powers that threaten to destroy them. Smith calls them "mechanisms of survival."[17] He selects four mechanisms of survival that have been identified in groups under diverse exilic and colonial conditions. These mechanisms are comparable to some of the defenses we find within our own communities today: the first of these responses is a new structural adaptation or way of reorganizing people's leadership. Among the biblical examples that Smith associates with this response is the new way of organizing the *bene-ha-gola*—the children of the exile—or the transformation in the constitution of the assembly of the elder men. He highlights how the community had to make adjustments, to be more flexible, and to create new forms of adaptation to crises in order to develop an effective resistance. The second response that Smith analyzes has to do with changes in the patterns of leadership. The author points out changes between confrontational styles of old leadership vis-à-vis the new strategies of social resistance that were adopted in the exilic and postexilic periods. The examples that he discusses are found in the leadership exerted by the prophets Jeremiah and Hananiah (Jer 27–29), as well as the leadership of Ezra and Nehemiah. The third mechanism he identifies is the creation of a new literature of stories and folkloric traditions through "heroic stories" that offer new models to the group. The fourth mechanism of survival and the one that we are interested in here has to do with the creation and elaboration of priestly ritual practices.

In biblical critical studies, these practices have traditionally been interpreted as not very creative and as legalistic manifestations of priestly exilic and postexilic circles. They are reinterpreted by Smith as mechanisms of protection in order to survive in exile. After having examined these theories on the formation of tradition and priestly document, Smith questions Wellhausen's theses concerning his negative evaluation of the chore of priestly circles. Smith, on the other hand, shows that the purity rules in the legal traditions are priestly mechanisms of social survival and maintenance and concludes that "to dismiss this creativity as 'legalism' is to forget, or ignore, the sociopolitical circumstances in which it was formulated. Majority cultures rarely understand, much less appreciate, the actions of minorities to preserve and maintain identity."[18]

This study offers hermeneutical clues that can be very valuable for our communities who live under new and diverse situations of modern exile. It is important here to recall, as one Jewish writer reminds us, that as much as the Jewish people have kept the Sabbath, all the more have they been kept by it. The view on the Sabbath, far from being a legalistic expression of some conservative groups, represents a mechanism of survival.

CONCLUDING REMARKS

Needless to say, in our Hispanic/Latina communities, especially among some evangelical settings, the value and purpose of ritual practices are perceived, to a great extent, as means that restrain the freedom of the spirit and perpetuate hierarchical structures that hamper the free relationship with God and our neighbors and promote structures of dominance. Without trying to be exhaustive and to the extent that some truth can be drawn from these perceptions, I can point to other historical and sociological reasons that are important: (1) culturally, we have inherited varied cosmological perspectives, among them what has been identified as "Western individualism." Some of its historical roots are associated with the concept of Person in early Christianity, the Protestant Reformation, and the cosmology of modern rationalism. (2) The influence of the mainstream American society, which is an individually oriented society, that is, people and persons perceive themselves above the group and free to do whatever they believe is right. It fosters an uncritical rejection of traditional ritual practices, but then substitutes them with other rituals of the American way of life, which, though not regarded as rites, in fact are. (3) What is more interesting is the posture of some groups within the Hispanic/Latina community that have adopted a lifestyle that reflects rather individualistic visions of life instead of a communal one. These groups do not seem to worry about the relationship between individualistic cosmology of society and the influence that rituals can play in those visions. Influenced by a modern and postmodern individualistic liberal understanding of the world, our communities are uncritically discarding every ritual practice as antiquated, unnecessary, and oppressive and preserving very few tools to resist change and to perpetuate our values and traditions.

Ritual studies, as we pointed out previously, have demonstrated that although in most biblical traditions a clear criticism to the life that succumbs to ritualism and to religious hierarchical relationships oppressing the people of God is affirmed, there are other traditions that reflect a critical openness to the liberating role of rites amid the people. Using Jesus' remarks as the starting point for our reflection, we have intended to underscore the possible existence of groups among the early Christian community that may have explored an alternative model to relate the search for justice and its relationship with their legal traditions, a model considered "politically incorrect" for those who dominated the structures of power and even perhaps for those who fought against them, a model that transcended the paradigms reducing life to mutually exclusive alternatives. So here we find Jesus accepting the life in community as one of healthy tension. Tension between what "they ought to have practiced" (the traditional values, the orthodox view, the least thing expected of them), and "the other things" (the just, "the necessary things," what goes beyond the expectations of orthodoxy, what goes to the root of matters). Jesus invited them to rehearse a model that needed constant attention and revision in order to be pertinent.

It would be naive to think that developments, changes, and growth in our communities will only happen with the accusation and denunciation of injustices and the proclamation of justice and love. This is extremely important; but if we do not create concrete social infrastructures that enable just relationships and support and facilitate liberating spaces, it will be very difficult to reach our goals. In this sense, it is urgent that we dare to incorporate ritual traditions by means of which we foster values and relationships where we rehearse and enjoy the promises of the Resurrected One, traditions where we critically rehearse multiple practices (rites and ceremonies) that will help us to continue to reaffirm some values, transforming and changing others in order to foster and to perpetuate the values of the kingdom of God, which support cultures of peace, of reconciliation, of justice, and of ecumenical fraternity. In this sense, Jesus' words support and summarize what we mean: "It is these you ought to have practiced, without neglecting the others."

Toward a Hermeneutics
of the Diaspora

A Hermeneutics of Otherness and Engagement

Fernando F. Segovia

As the title for the present essay indicates, I believe that the time has come to introduce the real reader, the flesh-and-blood reader, fully and explicitly, into the theory and practice of biblical criticism; to acknowledge that no reading, informed or uninformed, takes place in a social vacuum or desert; to allow fully for contextualization, for culture and experience, not only with regard to texts but also with regard to readers of texts with a view of all readings as constructs proceeding from, dependent upon, and addressing a particular social location, however circumscribed.

I see this irruption of the flesh-and-blood reader into biblical criticism as a harbinger not of anarchy and tribalism, as many who insist on impartiality and objectivity often claim, but rather of continued decolonization and liberation, of resistance and struggle against a subtle authoritarianism and covert tribalism of its own, in a discipline that has been, from beginning to end and top to bottom, thoroughly Eurocentric despite its assumed scientific persona of neutrality and universality.[1] In effect, I regard the admission and intromission of real readers, of the contextuality and particularity of all readings, as an acceptance of the world for what it is, in the richness and fullness of its diversity, especially in this time of increasing and irreversible globalization in every sphere of life, including the theological and the interpretive—an acceptance of the other not as an imposed or defined "other" but as independent and self-defining.[2]

In this essay I should like to propose, therefore, the beginnings of a hermeneutical framework for taking the flesh-and-blood reader seriously in biblical criticism, not so much as a unique and independent individual but rather as a member of distinct and identifiable social configurations, as a reader from and within a social location.[3] The proposed framework is not conceived in essentialist terms as a master or totalizing narrative derived from the human condition and calling for universal applicability but as a contextual stance that is directly grounded in and informed by my own social location as a member of the diaspora, by which I mean specifically the massive dispersion of the children of the Third World, the world of the politically and/or economically colonized, in the First World, the world of the colonizers, of the political and/or economic center. In my own case, furthermore, such a location in the diaspora can be more specifically described in terms of my sociopolitical status as a Hispanic American, a readily identifiable and distinct social configuration within U.S. society. It is a framework that I refer to as a hermeneutics of the diaspora, a Hispanic American hermeneutics of otherness and engagement, whose fundamental purpose is to read the biblical text as an other—not to be overwhelmed or overridden, but acknowledged, respected, and engaged in its very otherness. It is a framework that is ultimately grounded in a theology of the diaspora (a Hispanic American theology of otherness and mixture) and that gives rise to a specific methodological approach—the reading strategy of intercultural criticism.

I see such a framework as forming part of that paradigm or umbrella model of interpretation within biblical criticism that I have characterized in terms of cultural studies. Thus, for example, the proposal calls into question the enduring and beloved construct of a neutral and disinterested reader in biblical criticism (a universal and informed reader) and opts instead for the construct of a flesh-and-blood reader (a real reader who is always situated and engaged, socially and historically conditioned, reading and interpreting from a variety of different and complex social locations). Such a reader is not universal and may or may not be informed, that is to say, may or may not possess sophisticated training in criticism and theory of whatever sort. Moreover, the proposal also calls for engagement in a joint critical study of texts and readers of texts, for analysis of textual as well as interpretive perspectives and ideologies. As such, it looks upon a critical analysis of the biblical texts to be as important as a critical analysis of their readers and readings. Furthermore, the proposal regards all models of interpretation and strategies for reading, all retrievals of meaning from texts, and all reconstructions of history behind texts as constructions, formulated and advanced by flesh-and-blood readers. In other words, no model, retrieval, or reconstruction is seen as beyond interpretation and controlling interpretation. Finally, the proposal forms part of a much larger process of decolonization and liberation taking place in the discipline since the mid-1970s; in fact, it extends such a process from the realm of theory and methodology into the realm of human diversity. As such, it continues to break down the traditional and fundamental Eurocentric moorings and boundaries of the discipline in favor of a multidimensional and decentered mode of discourse, a global discourse in which all readers have a voice and engage one another out of their own respective social locations, out of their own otherness.

In what follows, then, I begin with an analysis of the social location of the diaspora and my own position within the diaspora as a Hispanic American;

then, I proceed to outline the basic contours of the proposed hermeneutics of the diaspora.

THE DIASPORA AS SOCIAL LOCATION

The Context of the Diaspora

Diasporas are not all the same: they are highly complex and multidimensional realities. A beginning distinction in this regard is, I believe, in order and helpful. At its most general level, the diaspora represents the sum total of all those who presently live, for whatever reason, on a permanent basis in a country other than that of their birth. Diasporas involve migration, therefore, and are, at their very core, political phenomena, involving changes in sociopolitical status and/or affiliation. As such, they affect the world as a whole: the First World; the Second World, or the former communist bloc; and the Third World. At the same time, the reasons for expatriation and the resultant status of the expatriates vary enormously in each case.

Thus, for example, with regard to the first two types of diaspora, the reality of expatriation for academicians or highly trained professionals of the United States or Western Europe who choose to live their lives on the other continent is very different from the reality of the former political refugees from behind the Iron Curtain who fled to and settled in the West or the reality of the unemployed masses of workers from Eastern Europe now seeking employment in Western Europe. I belong to neither one of these realities and cannot speak for them, although I suspect that the ongoing diaspora involving the former denizens of the communist bloc has a great deal in common with the diaspora of the Third World; after all, such a situation can ultimately be described as well in terms of a colonizer/colonized relationship, given the hegemonic role and power of the former Soviet Union in these countries and the devastating economic conditions left behind by the imperial center after its collapse and withdrawal.

It is with the third type of diaspora mentioned above, therefore, that I am specifically concerned, that is, with that large and growing segment of people from the Third World who are forced to live—for whatever reason, though usually involving a combination of sociopolitical and socioeconomic factors—in the First World, whether in Europe, Japan, or the United States.[4] By and large, these are the children of colonialism and neocolonialism: people from the world of the colonized who now have to live in the world of the colonizers, from the world of the poor and undeveloped/developing South who now have to live in the world of the rich and developed North. Given the traditional relationship between colonizers and colonized—a relationship profoundly marked by a set of binary oppositions ultimately grounded in those of center/margins and civilization/primitivism—such a reality is global and comprehensive. At the same time, to be sure, within such a reality, distinctions have to be made, based on a number of different factors: despite overall similarities, it is far different to be a farm worker than to be an accountant or engineer, to have "colored" skin rather than "white" skin, and to be female rather than male. It is this diaspora in which I find myself "thrown" (*arrojado*) as a human being, as a critic, and as a theologian; it is this diaspora, therefore, that serves not only as a fundamental constitutive factor for my social location but also as a point of departure for my critical and theological voice.[5]

In what follows I proceed to analyze my own position within such a diaspora as a Hispanic American, with an emphasis on the general characteristics or similarities of this reality rather than on its distinguishing features or characteristics.[6] Such a diaspora is, of course, a diaspora of the Western Hemisphere: the children of Latin America and the Caribbean who are forced to live in the North for a variety of interrelated and interdependent reasons. Within such a diaspora, those of us from the Spanish-speaking countries of Latin America have become known as Hispanic Americans. It is from such a corner of the diaspora that I set out to construct a hermeneutics of the diaspora, a hermeneutics of otherness and engagement.

The Context of the Hispanic American Diaspora

As a Hispanic American, I belong to a large group of people for whom biculturalism constitutes a fundamental and inescapable way of life.[7] Such biculturalism reveals two essential dimensions. On the one hand, we live in two worlds at one and the same time, operating relatively at ease within each world and able to go in and out of each in an endless exercise of human and social translation; on the other hand, we live in neither one of these worlds, regarded askance by their respective populations and unable to call either world home. Thus, our biculturalism results in a very paradoxical and alienating situation involving a continuous twofold existence as permanent strangers or aliens, as permanent "others." It is a situation that I have described elsewhere as having both two places and no place on which to stand.[8] This situation of double and reinforced otherness may be further delineated as follows:[9]

1. As Hispanic Americans, our present, permanent, and everyday world is that of the United States, whether we are born or naturalized citizens, legal or illegal aliens. In this world we immediately find—much to the surprise of those of us who are immigrants, given our image of the country from the outside as a bastion of freedom, justice, and opportunity[10]—that there is a script ready for us to play and follow, outside of which we dare venture only against great odds and with considerable opposition. This script involves a name, a pattern, and a value judgment.

First, the name does vary, with *Hispanics, Hispanic Americans,* and *Latinos* as recurrent options; the important point in this regard, however, is that we use none of these names for ourselves. The names are given to us and thus form part of the script itself. Second, the pattern behind the name is consistent and inflexible: regardless of geographical or social origins, we are all seen in terms of a rather monolithic and undifferentiated mass. Again, we have but little choice in this regard, with no amount of explanation seemingly capable of altering the established pattern. Third, the value judgment that underlies the pattern is not only similarly rigid and unchanging but also quite disparaging and destructive. Its overall contours encompass such attributes as lazy and unenterprising, carefree and sensual, undisciplined and violent, vulgar and unintelligent; its corresponding images in popular culture come readily to mind: the Puerto Rican gangs of the film *West Side Story;* the Mexican outlaws or *bandidos* of countless Westerns; the drug lords and pushers of *Miami Vice* and a host of other television programs; the happy-go-lucky Carmen Mirandas and Ricky Ricardos of this world. Thus, the name and the pattern are by no means neutral but reveal and convey a dominant perception of the group as primitive, inferior, and uncivilized. Once again, we find ourselves tightly locked into this external view of ourselves, with protestation or enlightenment as a seemingly useless enterprise. In our present, permanent, and everyday world, therefore, we begin as strangers and we remain strangers throughout—the undesirable "others," the ones who do not fit.

2. As Hispanic Americans, directly or indirectly, our former, traditional, and distant world is that of Latin America, even for those whose world was annexed by the United States, as is the case with Puerto Rico and the former Mexican territories of the Southwest. Contrary to popular perception in the United States, this former world of ours is a world of profound differences, incredible diversity, and great richness. First, in direct contrast to the homogeneity ascribed to us via name and pattern in our present world, we hail from many and enormously diverse quarters—many countries and areas, each with its own distinctive history, traditions, and culture—and we call ourselves mainly by our place of origin, for example, Dominicans, Puerto Ricans, Salvadorans. Similarly, in direct contrast to the judgment rendered against us, we represent, in varying degrees and configurations, a new *raza,* a rich mixture of races and cultures, encompassing European, African, Amerindian, and even Asian components. Ironically, such elements have perhaps never interacted before to the extent that they now do in the United States, especially given our present numbers as the equivalent of the fifth most populous nation in Latin America, so that in effect the emerging Hispanic American reality in the United States may in the end give rise to an even greater degree of biological and cultural mixture than ever before.[11]

Yet with each passing year in our present world, we realize that our traditional world is no longer ours: our association with it has become remote, at best intermittent, and passive. In fact, from the point of view of our former world, we encounter yet another script ready for us to play and follow, outside of which we can venture but not very far. The script has a name: the (willing or unwilling) emigrant or expatriate, such as the Mexican American *pocho* or the Puerto Rican *neorican;* an ironic pattern: getting ahead in the land of freedom, justice, and opportunity; and an even more ironic value judgment: culturally disconnected but economically superior. This script, however, is far more understandable, given our absence and distance, and much more benign, given an abiding sense of ultimate, even if conditioned, acceptance. In our former, traditional, and distant world, therefore, we gradually and inevitably become and remain aliens as well—the distant "others," the ones who left.

3. We are thus always strangers or aliens, the permanent "others," both where we came from and where we find ourselves. As such, we find ourselves always defined by somebody else—in our traditional world by those whom we left behind and in our present world by those with whom we live; silenced and speechless—without an autochthonous, self-conscious, and firm voice and without a home of our own—excluded and condemned by such external definitions and such lack of voice. On the one hand, we know and understand, however regretfully and painfully, the definition of those we left behind—a permanent and living association elsewhere does remove one slowly but surely from one's traditional world. On the other hand, we suffer and fail to comprehend the definition of those with whom we live—our permanent and everyday association is disdained and rejected. Such "otherness," bestowed upon us and defined for us, overwhelms and overrides us, depriving us not only of a present, past, and future but also of self-definition, self-appropriation, and self-direction.

Such a constitutive and alienating "otherness" can be, as is often the case, internalized and lived out, resulting in the classic pattern of the colonized: passivity, submission, obedience. To be sure, this process of internalization can and does range anywhere from the truly constitutive or existential (the full acceptance of the external definition as the self-definition) to the purely strategic or tactical (the surface adoption of the external definition as a way of survival). Such "otherness," however, can also be turned into a point of departure for the formulation of our own voice, a voice that not only makes explicit the spirit of independence, resistance, and rebellion that so often lies beneath the surface of the friendly and hospitable colonized but also gives rise to the classic pattern of the colonizer, the pattern of manifest destiny: self-confidence, self-expression, and self-determination. For me it is precisely this latter option that gives rise to the voice behind the theology of otherness and mixture, the hermeneutics of otherness and engagement, and the interpretive strategy of intercultural criticism.

Toward a Hispanic American Voice

Given this social location of ours as Hispanic Americans, *we* must claim our *otherness* and turn it precisely into what it is, our very identity, using it constructively and creatively in the interest of liberation, not only on our behalf but on behalf of others as well.[12] I would argue, therefore, that our theological and hermeneutical voice must be grounded in and grow out of this identity of otherness.

1. To begin with, this otherness does indeed have another and much more positive dimension. While our paradoxical situation does mean having no place to stand, it also means having two places on which to stand, a second fundamental dimension that cannot be overlooked or bypassed. The very source of our alienation becomes thereby the very source of our identity. While regarded as "others" in both worlds of our existence, the fact remains that we do live in both worlds and that we do know how to proceed, at a moment's notice, from one world to the other. In other words, we know both worlds quite well from the inside and the outside, and this privileged knowledge of ours gives us a rather unique perspective: we know that both worlds, that all worlds, are constructions, rather solid and firm constructions to be sure, but constructions nonetheless. We know from our very experience that "nature" is itself a construction and its "laws" conventions. We know what makes each world cohere and function; we can see what is good and bad in each world and choose accordingly; and we are able to offer an informed critique of each world—its vision, its values, its traditions.

This privileged knowledge allows us in the end to see our own reality as others in terms of construction, understanding thereby the attributes of and rationale for our perception as "others"; to use this reality to our own advantage, giving such otherness a voice of its own; and to do so critically, not in terms of "nature" and "laws" but rather in terms of our own power to construct ourselves and others, avoiding thereby all semblance of a new romanticism or a new imperialism, a utopian or messianic interpretation of our otherness, whereby such otherness becomes idealized or exclusionist. In the end, any such glorification of our otherness would only serve to define and silence those who are others to us, doing thereby unto others what others have done to us.

2. Giving a voice to this otherness of ours entails a threefold critical process of self-affirmation: (a) self-appropriation, or a reenvisioning of our past and our history with our own eyes; (b) self-definition, or a retelling of our present reality and experience in our own words; and (c) self-direction, or a reclaiming of our future and self-determination in terms of our own dreams and visions. Thus, the process entails, on the one hand, an active refusal to be bound by our imposed definitions, with a corresponding commitment to understand, expose, and critique such definitions; on the other hand, the process also entails an active determination to offer our own self-definitions, with a corresponding commitment not only to the self-affirmation of others but also to a critical exchange with such others and their own corresponding self-affirmations. As such, the process of self-affirmation envisioned is one that confers dignity, liberation, and openness not only on the group itself but on all other groups—a manifest

destiny that goes against the very grain of and redefines and reenvisions the very notion of manifest destiny.

3. In this process of self-affirmation, we must fully acknowledge, embrace, and integrate the fundamental characteristics of our otherness. First, we do well to remember our sociocultural past in a world where mixture is regarded as highly problematic and indeed offensive. We are a hybrid people, with biological and/or cultural miscegenation at our very core. This indiscriminate mixture, this *mezcolanza*,[13] brings together in many and varied ways the heritage of Europe via Mediterranean and Catholic Spain, of Africa and America, as well as of Asia (though to a much lesser extent). Though it is in large part because of such mixture that we find rejection in our present world, we must emphasize and embrace mixture: for us, mixture is life and gives life. Second, we do well to remember our sociohistorical and sociopolitical past. Our mixture is by no means the result of an irenic encounter and coexistence but rather of a harsh and cruel tradition of colonialism and neocolonialism. Such a tradition has given rise to a history of violence and oppression, tyranny and corruption. Yet, despite such history and tradition, we have also manifested an enduring commitment to freedom, life, and dignity. We must emphasize and embrace such a commitment: in the very midst of chaos and death, we struggle for life and enjoyment of life. Third, we do well to remember our sociocultural present. We find ourselves not only the target of sustained discrimination, socially and culturally rejected at all levels of life, but also in a situation of widespread social devastation—politically powerless, economically deprived, and educationally fragile. At the same time, we struggle to make a home under the democratic principles of the nation, hoping that our commitment to life can ultimately take root and grow. We must emphasize and embrace this struggle as well: despite often unbearable conditions, we continue to believe in and strive for our dream of freedom, justice, and opportunity in a new home.

This embrace of mixture, life, and struggle should ultimately provide us with an identity that recognizes the others but refuses to define them, as we ourselves have been and continue to be defined; that allows such others to speak and to define themselves, in contrast to our own silencing and silence; that is committed not to a placid exchange of views with these others but to hard critical exchange, including the *very* construction of others as others. Thus, the voice of our otherness becomes a voice of and for liberation: not afraid to expose, critique, and provide an alternative vision and narrative; grounded in mixture as something not to be eschewed and marginalized but valued and engaged; and committed to the fundamental principles of freedom and justice. From such a voice emerges a profound commitment not to overwhelm or override the other but rather to acknowledge it, value it, engage it—a theology of mixture and otherness, a hermeneutics of otherness and engagement, and a reading strategy of intercultural criticism.

TOWARD A HERMENEUTICS OF THE DIASPORA:
THE TEXT AS OTHER

The voice of *otherness* begins with contextualization and aims for it. In reference to biblical criticism, it argues that contextualization is imperative with
regard to the biblical texts as well as with regard to their readers and critics.[14] In
effect, it sees a genuine exchange with otherness—the otherness both of the text
and of other readers of the text—as impossible without a preliminary renuncia-
tion of presumed universality and objectivity and a corresponding admission and
acceptance of contextuality. It is a voice that seeks not a dehumanization or
rehumanization of the reader but a liberating and empowering humanization of
the reader, of all readers, by taking fully into account the experience and culture
of readers in the act of reading and interpretation. Such is the basis for a diaspora hermeneutics of otherness and engagement, from which emerges the proposed reading strategy of intercultural criticism.

Its theoretical foundation in literary criticism is that of reader-response criticism, involving a fundamental position to the effect that no text is read, understood, or interpreted without a reader and a corresponding view of meaning as
the result of interaction between the reader and the text. Within this overall
theoretical orientation, a broad interpretive spectrum can be readily outlined,
ranging from a reader-dominant pole (with meaning coming primarily from the
reader either as an individual subject or as a member of an interpretive community) to a text-dominant pole (with meaning coming primarily from the text in
terms of its own strategies and constraints).[15] Within this theoretical spectrum,
I would locate intercultural criticism to the left of center, toward the reader-
dominant pole, with a view of meaning as the result of interaction between a
socially and culturally conditioned reader and a socially and culturally conditioned text, with such a reader as an inevitable and ever-present filter in the
reading and interpretation of such a text. In what follows I should like to explore
these three basic dimensions of intercultural criticism.

First, the text is to be regarded, like any contemporary social group: as a
socially and culturally conditioned other. The question of access is crucial.
Rather than positing any type of direct or immediate entrance into the text, the
hermeneutics of otherness and engagement argues for distantiation from it as a
working desideratum, emphasizing thereby the historical and cultural remoteness of the text. Such a hermeneutics begins, therefore, by recognizing that the
biblical text comes from a very different historical situation and cultural matrix,
a very different experience and culture; that all texts, including the biblical
texts, are contextual products; and that no text—not even the biblical text—is
atemporal, asocial, ahistorical, speaking uniformly across time and culture.

This operative attitude of distantiation grows out of our bicultural reality
as Hispanic Americans. First, this experience shows us that all reality is

construction and, as such, profoundly historical and cultural. Second, this experience further shows us that external perceptions of ourselves as "others" revolve around the stereotypical and fail to respect our otherness, readily overriding and overwhelming our sense of identity with disastrous and lasting consequences for us both as a group and as individuals. Out of such experience emerges a key element in the theology of mixture and otherness: a commitment to understand those who function as others to us—the many social groups with whom we relate and coexist, even within our own social configuration—in terms of their own words and visions, by allowing them to speak on their own, to create their own narrative, and to define their own identity. Out of this experience emerges as well a key element in the hermeneutics of otherness and engagement: a commitment to understand the biblical text—or any other text for that matter—as an other to us, with its own words and visions, allowing it to speak on its own, to unravel its own narrative, and to define its own identity. In effect, if contemporary and coexisting social groups prove to be so different from and so puzzling to one another, then one is justified in calling into question any type of immediate and unqualified identification with texts that come from a very different historical situation and cultural framework.

For intercultural criticism, therefore, the contextuality and otherness of the text must be acknowledged, valued, and analyzed. This process of distantiation is helped immensely by a view of the text as a literary, rhetorical, and ideological product in its own right: an artistic construction with underlying strategic concerns and goals in the light of its own point of view, its own vision of the world and reality, within a given historical and cultural matrix. As such, a consideration of the text as other should avail itself of any variety of literary and sociocultural methodologies that allow us to bring this multidimensional character of the text to the fore. The ultimate aim of such an enterprise would be an understanding of the text as a whole, as a world of its own, as a construct within a more comprehensive historical-cultural framework—no matter how strange or remote.

Second, the reader is also to be regarded as socially and culturally conditioned as an other to both text and other readers. The question of critical honesty is crucial. Rather than seeking after impartiality or objectivity, presuming to universality and claiming to read like anyone or everyone, the hermeneutics of otherness and engagement argues for a self-conscious exposition and analysis of the reader's strategy for reading, the theoretical foundations behind this strategy, and the social location underlying such a strategy. This hermeneutics further begins, therefore, by recognizing that the reader, like the text, comes from a specific historical situation and cultural matrix, a specific experience and culture; that all readers are contextual products and that such different social locations can and do influence the process of reading and interpretation; and that no reader—not even an ideal or highly informed one—is atemporal, asocial, or ahistorical, speaking uniformly for all times and cultures.

This attitude of self-conscious reflection grows out of our bicultural reality as Hispanic Americans. First, this experience shows us that all reality, as construction, has its own way of seeing and acting and that such vision and behavior have in turn their own historical and cultural roots. Second, this experience also shows us that it is possible to live and function with relative ease in more than one reality, putting on and removing the proper lenses of each reality or world as the occasion warrants. From such an experience, once again, an important element in the theology of otherness and mixture comes to the fore: a commitment to acknowledge and allow for the voice of otherness in a world of incredible diversity. From such an experience, furthermore, an important element in the hermeneutics of otherness and engagement comes to the fore: a commitment to see readers, all readers and readings, as distinct and autonomous voices within such a rich diversity. In effect, if we ourselves know how to "read" reality with more than one lens, then one is fully justified in positing an enormous variety of such lenses and readings, both in the present and in antiquity.

For intercultural criticism, therefore, the contextuality and otherness of readers must also be acknowledged, valued, and analyzed. This process of conscious self-reflection is helped immensely by a view of the reader as a product, a "text" as it were, in his or her own right: a historical and cultural construction involving a view of the past, the present, and the future. Consequently, a consideration of the reader as other should avail itself of any variety of social and cultural methodologies that would bring to the fore this multidimensional identity of the reader, with a systematic and sustained analysis of such factors as socioreligious tradition and affiliation; ideological stance; sociopolitical status and affiliation; socioeconomic class, gender, racial, or ethnic background; sociocultural conventions; and socioeducational attainment. The ultimate aim of such an analysis would be an understanding of the reader as a whole, as a world of his or her own, as a construct within a more comprehensive historical and cultural matrix—again no matter how strange or remote.

Finally, the interaction between such a text and such a reader is to be regarded not as a neutral encounter between two independent, socially and culturally conditioned entities or worlds but rather as an unavoidable filtering of the one world or entity by and through the other, of the text by and through the reader. In this regard, both the question of access and the question of critical honesty are crucial. Despite the attitude of distantiation from the text, the hermeneutics of otherness and engagement argues that the historical and cultural remoteness of the text as an other is in itself not a reconstruction but a construction of the past on the part of the reader. Despite the attitude of conscious self-reflection, this hermeneutics further argues that such a construction of the past is dependent as well on the reader's own social location. The hermeneutics of otherness and engagement continues, therefore, by recognizing that the very process of distantiation ultimately comes out of a specific historical situation and cultural matrix, a specific experience and culture; that the results of such a process are likewise contextual products, influenced by the social location of the reader in question; and that no process of distantiation—not even a properly informed and self-conscious one—is in itself atemporal, asocial, or ahistorical.

This attitude regarding the interaction between the reader and the text again grows out of our bicultural reality as Hispanic Americans. First, this experience shows us that all reality, though constructed, is quite resistant to change, that it is not at all easy to go against or deviate from historical and cultural roots. Second, this experience further shows us that the external perception of ourselves as "others" stubbornly resists any type of critical questioning or enlightenment, often turning the whole exercise of conscientization into a frustrating Sisyphean task. Third, this experience also shows us that such a fundamental sense of reality as construction is very difficult to attain within a monocultural matrix. Out of this experience emerges a key element in the theology of mixture and otherness: a commitment to critical dialogue and exchange with the other, subjecting our respective views of one another and the world to critical exposure and analysis. Out of this experience emerges as well a key element in the hermeneutics of otherness and engagement: first, a commitment to critical dialogue and exchange with the text as other, subjecting our respective views of the world to critical exposure and analysis; second, a commitment to critical dialogue and exchange with other interpreters of the text, both historical and contemporary, again subjecting our respective views of the text and its world to critical exposure and analysis. In effect, if contemporary and coexisting social groups prove so resistant to change with respect to one another, even in the face of sharp critique and protestations, then one is fully justified in seeing all reconstruction of the past as another form of construction, no matter how well-informed or self-conscious it may be, especially given the inability of the text to engage in a similar process of critique and protestation.

For intercultural criticism, therefore, the interchange between the reader and the text must be seen in terms of both construction and engagement. On the one hand, the process of distantiation is helped immensely by a view of all reconstruction as construction. In other words, even when attempting to understand the text as an other to us, historically and culturally removed, we ultimately play a major role in the construction of such otherness; thus, even when considering the text as a literary, rhetorical, and ideological product, we ultimately have a major hand in the very identification and articulation of its literary structure and development, its rhetorical concerns and aims, its ideological thrust, and its relationship to its historical and cultural matrix. On the other hand, the process of self-reflection is helped immensely by a comprehensive and critical engagement both with the text as other and with others regarding their own constructions of the text. First, an understanding of the text as an other to us demands critical engagement with it—a thorough evaluation of its world, strategy, and applicability in terms of the reader's own historical and cultural context; the goal of such an engagement is none other than that of liberation itself. Second, in attempting to understand the text as an other to us, it is necessary to understand as well how the text has been interpreted by others, by readers in a variety of different historical situations and cultural frameworks. Such an understanding also demands critical engagement with these others—a thorough evaluation of reading strategies, theoretical orientations, social locations, as well as interpretive results, reception, and aftereffects; again, the goal of such engagement is none other than liberation itself.

CONCLUDING COMMENTS

Such then are the essential characteristics of the envisioned hermeneutics of the diaspora, a hermeneutics of otherness and engagement, and the basic principles for its proposed methodological approach, the reading strategy of intercultural criticism.

I see this hermeneutics of the diaspora—specifically grounded in and informed by the social location of Hispanic Americans—as having a manifest destiny of liberation and decolonization. Thus, it begins with and aims for contextualization—it puts aside and calls into question any claim to be objective and scientific, neutral and impartial, universal. Likewise, it opts for humanization and diversity—it resists both dehumanization, any divestiture of all those identity factors that constitute and characterize the reader as reader, and rehumanization, any attempt to force all readers into one and the same particular and contextualized discussion. Finally, it seeks to acknowledge, respect, and engage the other—it opposes any attempt, implicit or explicit, to overwhelm or override the other, to impose a definition upon it, to turn the other into an "other."

I also see the reading strategy of intercultural criticism not as the sole, proper, and definitive strategy for reading from within the diaspora of the Third World or even the diaspora of Hispanic Americans in particular, but as one such strategy among many, as one way of approaching and interpreting the biblical texts, with a similar dream and task of liberation in mind. Indeed, were I to argue otherwise, the results would be distinctly counterproductive: I would be going directly against the enormous diversity to be found not only within the diaspora itself but also among Hispanic Americans in particular; I would end up advancing yet another master or totalizing narrative, universalizing my own strategy and project for all, and thus effectively ruling out other such strategies and projects arising out of the same social location; and I would be defeating the whole project of liberation and decolonization, preventing others from speaking out in their own voices and thus in the end overwhelming the very otherness I set out to rescue and bring to the foreground. At the same time, I would argue that all such strategies should strive to engage one another as well as other strategies in critical dialogue. In fact, were I to argue otherwise, the consequences would be, once again, distinctly counterproductive: I would be ultimately abetting a gradual and inevitable absolutizing or totalizing of such strategies into master narratives, through both an avoidance of much-needed criticism and a failure to benefit from the voices and perspectives of others.

In conclusion, I believe that a hermeneutics of otherness must go hand in hand with a hermeneutics of engagement, and that I see as the very essence of the proposed hermeneutics of the diaspora.

CHAPTER 6

"EL HOGAR" AS MINISTRY TEAM

STEPHANA(S)'S HOUSEHOLD

Aida Besançon Spencer

Two renowned colleagues in ministry are John of the Cross and Teresa of Avila. Fray Juan de Santo Matia (Saint John of the Cross) founded the first community of friars along the order of the Way of Perfection after being discipled by Saint Teresa at Valladolid, Spain. Their ministry was to build up Christians by prayer, as Saint Teresa explains:

> To make the captains in this castle or city—that is, the preachers and theologians—highly proficient in the way of the Lord. . . .
> Do you think, my daughters, that it is an easy matter to have to do business with the world, to live in the world, to engage in the affairs of the world, and, . . . yet inwardly to be strangers to the world, and enemies of the world, like persons who are in exile?[1]

Justo and Catherine González are also colleagues in ministry. They each have their specialties, yet they encourage each other and influence each other and work together. Doing theology in community is one aspect of Hispanic American life that can bring insight into the biblical text. For instance, in *Mañana*, Justo concludes that those of us who believe in the Triune God must manifest similar love for each other: "We are created in for-otherness."[2] Understandably, then, one aspect of reading the Scripture "in Spanish" is to be aware that "God is addressing all of us as a community of faith."[3] Reading the Scripture *for* the community is not too far from serving the God of the Scripture *in* community. For Hispanics, family and community (*el pueblo*) are very important. Whenever I travel to the Dominican Republic and listen to the radio, I am amazed at how frequently I keep hearing about "el pueblo" this and "el pueblo" that. The announcers appeal to their listeners in community as much as to each of them as individuals. Christianity has the theological undergirding to make a community for others a reality.

What reading of the biblical text might be one that reflects marginalization? Only recently has much work been done to study the ministry of households.[4] In light of the communal emphasis in Latin America and the specific example of

Justo and Catherine, I would like to explore what we can learn in the model of Stephana(s)'s household in 1 Corinthians. Often discussions such as these fall under the genre of "house churches" or "household codes." However, what I want to unlock is not so much the church *in* the house as the house *for* the church, a ministering team.

Stephana(s)'s household is mentioned only in passing in Paul's First Letter to the Corinthians (1 Cor 1:16; 16:15-18). However, much can be gleaned from these few sentences: what is Stephana(s)'s household? what is unique about this household? and how should it be treated?

WHAT IS STEPHANA(S)'S HOUSEHOLD?

Paul describes this social unit with two synonyms: *oikia*, "household" (1 Cor 16:15) and *oikos*, "house" (1:16).[5] Both words can be used to refer literally to the home in which people live; however, *oikia*, which is more frequent in comic and Attic prose, strictly refers more to a house, as opposed to a set of apartments or room (*oikos*).[6] According to Xenophon, who lived in the fourth century B.C., in Attic law, *oikos* is everything a person possesses, even if situated in different cities, whereas *oikia* is the dwelling house (*Oeconomicus* 1.5).[7] Similarly, Aristotle uses *oikia* to describe the homestead (*Politics* 11.111.8). Although Aristotle uses *oikia* and *oikos* as synonyms, *oikia* seems to refer primarily to the household. Both terms are also used in the New Testament to refer to the household—the people who live in the house. Peter Lampe defines a "household" as: "(a) those persons who were economically dependent on one master to whose authority they felt subjected (this could include children, even adult sons, slaves, freedpersons, and 'clients'), and (b) the spouses of all these persons, including the master's own spouse, as long as these couples lived together."[8]

Aristotle's writing supports Lampe's definition. Aristotle writes that the household (*oikia*), the "partnership" for "everyday purposes," in its "perfect form" consists of slaves and free persons, "master and slave, husband and wife, father and children." The smallest unit of the household (*oikia*) is "a house [*oikos*] and a wife and an ox for the ploughing—for the ox serves instead of a servant for the poor." The household (*oikia*) is under the "royal rule of its eldest member" (*Politics* 1.1.6-7; 1.11.1). The household might include twenty to thirty people.[9]

For example, when the royal official's son in Capernaum was healed and the whole "household" (*oikia*) believed, the slaves who relayed the message to the official were also part of that household who "believed" (John 4:46-53). Jesus used the fact that heirs are permanent members of a household (*oikia*), while slaves are temporary, as a way to describe sin (John 8:35). Cornelius sent two of his household servants (*oiketēs*) to fetch Simon Peter at Joppa. Before they heard Peter's message, Luke describes them as part of a whole house (*oikos*) who were devout and God-fearing (Acts 10:2, 7; 11:14). Thus, an ancient household could be much larger than a nuclear family. It would be more like an extended family with all the workers in the family business who lived in a housing complex.

Therefore, since Stephana(s) is termed a household (*oikia*), it too, was a partnership, a large group of people, not all related by blood ties, dwelling and working together (1 Cor 16:15). The "house" (*oikos*) of Stephana(s) (1 Cor 1:16) was among the people Paul baptized. Possibly, the term *house* is more of a synecdoche, a part representing a whole,[10] a household baptized as a unit together. It is comparable to a people group (e.g., Acts 2:36), like the households of Cornelius, Lydia, and Crispus (Acts 10:2; 11:14; 16:15; 18:8), who were saved and baptized at one time.

Who is Stephana(s)? Most translators assume *Stephana* (Στεφαν) in 1 Corinthians is a man and the persons to whom one is to be subject (16:16) are men.[11] However, the plural of the masculine *houtos* ("this") easily could be generic referring to men and women.[12] *Stephanos* is a common ancient name for a man. Paul did not literally write *Stephanas*, rather, he wrote *Stephana*, in the genitive, the case of relationship ("Stephana's household"). Thus, scholars have had to posit the nominative form of *Stephanas*.[13] In the ancient materials now collected for us, *Stephanas* and *Stephana* are very unusual. The common masculine name "Stephen," or *Stephanos* ("crown"), is declined in the genitive *Stephanou* (e.g., Acts 22:20). Masculine nouns ending in *a* may be either Attic or Doric. Attic nouns are declined in the genitive as *Oniou* from *Onias* (2 Macc 3:1; 4:7). However, Doric *a* nouns make the genitive *as* or *a*, as a nickname, as in *Barnaba* (Acts 11:30; Gal 2:1; Col 4:10) from the nominative *Barnabas* for "Joseph" (Acts 4:36; Gal 2:13). *Stephana* could also come from the feminine *Stephanē* or *Stephana* ("wreath") or *Stephanas* ("wreath-maker"). Maidens wore on their heads the same kinds of "wreaths" with which the statues of the Ephesian Artemis was adorned (according to Dionysius of Halicarnassus II.XXI-XXII). Dionysius associated "garlands" with dancing "maidens," not men (VII.72), as did Homer (*Iliad* XVIII.597). Indeed, one early Christian prayer in a theater in Aphrodisias—"Lord, help"—was scratched by a *Stephana* (*euchē Stephana*).[14] Greek inscriptions have been found for both of these names: women, *Stephana* or *Stephanē*, and men, *Stephanas*.[15]

Thus *Stephana(s)* could theoretically be either a man who is described with a nickname, "Stevie," or *Stephana*, a woman, "Stephanie." In the New Testament, Lydia is also described as a leader of her household (Acts 16:14-15, 40). According to Peter Lampe, inscriptions of female heads of households in Asia Minor indicate they could be married women or widows who continued their husband's business after his death.[16] Indeed, Paul recommends that younger widows, who were unable to keep their vows of prayer, should marry and become heads of their households (*oikodespotēs*, 1 Tim 5:14).

Therefore, Paul concludes his First Letter to the Corinthians describing four ministering teams: two single men, one household, and one couple: Timothy

(1 Cor 16:10-11), Apollos (16:12), Stephana(s)'s household (16:15-18), and Aquila and Prisca (or Priscilla) (16:19). The variety of structure is impressive. Stephana(s)'s ministering team is described as a "household," whereas Priscilla and Aquila are described as having a church "abiding in their house" (Rom 16:5; 1 Cor 16:19).[17]

WHAT IS UNIQUE ABOUT STEPHANA(S)'S HOUSEHOLD?

Paul describes the household of Stephana(s) with two extended adjectival clauses: "it is a first fruits from Achaia" and "for ministry to the saints, they appointed themselves" (1 Cor 16:15). Where were "they" from? They had traveled from the province of Achaia or Greece (now southern Greece) to Ephesus (1 Cor 16:8, 18). They could have come from Athens or Corinth or Cenchrea or some other city in Achaia (Acts 17:15–18:18). Corinth seems likely since the church in Corinth knew this household and the household represented Corinth (1 Cor 1:2; 16:15, 17).

Paul uses metaphorical language to describe this household: "first fruits." The firstfruits were the first of the produce and the firstborn of the children who were dedicated to God (Exod 22:29-30; 23:19). Paul also uses the firstfruits as a figurative model of what will happen to others. For instance, Christ "has been raised from the dead, the first fruits of those fallen asleep. . . . Similarly, also, in Christ, all will be made alive" (1 Cor 15:20, 22). Christians who have "the first fruits of the Spirit" know they will eventually be divinely adopted (Rom 8:23; see also Rev 14:4). Probably, Stephana(s)'s household was not the first from Achaia to believe in the Lord. Luke records Dionysius and Damaris and others in Athens who believed (Acts 17:34) and Crispus's household in Corinth (Acts 18:8). No mention is made of Stephana(s) in Acts. Moreover, the second adjectival clause explains the first clause: as "first-fruits," they *ministered*. They dedicated their lives to serving God. In the same way a farmer might bring the first harvest to the temple, this family was a harvest of the outreach of Paul's own ministering team. This household was the first to dedicate themselves to ministry and served as a model for others.

The second adjectival clause presents several marvels. Neither Paul nor Silas nor Timothy nor Priscilla nor Aquila nor any other "leader" "appointed" (*tassō*) these people. They "appointed" or "set aside" *themselves*. Paul uses the plural reflexive pronoun. *Tassō* is a military term. For instance, a centurion in Capernaum described himself as "a person under authority, having *placed* under me soldiers." Therefore, he could command these soldiers to travel around (Luke 7:8). Similarly, God appoints governmental rulers (Rom 13:1). In the New Testament, the object or goal of the "assignment" is often service in Christ's name. For example, the Lord "appointed" Paul and Barnabas "to be a light for the Gentiles" (Acts 13:47); the church at Antioch appointed Paul and Barnabas and others to go to Jerusalem to discuss the place of circumcision (15:1-2). In contrast to these examples, Stephana(s)'s household enrolled or assigned or appointed themselves to service. They enlisted in the "battle" for God's reign, forming themselves into a battalion. Apparently, Stephana(s), the head of the household, did not make this decision alone because Paul uses the *plural* verb: "*they* appointed." They made a decision (aorist tense) at some past specific time to become the firstfruits for ministry.

How did they go about making this decision? We do not know. All we know is that it was a communal voluntary decision. Lampe describes the ancient household as involved in social welfare, education, work, and law. The whole household would often be involved in one business.[18] For example, when Simon Peter, James, and John were all involved in a fishing partnership (Luke 5:10), they functioned as a "household." Thus, Stephana(s)'s household decided to devote themselves to the business of ministry! Ministry to the "saints" would be comparable to today's clergy who devote themselves to help laypeople to be lights in the world. Apostles, prophets, evangelists, pastors, and teachers are examples of people who "prepare the saints for a work of ministry, for upbuilding of the body of Christ" (Eph 4:11-12).

What might be an illustration or example of the type of ministry to the saints that Stephana(s)'s household did? The next sentence seems to present such an illustration.: "I rejoice upon the arrival of Stephana(s) and Fortunatus and Achaicus, since your lack, they themselves filled, for they refreshed my spirit and yours" (1 Cor 16:17-18a). They sent three members of their household to minister to the Apostle Paul. We do not know for certain they were all members of the household, but we do know Stephana(s) was.

Moreover, Stephana(s) is mentioned first in the group of three. In addition, *Achaicus* means "from Achaia." Since the household is mentioned in the earlier sentence, would it not appear likely that all three are members of this household? In that case, all twenty to thirty or so of the members of the household did not travel from Achaia to Asia, but three of them did. These traveled as representatives of the entire household.

Even though Stephana(s) is the first name mentioned, the "and" (*kai*) connects each as equals. What did they do? First, they represented the Corinthian obligation to serve ("your lack"). Second, they refreshed Paul's spirit. Third, they refreshed the Corinthian spirit (1 Cor 16:17-18).

Paul uses imagery of filling a vessel up to the brim (*anaplēroō*)[19] as if the Corinthians drank up water or ate up a harvest, and Stephana(s)'s household "filled up" the void of the water or the harvest (16:17). Did Paul then expect all the Corinthians to dedicate themselves to God or to serve him in particular in appreciation for having heard the good news from Paul (Rom 15:27)? The household's ministry to Paul was not simply physical; they refreshed Paul's "spirit." The "spirit" is that aspect of a human person that is self-examining, that hearkens to God's Spirit (1 Cor 2:10-11; 14:15). The household gave the type of refreshing that only comes through Jesus, the living Lord (Matt 11:28). Gerd Theissen suggests that "in Ephesus Paul received some material support from Stephanas." However, he agrees that refreshing Paul's "spirit" does not "sound much like material gifts."[20] Theissen builds his first argument from "lack" (*husterēma*). *Husterēma* can refer to financial need, as in the material "needs" of the saints in Jerusalem or of Paul (2 Cor 9:12; 11:9). However, here "lack" is not literal, not only because Paul's "spirit" was refreshed but also because Stephana(s)'s household fulfilled the Corinthian "lack" (1 Cor 16:17).[21] The household would probably not be fulfilling the Corinthian financial needs since, at this time, the Corinthians were doing well financially (2 Cor 8:14). In addition, Paul was not accepting contributions from the Corinthians (2 Cor 11:9). "Filling up a lack" (*anaplēroō* and *husterēma*) as a phrase is a figurative way to describe ministry. Epaphroditus, who represented the Philippians, did much more than bring their financial contribution to Paul. He fulfilled (*anaplēroō*) their spiritual obligation (*husterēma*) to serve Paul (Phil 2:30). Paul, Silvanus, and Timothy wanted to see the Thessalonians face-to-face so they could "meet the *needs* (*husterēma*) of their faith" (1 Thess 3:10). The Galatians are to bear one another's spiritual burden and in this way "fill" (*anaplēroō*) Christ's law of love (Gal 6:2).

How were the *Corinthians'* spirit refreshed? Because, the Corinthians' obligation was fulfilled (v. 17)?[22] Or, perhaps, because Stephana(s)'s household had already ministered among the Corinthians before they came to Paul in Ephesus? Similarly, when Paul commended Phoebe, a minister of the church in Cenchrea, to the Romans, he too describes her as having been "a leader over many, even myself" (Rom 16:1-2). Both Phoebe and Stephana(s)'s household were commendable to others because they had earlier ministered to Paul himself.

What exactly did Stephana(s) and Fortunatus and Achaicus do to refresh Paul's spirit? Again, we do not know for sure; however, even today many of us have been refreshed by Christian "pastors" who have listened and observed our spiritual needs, prayed for us, spoken God's message to us in moments of need, and also helped us materially. Paul is in Ephesus in Asia. In 2 Corinthians 1:8-9 he describes how his and his coworker's time in Asia was one of hardships and great pressure, far beyond their ability to endure. They despaired even of life. In their hearts they felt the sentence of death had been passed on them. Possibly, Stephana(s)'s household was an instrument of God's comfort to Paul during those difficult times (2 Cor 1:6). "Refresh" (*anapauō*) is the same verb used to describe what Jesus promised to those who are weary and heavily burdened (Matt 11:28-29). It is the type of ministry Philemon did with his church for which Paul asks (Phlm 7, 20). Titus's spirit was "refreshed" when some of the spiritual problems at Corinth were resolved (2 Cor 7:13). "Refreshing of the spirit" is an emotional and intellectual version of receiving literal physical rest (Matt 26:45; Mark 6:31), and such a term is very appropriate to use in describing the type of ministry done with Paul by the representatives of Stephana(s)'s household at this time of great spiritual hardship.[23]

Stephana(s)'s household is not the only household to minister to Paul. When Paul was in prison, probably his second and final imprisonment in Rome, Onesiphorus's household (*oikos*) "repeatedly refreshed" (*anapsuchō*) Paul. The third person singular verb could refer to Onesiphorus alone or to the entire household: "he/it refreshed," "was not ashamed," "sought," "found," "served" (2 Tim 1:16-18). Paul reminds Timothy, as he reminded the Corinthians, how he *knew* about this ministering household who made an extended effort to reach a needy Christian, Paul, himself. Onesiphorus's household normally served in Asia, while Stephana(s)'s household normally served in Achaia.

HOW SHOULD STEPHANA(S)'S HOUSEHOLD BE TREATED?

How, then, should the Corinthians respond to Stephana(s)'s household appointing itself to ministry? Outrage? This introduces another marvel. The Corinthians were "also" to place themselves in subjection to this household (1 Cor 16:16). The purpose of Paul's encouragement, which he affectionately addresses to his "brothers and sisters" (16:15), is for the Corinthians to cooperate with this ministering household, as well as all coworkers and hard workers. "Subject" (*hupotassō*, v. 16) is the same verb as "appoint" (*tassō*, v. 15) with a prefix (*hupo*, "under"), which suggests the interrelationship of these two actions: the household "places" (*tassō*) itself for service to the saints; therefore, in turn, the saints "place themselves under" (*hupotassō*) the household serving them. Humble cooperation with those people helping one seems to be the point here. Paul uses the middle case, which signifies something done to oneself ("put *yourselves* in subjection"), *not* something done to others ("put *others* in subjection"; see also Eph 5:21). Similarly, cooperation with one another for a larger goal seems to be Paul's admonition to prophets: "spirits of prophets to prophets are subject" (*hupotassō*) (1 Cor 14:32). An appropriate image is the *hupotaxis*, the "*drawing up* of light-armed *behind* the phalanx."[24] The general of the army is Christ; the phalanx in Achaia are those who devote themselves to ministry; the lightly armed soldiers are the Corinthians, who must be ready to cooperate in the goal to fight the enemy, Satan.

Paul uses "coworkers" (16:16) as a metaphor for those devoting themselves to the ministry of the saints. For instance, in 1 Thessalonians 5:12-13, he exhorts the Thessalonians to pay proper respect to "coworkers" and "leaders" and regard them very highly. In the genitive case, a "coworker" is a "person of the same trade, a colleague."[25] Thus, Timothy, Apollos, Prisca, and Aquila would be "coworkers" (Rom 16:3, 21; 1 Cor 3:4, 9; 16:10-19) but not full ministering households. Timothy and Apollos minister as single persons, while Prisca and Aquila minister as a couple. Paul in no way describes here a permanent hierarchy of one person above and many people below, as sometimes happens in our churches. As Justo observes about Genesis, here "there is no hint of subordination."[26] Rather, Paul describes *many* people "above": a household, coworkers, hard workers. And, any subordination is a voluntary, mutual, temporal act.

Thus, in this pericope, Paul first introduces what Stephana(s)'s household has done (1 Cor 16:15), then what the Corinthians should do (v. 16), again what the household did (vv. 17-18a), and finally, in conclusion, what the Corinthians should do (v. 18b): "therefore, acknowledge [become fully acquainted with] such people." *Epiginōskō* means "to know thoroughly" or to "recognize, acknowledge, approve."[27] What does it mean here? "Acknowledge" is implied by the earlier verb *hupotassō* ("subjection"). "Know thoroughly" is implied by the cooperative mutual nature of the relationship between the household and the saints in Corinth. Paul began this pericope with a synonym of *epiginōskō* ("you have known" *oida*, v. 15). According to Joseph Thayer, *oida* implies more a knowledge coming from a mental perception, whereas *ginōskō* (v. 18) implies a knowledge coming from personal experience. The prefix *epi-* heightens the extent of knowledge: "mental direction toward."[28] Thus, Paul begins by stating that the Corinthians have known (*oida*), at a more superficial level, Stephana(s)'s household. In light of their (a) being a firstfruit from Achaia, (b) setting themselves aside for ministry to the Corinthians, (c) filling the Corinthians' lack, and (d) refreshing Paul's and the Corinthians' spirits, the Corinthians should get to know them thoroughly (*epiginōskō*), become thoroughly acquainted with them. From having a child's love, they should move to an adult love, which knows thoroughly (*epiginōskō*, 1 Cor 13:12).

Paul had both summarized his letter and introduced 1 Corinthians 16:15-18 with the brief sentence: "let everything among you be done in love" (v. 14). Thorough knowledge is one aspect of *agape* love (1 Cor 13:12), along with actions that are not envious or seeking only one's own interests (vv. 4-5). The type of ministry done by Stephana(s)'s household was one model of a group that all things bore, believed, hoped, persevered (v. 7); they *loved* for the sake of the Corinthians.

Stephana(s)'s household then is a beautiful example of how believers can minister "in for-otherness," manifesting the Triune love for each other. God addressed them as a house (*oikos*), which became a community of faith in being baptized, a church in the house. They then responded as a household (*oikia*), which chose to become a partnership that voluntarily dedicated itself to ministry to other Christians, a house for the church. Paul then exhorted the Corinthians to enter too into a voluntary, personal, mutual submission in ministry, a church for the house. Then indeed all would have been done in love.

The Latin American church has its potentialities and difficulties in following the model of the ministering household. Latin Americans are aided by a pronounced emphasis on family, extended family, relationships, and strong women. Latin Americans are deterred by an ecclesial emphasis on hierarchy and patriarchy.[29] The household model is not for every family. It must be done from free wills. But for everyone it is a reminder that even ministering singles and couples are parts of a larger Christian community who are all coworkers of the same one God (1 Cor 3:9), doing everything in love.

SUBVERSIVE AND LIBERATING MEMORIES

CHAPTER 7

VOCACIÓN Y COMPROMISO

THE ECUMENICAL VOCATION AND COMMITMENT OF A CHRISTIAN HISTORIAN

Carmelo E. Alvarez

The twentieth century was a great century for ecumenism. Many ecumenists call it the "great ecumenical century." It was an era that challenged the capacity and vision of many Christian historians in trying to understand and respond to the writing of the history of Christianity with new eyes and new perspectives. Most of the traditional writing of the history of Christianity was centered in Europe or North America.[1] One of the real efforts made by Justo L. González from the very beginning of his career, as a teacher and writer, was to address this issue. Justo has attempted in all his works to be ecumenical, not only in perspective but primarily in his vocation and commitment as a servant to the church and the world. Our primary objective in this article is to try to demonstrate how these three principles are intertwined in Justo González's thought and life.

Vocación (vocation) means accepting the highest calling from God to be servants of the people of God. By God's initiative and in grace, we put our talents to the service of others. The gifts of grace and of faith are shared with the Christian community for its edification and formation. As obedient servants we open ourselves to God for whatever task or mission, even when we dislike the task at hand. Our sense of obligation and responsibility, then, becomes a humbling experience. And when we are expecting frustration and deception, joy and satisfaction surprise us.

Compromiso (commitment) means that taking an obligation and devoting one's life in mind and heart a person has a positive attitude and the clear conviction that God's presence will lead to fulfillment and completion. *Compromiso* requires for thoughts and actions to be driven by a passion that is more than personal emotion or impulse (and both are needed in a way!), a real *entrega*. The word *entrega* conveys a sense of surrender, to devote energy and time to a cause. It means that our praxis of faith leads to the correct reflection and a transforming action. A faith that is not reflected theologically can lead to ignorance, and a theology that is not based in faith can lead to error. That's why any commitment must be based on the solid ground of faith and the right direction of theology.

The ecumenical perspective in the writing of church history is of a tremendous importance for Justo González: "This question concerns me deeply, for I have devoted all my adult years to research, teaching, and writing on church history."[2] For González an ecumenical perspective is one that is always in the making, a process more than a finished product. The Christian historian is called to view the past from the present situation, "we must be humbled by the reminder that ours is an extremely fragile enterprise, as we seek to penetrate the past without leaving the present."[3] It has the power and the promise of helping us to define who we are as we also try to define others.

We study history in order to discern the liberating and oppressive forces present in historical processes and to try to understand the moral values and the theological options involved in order to affirm an ecumenical vocation.[4] Any ecumenical perspective means that we live in a creative tension between the particular and the global, toward a true catholicity.[5] An ecumenical perspective means that the Christian historian aims at "telling the story" from a global perspective that is inclusive in scope and intentionality, "according to the whole," truly catholic. In our quest to write ecumenical history we need to get at a "consensus" that will both respect the particular and recognize the differences, being united in the one faith we profess.[6] These guiding principles provide the theological and methodological foundations for González's work as a church historian.

Justo L. González has dedicated his entire academic life to forging an ecumenical vocation and commitment as a Christian historian. His first experiences as a teacher at the Evangelical Seminary of Puerto Rico and at Candler School of Theology in Atlanta, Georgia, urged him to write textbooks. The first one was *Historia del Pensamiento Cristiano*. This textbook was published as part of Biblioteca de Estudios Teológicos (Library of Theological Studies), a project sponsored by the Fund for Theological Education of the World Council of Churches. His *Historia de Las Misiones* was part of this project too. A short book, *Revolución y Encarnación*, offered a theology of history from the perspective of the incarnation and a social ethic of service and commitment. The three volumes were published in English as *A History of Christian Thought*.[7] *A History of Christian Thought* has more than nine printings in the United States and was translated into Korean in 1988. A Chinese translation is in progress.

An important project was *Y hasta lo último de la tierra*, which is the story of Christianity for lay pastors and church leaders with nonprofessional theological training. These ten volumes were published in two volumes as *La Historia del Cristianismo*, and in English as *The Story of Christianity*. The English and Spanish editions of these textbooks are used in seminaries and Bible institutes in the United States, Latin America, and the Caribbean. Three important additions in the last few years are: *Bosquejo de Historia de la Iglesia*, *Church History: An*

Essential Guide (This is the English version of *Bosquejo de Historia de la Iglesia*), and *Christian Thought Revisited: Three Types of Theology*.[8]

I am using these examples to demonstrate the extraordinary capacity of Justo González as a writer and his real commitment to providing relevant sources for the study of church history for seminaries, Bible institutes, and programs for lay training. It is clear that his passion for teaching is complemented by a solid discipline in scholarship, as a researcher and writer.

Very closely related to this teaching and writing capacity is Justo's role as a mentor. Justo González has modeled for us the role of mentoring and guiding young scholars and theological students. His love for teaching and the joy he brings to the classroom, informal conversations, and jokes reflect a joyful spirit. Justo is a natural facilitator, sharing his insights and experiences, encouraging the young teacher, and many times challenging those of us who think we really know how to teach! Justo González knows how to befriend, not patronize, maintaining the integrity of friendship without compromising the integrity of serious scholarship. Justo has been able to develop a mentoring process beyond the individual relationships expressed in educational organizations: The Hispanic Summer Program (HSP), AETH (Association for Hispanic Theological Education), and the Hispanic Theological Initiative (HTI) are excellent examples of an institutional mentoring.[9]

This ecumenical vocation and commitment is expressed in four dimensions of the faith: Christian tradition, Hispanic identity, confessing the faith, and confession. The Christian tradition is clearly defined as a historical-theological heritage,[10] the Hispanic identity is expressed as a cultural-anthropological heritage,[11] confessing the faith means searching for truth (*fides quaerens intellectum*) in theological reflection[12] and making a confession professed in a resounding credo.

HISPANIC CREED (BY JUSTO L. GONZÁLEZ)

We believe in God, the Father Almighty
Creator of the heavens and the earth;
Creator of all peoples and all cultures;
Creator of all tongues and races.

We believe in Jesus Christ, his Son, our Lord,
God made flesh in a person for all humanity,
God made flesh in an age for all the ages,
God made flesh in one culture for all cultures,
God made flesh in love and grace for all creation.

We believe in the Holy Spirit
through whom God incarnate in Jesus Christ

makes his presence known in our peoples and our cultures;
through whom, God Creator of all that exists,
gives us power to become new creatures;
whose infinite gifts make us one people:
the Body of Christ.

We believe in the Church
   universal because it is a sign of God's Reign,
   whose faithfulness is shown in its many hues
   where all the colors paint a single landscape,
   where all tongues sing the same praise.

We believe in the Reign of God—the day of the Great Fiesta
   when all creation's colors will form a harmonious rainbow,
   when all peoples will join in joyful banquet,
   when all tongues of the universe will sing the same song.

And because we believe, we commit ourselves:
   to believe for those who do not believe,
   to love for those who do not love,
   to dream for those who do not dream,
until the day when hope becomes reality.[13]

Finally, our existence, our vocation, our whole life, is a movement toward the mystery of life: God. I am convinced that Justo Luis González as a teacher, writer, and ecumenist loves and appreciates these words from Saint Augustine in the *Confessions:* "For behold, You have taken delight in truth: and he that does truth comes to the light. I desire to do truth in my heart, before Thee, by confession: with my pen, before many witnesses" (*Conf.* X, I. I). To this supreme vocation Justo and all of us have been called! By God's grace we know who we are and whose we are. *Gracias sean dadas a Dios ahora y siempre. Amén.*

CHAPTER 8

VIEWS FROM THE MARGINS

CONSTRUCTING A HISTORY OF LATINA/O PROTESTANTISM

Edwin David Aponte

RELIGIOUS HISTORY AND MARGINS IN THE UNITED STATES

Conversations in the latter half of the twentieth and in the early twenty-first centuries about the religious history of the United States and the formal writing of that history show that there is a growing, if sometimes reluctant, acknowledgment of the multicultural realties of the nation. As the 2000 U.S. Census shows, the United States is increasingly and probably irreversibly diverse. The demographic changes that have occurred since 1965 have produced many evaluations and conversations on this increasing diversity, ranging from puzzlement, lionization, and suspicion of it to jeremiads against it. One part of this ongoing reappraisal is a growing acknowledgment of the existence of social "centers" and "margins." At the very least, "melting-pot" paradigms that have been used for identification and interpretation of very diverse communities are problematic and insufficient for describing those multicultural realities. There is a growing awareness that there can be multiple perspectives on the same event or that, depending on particular contexts and starting points, some stories of American religion and culture receive more attention than others.[1]

Nonetheless, despite some openness to alternative ways for historical understanding, there is still a widespread tendency to view "American" religious history and culture, and especially the written history, through a lens of a few Protestant denominations believed to be the normative U.S. American religious mainline or cultural mainstream. There may be a general (and sometimes grudging) acknowledgment of multicultural religious realities present in the social and cultural landscapes, but this does not necessarily mean a change in the retrieval and telling of American religious history that allows for a meaningful place for diversity. It is not solely a question of identifying diverse landscapes or noting the restructuring of U.S. American religions in telling or retelling the stories of North American religions and cultures, but of affirming the existence of alternative perspectives on landscapes and structures rarely acknowledged in the past.[2] What is necessary is not simply an acknowledgment of the historical presence of overlooked others but also an acceptance that stories from previously overlooked margins and perspectives are worth knowing and indeed are important for fuller historical understanding, to say nothing about the common good of the larger collective society.

While acknowledging the diverse nature and varied perspectives of life and culture in the United States, it also is evident that there are some groups that simultaneously are identified as "marginal" in relation to those that dominate society culturally, politically, economically, and religiously.[3] From the perspectives of socially, culturally, and religiously dominant centers the margins are those peoples and areas on the periphery of life, that is the life of the social and cultural center. In some talk of social-cultural centers and margins it seems almost as if a theory of a flat world is still at work. Areas of cultural importance and dominance are at the center of a tabletop world; the cultural margins are at the dangerous edges where nothing of much importance happens and beyond which the world drops off into nothingness.

However, the margins are more than edges between social and cultural centers and nothingness. These so-called marginal groups occupy not just geographic regions away from the cultural center; the margins are also border areas with other concurrent cultural areas of alternate discourse and activity. Furthermore these margins and border areas are not restricted to remote geographic spaces, but also can be understood as a type of social borderlands, liminal areas of multiple discourses, of crossroads and bridges, boundaries simultaneously fixed and fluid, social regions of immense diversity and complexity.[4] The social margins/borderlands may exist physically side by side with a dominant culture while at the same time be ignored by that ascendant culture. Social and cultural borderlands or margins are anything but cultural backwaters of little importance, but rather they are places where individuals and communities craft and live out multiple identities and experiences that challenge dominant categories of perceiving, knowing, living, and storytelling.[5]

Within the United States, growing diversity and complex social identities pose challenges for the constructing of religious histories according to an imposed normative lens of American religious history and culture.[6] There is a dynamic richness present in the borders and margins that may be unknown to those with cultural dominance at self-appointed centers. And since the borderlands and margins may be little known to the dominant social centers, when the latter constructs the narratives of U.S. American religious life the peoples of the margins may have their stories misrepresented, if indeed they are told at all. The formal dominant narratives exhibit power as they tell the story of religious life and culture from a particular perspective. Whether it is power to help or to harm depends partly on how inclusive the narrative or storytelling is. The identities and descriptions imposed casually by dominant social-cultural centers may be fair representations or they may be outrageous stereotypes. One way to discern the difference is to seek the views from the margins.

Another important aspect in presenting a fair representation within religious histories is to be aware that the margins as social borderlands are not static settlement, but rather places of creativity and movement. Within this churning, innovative social activity, the margins as social borderlands have distinctive stories and ways of understanding punctuated by struggles and triumph, populated by peoples who are immigrants, migrants, cultures in diaspora, and those who have always been present.[7] Latinas/os or Hispanics are among those at the margins of dominant society in the United States.[8]

The 2000 U.S. Census lists the total population of Hispanics or Latinas and Latinos as numbering 35,305,818, or 12.5 percent of the total population with the prospect of an increase to 25 percent of the total population by 2050.[9] Nevertheless in many ways Latinos and Latinas are still perceived to be at the cultural margins, not only socially but also religiously. If for no other reason than sheer numbers (of course there are other reasons) it is essential to better understand the religious history of this growing segment of the population of the United States.[10] Unfortunately, dominant historical and sociological perspectives on Hispanic or Latina/o communities often use interpretive models that do not consider Latina/o religious dimensions and perspectives. Not only are Latinas/os relegated to the social and cultural margins, among some academics and public policy-makers religious life is deemed not important for serious study or discussion.[11]

In order to combat this type of double prejudice with its predisposition to exclude the margins/borderlands and thereby overlook Hispanics/Latinas/os, there is a need for alternative methodologies of analysis and understanding from the very margins that dominant perspectives undervalue. Such views from the margins can adequately take into account the realities of the social borderlands in ways that are recognizable to the peoples of the social borderlands who daily negotiate the center/margin paradigms of dominant society. The religious history of the United States cannot be adequately and fully understood without looking at Hispanics or Latinas/os, one of the groups on the margins and in the social borderlands.

LATINAS/OS AND AMERICAN RELIGIOUS HISTORY

The combination of changing demographic realities and an awareness of realities overlooked in the past contributes to what Justo L. González calls "the changing cartography" of church history.[12] Part of the changing context is greater awareness of both the polycentric nature and the fact that interdisciplinary approaches are needed to construct a fuller picture. González states that "it is no longer possible to separate the history of the church from the history of missions or the history of the expansion of Christianity."[13] One perspective that can be used for the changing geography of church history is that of the "little stories." This perspective draws on the work of Alex García-Rivera about religion on the margins. García-Rivera analyzes aspects of Latin American religion in the form of devotion to San Martín de Porres.[14] García-Rivera asserts that much of Latin American history and theology has focused on the "big story," that is, the stories of dominant society, while the little stories of the grassroots have been ignored, suppressed, and/or trivialized. However, the power of the little stories (in this case the life of the marginalized mulatto San Martín) is so great that popular religiosity overcomes attempts to suppress it and supplant it with a dominant story and practice of religion. So while the power of dominant societies may be manifested in its focus on "big stories," an alternative power source is present in so-called marginal communities as they embrace the "little stories."

U.S. American religious history has focused on the "big stories" and the "significant individuals" (usually male) that figured prominently in those big stories of dominant groups in American religion and society. A view from the margins brings the needed reminder that historical religious life in the United States has always had "little stories." As García-Rivera states,

> The "little stories" thus may be the antidote for the contemporary malaise affecting our society's specialists—the twin complaints of lack of meaning and irrelevance. The "little stories" promise the possibility of the return to the "Big Story," a return of meaning and relevance in our present social restlessness and lack of direction.[15]

It is from within the margins with its many "little stories" that more complete histories of Latina/o Christianity in the United States can be constructed. As an example, Latina/o Protestantism is itself a minority group (albeit a significant and growing one) within a minority group in the United States. Retrieving the histories of Latina/o Protestantism not only illuminates the inherent richness present but also contributes to a fuller understanding of the stories of Latina/o Christianity, Hispanic religion, and culture, as well as the larger church in the United States. Such a retrieval also calls for a revision of the ways stories of American religion and culture have been told in the past, as well as suggestions for future retellings.

A word of caution is necessary at this point. Focusing on the "little stories" of the margins and borderlands may be misunderstood as seeing those stories having only limited relevance, that they are stories for "over there" and "those people." If so limited by such a paternalistic attitude, the testimonies of oppression experienced by the margins may not affect the center.

LATINA/O PROTESTANTISM AS ALTERNATIVE
SOCIAL AND CULTURAL SPACE

Social margins as cultural and social borderlands are the places where many cultures meet, not just in a geographic sense or political boundaries, but rather as a fluid place of consciousness, indeed of alternative consciousness. The meetings of cultures may also produce the transformation of cultures. Within the borderlands are found different perspectives on identity and interaction, space and history, on cultural formations. For some, literal and cultural borderlands are desolate and empty. From the perspectives of borderland studies, models of interactions include alienation, coexistence, interdependence, and integration. In this context Juan Flores comments on the nature of borderlands as the positive cultural space of identity for Latinas/os.

> Contrary to the monocultural dictates of the official public sphere, the border claims that it is "not nowhere." This first gestus of Latino cultural practice thus involves an emphatic self-legitimation, a negation of hegemonic denial articulated as the rejection of anonymity. Though no appropriate name is available in the standard language repertoires, whether English or Spanish, namelessness is decidedly not an option.[16]

Latina/o reality construction in the everyday "not nowhere" of the margins/borderlands counters many dominant public perceptions of U.S. Hispanic realities. The actual lived experiences of Latinas and Latinos in their social and historical contexts cannot be ignored in constructing religious histories of the communities. Within the actual lived contexts that others may label as "no where" or marginal, Hispanic/Latina/o identities are created and sustained. Latina/o Protestantism is one expression of the ongoing formation and practice of ethos and identity within the "not no where" of the social borderland. The borderlands and the margins are not simply a trope of postmodern vagueness and infinite meanings, but rather places of social, cultural, and religious communal discourse, a public stage where all the action takes place.[17]

One place to begin a new understanding of Hispanic/Latina/o religions is found in conversations concerning modernity, postmodernity, and postmodernism, and specifically the nature of public spheres and subaltern counterpublics.[18] Viewing Latina/o religion and especially Hispanic/Latina/o Protestantism in its own social space means reconsidering the nature of the public sphere and its relationship to the margins, as well as the identities of the participants of these different arenas.

The term *public sphere* finds its contemporary roots, usage, and definition in the writings of Jürgen Habermas. The public sphere is the place where individuals in community negotiate what are the common good and the rules for governing and maintaining the civic community and shared identity.[19] Habermas claims that through a new public sphere governed by reason and unfettered public exchange the goal of pragmatic attainment of the public good, or accomplishing what is best for the common civil society, can and will be realized. Habermas views this new public sphere as being of a universal nature where all individuals in community participate and address public issues in their common life together.[20]

In many ways this Habermas project is an outgrowth of modernity stemming from the European Enlightenment and, as such, various postmodernists have criticized Habermas.[21] Among them Jean-François Lyotard questions whether Habermas is justified in allowing the possibility for emancipatory actions, as well as placing too great an emphasis on the positive potential of rational dialogue in society. The concern of some postmodernists is that Habermas's proposal actually is an extension of the discredited Enlightenment project of modernity, which is judged by many to have produced injustice, inequity, enslavement, death, and anything but emancipation for masses that are not part of dominant elites. From a postmodernist critical perspective a modernist vision of the common public sphere is really not open to everyone in society and ultimately does not contribute to the desired common good, emancipation, or liberation in any broad and meaningful way.[22]

In addition to the criticism of an unexamined modernist conception of what is meant by the public sphere, Nancy Fraser further criticizes Habermas's conception of the public sphere as limited because it neglects gender issues.[23] Fraser agrees that the concept of the public sphere is useful, but she is critical of Habermas for an idealization of a male-dominated bourgeois public sphere while at the same time ignoring the concurrent existence of other public spheres. Fraser calls into question Habermas's claim of a universal homogeneous public sphere accessible to all in society, and she argues that it is actually a fiction advancing the parochial interests of dominant groups excluding scores of others, including women.

By bringing a gender critique into the discussion of public spheres, Fraser argues for the recognition of a plurality of competing alternative publics. Not only does Fraser identify the reality of many public spheres, she also advocates for this plurality of publics on the grounds that it enhances participatory parity, thereby promoting the public good in a more inclusive sense. Developing this concept further, Fraser calls these various heterogeneous public spheres subaltern counterpublics, which are areas of alternative identity and discourse, coexistent with and in opposition to imposed identities and interpretations of dominant publics. Fraser's vision of subaltern counterpublics is that "they are parallel discursive areas where members of subordinated social groups invent and circulate counterdiscourses to formulate oppositional interpretations of their identities, interests, and needs."[24] Subaltern counterpublics function as sites of gathering, articulation, creation, regrouping, and withdrawal, as well as bases from which their participants foray into dominant "official" publics.

A similar critique of the idealized monolithic public sphere emerges from Latin America. Following the interdisciplinary work of the South Asian Subaltern Studies Group, the Latin American Subaltern Studies Group has developed further the concept of subaltern counterpublics.[25] Both groups call for a new type of historiography that questions assumptions, both casual and ideological, which show preference for the dominant views.[26] In this type of analysis subaltern counterpublics are recognized as distinct from dominant discourses and producing social effects that are internally recognizable, even while invisible to larger publics. In the jazz-like cultural performance of subaltern counterpublics, there is creativity, change, and improvisation, always calling into question traditional approaches as alternative public space is constructed.[27]

Speaking about another community outside dominant society or public sphere in the United States, Higginbotham sees the black church as an alternative public space within the African American community. While recognizing the utility of the concept of public sphere as a descriptor and tool of analysis, Higginbotham also agrees with other critics of Habermas, particularly those advocating the need to speak of a plurality of public spheres, some of which are oppositional or alternative counterpublics. She views the black church as creating its own heterogeneous public space while simultaneously engaging from its own base the dominant public space.[28]

In a similar way Latino Christianity generally, and specifically Hispanic/Latina/o Protestantism, also can be seen as a complex of heterogeneous subaltern groups that create their own alternative public spaces and produce social effects, demonstrating both a type of public character and an important role of the Latina/o church within the larger community. Latina/o Protestantism meets the definition of a subaltern counterpublic on the margins of dominant groups with power in a society.[29] In its many manifestations Latina/o Protestantism as subaltern counterpublics recognizes and resists the status quo hegemony with its efforts of social, economic, and cultural dominance and colonialization. Reflective of the cultural borderlands existence of Latinas and Latinos in the United States, Hispanics pass in and out of many public spheres, while simultaneously creating and maintaining their own alternative public spheres or social spaces.

Furthermore, Hispanics in the United States and Latina/o Protestants in particular are self-aware of their alternative identities.[30] They know in ways that members of dominant centers may not that there are multiple public spheres because Latinas and Latinos cross the social and cultural borders every day. At times crossing cultural borders requires not only insight and astuteness but also resistance. Through this subaltern community's self-awareness of its resistance, more ways in which this Latina/o subaltern counterpublic assesses the effectiveness of this resistance to colonialization are revealed. As García-Rivera observes that cultural hegemonic forces and subaltern groups are in fluid rather than static relationships. A subaltern counterpublic sphere Latina/o Protestantism operates in ways that result in the status quo being, at times, mollified, bypassed, or challenged.[31] Recognizing Latina/o Protestantism as a distinctive subaltern counterpublic means that the most effective starting point of historical study is within this alternative public sphere. This is an important starting point for an alternative methodology for studying Latina/o religions. From the viewpoints of alternate "marginal" public spheres of Latina/o Protestantism—especially from within congregational cultures—alternative institutions, initiatives, and world-views can be seen.

Latina/o communities on the margins of dominant U.S. society experience the realities of poverty, violence, racism, economic oppression, and ongoing displacement. While Latina/o communities have an image imposed on them by the larger society (such as the federal government, the state, the city, social service agencies, universities, and mainline denominations), Latina/o Protestantism crafts its own identities and simultaneously empowers itself for the actions that produce behavioral and social results on both individual and corporate levels. Within the social, cultural, and religious borderland spaces throughout the United States, Latina/o Protestantism articulates critical and creative emancipatory actions within an alternative public sphere.[32] The traditional master paradigms of U.S. American religious life not only fail to predict such identities and outcomes, in some manifestations these dominant assumptions do not even envision such a reality.[33]

Furthermore, Latina/o Protestantism as a network of alternative public spheres is not only an arena for a parallel social life; it also manifests characteristics of resistance against the dominant cultural public spheres. Otto Maduro observes that some religions play significant roles in the struggle against hegemonic domination as he speaks of the relationship between religion and empowerment of Latinas/os, particularly as one takes seriously the Latina/o religious communities' self-perspectives.

> Religion could be—besides and, at times, despite other functions—a possible medium, among others, for the articulation and proactive stimulation of a people's empowerment, that is, for the actualization of their capacity to transform their social environment in consonance with their own interests. This might be particularly true in the case of U.S. Hispanics, for whom all too often our religious traditions and institutions occupy a central place in our worldview, one of our scarce sources for self-identity as well as for the ethical assessment of our typically alien environment.[34]

U.S. Hispanic religions are central to Latina/o worldviews. Such worldviews operate in self-initiated transformative empowerment in the contexts of alternative public spaces on the margins/borderlands of dominant society that oppresses, alienates, and determines that some will be pushed to the "fringes."

SUBALTERN AND METAMODERN

Speaking of Latina/o Protestantism as alternative public spheres struggling against hegemony is only part of the story in envisioning a culturally sensitive and effective historiography. Viewing Latina/o Protestantism as subaltern counterpublics on the margins and in the borderlands also means allowing for Latina/o understandings and interpretations of marginality. Just as it is inadequate and inaccurate to assume that there is one undifferentiated common public sphere, or that there is a finite set of subaltern counterpublics, likewise it is not appropriate to assume a sole, fixed understanding of the margins. Marginality can be understood differently from different perspectives. Justo L. González observes that marginality is an interpretive, heuristic device that is reworked in Hispanic/Latina/o contexts. González states that when speaking of marginality within Hispanic/Latina/o religious communities one should remember that

> First, since we live in a polycentric society, most of us stand at the margin in some relationships, and at the center in others. As Hispanics, we stand at the margin of the dominant cultural and political trends in our society. Yet those of us who are educated, or male, or wealthy stand at the center in other relationships. Second, marginality is not always entirely imposed. Many Christians in the early church remained marginal to the affairs of their society because fuller participation would have involved them in idolatry and immorality. Likewise, Hispanics and other cultural minorities often feel the need to make a space for themselves and their culture—a space at the margins of society, and yet a space in which we can be ourselves in ways we cannot be when totally immersed in the dominant culture. Thus, the marginality imposed from outside is often reinforced by a self-created marginalization.[35]

Therefore marginality may not always have a simply negative and static connotation, but rather it is a more complicated concept referring to a dynamic cultural space of creativity. Not only are alternative public spaces created but also alternative self-understandings as one engages the dominant public sphere. The power of Latina/o alternative public spheres is seen in the reinterpretation of the margins. Imposed identities are not accepted as the only identities. Recognizing the complexity of life in the margins helps avoid essentialist reductionism. Furthermore, the polycentric nature of society raises the possibility that the same person or group may be in the margins or at the centers depending on where the starting point is in the cultural landscape. As subaltern counterpublics in a polycentric society Latina/o Protestantism uses "self-created marginalization" in creating and protecting its own life-worlds, as well as its engagement (not retreat) with dominant public spheres.

Caution should be exercised when any particular expression of Latina/o Protestantism is viewed as a subaltern counterpublic sphere. While there is some help from this perspective in constructing histories of Latina/o Protestantism, at the same time such an assessment is postmodern; and in many ways discourses about modernity and postmodernity represent the parochial conversations of dominant social and cultural elites. When such dominant elites discuss marginalized peoples within the cultural landscape, the starting point for a fuller understanding ought to be from the marginalized peoples and not the prejudged assumptions of the elites.

A critique of the Enlightenment modernity of dominant public spheres reflects the failure to recognize fully the polycentric nature of society. On the other hand, postmodernity proclaims a desire to correct the imperialistic, arrogant, positivistic claims of modernity. As such, some forms of postmodernism claim solidarity with the peoples of the modernist margins. However, for all its avowal of solidarity with diversity and the margins, various expressions of postmodernity still retain the perspectives of dominant cultural elites with assumptions that most persons and groups have made the same journey from modernism to postmodernism.[36] Some postmodernists proclaim with great enthusiasm their discovery that there are alternative social spheres and perspectives from that of the dominant discourses of society. Some postmodernists go on to declare that there are no master narratives, that everything is relative, and that all perspectives are of equal value. There is a certain ironic curiosity to such a postmodern position. On the one hand there is a postmodern conviction that all perspectives should have equal consideration. On the other hand, often there is exhibited the arrogance of dominant elites that do not "get it" and at an existential level assume a common perspective, experience, and intolerance for those who do not agree with them. It is at this point that González provides a Latino corrective on postmodernity and thereby helps illuminate Latina/o religions and cultures in a pluralistic society with a status quo of social and economic classes. González states that

> when referring to those whom modernity marginalized, I prefer the term "metamodern" rather than "postmodern." This is not just a matter of substituting a Greek for a Latin prefix. Although the two do coincide in many of their meanings, "meta" also has the connotation of "beyond," and it is in that sense I employ it here. We have always existed at the edges of modernity. We are not those who profited from modernity and who now feel it necessary to promote a postmodernity in which all metanarratives, as well as all principles of truth and justice, are equally powerless to challenge and to transform the status quo. We are those whom modernity colonized, those whom the colonial powers saw as objects of modernization, those whose metanarratives were assaulted and suppressed in the name of the great modern metanarrative. We are those who must still believe in the metanarrative that justice shall prevail and the crooked will be made straight.[37]

From this perspective, U.S. Hispanic religions and culture are in a sense "beyond" both the modernity and the postmodernity of the dominant society. More specifically, as subaltern counterpublic spheres, Latina/o Protestantism is also a metamodern reality, victimized by colonization and racial and class apartheid that came as part of modernity.[38] A postmodern historiography claims a homogenized, idealized sameness of all perspectives and experiences of the past. A metamodern perspective sees that, contrary to its own claims, postmodernism acts in the best traditions of the European-American Enlightenment when it declares on behalf of all (including the borderlands) the foundational creed that metanarratives are passé and no longer have legitimating existential power.[39]

Postmodernism has focused on local narratives in which some local narratives and stories are still more equal than others. Despite the postmodern turn, Latinas/os remain on the margins and their local narratives are still largely ignored, or even worse trivialized. In a parallel analysis Enrique Dussel confronts the mythology of modernity through an approach he terms *transmodernity*. By transmodernity Dussel articulates an approach that seeks to go beyond the exclusionary limits of modernity and "deny the irrational sacrificial myth of modernity as well as affirm (subsume in a liberating project) the emancipative tendencies of the Enlightenment and modernity within a new transmodernity." Reason, and indeed Enlightenment reason, is not rejected out of hand per se, but rather the violent imposition of "Eurocentric, developmentalist, hegemonic reason."[40] González further develops his understanding of marginality under the rubric of "incarnate marginality." He writes that living out an incarnate marginality means that "we must affirm that the proper place for those who follow Jesus Christ is the margin rather than the center; it is the valley rather than the hilltop; it is the cross rather than the throne."[41] A restrictive postmodern does not make allowance for this type of understanding.

While there is some value in postmodernism, especially in its critique of the shortcomings and arrogance of modernity, the postmodern critique itself must be viewed critically, especially with regard to its own debt to modernity.[42] Sometimes postmodernism exhibits a very modern hubris in its attitudes toward those who are "beyond," in González's words, those on "the edges of modernity." Earlier it was argued that in constructing a historiography for Latina/o Protestantism there is help in considering it as a subaltern counterpublic. As such, Latina/o Protestantism lives a metamodern reality in contexts that are simultaneously modern and postmodern. Latina/o Protestantism is a metamodern reality in which issues of racial/ethnic identity and racial oppression are two significant factors in the creation of a Latina/o Protestant subaltern counterpublic. In its pivotal location in the vibrant social margins beyond the central concerns of both modernity and postmodernity, Latina/o Protestantism is a subaltern counterpublic that was not consulted when the postmodern turn took place. Indeed, in the face of the "noncanons" of postmodern canonicity, Latina/o Protestantism unashamedly holds on to its metanarratives, which were not the metanarratives of discredited modernity, nor a relative postmodernity that leaves no room for a standard of salvation, liberation, and justice.[43] The still operative metanarratives of Latina/o Protestantism while ignored by modernity and postmodernity have sense-making and action-producing power for those communities that hold them. As a metamodern phenomenon, Latina/o Protestantism exists beyond the usual social, historical, and theological explanations, whether they be modern or postmodern. As a metamodern subaltern counterpublic, Latina/o Protestantism is deeply aware of the status quo, recognizes and deals with it, but also can challenge its hegemony by drawing on alternative assumptions and narratives. Latina/o Protestantism finds strength and resources within its own understandings of "big stories" and mines the "little stories" of alternative communal public spheres.[44]

As a metamodern reality, Latina/o Protestantism creates and maintains its own sense of identity and strives for the common good of its counterpublic sphere, and whenever possible contributes on its own terms to the common good of the dominant public spheres. Any effort to relate the stories of these communities should take into consideration the alternate public spheres and metamodern realities on the margins.

The use of the term *metamodern* emphasizes the "beyond-ness" of the experience of Hispanic/Latina/o Protestantism. Metamodernity is another way to talk about life on the margins, in the social borderlands, the alternative public spheres. Latina/o Protestantism is a distinct subaltern counterpublic sphere and a metamodern reality not considered in the colonial discourses of modernity, nor in the postcolonial discourse of postmodernity. Latina/o Protestantism refuses to give up its metanarratives, which are central to its ethos/worldview and has been a source of life, liberation, and empowerment in the midst of ongoing oppression.

TOWARD A HISTORIOGRAPHY OF LATINA/O PROTESTANTISM

Understanding Latina/o Protestantism means opening up the historiographic task by recognizing the importance of cultural perspective and identity, not only of the observer but also of the metamodern perspective of the participant. The metamodern emphasis is a perspective of analysis rather than a theory of analysis.[45] As a critical methodology in the study of Latina/o Protestantism, metamodernity means seeing and listening to the perspectives and the understandings of those outside or beyond dominant culture. It means assuming not only the existence of those stories but also their inherent value. A metamodern approach to the history of Latina/o Protestantism also implies the possibility of new ways of gathering and analyzing information as well as new ways of presenting this segment of the history of Christianity. The historical narratives and related discourses of Latina/o Protestantism not only are informative of those communities but also provide insight into the theologies, ideologies, practices, processes, structures, and institutions of both Hispanic and non-Hispanic communities.[46]

By intentionally starting from a metamodern perspective, religious life on the margins and in the borderlands is recognized as significant not only for local communities but also for broader publics. The realities and perspectives of Hispanic/Latina/o Protestantism reveal abundant innovation, alternative approaches, and diverse movements with wide appeal and participation. The "little stories" from this part of the margins/borderlands will surprise many with its challenges of historical and theological stereotypes of the dominant centers.

A repositioned metamodern view from the margins of the North American religious landscape provides better understanding of Hispanic/Latina/o Protestantism in the United States in part by introducing new data and evidence into the construction of the history of American Christianity in the United States.[47] Some of the new evidence is the distinctive awareness and contextual responses to its specific social and historical settings that will influence the production of new histories. Simultaneously, a metamodern approach starting with the "beyond-ness" of Latina/o Protestantism can be a corrective in the study of North American religions and cultures. Furthermore, a metamodern approach fosters new insights into dominant religious power centers, denominational stories, concepts of mainline and mainstream, the religious life-worlds of other racial/ethnic groups, and alternative perspectives on multiple restructurings of North American religions calling for a reinterpretation of religious life in North America. Instead of being peripheral or being on the edge of nothingness, constructing history with a view from the metamodern margins where significance is constructed by and for so many. It means going where the action is, action that affects all in society.

THE STATE OF U.S. LATINA/O THEOLOGY

AN UNDERSTANDING

Orlando O. Espín

My task is to share with you some ideas on where U.S. Latina/o theological reflection has been over the last two decades and where it might be going in the foreseeable future.[1] Obviously, I cannot foretell the future nor do I have the only possible interpretation of our theological past. This is "an understanding" (emphasis on the indefinite article), a descriptive snapshot of U.S. Latina/o theology at the dawn of the twenty-first century. It cannot be thorough or exhaustive.

I am going to try to *describe* for you some trends, issues, and characteristics I have seen over the past twenty years, as well as some trends, issues, and characteristics I see developing into the near future. Therefore, I will not be offering you a long list of publications and their contents. However, I will be making some evaluative observations that might be helpful to you in assessing the past and possible future of U.S. Latina/o theology. Needless to say, this panoramic description is necessarily incomplete, representing only my own perspective—and even then, only telegraphically. I have tried to cover both Protestant and Catholic trends, issues, and developments; and I readily recognize that my own research interests and questions, and my denominational affiliation, as well as my professional training in systematics, have probably influenced my choice of trends and issues and blinded me to others.

In the two parts of this presentation I have followed no particular order when presenting and discussing trends and issues within Latina/o theology, both in the past two decades, as well as those that seem to be emerging. In other words, I have avoided prioritizing the issues, trends, and difficulties. I am thus making no claim that these are the only important ones. I will be surprised if some of you *don't* tell me, after I finish, that I forgot this or that issue, this or that trend, and that my explanation of something is incomplete or superficial. I am guilty as charged!

WHERE HAVE WE BEEN?

When was U.S. Latina/o theology born? Where was it born? Who started it, and why? These are questions I will leave to the historians among us.[2] I have chosen instead to focus on roughly the last two decades, not because of any claim on my part that Latina/o theology is *only* twenty years old, but because that seems to be the period when we note the clear emergence of the distinct theological literature and reflection we now call "U.S. Latina/o theology."[3] Some of our colleagues have argued that this movement began back in 1972 when Virgilio Elizondo published a brief but important article on Mexican American religious education.[4] Others have suggested that the movement began even earlier, with Justo González's publication of a book on the history of Christianity in the Latin Caribbean.[5] Whatever the arguments for one or the other suggestion, no one can deny that both of these respected colleagues, by their vision and their efforts, made it possible for Latina/o theology to begin. Also, we cannot forget the contributions of the late Orlando Costas (among Protestants) and of Edgard Beltrán (among Catholics).

In any case, the 1980s saw the coalescence of different trends and sources into an identifiable theological movement, which blossomed in the early 1990s. One cannot overestimate the importance of the Academy of Catholic Hispanic Theologians of the United States, the *Journal of Hispanic/Latino Theology*, La Comunidad (Community of Hispanic Scholars in Theology and Religion), The Fund for Theological Education, *Apuntes,* and the networking and hard work that ultimately led to the immensely successful Hispanic Summer Program and Hispanic Theological Initiative (HTI).

When we look at the body of literature produced by Latina/o theologians during the past twenty years, what do we find? Where has Latina/o theology been over these last two decades?[6] Several issues, characteristics, and trends seem to have dominated this period. As we review some of them, please do not lose sight of the fact that over these two decades changes and developments did occur. And please remember that the following list does not attempt to prioritize.

We Are We, and Not They

Perhaps we could start by remembering that Latina/o theology was born at the intersection of European and European American theologies, on the one hand, and of Latin American theologies, on the other—an intersection that did not occur in either Europe or Latin America but in the United States, and here does not occur in either Europe or Latin America but in the United States, and here not among Anglas/os but within the extraordinarily diverse context of the U.S. Latina/o communities.[7] Furthermore, Latina/o theology (from its inception) always understood itself as being neither a copy, translation, nor adaptation of earlier intellectual traditions.[8] Latina/o theologians began their work critiquing the universalizing and colonizing pretensions of European and European American theologies, as well as recognizing that we were not in Latin America (thereby questioning as well the temptation to simply translate or adapt Latin American theologies to our U.S. context, in spite of the fact that we borrowed heavily from Latin American liberation theology). I don't think that at that time we had read postcolonial theory, but postmodern thought was certainly gaining ground. In any case, when the Latina/o theological critique of dominant theologies began, with the tools we had then (mostly borrowed from the Latin American critique of ideologies),[9] it began by insisting that, theologically, "we are we" and therefore "we are not they." This led to a number of publications on the significance of culture, particularity, and ethnicity for theology—and this is the first set of trends and issues raised during the first two decades.[10] We needed to open "our" space, speak with "our" voice, discuss "our" issues. Although never pretending that we were the only partners in the theological conversation, we insisted on being included: thus, ethnicity, particularity, and culture—the uniqueness of these among Latinas/os and their implications for theology and for the defense of our people—became the first issues we raised.

Mestizaje

Together with ethnicity, particularity, and culture came the development of other categories, the most important of which was *mestizaje*. It became the main category of Latina/o theologizing.[11] What had been a denigrating label (*mestizaje* and the condition of being *mestiza/o*) was transformed into a self-descriptive reason for pride. Furthermore the reality, history, and processes of *mestizaje* became the tools through which much was then examined, in that first attempt, to show that we, as *mestizas/os*, were therefore "distinct," "different" from Latin Americans and European Americans, not because they themselves were not *mestizas/os*, but because our particular manner of being *mestiza/o* made us different from them.[12] Our cultures were then studied as *mestiza* cultures, and our religion as a *mestiza* religion. Christ became the *mestiza/o* savior, and *mestizaje* became the cornerstone of his and our identities. The church, too, was to be *mestiza* if it wanted to be truly Christian. And so on. To be Latina/o became synonymous with being culturally (if not racially) *mestiza/o*, and that which was not *mestiza/o* was somehow not "really" Latina/o. I am in no way challenging the contributions of *mestizaje* theory and the many avenues of thought and creativity it opened for us. And I am not denying either that many Latinas/os are in fact *mestizas/os* in one way or another. What I am pointing to is the "romantic" dimension and use of these categories,[13] at least as often employed by Latina/o theology over the last two decades, and the "veiling" that was caused by promoting *mestizaje* as an essentialist definition of *latinidad*—it hid all sorts of denigrating, violent, and dehumanizing behavior, which Latinas/os themselves engage in, as well as displaced the necessary recognition of Latina/o internal diversity and our own racism and biases. The use of *mestizaje* got us to see ourselves with pride and as a distinct human group in society, but the violent history of *mestizaje* led many to further define *latinidad* by victimization.

To Read the Bible "in Spanish"

During the first two decades of Latina/o theology, an enormous amount of work went into identifying the sources of a distinctly Latina/o theology.[14] Obviously, Scripture became the primary source, but Latina/o theologians soon discovered that how we read or interpret Scripture, and more specifically from which perspective and for whose benefit, is an extremely important and theoretically difficult issue to tackle. To borrow Justo González's question, how do Latinas/os "read" the Bible in Spanish?[15]—referring not only or mainly to the Castillian language but to the complex cultural and epistemological issues at stake. The struggle for a Latina/o exegetical model, and the hermeneutical grounding for it, is far from over; in fact, it has only begun. But the issues have been raised and acknowledged. My suspicion is that over the past twenty years we knew that the historical-critical method was insufficient for our cultural contexts, but we did not articulate and ground the bases for this assumption, nor had we a different methodological or hermeneutic alternative. In spite of this, I think we were and are still on target with our suspicion of the dominant exegetical model and of some of the more postmodern alternatives offered by the dominant academy.

Who Are "the People"?

In its quest for the sources of a distinctly Latina/o theology, our movement turned to Latinas/os themselves—to their faith, their Christian experience, their Christian expressions, and some to the Latina/o intellectual tradition. And it is in this quest that many of us began to work through such issues as popular religion, epistemology, praxis, spirituality, *lo cotidiano*, and so on. Any one of us in the first generation of Latina/o theologians (that is, those of us who have been engaged in theology over the past two decades at least) can readily confess that our work in these and other areas is far from over and far from sufficient—new answers raise many more questions, which in turn lead to newer areas and further questions and answers. However, many of us will admit that if we were to read today what we wrote twenty years ago we would find it perhaps somewhat "romantic," and evidently in need of further development. This, of course, could be said of many theologies anywhere on the planet, but the fact remains that we need to do more on each of the areas we proposed as theological source. One example will suffice. Over the last twenty years, what have we meant by, and how have we explained and reasonably legitimized, the meaning of the term *people*, and of its adjective *popular?*[16] During the past two decades, although less so in the more recent past, we have simply assumed that we all knew and understood the meaning of *people* and fully understood its legitimacy as a theological source and even as an analytical category. By which criteria, and grounded how, have we claimed all those things for the "people" and for whatever might be "popular"? We still have some serious work to do. My suspicion is that we assumed the category *people* to have been exhaustively analyzed in Latin American liberation theology, and thus borrowed its use without further analysis. The maturity of U.S. Latina/o theology is now demanding that we look into *people* again without many of our earlier assumptions.[17]

Social Reality and Faith Expressions

There is no question in my mind that Latina/o theology has always tried to be sensitive and responsive to the social, economic, and political realities of Latinas/os in the United States.[18] Our theology has also been just as sensitive to popular expressions of the Christian faith. We have frequently included data on U.S. Latinas/os made available to us by the social sciences and attempted (with varying degrees of success) to theologize from the reality described by the data. We have tried to step behind the external expressions of faith (some of which might not be pleading to our understanding of Christianity) and there listen to the faith of everyday Latinas/os, not by pretending that Christianity could somehow exist without expression, but by not equating the former with the latter. Why and how Latinas/os believe are not idle questions in and for theology. Indeed, to understand how Latinas/os "construct" what they hold to be real and good and important is crucial to the Latina/o theological movement. The first twenty years began the process of study of popular religion and the incorporation of social scientific interlocutors into our theological dialogue—both in a clear and conscious attempt at listening to our people, recognizing in our communities' life and faith a source for our theology.[19] But again, a dosage of "romanticism" seems present in these earlier discussions, as well as some analytical assumptions that today are being challenged by the very theologians who originally proposed them.[20] Is the use of social scientific data as a means of accessing social reality, as well as the theological study of popular religion, to be discarded or put aside now? Not at all! On the contrary, these are today more important than ever. What I am suggesting is that some of the approaches employed and some of the analytical categories assumed must be thought about more carefully. How could one conceivably do theology (*any* theology) today while disregarding the social reality or the faith expressions of the very Christian communities one claims to be serving through theology? How can anyone do theology today (*any* theology) and not consider the believing people's faith and life as theological source?[21]

Theological Traditions and Ecumenism

There seems little doubt that U.S. Latina/o theology was born within various Christian denominations. Some of them, perhaps, have had a greater impact or a greater output; but it seems that most Christian ecclesial traditions have been involved in our movement. From the start, and I don't think I exaggerate, Latina/o theologians have been sensitive to the ecumenical needs of our communities, as well as respectful of intra-Latina/o denominational differences. The truly fraternal and sororal spirit evident among Latina/o theologians (which, unfortunately, is not always paralleled at the congregational level) opened within our movement not only the opportunity for excellent transdenominational friendships but also for such transdenominational programs as the Hispanic Summer Program, the Hispanic Theological Initiative, and our two theological journals.[22] This in turn has contributed to the birth of a respectful and sensitive theology (ecumenically speaking). To me, for example, it is always a privilege when I can honestly discuss any theological issue—even those issues that might seem to interest mainly members of my own Roman Catholic Church—with Justo González (a Methodist), Daisy Machado (a Disciple of Christ), Samuel Solivan (a Pentecostal), José David Rodríguez (a Lutheran), Teresa Chávez-Sauceda (a Presbyterian), Loida Martell-Otero (a Baptist), and Ismael García (a United Church of Christ theologian), among many others. This shared respect and shared interest in each other's traditions have affected Latina/o theology over the last two decades, and increasingly more so. This is a gain that our respective denominations will do well to heed. God is saying and doing something here!

But just as I have emphasized the ecumenical spirit among most U.S. Latina/o theologians, I want to also underline that most of our published works bear the mark of our denominational affiliations: we write from within our traditions, and this (at least in my mind) is both a plus and a minus. We are familiar with the work of European, European American, and Latin American theologians of our denominations. Catholics know their Catholic theologies; Protestants know their Protestant theologies; and no one is embarrassed to engage their own theological traditions in dialogue and mutual critique. We do not hide who we are. We have not made excuses for the theological and ecclesial traditions of our denominations because we understand all of them to be limited human efforts at understanding what is often beyond all understanding, just as we understand these theological traditions to be bearers of much wisdom and insight. The same self-honesty that led us to demand our voice and our space as Latinas/os in society and in the academy has also made us appreciate the denominational traditions that nourished us and announced the gospel to us. Most Latina/o theology, over the last two decades, has been denominational as well as ecumenically respectful. But, the next step will have to be the construction of a truly ecumenical, Latina/o theology that can be received by most (if not all) as reflective of their faith and of our common heritage. There is a growing need to show that the ecumenical spirit can be translated into actual theological works.[23]

Feminist Contributions

There is no question in my mind that one significant dynamic within Latina/o theology, over the last decade or so, has been the ever increasing reception and incorporation of methodological concerns and issues raised by feminist critical theory. From the growing interest on *lo cotidiano* to the critique of gender roles to a whole other set of critical issues originally raised by Latina feminists outside the theological academy (think, for example, of the growing importance and discovery of *nepantlah* among us, as an analytical category, which can be traced to our reading of Gloria Anzaldúa's and Pat Mora's retrieval and creative uses of this ancient Nahuatl term). Latina feminists have begun to affect Latina/o theology (and not just that theology done by women), with particular emphases on *lo cotidiano*, *nepantlah*, and epistemological critique.[24] However, we would be daydreaming and lying to ourselves if we thought that this increased awareness and reception of feminist concerns and issues has occurred without tension, that it's a "done deal," or that most of feminist critical theory has been understood, assimilated, or even read by most Latina/o theologians (who are males).[25] Unfortunately, much Latina/o theology pays lip service to feminism, while ignoring it methodologically. We are certainly not where we were twenty years ago, but we are not even near where we should be.

The Validation of Our Theology

As Latina/o theology grew during these twenty years, it became important to ask, who validates our theology? Who says and confirms that we are doing what we should be doing? Questions intimately connected with another one: who benefits from our theology? These are not just theoretical questions; these are eminently ethical issues. Theology (all theology) is ethical or it is not "theology." Latina/o theologians work under the same pressures and demands as all other theologians: we have to publish and teach, go through review processes, struggle for tenure and professorial ranks, deal with boards and deans and publishers, and so on. We all know what academic life is like and what are its exigencies. The point I am making is that Latina/o theologians are responsible to the theological academy, and we are judged by the standards of that academy.[26]

Our work must be scholarly rigorous, self-legitimizing, publishable (and published), and so on. We cannot allow ourselves to publish second-rate scholarship and pretend that it is good enough "because we are Latinas/os, speaking from the Latina/o experience." To claim such nonsense is to justify racism and biases, as well as to cheat our people of the best we can and should offer them. We, Latinas/os in the academy, have exactly the same requirements as everyone else, and so does our scholarship—although we know that this is not *really* true. We often face, in our various institutions, the biases of colleagues and administrators who consistently demand more of us than they would demand of themselves, as if requiring us to "prove" to them that we can be considered their equals. Women know exactly what I am talking about, because they often face these "extra demands." I have heard this extra weight put on our shoulders referred to us as the "Ginger Rogers effect": if you recall the famous dancing pair of Ginger Rogers and Fred Astaire, most people thought that he was the lead dancer, and perhaps the better one of the two. Astaire might be better known than Rogers, but what people very often forget is that Ginger Rogers did exactly the same pirouettes and dance steps as Fred Astaire, but backward and on high heels! Latinas/os in the theological academy today face these "Ginger Rogers" demands. We must continue fighting this inequality, yes, but meanwhile we must make sure that we have the scholarly rigor and depth that will make our theology withstand critique from the dominant culture's intellectuals.

However, and this is an extremely important "however," even when granting that we do need to have our theology validated by the academy, *that* is not the real and most important validation we require and seek. Indeed, there is another validation that is the key to our not being co-opted by the dominant academy's acceptance or applause (or by the dominant academy's politically correct need to convince itself of its own openness). I am speaking of the validation that comes from our Latina/o theologians that asks whether our work in fact furthers the goals of *our* people: their struggles for equality and dignity, for decent housing, education, and health care. An equally necessary question is whether our theology prophetically challenges our people to grow beyond *our* biases, *our* idols, and *our* sins. If the social, political, economic, and religious reality of Latinas/os is not positively affected by our theological work, then the applause or acceptance of the academy means nothing. Or perhaps it means that we have betrayed our communities' trust. Evidently, theology is not a recipe or an immediate "fix" for what needs to be immediately changed or for what needs to be affirmed, but the requirement of validation by the people remains.

Teología de conjunto

By *Teología de conjunto* I mean that manner of doing theology that has become so frequently identified with Latina/o theology. A group of theologians (i.e., a *conjunto*) gather (sometimes with pastoral agents or with scholars in other fields) and, together, "create" theology—each bringing his or her own expertise to the group, but all working together for the same purpose and on the same topic.[27] The product of this effort, consequently, does not belong to any of the individual theologians but to the group. The effort, then, must be validated by Latina/o communities. There are a few models of *Teología de conjunto*, but they all emphasize the communal, conversational, shared style of doing theology. Needless to say that during the past twenty years much has been written by theologians individually; therefore it would be inaccurate to assume that all Latina/o theology has been created as *Teología de conjunto*. But even the individual works have involved and been built upon a great deal of consultation and conversation. Nevertheless, *Teología de conjunto* has been slowly becoming a more frequent model for our theologizing, and some very important individual and collective works owe their existence to this model. I would add here something that is very important, in my view, and that has characterized most Latina/o theology during these last two decades: Latina/o theologians have not competed with each other. If anything, we have been supportive of and dialogical with each other's work. We have critiqued each other—sometimes fiercely but usually in private—but have not tried to destroy our colleagues, their careers, or their ideas. I certainly hope that, although our mutual critique might need to move into a more public forum,[28] we will continue to be supportive of our colleagues.

Working within Traditional Disciplines

Last, in this section on the past twenty years, it seems evident that we must also recall the contributions made by Latina/o theologians to and within the traditional disciplines of professional theology. I think we will find publications in most of these disciplines, more often scholarly articles and occasionally books (which is itself a cause for some concern). We are few, but the body of literature produced seems to suggest that we have been extremely active.[29]

What traditional theological subjects have we discussed during these twenty years? I think that theological methodology has been paramount (and here I include questions not only on method but also on the grounds and assumptions of method, as well as hermeneutical and epistemological issues, and so here, too, I include much of the feminist contribution) and for understandable reasons. Following, in no particular order, we have published in fields such as trinitarian and pneumatological studies, social ethics, revelation and tradition, popular religious practices, Christology and theological anthropology, church, ecclesiology and doctrinal history, spirituality and the spiritual grounds of theology, Mariology, grace and sin, justification and salvation, and praxis and aesthetics (although these could be understood as part of the methodological focus of so much of our theology). I have probably forgotten some fields, but I think this brief list gives us an idea of Latina/o theological productivity over the last two decades as it also suggests which areas of theology we have barely touched. Although an argument might be offered that biblical studies fall within overall theology, I have on purpose not included them in this brief list because I think that most biblical scholars would have some serious reservations about being told that their disciplines are only a "subsection" of overall theology.

The Christian churches in the United States are changing their demographic makeup. Indeed, some of our denominations would either shrink, stop growing, or not be able to understand themselves without the ever-growing Latina/o presence within their ranks. Theological research into Latina/o culture and faith is an urgent and necessary task for the churches and for academic theology. Indeed a reinterpretation of American Christianity's future and ethos, given the new cultural and demographic realities in church and society, is fast becoming an equally unavoidable task. Although some gains can be indicated, most of our denominations and most of the theological academy still consider us a fringe—unimportant to otherwise "real" theology and at best a pastoral problem to be solved but not a theological partner to be engaged. The last twenty years have been extremely productive, but don't daydream yourselves into thinking that the churches and the academy are paying serious attention—most are not. We have an enormous task ahead of us. Demographic growth will be on our side, since one out of every four Americans will be Latina/o in less than fifty years; but still, we will not be able to count on those millions of Latinas/os being Christian if the churches and theological faculties continue to ignore or dismiss our people's needs and contributions. Furthermore, if we Latinas/os insist on defining ourselves as an immigrant community, we are going to be banking on the past and not on the future. Whether we like to admit it or not, much of our theology so far has spoken from and for the reality of immigrants, and we have yet to consistently address the reality of the majority of Latinas/os who (says the U.S. Census Bureau) are already American-born.

We have had a very busy, creative, and extremely important past two decades. But we are far from done, and the questions and demands keep growing. Mercifully, and in great part thanks to the Hispanic Theological Initiative, the number of Latinas/os engaged in professional theology keeps growing, but we are still too few.

WHERE ARE WE GOING?

After this very quick and admittedly insufficient panoramic description of the last twenty years, where is Latina/o theology going? Many of the trends and issues I will be mentioning shortly have not been sufficiently considered yet by our theology, probably because of the limited resources at our disposal, as well as our limited numbers.

Let me list the trends and issues I see developing in Latina/o Protestant and Catholic theology, raising some questions associated with each that indicate some of the issues that, in my mind, Latina/o theology has to research and reflect upon in the future. For the sake of clarity, I have grouped these trends and issues, and some of the questions raised by them, into ten areas. I should also add that I have not tried to place them in any particular order of importance.

The Theological Study of "Popular Christianity"

I do not think I exaggerate if I say that we will be seeing further studies on what has come to be known as "popular religion" (both Protestant and Catholic). I think Latina/o theologians have already established its importance and role as a source of a theology done *latinamente*—even Protestant theologians have begun to recognize that there is such a universe of faith expressions that can be legitimately understood as "popular Protestantism." Indeed, I think some Latina/o theologians have convincingly argued that *all* theology must pay methodological attention to the people's faith and faith expressions if this theology does not want to become a dialogue among specialists without reference to or resonance in the wider, living church. Method in theology is not free from ethics, and consequently our theology (which has chosen to be on the side of the poor) must make a methodologically serious study of the religion of the poor. This is not "political correctness," this is a matter of faith and of loyalty to the gospel.

Popular Christianity is not a collection of beliefs or practices, no matter how exotic or quaint, orthodox or heterodox by our denominational standards. Popular Christianity is, first and foremost, an epistemology, a way of imaging reality and of constructing knowledge.[30] It is a bearer of culture and identity. It too is listener and witness to revelation in culturally authentic and specific ways that, among Latinas/os (as among all peoples), bear the impact of both grace and sin. The rites, beliefs, and symbols commonly associated with popular Christianity are *not*, in and of themselves, what is important in this religious universe; rather, they are like doors through which we may sense the faith of our people and their daily struggles for life. Because of this, some Latina/o theologians have argued that popular Christianity is a source for an authentically Latina/o theology. But the thorough theological study of popular Christianity is today far from sufficient. We still need to access and reflect on the worldviews, identities, cultures, grace and sin, pains and sufferings, and so much more, which are expressed, experienced, embodied, and somehow constructed in and through popular Christianity.

There are numerous theological issues still unresolved and in need of further research and reflection. For example, what is the relationship between popular Christianity and the development of doctrine, as well as in the development of denominations? What is popular Christianity's role as "receiver" of and witness to revelation? Or, is there no such role? Whose experience and whose

Christianity defines "popular Christianity," and by which criteria (and set by whom) do we define it as "popular"? Can what we say of popular Christianity among Latinas/os be legitimately "extended" to other milieus within the wider church? Does popular Christianity have within it room for the prophetic voices that might challenge it? How does Latina/o popular *Catholicism* relate to Latina/o popular *Protestantism*, beyond the evident fact that both are Latina/o?[31] Needless to say, I could go on and on speaking about popular Christianity since it has been my area of study for over two decades. I do want to add, however, that Brite Divinity School and the University of San Diego will soon begin a joint, comprehensive, and ecumenical research and publication project dealing with these and many other questions regarding Latina/o popular Christianity.

Epistemology

Another area that I believe is becoming increasingly important, and which requires further study, is epistemology.[32] What I have just indicated about the reasons for the theological study of popular Christianity suggests our growing interest in epistemology, although it is by no means the only reason. By *epistemology* I mean, generally, the processes by and through which Latinas/os image the "real" and construct knowledge (and, specifically, *theological* knowledge), why they do it in those ways, and for whose benefit. No one in Latina/o theology doubts the existence of Latina/o cultures in their rich variety. The questions on epistemology have to be addressed precisely because culture assumes that there are indeed specific ways of imaging the "real" and of constructing knowledge that, in turn, shape and identify culture.[33] The study of epistemology is deeply connected to much of what Latina/o theology has been doing over the past two decades and will inevitably become an even more important concern. As an example of the growing interest in this field, I can mention a multiyear project recently begun by the Center for the Study of Latino/a Catholicism at the University of San Diego, which will bring together Protestant and Catholic theologians, philosophers, historians, and social scientists for the sole purpose of reflecting on and mapping the epistemology (or epistemologies) undergirding Latina/o theology. This a massive research effort with potentially crucial results for our discipline. Any study of epistemology, furthermore, will lead to some substantive questions on salvation, revelation, and so on, because these theological topics stand on how humans culturally understand and image what to them is real.

Critical Feminism

We are already witnessing a growing dialogue within Latina/o theology, with feminist critical theories, and with the slow but increasing incorporation of this theoretical work into our theological method. This dialogue, I think, will continue and grow, as will its effect on Latina/o theology. We are certainly moving in the right direction, as many epistemological discussions among us are demonstrating. But I believe that it is not enough for Latina/o theologians, most of which are men, to include references to issues raised by many of our women colleagues, nor is it enough to occasionally address questions raised by feminist critical theories. The big issue here is whether we have understood well enough, and whether the dialogue with feminist theorists (within and outside Latina/o theology) has truly been sufficient, to transform Latina/o theology *methodologically*, thereby making the latter truly inclusive, truly liberative of both men and women, and truly reflective of Latina/o humanness. This, therefore, is a question of *method* (applicable to our entire discipline), and *not* mainly of being sensitive to women's concerns.[34] The epistemological questions raised earlier (as well as most others in this paper) all have a bearing upon and are themselves affected by the issues just mentioned here. It is now impossible to do Christian theology pretending that the challenges posed, the issues raised, and the contributions made by critical feminist theories can be either ignored, downplayed, or methodologically excluded.[35]

Questions of Class, Race, and Culture

Another trend, deeply connected with the preceding ones, is the growing concern for class, race, and cultural issues. Perhaps Latina/o theologians have been too "romantic" in their references to, reflections on, and use of Latina/o culture; probably—although I hate to generalize because there have been exceptions. But what seems increasingly clear is that we have to get more critical in our analyses of culture, and we definitely have to extend these critical analyses to questions of race and class.[36] The broad fields of cultural and postcolonial studies have to be engaged more systematically, and our theological method has to deepen the critical sophistication of its cultural analyses. This, in turn, must increasingly bring to our attention, and hopefully provoke some serious reflection on, questions regarding class and race. Although this reflection has not been absent altogether, I do think we have to pay a closer and more critical look. With all due respect to the ethicists among us, we cannot let questions of class and race become solely "ethical" questions: in doctrinal, systematic theology (as in other theological disciplines) we also have to realize that class, cultural, and race analyses are unavoidable.[37] Furthermore, the growing reflection on what has come to be known as "interculturality" should affect our theological method and approaches.[38] As María Pilar Aquino has forcefully argued, interculturality must become a methodological axis in and for Latina/o theology. This intercultural methodology, I suspect, will open our academic field to sustained reflection, doctrinally and ethically, on globalization and its related phenomena, and it will arguably lead us to join ever-broadening dialogues across the country and the globe.[39]

Biblical Exegesis

I realize that I said earlier in this paper that biblical scholars often feel uncomfortable when their disciplines are lumped together with theology. The fact remains, however, that theology cannot survive without biblical exegesis. A concern that has appeared across denominational lines is the search for a specifically Latina/o "reading" of Scripture. There have been some significant steps already taken in that direction, and thus the realization that this "reading" is necessary is no longer an issue. But now there are other questions that call for further research and study. Do authentic Latina/o epistemology and exegesis (however these might be construed) receive and interpret the Scriptures in manners indistinguishable from the European and European American dominant reception and interpretation we were trained in? Or does it lead to a distinctly Latina/o understanding of the Bible (no less scientifically rigorous, but yet authentically Latina/o)? What would a Latina/o exegesis of Scripture look like methodologically, and on which grounds does it philosophically, socially, and theologically legitimize itself? How will the biblicists among us epistemologically ground a Latina/o exegetical method that incorporates the contributions of feminist exegesis, postcolonial theory, and cultural studies (for example) and still remain in communion with the faith and reality of Latina/o communities in our *barrios?* What other theoretical contributions, from other parts of the country and the world, should Latina/o biblical scholarship be in dialogue with, and why?

The Critique of Our "Idols"

Latina/o theologians have been very good in their critique of the "idols" and sins of dominant culture. But there is no question in my mind, or in the minds of a growing number of our colleagues, that we need to deepen our theological critique of *our* own Latina/o "idols" and sins (from domestic violence, homophobia, and *machismo* to political and religious *caciquismo,* racism and social naivete, and every other "idol" in between).[40] Is the defense of *latinidad,* necessary as it might be for minorities within a dominant culture, hiding and by complicity condoning the sins of Latinas/os? Are not our sins and idols in need of in-depth critique, as are the idols and sins of dominant culture? Has Latina/o theology been "romanticizing" Latina/o family life and Latina/o culture and history, thereby contributing to the perpetuation of our sins and idols; and if so, how do we defend our *latinidad* while we also seriously critique our own dehumanizing behaviors and attitudes? I need not say that this necessary turn in our theology has a potentially significant impact on a Latina/o theology of grace and sin, as well as on our reflections on Trinity, pneumatology, Christology, soteriology, and ecclesiology. There too are immense pastoral consequences.[41]

Church History

Another growing concern is for church history not merely as a retelling of past events (if that ever was how church history could be done) but as a theological reflection on the church's past—warts and all. We need this kind of church history from the Latina/o perspective, not only to work with the specifically Latina/o or Latina/o-related events but as the entirety of the church's long history could be interpreted *latinamente*.[42] What would the telling and retelling, constructing and reconstructing of the church's past look like if it were comprehended from the Latina/o perspective and various experiences of church? And further, how would church history look if it were told, retold, constructed, and reconstructed from the perspective of Christians from the so-called popular classes instead of from the perspectives of political and social, academic or denominational elites? What would church history, as a scholarly discipline, look like if it were methodologically constructed from the perspective of the people's daily life and concerns, and not mainly from the ideological (theological, philosophical, or political) concerns of the denominational and social elites? And what will all of these reconstructions and changed perspectives do to Latina/o theology's methods, sources, assumptions, and choice of thematic developments?

Tradition and "Traditioning"

Tradition and "traditioning," with all sorts of pastoral and doctrinal implications, is another area of growing concern among many Latina/o theologians. Evidently, theological studies on how Christianity "transmits" itself across generations and across cultures are not disconnected from what I have just said about church history, or about cultural, racial, and class analyses, or about epistemology, or about popular faith expressions, or about feminist critical theories, or about Scripture. Indeed, to study tradition and "traditioning" is to implicate all of theology and its methods and groundings, as well as Scripture and church history. I must admit, however, that concern for the Christian tradition and for the manners and conditions through which it is "transmitted" (that is, "traditioned") across generations and across cultural lines is theologically worded differently among Christian denominations. For some Protestant colleagues the very mention of the terms *tradition* or *traditioning* brings up ghosts that they feel bound to exorcise. Among Catholics, Episcopalians, and a number of other Protestants, the terms are commonly accepted.

Is there a Christian message all of us can speak of? Are there ways in which this message can be transmitted across the generations and across cultural lines, even though these ways of transmission are not themselves part of the message but, rather, time-honored ways of announcing the gospel and organizing the church in new contexts?[43] How and why we transmit the Christian message (and what the components are of that message) are concerns of *all* Christians, regardless of the terminology or categories employed by them. What is the Christian message? What are its necessary elements? Are there necessary expressions of the message, and which are they? Are there human behaviors required of those who accept the Christian message as word of God, and why? These and many other questions have to do with the theological study of "tradition" and "traditioning." Some Latina/o theologians have begun to ask, however: what is the Christian tradition and what would its contents be if we were to understand tradition and traditioning *latinamente*? How would the Christian message be "traditioned" (i.e., "handed over," proclaimed and received, and further elaborated) if the subjects and bearers of that message and its transmission were Latinas/os?[44] What is the role, if any, of popular expressions of faith within the overall transmission of Christianity, and for the development of doctrines, across generational and cultural boundaries? Given that Christianity cannot transmit itself mainly as a doctrinal universe, how does it "hand itself over" into this new century among U.S. Latinas/os, in our diverse churches, without losing authenticity and continuity and without becoming a vestige of our Christian or cultural past? We believe that God can and will speak to humankind in this new century, but what are the epistemological, cultural conditions for humans to understand that God is indeed speaking, and by which criteria do Christians determine that the message is identifiable as indeed "Christian"?[45] These questions, evidently, have much to do with many other related issues. However, I do want to suggest that some Latina/o theologians, if they wish to remain faithful to their Christian calling (and perhaps here I am fine-tuning some of my earlier remarks on our growing ecumenical sensitivity), have to somehow get over narrow terminologies and definitions (reminiscent perhaps of past denominational struggles within and among our denominations), and realize that Christians, together, and for the sake of our common evangelizing mission, must move beyond denominational and theological stereotypes and into more fruitful, accurate, and ecumenically sensitive understandings of theological terms and concepts, and of our one religion.

Theology of Revelation

A growing concern in Latina/o theological reflection, which is very much tied to much of what I have been mentioning here, is the need for a deeper and more sustained reflection on the meaning, conditions, and consequences of revelation. Latina/o theology assumes that there has been divine revelation, of course, but there are some very important questions behind this assumption. For example, what is revelation, if we were to think it from the Latina/o perspective? What are its contents, *latinamente hablando*? How does it occur, and how is it received, understood, and expressed among Latinas/os? Because all Christians believe that the definitive revelation occurred in and through Jesus of Nazareth, has all revelation ceased, or does it continue? If yes, or if not, how and why do we philosophically and theologically justify our answer? How, and by which criteria, are contents and processes of revelation determined or justified by our people? Who is the source of these criteria? How do we evaluate, and by which criteria, the legitimacy or adequacy of the *expressions* of revelation? Who are the witnesses to revelation among Latina/o communities, and how did they come to be regarded? And, very important, what is the relationship of culture, gender, race, and class to revelation (given that we cannot speak theologically of revelation without the human interlocutor and given too that this interlocutor is necessarily defined by culture, gender, race, class, and so on)? This line of questioning, of course, brings us back to issues I raised earlier on tradition and traditioning, on epistemology, on popular expressions of faith, on feminist theory, and so on, and could potentially affect the whole of Christian theology.

An Ecumenical Theology

One development to expect within Latina/o theology, in the foreseeable future, is the unfolding of an ecumenical theology, authentically Christian, therefore acceptable to most, and truly representative of the faith and cultural heart of our people. Probably, in the long run, this development will be the gathering point of all the others I have been mentioning, as it might also be our more lasting contribution to our churches and our people.

Protestant and Catholic Latina/o theologians have been involved in the process of creating a theology from the Latina/o faith and cultural perspectives, and even those projects that so far have been specifically identified as either Catholic or Protestant have included (and *not* for "politically correct" reasons) the contributions of colleagues from both sides of the denominational divide. I am not suggesting that this ecumenical theology already exists as a body of literature, although some articles have begun to appear in this direction, but the thrust and intent are definitely there. Collaborative efforts of such groups as the Group on Hispanic Religion and Culture (at the American Academy of Religion), the Hispanic Theological Initiative, the Hispanic Summer Program, *Apuntes* and the *Journal of Hispanic/Latino Theology*, and the University of San Diego's Center for the Study of Latino/a Catholicism have fostered substantive conversations and common projects. This ecumenical collaboration, I believe, will continue if Protestants and Catholics remain faithful to the clear prompting of the Spirit among us. However, and for the foreseeable future, there seems to be a felt parallel need to look *also* at our denominational theologies, almost (I dare say) in preparation for the coming of a truly ecumenical effort. The process of creating an ecumenical Latina/o theology will take time, lots of goodwill, breaking stereotypes, and plenty of hard work—but it is coming.

This is a long-term task, and we must make sure that we do not bring to this project a preconceived "theological map," although certain areas are beginning to unfold as points in the process and method of reinventing Christian theology from the Latina/o ecumenical perspective. Some of these points seem to be:

A. The need to construct a common theological vocabulary and methodology from *within* Latina/o reality, experience, and faith; not necessarily according to the canons of the dominant academy or according to Christianity's past inter-denominational battles, although not without the wisdom acquired from both the academy and church history.

B. The commitment to construct a theoretically and methodologically solid theology with intellectual rigor, validated by our communities, but without creating false dichotomies between intellectual work and pastoral or social action.

C. The need to avoid entrenching or "ghettoizing" our theology exclusively within Latina/o cultures or within denominational strictures, as if it could speak only *about* Latinas/os or in the language of one Christian tradition. One thing is to speak *from* the Latina/o perspective (as all theologies speak from their particular perspectives), and quite another is to speak exclusively about particular Latina/o concerns. One thing is to be enriched by the history and traditions of one's denomination, and quite another is to erase variety in theological topography and nomenclature or to assume that no other Christian church can speak or enlighten truth. We must avoid intellectual and denominational ghettoes (which includes our refusal to be pushed there).

D. The need to specify and broaden the definition and task of theology, constructing the latter to be a critical reflection on the praxis of the faith. Consequently, a Latina/o ecumenical theology would want to reconstruct all Christian theology and ethical theology not as a merely theoretical, speculative activity: our clear aim should be not new doctrines or new theories but new relationships; our methodologies cannot be principles to be applied to reality but guides to clarify Christian faith and its praxis. Method in theology is not free from ethics, and consequently our theology needs to be clearly (as Jesus was) on the side of the poor and oppressed, whether these be Latinas/os or not. We want an ecumenical theology that can honestly help transform the earth according to the will of God. Nevertheless, the service of the poor would require that a Latina/o ecumenical theology, *qua* theology, be theoretically solid and intellectually rigorous. The reinvention of Christian theology, from an ecumenical Latina/o perspective, will indeed be a long journey into uncharted territory, but we have *not* just begun to walk toward it.

E. The need to critically engage the theological academy's assumptions, disciplines, and methods. As I said earlier, we must avoid the theological ghetto.

Will the future one day confirm that we have dealt with all of these ten areas, and will historians show that my assessment of the past twenty years was sufficiently correct? I have no way of knowing. I do believe, however, that U.S. Latina/o theology is moving in the right direction by asking some very important questions, each with equally serious consequences for Christian theology and the church. There is much to do, and thank God there is the theological will to do it.

LATINA/O CHURCH HISTORY

A HAUNTING MEMORY

Daisy L. Machado

I am a Latina, born in Cuba and raised in New York City, more specifically in "Crooklyn" as Spike Lee has called that large and interesting borough. I am not part of the first great wave of Cuban refugees who arrived at the port of a then small, insignificant city in south Florida called Miami. My father and mother did not flee the 1959 Cuban Revolution but rather fled hunger, unemployment, and government repression. And like the millions of immigrants from Europe before them, they believed that in the United States life would be different and perhaps even better. My father had all of seven dollars in his pocket when he arrived at LaGuardia International Airport in July 1956. He spoke no English, knew no one in this country; but at twenty-five years of age he felt he could do anything.

And he did. He saved his earnings and brought his wife and daughter to this new and strange land. He worked hard and learned English. He was a factory worker, one of many of the millions of immigrants that make up the statistics collected annually by the Census Bureau. But to my sister and to me he was *papi*. And after telling us his wonderful bedtime stories, he would whisper in our ears that we could do anything, we could be anything, we could climb as high as the stars. He whispered how we were no different from the Jewish or the Polish or the Italian or the black children that made up our international community in Brooklyn. He helped us see beyond the poverty of our inner-city neighborhood and dream of being and becoming and doing and succeeding. "This is not Cuba," my dad would say. "Here in this country we do not need to fear the police or the government. We do not need to whisper our discontent. We can claim the *dignidad* that is ours to claim as human beings." He seemed so sure of himself. He seemed so sure that we would one day leave that ghetto and pass through the doors of opportunity and self-realization using the keys of education, hard work, and faith in God. My dad, though certainly not a sixteenth-century Puritan, knew all about the Protestant work ethic.

But my dad and my mom were very peculiar about one thing: they would not let us forget we were Cubans and in doing this they made us aware of the duality of our existence. Spanish was the only language spoken at home, even though they made sure we learned English and did well in school. We ate the foods of their childhood. We savored the spices of their far-away home. I was often annoyed that my mother did not think that cold cuts or peanut butter and jelly were really foods, and I often faced the taunts of my elementary school friends who could not understand why I didn't eat "normal" foods. And then something happened that only reinforced how much I did not belong to the big North American world in which I lived. In the fourth grade my teacher punished me for speaking Spanish with a classmate. She made me stand before the class and apologize for speaking that "nasty language." Right then and there it was evident to me that I was not like everybody else. I was different. I was an outsider. I did not belong.

And the search began. I wanted to understand why in a nation that promoted itself as a haven for immigrants, why in a nation that talked about God and had reminders of God even in its currency, there were still so many millions of outsiders, of people who did not belong and who were systematically kept on the margins. I worked as a social worker dealing with abused children and women, often testifying in the family courts in an effort to avoid further violence and pain. I translated for Latina/o clients in the welfare offices of the city of New York. I visited the homes of children, women, and men where poverty and racism had consumed all joy and hope. I had entered the belly of the beast and I knew there was no heart beating within it. I then entered seminary. My decision to begin theological studies was not only a response to my faith commitment to become a pastor but to work as a pastor through the church community, a place I believed that still harbored hope, to bring about change. I pastored inner-city congregations in communities surrounded by gang violence and a thriving drug industry, a place of abandoned buildings and empty lots littered with broken bottles and garbage. Was this the world my father wanted us to prepare for? Was this the world my father had brought us to with such deep aspirations for a better future? Was this *my America*?

I thought back to the many years of conversation with my father. I recalled the many heated conversations between us about politics during my years in college. I tried to recall his words and his expressions and then I began to understand. I began to understand my father's continued effort to make me believe in myself and who I was. I began to understand his insistence that I know who *I* was before I had to deal with the North American reality outside. That was why my father wanted me to be proud of my Spanish. Why he wanted me to understand the meaning of our migration to this country. Why he wanted me to learn that home and nation were more than a house or a neighborhood or a naturalization card. He wanted me to know that what I carried within me, my identity as a Cuban immigrant, my history as a *caribeña* (a person from the Caribbean), were not only of great worth but also were necessary in order to sustain me in a society and a nation that did not know *how* to include me.

118

Yo soy cubana-americana. I am a Cuban-American, not because a court document from the Department of Justice and the Department of Immigration says so, but because I truly do belong to *América*, that other *América* that is much larger than the borders of the United States of America (which continues to claim to be the only America with the capital "A"). The *América* that gave life to my parents and their parents is older than the first British colonies on the eastern seaboard of the North American continent. In the *América* I am talking about English was not spoken until a little over two hundred years ago. In that *América* people come in all the colors of humanity, a great *mestizaje* of indigenous, African, and European blood. And I have finally understood the full meaning of my father's subtle lesson: I live in the world of two Americas. José Martí had already written about these two Americas in his great work *Nuestra América*, published in 1891. It is ironic that over one hundred years later, Martí continues to map out for the more than twenty-four million Latinas/os living in this country a very important reality that must be faced: there is *nuestra América* (our America), and there is the America that will never be ours. It was now clear what my father was trying to do. He was trying to prepare me for my encounter with the other America. That is why he wanted us to know who we were and be able to celebrate the life-giving connection with *nuestra América;* to have a clear sense of belonging despite the fact that we would exist in the margins of the other America.

AMERICA LEFT ALONE

In the September 1992 issue of *The Journal of American History* there is an article by the editor, David Thelen, entitled "Of Audiences, Borderlands, and Comparisons: Toward the Internationalization of American History," whose purpose is to explore the benefits of inviting outside historians to "encourage exploration of alternatives to the narrowed academic conversations that shape our field."[1] Thelen then goes on to list the benefits of the writing of history for foreign audiences because it forces scholars to answer, "How do people use words, and ultimately create lives, out of materials from two or more cultures in the borderlands between those cultures?"[2]

The reason I mention this article is because it provides such a clear example of precisely how the other America perceives itself. It points to the mythology that this other America has created about itself and how the academy has helped and continues to help in perpetuating this national self-understanding. The question that I would pose to all who in one way or another participate and help create the history of both Americas is, why is it that only those who live in countries defined as "foreign" are invited to bring "new perspectives"? I find myself suspicious of those who continue to define *global* or *borderland* as an overseas event and not one going on right across the street in Newark or Hartford or Los Angeles or New York City. The history of missions in mainline or historic denominations has shown that there is a safety that comes with distance that has been at the core for funding and promoting foreign missions. However, when that same missionary work is redirected toward the racial ethnic populations within the country, funding is hard to come by and the work is done mostly as "special ministries" projects that are created to be of short duration. Can it be that the history told and examined by *americanos* who are Mexican, Cuban, Nicaraguan, Puerto Rican, Salvadoran—who are citizens of *las Américas*—poses a threat to the accepted national historical themes? Can it be that like the foreign missions of historic denominations, safety comes with distance and that Latinas/os are just too close for comfort?

What is going on in the other America? Some historians use the term to describe the process of creating a space between Americans (those with the capital "A") and all others as "American exceptionalism." Joyce Appleby, a professor of history at the University of California in Los Angeles, defines *American exceptionalism* as a process that "projects onto a nation . . . qualities that are envied because they represent deliverance from a common lot."[3] Appleby argues that while this exceptionalism helped to generate a national identity for the revolutionary generation of 1776, two hundred years later, however, it "foreclosed other ways of interpreting the meaning of the United States."[4] I think we need to pause here and examine what Appleby is saying. It is very important that at the threshold of a new century, Latinas and Latinos within the academy, as well as those preparing to serve our Latina/o congregations, need to critically and unashamedly examine the ways in which the theological education we have received (and we often teach) has served as an "intellectual wrap" that hides the reality of diversity that has been a part of the formation of this nation from day one. And I want to go even further here: I want to say that what is hidden is the reality of an American diversity that has been and continues to be much more than the commonly held notion that race in the United States is a black/white issue.

Why is this so crucial for the liberation and empowerment of Latinas/os, African Americans, Native Americans, Asian Americans? Because to continue to accept the new forms that this American exceptionalism has taken, in the debate about bilingual education or the debate about affirmative action or the debate about the militarization of the Rio Grande border or the debate about workfare versus welfare, by uncritically accepting these notions, we lose sight of very important realities. We lose awareness of the systemic use of racism in the courts, the corporations, the government of this country. We forget that there was a very intentional and planned ejection and extermination of the indigenous people throughout this country. We accept the criteria of progress as the only way to measure the worth of a person or a group of people or a nation, and simply dismiss those who do not measure up as useless or backward. We also suffer the grave loss of seeing with clarity how interconnected we all are. There can be no understanding of the slavery issue without also understanding the results of the mass killing of indigenous people in the Caribbean by the Spaniards years before there was a slave trade in this hemisphere. There can be no understanding of border issues and immigration from the south to the United States without examining the political and military maneuvering of the United States government in the unstable territory of the newly formed *República de México* in the nineteenth century. To fully capture the meaning of Fidel Castro's influence in the Caribbean and throughout Latin America, there is the need to also examine the foreign policy of the United States, not in the last forty years but at the turn of the twentieth century. The Spanish-American War of 1898, the warning made to Simón Bolivar—Latin America's most famous liberator— by the Monroe government in the 1820s to stay out of the Caribbean, the making of Puerto Rico into a colony, all these historical realities had to do with a U.S. political worldview that was fed by these earlier notions of exceptionalism. And these notions have not gone away despite the new millennium.

The idealization of the United States by the Europeans of the Enlightenment had a strong influence on the national myths. Today these myths have become as well-known and as palatable as "mom, the flag, and apple pie." The enthusiasts of democracy in the eighteenth century created a chauvinistic sense of importance and nationhood. The strength of this great national myth of the conquered frontier lay in its use of Divine Providence and the Bible. This use of Divine Providence and the Bible created an intricate rationalization, or to use Appleby's term, an "intellectual wrap," which carefully hid the real and intentional application of theories about race and gender. In the early years of the nation, men like Benjamin Franklin and Thomas Jefferson, followed by historians like Francis Parkman, George Bancroft, and Frederick Jackson Turner in the last ninety years, made the connection between the westward movement of the United States across the continent and democracy itself. The result of this was the creation of a direct correlation between God's Will for the newly emerging nation called the United States and the people who would become her citizens.

The myth that was created told of an almost primeval Western frontier, which could only be "conquered" by a particular or "chosen" people. And as this myth was told and retold it gave shape to both the *public* persona of the ideal American (with a capital "A") and to the *individual* persona of the ideal American (also with a capital "A"). It was becoming ever more apparent not only that God had chosen the United States to be the "ark of salvation" for the nations but also that its citizens possessed the unique and exceptional characteristics of intelligence, strength and hard work, an ability to overcome odds, a love of freedom, a rugged individualism, and an ability to develop and master technology. It was also told that the crowning glory of this new man (women were not included) was his capability to establish and protect democracy. There was however one major problem with all this: the creation of a "chosen" nation to be possessed by a "chosen" people necessitated a virginal land. God needed a "clean slate" to produce this new nation whose light would shine as an example to an old and corrupt Europe. And in order to create a "clean slate" one had to eliminate the value and importance of the people already there. The people already inhabiting the land were deemed less human by virtue of their skin color or their religion or their way of life. Once the categories that defined the "other" were firmly set, it then became much easier to forcibly move the native peoples from the Southeastern United States to the Midwest in what is today known as the Trail of Tears. The fact that the Native Americans had been categorized as lacking in worth, inferior, and destined to eventual extermination transformed their thousands of deaths along the Trail into further proof of their unworthiness to possess the land.

The same scenario was played out in the takeover of the Mexican territories by the United States in the nineteenth century. The colonization of Texas is a clear example of what type of thinking takes place in order to create the "clean state" necessary for the national myths of this country. By devaluing Roman Catholicism and seeing it as mere superstition, it became much easier for Stephen Austin to falsely pledge allegiance to the Roman Catholic government of Mexico when he entered the northern borderlands of the territory then known as *Coahuila y Tejas*. Austin and the first Euro-American settlers, who in the early 1820s moved into what is today Texas, not only displayed little respect for Roman Catholicism but were just as demeaning toward the *mestizo* people they encountered. The *mestizaje* of the *tejanos*, the mixture of indigenous, African, and Spanish blood, was believed by Austin to produce a people who were inferior, depraved, incapable of governing themselves, and sexually promiscuous. Austin wrote, "To be candid the majority of the people of the whole nation as far as I have seen them want nothing but tails to be more brutes than the apes."[5]

CONCLUSION

But how does this speak to us today? Indeed all this history seems so distant from the multicultural world we know. Social historians have been busy for over two decades recovering the memories of communities all over the United States. The biggest hit on public television stations in the spring of 1998 was the historical miniseries called the "Irish in America." Today we celebrate Martin Luther King, Jr.'s birthday as a national holiday. February is Black History Month. Cinco de Mayo has become a statewide holiday in Texas, even though most Texans—Anglos and Mexicanos—don't know that they are celebrating an event in the history of Mexico that has nothing to do with Texas. The media has even focused on the Chinese New Year providing the nation with some history and a glimpse at community celebrations around the country. The United States wears the badge of multiculturalism as a means to show that Americans (with a capital "A") have moved into a new day. But is this really so? How comfortable are the Euro-Americans in this country with the reality of diversity or multiculturalism or racial inclusiveness? And an even more difficult question, how much are racial ethnic people willing to give up in order to be accepted by those in the majority? What is the ultimate cost of this loss for the individual and for the community he or she comes from?

I say we still have a long journey ahead of us. The myths created in the past to forge a sense of nationhood have not gone away, they have merely been reworked and updated. Evidence of this can be found in the language of U.S. foreign policy today. We hear the president and members of congress describe the role the United States must play as a protector of the world's peace and democracy. However, at the end of the twentieth century there is no more "virginal continent" to conquer. The native peoples have been boxed into the reservations; the West has been forever won by the likes of larger-than-life male pioneers who continue to be resurrected on our television screens in the greatest of all Hollywood Western prototypes, John Wayne. Our worldview seems to have shifted, and we think in terms of popular television programs like *Star Trek: The Next Generation, Deep Space Nine,* or *Voyager.* Our televisions bring us aliens from other galaxies with funny sounding names like Changelings, Bajorans, Klingons, Ferengis, and Cardassians. And while many think these programs are about an imagined future, I argue that they may also be seen as a revisiting of our past.

In the races of the different television aliens and their particular characteristics, we find embodied the struggles, the concerns, the hatred, the violence, the greediness, the untrustworthiness, as well as the hopes, dreams, aspirations, and visions we find in ourselves. Because these beings are portrayed as distinct from who we are as a nation, or as a racial group, or as humans, it is safe to become moral critics of their behavior. However, more than fiction, these strange-looking aliens are a reminder that this country has never been one nation made up of one people with one vision—that has been the ideal and never what the United States has really been. If knowledge is indeed power, and history, as Joyce Appleby says, "exercises that power by awakening curiosity, stretching imaginations, deepening appreciation, and complicating one's sense of the possible,"[6] then we must boldly take possession of that knowledge by recovering the diversity of the history of both Americas. It is not about political correctness or liberal politics. What is at the core for Latinas and Latinos is the ability to free ourselves from the restrictions imposed by the ideological imperatives of an idealized history that serves to exclude and marginalize. What I am referring to is the ability to redefine what has been called by dominant society as the "norm" and acknowledge that Latinas/os are also "normative" because our ancestors have been the permanent residents of this hemisphere for centuries. We are not the aliens. We are the heirs of a rich and diverse history that has been over five centuries in the making. We are the daughters and the sons born of the interactions of diverse races and cultures who as a whole make us who we are today. We refuse to be haunted by a national historical memory that barely includes us as a people so that we remain faint figures of an ancient past. The new millennium demands that Latinas/os be seen, heard, understood, and embraced. After all, this is *nuestra América*, and we are its proud citizens.

LEADERSHIP IN THE LATINA/O COMMUNITY

A BRIEF LOOK AT THE MEANING OF LEADERSHIP FOR TODAY

Zaida Maldonado Pérez

The list of needs faced by the Latino/Hispanic communities is staggering.[1] Among the most pressing and challenging are issues of immigration; language skills; stereotyping by non-Latinos; discriminatory practices; deficiencies in the education system that serve our communities; disproportionately low numbers of Latinos with high school, undergraduate, and/or graduate degrees; the highest proportion of teen pregnancies among racial/ethnic groups;[2] rising numbers of single-parent households; and an all-pervasive institutional and systemic racism that egregiously curtails and impedes creative, intelligent, energetic Latinas and Latinos to develop to their fullest potentials. Given these incredible challenges, we need to stop and ask, what does it mean when we talk about "leadership," whether secular or religious in the Latino/Hispanic community? Who or what makes a *líder?*[3] And, how can our seminaries help us equip our *líderes* for the kind of service that will advance our communities—and theirs?

THE "COMMUNITY SERVANT": THE SERVANT LÍDER MODEL

In a recent report by the National Community for Latino Leadership (NCLL) entitled, "Reflecting an American Vista: The Character and Impact of Latino Leadership,"[4] Latinos express their understanding of what constitutes "effective and meaningful leadership."[5] The main characteristics were summarized under what the NCLL calls "The Four C's of Latino Leadership," that is: Character, Competence, Compassion, and Community Service. According to the NCLL, "character" and "competence" are in line with the general views of the mainstream population. "Compassion" and "Community Service," however, do not coincide with mainstream perspectives.[6] This makes the notion of "community servant" (with "compassion" falling under "servanthood") vital to the Latino understanding of "leader" or "leadership."[7] Specifically, the "community servant" metaphor speaks to the kind of leadership model for which our communities yearn, that is, a *servant líder* model that also displays integrity of character, competency, compassion, and caring in their service as leaders. This model is in direct opposition to the kind of *caciquismo*[8] that permeates some of our churches and communities. Unfortunately, neither space nor time will allow me to explore either of these leadership models in depth. What follows is a brief exploration of what the *servant líder* model might entail from my perspective as a Latina.

Merriam-Webster's Third New International Dictionary defines *leader* as someone "who has commanding authority and influence" over others. When placed alongside this definition, the Latino understanding of *líder* as a "community servant" will seem upside down, less effective, and probably less glamorous. If a *líder* is a "community servant" then, in the eyes of the Latino community, if even ideally speaking, the *líder* should be someone who serves. Who does he or she serve? He or she serves the community. If this is true, it follows that the true *líder* should be the community itself. It should be the community that dictates the needs, that works together with the servant *líder* to devise strategies and call each other forth to make things happen. The "community servants," on the other hand, are there to hear, help discern, and, in some cases, better articulate those needs and give guidance. Their gifts should be placed at the disposal of the community—not always as these servants see fit but as the *community* may see fit and necessary. This does not presume, however, a kind of blind, unthinking service. A community servant should work not for the approval of the community but for the improvement of the community. This calls for a dialectical approach that allows for supportive but also challenging interchanges between servants and their communities. The call to service goes hand in hand with the call to be prophetic.

Finally, in the community servant model, power and authority are wrought in the collective birthing of solidarity in mission and in purpose. Furthermore, whether persons or institutions, the true servants will distinguish themselves by virtue of the respect and trust they have earned in this service.

This view is contrary to the *caciquismo* style of leadership, which imposes authority and control over those they purport to serve. In this setting, the *cacique*-type leaders dictate their wishes, prescribe the method(s) for action, and determine who is in or out, worthy or unworthy. These so-called leaders usually find the basis for their *caciquismo* in particular theological interpretations that are further sustained by sexist cultural mores and values. While we may not be able to do away with *caciquismo*, it *is* possible to create the possibilities for *servant líderes* to emerge. This brings us to other important questions, how and where are Latino community servants formed?

THE CHURCH AS LOCUS FOR DEVELOPING LEADERSHIP

Most Hispanic leaders are made and rise up from *within* their communities and, in particular, their church communities.[9] It is there where they are given the safe space to develop, to take risks, and where their gifts are nurtured and affirmed.[10] The call to be a "community servant," secular or otherwise, is not only an honor, it is *a vocation* not unlike that modeled by Jesus. In the NCLL study, *Persona de Fe* (Person of Faith, Religious or Spiritual Person), for instance, is one of the qualities listed under those most important to Latinos.[11] It is this religious grounding, this perspective of *líder* as community servant *called* to embody the kind of self-giving that Jesus modeled, that makes the definition distinctively *Latino*. It is also this distinction that should determine the source of authority. The community servant's authority does not come by, or hinge upon, a person's level of education, place in academia, or social or political hierarchy. It does *not* depend on "status." Community servants are *discerned* by the community by virtue of their calling; they are not "assigned" or picked as one might assign or pick committee chairs based on expertise.

Having said this, I need to clarify that it is not a matter of eschewing education or expertise; Hispanics value education and want more of it for us and for our children.[12] Rather, it is the ability to display *another* kind of education that consists of the wisdom passed on by the community. It is a wisdom that calls for upholding that enduring part of the faith, values, and cultures that have made them who they are. These help them not just survive but also feel the gift of grace even amid daily unjust and trying circumstances. Determination and boldness, for instance, are characteristics born from the knowledge of a faith that reminds us that the servant—with the leading and support of its community—is able to "do all things through him who strengthens" her or him (Phil 4:13). (Or as my Roman Catholic friend says, "con la ayuda de Diosito" se puede todo. [With the help of God—using the diminutive to mean "dearest God"]). But, it is also a wisdom that calls for careful scrutiny of those values and cultural mores that we hold so dear. This collective wisdom, informed as it is by our faith, aids the community in recognizing that the problems we face are expressions of sin and that this sin cannot be effectively countered with just "expertise." Only divine intervention, working through the community, can work the kinds of miracles needed to change the heart and ways of those who sin by obstructing the path to true liberty and justice for all. Leadership, whether secular or religious, is a faith thing.[13]

Finally, unlike the *caciquista* who feels accountable only to God, community servants assume accountability to God through the community that nurtured them and through the faith and values of that community, especially when these help their task to faithfulness.

Leadership as the ability to "command authority and influence over other," as Merriam-Webster defines it, comes at the price of servanthood. However, leadership modeled after Jesus demands a servant heart, a willingness to let go of self-interest. It means working on behalf of the community of others, that is, those who clean our kitchens, mow our lawns, empty our garbage, and clear our tables. *¡Que Dios te lo pague!* (May God repay you), for instance, is an expression often extended to community servants as a way of recognizing that the service rendered is invaluable and can never be adequately repaid. Only God can justly recompense the servant. It's not a tit-for-tat (*Esto por aquello* or *hoy por ti, mañana por mí*) kind of thing but an understanding that we give by grace what we receive by grace.[14]

We have addressed, if even briefly, the question of what Latinos understand by the word *leadership* and how its meaning stems from, and is intertwined with, our religious understanding of servanthood à la Jesus. This helps to explain why community servants in our Latino communities, in the main, are usually the pastors, priest, religious, and lay religious leaders. This has serious implications for seminaries and denominations. If our future depends on the effectiveness of our religious leaders and the viability of the churches from whence these leaders spring and find nurturing, then, we must ask, what are our seminaries and denominations doing to help develop and sustain effective leadership? What is needed in our seminaries and denominations to help and support the work of our community servants and help us move from creative survival strategies to creative futures?

WHAT DOES THAT SERVICE ENTAIL?

In a recent proposal to The Pew Charitable Trusts for a Hispanic Church Research Proposal, Edwin Hernandez refers to the deep-rooted religious commitment of the Latino community as one of its most important characteristics. "Although other racial and ethnic groups also manifest strong religious faith," Hernandez comments, "in the Hispanic community, because of the relatively weak state of other institutions, the church plays an especially critical role. Churches," he continues, "are among the most viable and dynamic institutions in the Hispanic community, nurturing cultural and civic values and behavior, and inspiring and organizing community involvement, often in distressed urban neighborhoods."[15]

The strength of these religious institutions depends greatly on their capacity to produce community servants who will work and challenge our communities to move beyond the statistical realities that impoverish and compromise the future of our children and our communities. But these churches and their denominations cannot do it alone. We need seminaries to allow us to help them create the kinds of programs and incentives that will not only attract Latino leadership, but also give them the skills and knowledge they are, generally speaking, not currently getting from their theological education.

Second, the needs of our communities are too variegated, too complex for any one person, denomination, or seminary to address effectively or otherwise. The answer must be found in community by building creative alliances, networks, and consortiums.[16] If education is to nurture leadership in the community, then it needs to take on a community servant model rather than a consumer model. We need a communal leadership, a synergistic cooperation of persons, and public and religious institutions pulling together, learning from each other and "visioning" the future together. This is a kind of lateral leadership of shared power, resources, knowledge, and hope—there has to be hope.

Finally, and now I am speaking primarily to my Latino sisters and brothers, we need community servants who will not be afraid to challenge discriminatory practices within our cultures (both Anglo and Latino), including theologies that keep women from developing their God-given talents, from fulfilling their own calls—wherever that may take them; and from being the kinds of role models our *muchachitas* and *muchachitos* so desperately need. Women have been and continue to be the strongholds in our communities and churches. Yet, their services, gifts, and talents are rarely acknowledged or allowed to flourish. Let us deal frankly and boldly with domestic violence against our women, daughters, and mothers. Let us dare to speak candidly about issues of sexual identity, about AIDS in our communities, about drugs and gang violence.

REGARDING SEMINARIES AND DENOMINATIONS

Latinos want institutions with a servant heart—institutions that understand their call to diversity as part of their call to faithfulness.[17] We look for and need persons and institutions that will join our *líderes* to work with and service our communities by being attentive to their needs, by being willing to refashion, restructure, and re-create themselves in light of those needs. We want to help institutions form coalitions, networks, and alliances that will enhance that service even as they provide service to each other. We need intentional and well-informed efforts that become a part of the institution and/or denomination at every level. We want to help train servant leaders who will help us discern and develop more leadership, not hoard it for themselves (*a lo cacique*). We need and want to see more Latino faculty involved in the training of those Latino and non-Latino servants who will work with our parishes and our Latino and non-Latino communities. And, for this to happen, we need to work together as seminaries and churches to identify, encourage, and support Latinas/os to pursue what for many of us is still but a chimera: a master of divinity and a PhD in theology.

These undertakings can be very messy and time-consuming. In a consumer-oriented society, such a long-term investment may seem foolish. However, our "business" or calling should not be "business as usual." There are enduring as well as numerous blessings for all involved. We were called to sow; others may do the reaping. In the meantime, our calling is to be faithful. Let us dare to be compassionately messy and even fools for God! ¡Y, *Que Dios te lo Pague!*

III

LIBERATING TRUTH

THE TRUTH OF GOD

A GLOBAL RELIGIOUS FAMILY

Virgilio Elizondo

It is a great privilege to be invited to contribute to a work honoring Justo González—a unique scholar, teacher, pastor, and friend; *Un verdadero discípulo del amor infinito y gratuito de Dios.*

To work for a unity in diversity of various peoples and religions, precisely in the context of the history of religions and the present status of religion today, is indeed a courageous and daring endeavor. Unfortunately, when we look at the historical record and even at the contemporary situation of the planet, it is a scandal that religions have served more to divide and destroy people than to unite them and give them life.

RELIGION: THE GREATEST THREAT TO WORLD PEACE

If there is nothing more beautiful than the love and service of others for the sake of the love of God, there is nothing more cruel, bloody, and destructive than the hatred of others for the sake of God! This has been the great scandal and sin of religions—the intolerance of other religious traditions to the point of war, murder, and annihilation. The religions of the world have produced much good and beauty; they have developed great insights and truth about the human and especially about the human in relation to the cosmic, the divine, the eternal, and the absolute. They have given many insights into God and the ways of God but no one alone has exhausted the mystery of God! Religions can become quite arrogant in their own understanding of God and violent in the defense of their convictions—as if God needed human beings to defend God.

In a very provocative and much-debated article published a few years ago in the journal *Foreign Affairs*, Samuel P. Huntington claimed that the final and ultimate world war, which would annihilate humanity from the face of the planet would be a religious war. Many disagreed, and I hope and pray that he is wrong. However, looking at the present situation of religion in the world today, I fear that he might just be right! Look at the greatest conflicts in recent times.

They have not been ideological, but religious. Today, it is not the war between Communism and the Free World, but between different religions that is threatening the survival of humanity. In the name of the sacred we are destroying the secular! Today it is religion that is the great threat to world peace and to the building of a world community of cooperation and concern. Give rivaling religious groups nuclear weapons, and they will certainly start and escalate a nuclear global war like we have never seen before and will never see again—there will be no one to see it.

The New Beginning

Yet Justo is not a prophet of doom but a bearer of good news. The unity and diversity that our Latinas/os in the United States have been struggling for is precisely the good news we have to offer humanity today. Our own United States is a marvelous example of religious cohabitation and cooperation. But there are other new beginnings taking place, such as the work of Justo through the Hispanic Theological Initiative. Such efforts will not only reverse the tide of religious hatreds and wars but will dare to create something new. New beginnings are taking place, not just at the highest level of the officials of our religions but from among the ranks of the poor who, full of the Spirit of truth and wisdom, know in their hearts and souls that something new needs to take place. They who have suffered the violence of economic and social oppression and have been consoled only by their religious convictions do not want their religious convictions to become a new source of the oppression of others. Out of their very suffering, and quite possibly purified by that very suffering, they are offering something new to humanity. This was the way of Jesus, and it must be our own way today.

Several years ago, in the midst of the Gulf War, my people at San Fernando Cathedral—a cathedral of the poor of San Antonio, a cathedral that is beautiful and magnificent, not because of the beautiful stained glass windows or the beautiful stone walls, but precisely because here the poor of the city know they are at home—came to me with a very special request. Why not reverse the world trend of religious wars and organize a multireligious prayer service, and why not do it on Thanksgiving Day? As they told me, Thanksgiving Day is a very sacred day in the United States, yet it is not a holy day of any one religion. So why not use this day to celebrate that which is truly sacred and new about the United States: a space where all the religions do not only coexist in the same space in peace but, even more than that, learn from each other and work together for the betterment of the people.

So, we gathered Muslims, Jews, Buddhists, Hindus, Native Americans, Mainline Protestants, Fundamentalists, and Catholics and invited them to pray together. It was a phenomenal experience. One old-time Catholic commented after the service: "The painting of the *Last Supper* is my favorite. Today, I had the experience I was at the last supper at the end of time." The wife of the rabbi commented: "During the prayer service, I had the feeling that we were inside Noah's ark about to begin the new creation." A simple beginning, but there is where the greatest breakthroughs take place.

At the same time, in another part of our hemisphere another great breakthrough was taking place. In Brazil, during the annual national gathering of the leaders of the basic Christian communities, which gather together the poorest of Brazil, the opening liturgy was presided over by a Candomble High Priestess and cocelebrated by the Catholic Archbishop of the area along with the Episcopal Bishop, other priests, and community leaders, and with religious leaders of many of the native religions. It was a fabulous experience of the spirit that empowers us to go beyond our divisive boundaries and join together in that which is greater than any one of us: the God of life who is greater than the best expressions of God of any one religion. We were united in prayer and celebration around that which is most common to all of us: our humanity.

In the Ecumenical Association of Third World Theologians, I have had the stretching experience of meeting with people of the various continents and of various religions, all of us searching together from within our own religious and ethnic traditions for how we can work together for a new world of justice, compassion, and love. How can we put our religious traditions at the service of humanity rather than allowing them to be the very source of the destruction of humanity. Out of the struggles of the poor of the world, a new force for unity is emerging, a new force that goes beyond the limitations of any one religion and is finding ways of joining forces for the sake of humanity.

Right here in our own country, Justo had the vision to begin a joint theological education program for Christian ministry that would bring future ministers of the Christian family to live, study, pray, and celebrate together. Thus, the differences and prejudices that presently divide us might be transformed into sources of enrichment rather than division, of fellowship rather than distance. This project is truly something new and offers much hope not only for our Latinas/os but for humanity—out of our suffering of division we are now called to usher in a new unity.

These are small but very significant signs of a new beginning, which is being brought about by the great Spirit of life, which is triumphing over the great sin of all our religions: making of our own religious expression an idol to be adored and therefore a justification for the death of those who refuse to adore! Making our expressions of God the same as God! What an insignificant God it would be!

Through these programs we are making a new beginning through our intellectual intercourse, which is allowing us to go beyond our prejudices and helping us to understand and appreciate one another not only in the things we have in common but even more so in our differences. It is precisely in our differences that we can both come to appreciate our own all the more and equally be enriched by the differences of the other. This form of dialogue is an important first step in transforming religious rivalries into a new community of understanding.

But in our ecumenical get-togethers we are celebrating a deeper level of unity: through prayer we are entering into spiritual intercourse, we are "compenetrating" one another's soul and entering in a mystical way into one another's most sacred space, the realm of the sacred. This is bound to produce great fruit. Praying together in a common space will allow each one of us to experience together the great Spirit of Life, which is greater, richer, and more beautiful than any one of our individual expressions of it. It will lead us into new and deeper levels of understanding and appreciation that the best of dialogue is not capable of.

But there is even a deeper level of communication and that is the biological intercourse that is taking place as individuals from different religions meet, fall in love, get married, and produce children. This love brings very diverse persons together in the deepest and most sacred of all unions, the conjugal bond. It is beginning to produce a new humanity that will be at one and the same time Muslim and Christian, Jewish and Buddhist, Hindu and Candomble, and any variety of combinations. Love is piercing through the most dogmatic divisions that have kept people apart, and a new humanity is in the making. Old religious absolutes will not stop this. It is the movement of love. Can religions help to make this something positive, or will each one of us be so much in love with ourselves, with our own religiously created idols, that we will become enemies of the new humanity rather than artisans of it?

New Role of Religion

God is greater than any one of our best expressions of God. I do not mean to relativize the notions of the sacred of any religion, but I do want to affirm that no one truth, no matter how true and orthodox it is, can exhaust the mystery of God. In fact, I believe that each of the great religious traditions can add to and enrich the understanding of God in each one of us.

I first came to an appreciation of this through what originally seemed to be a very simple and pious devotion of the Mexican people: Our Lady of Guadalupe. As I pondered more and more on the Guadalupe event precisely at the very beginning of what we now know as America, it became evidently clear that Guadalupe was much more than a very tender and beautiful Mexican devotion. At the moment when two great peoples, the peoples of Europe and the native peoples of the Western Hemisphere were first coming together, each with centuries of revered, but very different religious traditions, God gave all the religions of the world a great gift through Our Lady of Guadalupe. For in her and through her, two great religions, the Christian religion of Europe and the

Mesoamerican religions of the Western Hemisphere, were not only reconciled to each other but even purified each other and enriched one another. Guadalupe gave to the religions of the world a new way of relating to one another: no longer by way of radical opposition, but by way of enriching synthesis! Guadalupe is a beautiful symphony of various religious traditions that came together in and through her.

For religions to offer life in today's global community, we need to take a new look at how they relate to each other. To begin with, we cannot relate properly with one another unless we know who we are! Hence the first step is to reclaim and reaffirm our own tradition. I love being not just a Catholic but a Mexican Catholic. I love the religious traditions I received from my parents and ancestors. I do not want to lose my love of Jesus, Mary, and the saints. I do not want to lose the power of participating in the popular rituals of my people, where I experience such a deep sense of belonging and eternal life. I do not want to lose my sense of being part of a world family through the unity of our symbols: the pope, the bishops, the sacraments and many other elements of my Catholic faith.

Yet as much as I love my Catholic tradition, I have been greatly enriched by my contacts with persons of other faith traditions: with the Jewish people and their great prophetic tradition of social justice; with American religions and their sense of the sacredness of all creation; with fundamentalist Christians and their love of the Scriptures; with traditional Protestants and their love of preaching; with Buddhists and their exciting sense of meditation; and with the Muslims and the seriousness with which they take their faith.

I still have much to learn from others, yet the more I learn from them and the more I am enriched by them, the more I appreciate my own Mexican Catholic tradition. I am no less of a Catholic because of my contact with others and my learning from them, but I believe that I am much more of a human being!

Each one of us is called upon to affirm and love our own religious tradition. Yet in this very love, we are called upon to be self-critical, to see the limitations, prejudices, and even the sins of our tradition. It is only by a loving self-criticism that we can begin to affirm yet transcend the limits of our own tradition.

But just as we are called to reaffirm our own beloved tradition, so are we called to develop a spirituality of openness to the beauty of otherness. Each religious tradition has something of value to offer the others. Each one of us has to die a bit to the absolute nature of our own tradition, and without reducing it to a superficial relativization we can both contribute to others and learn from them. For us as Catholics a tremendous step forward was made in this direction when the Second Vatican Council recognized that there was truth in other religions. Before that, we had seen ourselves as the sole bearers of truth and the other as simply false. Without in any way giving up our claim to truth, we recognize that there is truth, goodness, and beauty in the others.

We also need to trust in the great Spirit that is guiding us toward a deeper unity, one that human history has never known before. We must be open to new expressions of religion; we must work to create a new symphony composed of the various religions of the world. No one religion will dissolve into the other any more than one instrument dissolves into another. Together we will make great music and the conductor will be the basic good of humanity, a humanity where there will be no more exploitation of anyone, no more enslavement, no more violence. The truth of any religion will not be its dogmas, creeds, or doctrines but its loving concern for the unity, justice, and advancement of the human family. Thus we will not have a sort of panreligion, but a beautiful mosaic of all the religions of the world together radiating the beauty and glory of God like we have never witnessed before. We are beginning; we have a long way to go, but it is our sacred responsibility to make of religions a source of life and never again a source of bloodshed, division, and death.

Let us celebrate together the unique elements of each without being exclusively any one of them. Let us celebrate what is indeed beginning, even though it has a long way to go. To the degree that we can accomplish this, religion will no longer be a threat to the human family, but the very force that will ensure the survival and creation of a new humanity of care and concern.

Thank you, Justo, for the great contribution you have made toward this new and daring beginning.

BETWEEN BEING AND HAVING

REFLECTION ON THE RELIGIOUS AND MORAL FOUNDATIONS OF HUMAN DIGNITY

Ismael García

PRELIMINARY OBSERVATIONS

My purpose in this presentation is to analyze the meaning of the term *dignity* in the religious, social, and political discourse of Puerto Ricans. Although the social context in which I presently find myself—that of a Puerto Rican in the United States—is significantly different from those on the island, I assume a cultural and religious continuity between both communities that allows me to generalize concerning some of my claims on the meaning of our sense of dignity.[1]

Our language on dignity reveals a duality. In the first place, the term *dignity* expresses our conviction in the inherent and absolute value of all human beings. This implies that in our personal actions and in social relationships we have to express our conviction that every individual is our equal in value and, therefore, is worthy of our recognition, respect, consideration, and care. This value brings with it certain obligations that limit and put conditions on the way in which we should relate to other people. The existing dignity in all human beings carries with it the obligation not only not to interfere in an invasive manner with the liberty of the other but also to assist others when this is necessary for their self-realization. Our *ay bendito* expresses this feeling of sympathy with the pain of our neighbor and the benevolent inclination to help.

This conviction about dignity has religious roots.[2] From the perspective of our Christian faith, human dignity is *a value that has been given to us*, a value that we affirm and justify in theological terms. By faith we declare that human dignity is founded in our being created in the image and likeness of God. The fact that God revealed God's purposes in the person of Jesus, the Christ, is indisputable proof of the value that God has invested in human beings. Furthermore, our consciousness of the faithfulness of the love of God toward us, despite our sin, rejection, and transgression, points to the innate, absolute, and permanent character of our dignity. From the perspective of our faith, dignity is innate to our being and cannot be lost under any circumstance.

In the second place, the term *dignity* affirms historical-cultural and moral-political values that are inevitably relative and contextual.[3] If it is true, from a religious perspective, that dignity is innate to our being and that neither the state or society can give it to us or take it away from us (in the best cases society and the state can only recognize and respect our dignity), it is equally true that, from the historical-political-moral point of view, the state and society do have the capacity to make our dignity decrease or flourish. The way we act and treat our neighbor, the rules and social structures that we create to organize our relationships with others, and the goals and visions that we follow as individuals and society, affect, in a significant manner, our sense of dignity and the possibilities of realizing our potential as worthy beings. Therefore, dignity is not only a *given*, it is also a historic *task*.

It is within the context of specific historical-political struggles that we discern those necessary conditions, material and spiritual, for human beings to obtain their fullest realization. Thus, the importance of the struggle for the revindication of civil rights and human rights: we struggle for rights that are defined and redefined in a more concrete manner in our historic living, where we continually create and re-create our social and natural world.[4] Our notion of human dignity, therefore, always relates with our sense of justice and the values of equality, liberty, and community.

This dual meaning of human dignity, as *given innately* to our being and as a *historic task or project*, points to a dialectic relationship. This dialectic is made evident when we examine the language that our community uses to justify its diverse struggles for emancipation. We appeal to our sense of dignity and the sense of self-respect that always accompany it, as *motivation* that sustains us in the *task* of fighting and resisting those forces that we identify as oppressive and dominant. At the same time, the reason for being and that which justifies our historical struggles is the realization (personal and public) of that dignity that *has been given to us*. Dignity is the beginning and end of our struggles. That which is *given* is found and is deepened in the *task*, and the task is made possible by that which has been given to us. If it is true that this argument has a circular character, I believe that it is not a vicious circle. The circle makes us conscious of the fact that within the context of the struggle to increase our liberty, equality, and community we discover and deepen our sense of dignity.

DEVELOPMENT OF THE THEOLOGICAL DIMENSION

In our religious tradition we confess that everything that God has created is essentially good (Genesis). Evil, although it exists, does not have a being. As Saint Augustine affirms, evil is the distortion of that which is essentially good. Evil does not exist in itself, but is dependent of what is right and good. As divine creation, therefore, human beings are essentially good, valuable, and, consequently, worthy of recognition, respect, and care. In our faith community, respect, recognition, and dignity is revealed in the experience of the many and diverse services, opportunities, and responsibilities that God gives us. It's no accident that Jesus, in the context of his crucifixion, announces to his disciples that part of his salvific mission is to prepare for us a place in the reign of God. This divine service affirms our sense of dignity and also points to the fact that being worthy is found in serving and contributing to the well-being of others.

Our value and dignity also is manifested in the fact that God makes us participants of God's providential plan. God assigns us to be God's people and to be God's blessing for all nations. God calls us to be historic actors, creators of communities where life is given and where free and responsible agents flourish. This is how God affirms that God wants the best for us and that we are of real importance to God. And it is also here where we "awaken" to the fact that our condition as free and responsible creatures—that is, as moral beings—is fundamental to our sense of dignity.

The awareness of being redeemed also grounds our sense of dignity. In principle, no one is at the margin of divine redemption and, consequently, humanly and politically speaking, we are never justified to abandon that person we consider as lacking (or as we use to say pejoratively *chusma*). Redemption reveals the unconditional character of dignity. This is an integral part of our being and it cannot be lost, no matter our intelligence and intellectual capacity or lack of, no matter our moral capacity or lack of, our social position, our natural or acquired talents, our potentials, and so on, no matter how sinful we are. We are all equally worthy, since nothing alters the fact that we are all creatures redeemed by God. Redemption, though, is not passive nor, as Bonhoeffer would say, is it cheap.[5] The state of being redeemed does not destroy, nor does it diminish our integrity as moral beings. The sense of dignity that provokes redemption implies a divine and human commitment, with the task of reforming and/or transforming: our immorality into moral behavior, our sin into faithful commitment to God, our ignorance into critical intelligence, our laziness into personal discipline.

Our faith radicalizes our sense of dignity. It makes us aware of our value, not only because God values us, but because within ourselves, in our being, God has transferred and deposited in us an absolute value. We have value not only in our relationship with God but also in our being and existing.

SOME IMPLICATIONS OF OUR THEOLOGICAL CONVICTIONS

On the level of motivations, dignity implies that we have to free ourselves from attitudes that justify relationships of oppression, such as the attitudes of superiority or inferiority. ("He thinks he's better than everyone else," "he has an inferiority complex.")[6] Such attitudes sustain and promote hierarchical structures, in which from our social class, educative level, national membership, religious identity, or racial constitution, some see themselves as basically superior or inferior to others and as meriting or not meriting certain rights and privileges. From our theological perspective, such attitudes and motivations are a denial of our status as children of God and as brothers and sisters.

A manifestation of the attitude of false superiority is the pharisaical temptation, which is particular to the church and Christians, to identify our beliefs and practices as the only true and faithful ones to the divine purpose. This exaggerated identification of our visions and interpretations with the divine purpose, loses its perspective of our finite and sinful condition. It loses from sight the importance of self-criticism and of the necessary humility to recognize the ambiguity that is present in all of our religious beliefs and in our moral practices. Nationalism and uncritical political partisanship are also secular manifestations of this pharisaical tendency. The superior attitude makes us defensive and indifferent to the claims, necessities, and cares of those who are different and who think differently. It also motivates us to promote our interests at the cost of the well-being of others and of society. Prophetic criticism makes us recognize that those who gather great power, riches, and social prestige are particularly tempted to believe that they are better than others and see themselves as unconditionally good and to convert their needs into absolute rights that others have to serve. Culturally they see and promote themselves as the examples to follow, the model of what human beings are. And they assume that they have the right to destroy, punish, or ignore all who identify themselves as different and less than they.

False humility and submission also feed on inferior attitudes, which are a denial of our status as creatures of God. This is the temptation of those who are weak and oppressed. Historically and politically speaking, false humility and passivity are attitudes that help to consolidate oppression, evil, and injustice. They encourage the lack of critical combativeness and the lack of political organization and militancy, while promoting in their place a social conformity that denies our being historical actors with genuine interests and points of view worthy of being taken into consideration or free beings capable of expressing and exercising their interests in a responsible manner. Speaking theologically, this abandonment of the historical responsibility is converted into an obstacle to the historical purposes of God. We, as Christians, have to rediscover that Christ called us to be humble before God and not before others. Because of this, the militancy of Jesus against the religious and political leaders is not contrary to his humility as Son of God. One of the principal challenges that we confront today is to rediscover our faith as a historical imperative.

It is indispensable to note that the superior and inferior attitudes that motivate forms of oppressive behavior, *do not* constitute the heart of oppression. Oppression has an inevitable structural dimension.[7] It is not our motives but our practices, particularly those that gain institutional status, that incarnate in social structures and foment oppression. Oppressive motivations and attitudes are products of social structures and practices; at the same time these motivations and attitudes consolidate and perpetuate oppressive structures. This is why an ethic that insists on the formation of human character recognizes that it is indispensable to create just structures to create just human beings.

The dialectic that is given between the religious dimension of dignity (*what's given*) and the historical-moral dimension (*project or historical task*) manifests certain *logical* ambiguity. If it is correct that nothing or no one can take away the dignity that God has incarnated within us, the logical implication seems to be that it does not make sense to resist or battle against attitudes, practices, and oppressive structures since these do not affect our dignity. Nevertheless, humanly and politically speaking, we, by intuition, know that this cannot be correct. Intuitively we know that the way in which we are treated and the relationships that we establish with each other, *do* affect our dignity and affect it in a significant manner. How can we resolve this ambiguity? If we accept that this ambiguity is not essentially logical but that it is of a practical nature (historical-moral), we can affirm that it is true from a religious point of view that our value is unconditional and absolute; this in no way denies the importance and the impact of the social and historic context in which we confront the diverse challenges of establishing conduct of relationships. From a practical point of view, our relationship with other people does not end with recognizing them as absolute value. Proper relationships between human beings are defined in light of what we value in the human being. What we value in a human being is not only their relationship with God, although this is fundamental, but also the value that God has deposited in us as creatures. It is our interpretation of the value of a human being that permits us to define the proper type of relationship and treatment and that sustains their dignity as a valuable being.

What do we value in a human being? The *first thing* that we value in a human being is *his or her existence* as a creature. The physical existence of human beings, their incarnation, presents a set of obligations related to their physical-corporeal well-being. To remain indifferent before the physical necessities of others becomes a basic fault to our dignity and the dignity of others. A major fault is denying or demonstrating disdain toward the physical well-being of others. Thus, we derive the language and preoccupation for the right to existence that rules in all national and international codes regarding human rights.

The *second thing* that we value in human beings is their *particularity*. Dignity implies that we have respect for every individual in their difference, in their character as the unique and distinct being that they are. This carries the obligation to contribute to the promotion of the integral self-realization of others. Every human being has rights, not only to life but also to services and to educational activities and social and cultural spaces that promote the individual self-development and the self-development of their group. It is contrary to our dignity and the dignity of others to convert ourselves into obstacles to the possibility that others can self-develop and make their creative contribution. It is because of this that the right to self-development constitutes another human right that enjoys a certain universal acceptance.

The *third thing* that we value is the capacity of every individual *to act* in an autonomously creative manner. This allows us to affirm the right to self-determination. Each individual has a right to spaces of privacy where he or she decides how he or she wants to live and the vocation he or she wants to follow. Socially speaking, we have to create political, social, and economic institutions with a democratic character that would provide to individuals and social groups multiple and varied occasions where each one can actively participate in the processes that would determine the future of the community and in which people can define their personal life plan. This list of rights is minimal. And it is important to emphasize that the right to existence, the right to self-development, and the right to self-determination are mutually related, to the point that if one of these rights is not honored we can lose them all.

DEVELOPMENT OF THE MORAL
HISTORICAL DIMENSION OF DIGNITY

As we noted before, it is through the processes of resistance against those forces that diminish our dignity—that is, in the context of the different struggles for liberty, to foment equality and increase the well-being of our community—that our human and civil rights are discovered and that define more plainly and profoundly what we mean by the term *dignity*.[8] Therefore, dignity is related, on the one hand, to the right to have a minimum income that would permit all working people to live and sustain their family. It is preferable that our income be the result of work and the social contribution of those who work. But in those cases where work cannot be provided, each person should be provided with an income that would allow them to participate fully in their social and political context. On the other hand, dignity is related with the right to participate in those processes where the destiny of the community, the goals that are desired, and the priority between these goals and the sacrifices that these goals imply are debated and decided. A basic democratic principle is that we should actively participate in everything that significantly affects our life. In addition, we should frequently reevaluate the social goals that we pursue. Finally, dignity is tied with the right to self-development, which implies access to education or other forms of training and which enjoys diverse cultural capacities that allow us to develop our own.

Although I categorically affirm the importance of human and civil rights in the process of consolidating and deepening our sense of human dignity, it is important to maintain a critical attitude regarding this affirmation. In our political-social context, human rights suffer from an atomistic individualism that is antibiblical. What is worse, our understanding of human rights tends to encourage a competitive aggression between factions of society. Presently, our social life is mainly defined in conflicting terms. When we claim "my rights" this normally leads us to seek our well-being at the cost of the well-being of others. However, I insist that, from the perspective of our Christian faith, and from the perspective of the poor, the potential exists that these rights are redefined in such a way that they are converted in occasions where equal relations and mutual respect are established. These can be ways to foment human brotherhood and sisterhood that is inspired under the status of being a child of God. These rights, under the influence of the biblical vision, allow us to recognize the obligation to serve and take care of the neighbor. In the biblical context, these are rights that emphasize mutuality and reciprocity and promote an egalitarian vision of society. Finally, they are rights that serve justice and the creation of pluralistic and diverse communities, where the various social groups negotiate integration and mutual promotion.

SOME IMPLICATIONS OF OUR
MORAL NOTIONS OF DIGNITY

When we examine spheres of our existence, we discern different levels of significance in our sense of dignity.

On a personal level, dignity is manifested in self-discipline, in our commitment and contribution to social well-being and in the responsible use of our liberty that defines us as moral beings. Personal discipline and work that contributes to social well-being and to moral responsibility are component elements or constituents of our sense of personal respect. This is where the terms *don/doña*, used to express respect, point to a value not always related to economic success but to the recognized social status given to persons who contribute to the community and who demonstrate respect and consideration to the neighbor and a measured sense of self-esteem. Self-discipline motivates us and contributes to our developing our capabilities and potentials through which we obtain our self-realization as creative beings. It is vital, therefore, that we have some *sense of self-esteem*, of appreciation of ourselves, and of an awareness of the legitimacy of our right to realize those values that give meaning to our life. Self-esteem helps us to avoid self-hate, it frees us from the sense of impotence and inferiority, and allows dignity to be converted into a historic emancipating force. Without this sense of self-esteem we cannot genuinely contribute to the well-being of others nor to the well-being of our community.

On a social level, dignity is related to our sense of justice. In general terms, social justice is defined as the inclination to contribute to the well-being of others and, at a minimum, not take advantage of the bad fortune and the weaknesses of others. Beyond our self-esteem, or better said, that which makes self-esteem genuine and not egotistical, is our inclination to serve others, even when this service implies a level of personal sacrifice. In the social sphere or ambiance, dignity motivates us to create a more democratic and egalitarian society. It is the creation of social egalitarian structures that allows us to recognize and relate to one another as persons of the same value.

The blessing of the just shows the social actions that are worthy of Christians. It is not a matter of dignity to tolerate or accept suffering that is a product of injustice. This suffering, particularly when it is put on the innocent and weak, has to be fought militarily and openly. On the other hand, suffering that is a consequence of the struggle for justice, that always implies social change, has to be tolerated with determination and valor. Only suffering that results from our practical testimony of the justice of God, suffering that comes from trying to better the condition of the poor, has a redemptive character. Suffering that is born from injustice that is imposed on the poor diminishes the dignity of all.

To be treated with dignity requires the just distribution of social recognition and leadership and the just distribution of the social costs in such a way that these costs do not always fall on the weak and the voiceless. Nothing diminishes more our sense of dignity as the lack of social recognition. Anonymity, one of the most significant social crises of our time, gives us the feeling of being instruments of the vision and plans of others. Dignity requires the multiplication of spaces and occasions where people can exercise leadership and can be recognized as productive members of our society.

On a cultural level, dignity is manifested in the battle for cultural affirmation and in the struggle against cultural discrimination. In principle, each social group should have the necessary space and resources to live in the light of cultural values that their identity provides. It is because of this that our struggles for the preservation and development of our tongue, our language, are so important. Our sense of dignity is joined with the loyalty to our tradition and ways of life. The process through which we contribute to our cultural artistic tradition and to the system of values and visions of our culture is also that which allows us to deepen our sense of dignity. More than just the adaptation and repetition of traditional values and visions, this process demands the creative and responsible use of our liberty, the liberty to redefine our culture in such a way that it allows us to confront the particular demands of our historic moment.

The Apostle Paul understands the importance of culture in the formation and development of dignity. Of more importance, Paul makes it clear how cultural diversity pleases God. Cultural diversity expresses not only human creativity but also the immensity and complexity of God's creativity. To Paul every culture, although relative, is valuable, precious; and in principle, every cultural group fits within the purpose of God. This is why he accepts the continuation of Judaism as an integral part of the purpose of God. And he affirms that neither do the Jews have to deny their culture to be faithful to the message of redemption of Christ, nor do the Gentiles have to become Jews. Paul recognizes that the integration between the various cultural groups is important for the creation of the new community, the church; but the cultural assimilation is not necessary for the church to show its loyalty to Christ. Cultural diversity is not seen as an obstacle but is seen as an occasion to creatively *negotiate* a common life and new forms of being in community. The new identity of the community is not based on cultural chauvinism, nor on cultural abandonment, but on its service to the needy and the recognition and respect to the integrity of the other, including their cultural identity.

On an economic level, to be treated with dignity requires that all social members have access to those resources and to resources (medical, housing, work, education) that would lead to their complete participation in all social spheres. As we mentioned before, in a society such as ours in which money has so much importance, everyone should have access to a minimum quantity of capital. It is important to recognize, however, that from our perspective of faith, having should always be at the service of being, and it is a violation of our dignity to find our significance in the mere act of consuming and acquiring social goods.

On a political level, if it is true that having is at the service of being and acting, the political dimension enjoys a certain amount of priority in the foundation of the dignity of the person. From a political perspective, to be treated with dignity is joined with the creation of a pluralistic society that recognizes, cares, and provides so that each group can preserve its distinctive elements. Dignity requires that each group have the right to a voice and active participation within all those centers of decision (political, economic, social, and cultural) that affect the destiny of the community. There are few experiences that make us aware of our dignity like the experience of struggling for the vindication of the rights of the community, in particular, the right of its weakest members, especially when they plainly participate in the process of change and integration to the society. When we discover our capacity to organize religious, social, and political movements that realize the proposed goals and aims—and that increment the possibilities of life—and provide meaning for a greater number of members of our community, our sense of dignity grows and is deepened.

On a moral level, dignity implies a commitment to a morality that is dialogical, which emphasizes personal encounters and debate in a context that is socially safe and of mutual respect. Dialogue is necessary and indispensable because the other is particular and distinct to me. The basic assumption is that the others that surround me are strange and mysterious. At the same time dialogue is possible and potentially fruitful because the other is, as a moral being, my equal. In dialogue we discover ourselves, and we mutually reveal ourselves. In this process we have the occasion to discover our humanity; it allows us to recognize that, morally speaking, we are all "ends in ourselves." More significant is that an authentic dialogue can make us aware of and incline us to take into consideration the interest of others when we foment our personal interests. From a moral perspective, dignity is related to the development of the virtues of acknowledgment, the attention to the claim of another, hospitality, constructive criticism, and other virtues that promote mutuality.

CONCLUSION

A few final reflections are regarding the religious foundation of human dignity. If it is true that some religious practices are an integral part of the conservative and reactionary forces of society and they justify oppressive practices, then, in its root, every true faith incarnates a liberating critique that points at the direction of greater inclusiveness, pluralism, and justice. The salvific purpose of God, the good news, empowers us to create new ways of relating beyond the limits of the status quo. In the true God we find the vision and strength to overcome anything that appears impossible. The God that creates and is concerned about history is a historic liberating *force*.

From a religious perspective, dignity is intimately related with the virtues of hope and faith. These virtues sustain and motivate us to continue in the complex and painful struggles that promote social well-being and that create conditions to realize more inclusive forms of community. This is the reason that our saying "de la esperanza vive el pobre" ("the poor lives by faith") is so proper. When the poor truly believe that they are creatures of God and creatures who deserve to be treated with dignity, this sustains their struggles against social oppression and for the creation of a more just society. And when we see the poor as a child of God we can take more vertical postures and solidarity toward fomenting our dignity. This is the God who reveals to us that dignity is deepened and made more evident when we overcome all the barriers that maintain us separated and in conflict and moves us in the direction of providing one another the resources and services that allow us to have a full life.

It is in the religious sphere that the possibility exists to redefine the moral values that allow us to deepen our sense and commitment with the realization of human dignity. Our faith allows us to reinterpret *freedom* in a more inclusive manner than the capacity to do what one wants—*licentiousness*—and beyond the right to no intervention. In the Christian context we can proclaim freedom as an affirmation to our *creativity* and our commitment to the creation of a community of help and mutual support. Freedom is related to our inclination to serve and care for one another, as the Apostle Paul reminds us. Our dignity is deepened and consolidated not in my self-development and self-realization but in my capacity to contribute to the development and well-being of others as an integral part of my own development and dignity.

Our faith allows us to visualize *social equality* beyond the notion of uniformity and homogeneity. Christian equality emphasizes the recognition and respect of those differences that connect to our identity. Since we are not identical, equal recognition and respect carry a distinct treatment and the disposition—in spite of the differences—to seek to negotiate a life in common. It is precisely our differences that allow us to contribute to the well-being of others, creating and sustaining the community.

Finally, our faith allows us to conceptualize *community* in more constructive terms than the demand for mere conformity to the status quo and the personal sacrifice for the common good. Community is more the context for the integral realization of our individuality and particularity. Diversity and pluralism is that which define community as a proper context for the prosperity of human dignity. It is the communal participation and our productivity that foments communal life.

To be worthy and have dignity are two faces of the same coin; one is not discovered without the other. If one does not have, one cannot be, but our being worthy is not simply our creation. Dignity is a gift of God and in great measure it is a manifestation of the grace of God. As with many other manifestations of the grace of God, we discover and deepen dignity in our historical becoming and through our social struggles, struggles that, when they serve the poor and those to whom dignity is denied, are means of conversion and renewal to the divine purposes.

BEYOND THE FRONTIER MYTH

Roberto S. Goizueta

L egend has it that once, when asked what he thought about Western civilization, Mohandas Gandhi responded, "It would be a good idea." What we call "Western civilization" has, no doubt, enriched human life beyond measure. Western ideals have inspired men and women to spiritual, intellectual, literary, and aesthetic accomplishments that give expression to our human nature at its most noble. The twentieth century, particularly, was a century of unprecedented progress. Individual freedom, civil rights, and human equality are no longer unthinkable anathemas but fundamental axioms that shape our everyday lives and social institutions.

Despite the many undisputed advances of Western civilization, however, we are all painfully aware of the disquiet and anxiety that pervade contemporary Western civilization. Scratch the placid, well-heeled surface of our culture and one soon uncovers disturbing signs of another reality. Scratch the sanitized, efficient surface of the modern machine and one discovers six million scarred, emaciated Jewish corpses. Scratch the manicured surface of modern suburbia and one discovers the wan, baleful stare of the doped-up, pierced-through, suicidal teenager—or the bloodshot, empty stare of the abandoned, abused, stressed-out housewife. Scratch the egalitarian surface of modern democracies and one discovers the depressive boredom that comes from powerlessness. Scratch the ebullient surface of Wall Street and one discovers the desperate faces of the permanent underclass. Scratch the digitized surface of the computer age and one discovers the passive glare of the virtually real child.

To be living in the late modern, or postmodern period, is to have discovered, in the words of the German Jewish philosopher Walter Benjamin, that "every great work of civilization is at the same time a work of barbarism."[1] The legacy of Western civilization is, at the same time, a legacy of barbarism. How do we know? Because the victims of that barbarism are in our midst—and their faces and voices are finally breaking through the placid surface. The corpses are themselves speaking out from the grave. Their long-repressed cries are breaking through the complacent silence. And the victims are asking us how we, as a society, will respond to their cries. At the dawn of a new millennium, this is the question on which the future of Western civilization will depend. Every other question will eventually become irrelevant unless and until we can effectively address this single question: how will we, as a society, respond to the victims of our own progress, the victims of our successes, the victims of our achievements?

Above all, we must first acknowledge the historical fact that the many achievements of Western civilization have, indeed, come only at great cost. In the face of the millions upon millions of victims, dare we continue to beat our breasts and speak self-righteously of the "victory of capitalism" or the "victory of Western ideals"? Or can this society, without denying the obvious achievements of Western economic, cultural, and political ideals, summon the courage to look into the eyes of those victims and see itself reflected therein?

In this chapter, I will suggest that U.S. Hispanics in general, and U.S. Hispanic theologians in particular, can be important contributors to our nation's struggle to confront the ambiguities of its own history in order to move toward a more faithful realization of its noble ideals in order to strengthen Western civilization. What I will argue is that, in the United States, the noble ideals of Western civilization have taken a particular historical, ideological form, which undermines their realization in the long term insofar as this ideological form precludes the very acknowledgment of historical ambiguity—itself a precondition for the realization of those ideals. More specifically, the modern *frontier myth*, or ideology, still underlying U.S. culture impedes our society's ability to promote "life, liberty, and the pursuit of happiness" at a time when the frontier has been replaced by the "border" as the central symbol of U.S. identity *ad extra*. In other words, late modernity is a world of borders; but, given our history, the profound fear of immigrants reflected in recent legislation suggests that U.S. society continues to view these borders through the lenses of a frontier myth, open to economic expansion but closed to human immigration. The consequent distortion has devastating consequences, among them the inability to acknowledge historical ambiguity. Conversely, the Latina/o experience is one that, as Justo González has argued, allows for ambiguity and reflects an understanding of the border as a true meeting place, where different cultures interact.

THE FRONTIER

> I am become a name;
> For always roaming with a hungry heart
> Much have I seen and known,
> . . . .
> I am a part of all that I have met;
> Yet all experience is an arch wherethro'
> Gleams that untravell'd world whose margin fades
> For ever and for ever when I move.
> How dull it is to pause, to make an end.

To rust unburnish'd, not to shine in use!

. . . .

And this gray spirit yearning in desire
To follow knowledge like a sinking star,
Beyond the utmost bound of human thought.

. . . .

                              Come, my friends.
'Tis not to late to seek a newer world.
Push off, and sitting well in order smite
The sounding furrows; for my purpose holds
To sail beyond the sunset, and the baths
Of all the western stars, until I die.

. . . .

To strive, to seek, to find, and not to yield.[2]

With those words from Tennyson's "Ulysses," the American historian Frederick Jackson Turner ended his commencement address at the University of Washington in June 1914. Tennyson's words evoked for Turner those frontier ideals that had served the United States so well until the end of the nineteenth century: "to seek a newer world . . . to sail beyond the sunset . . . to strive, to seek, to find, and not to yield."

Indeed, it does not take much imagination to see reflected in these words not only the spirit of Daniel Boone and Andrew Jackson but also the spirit of Christopher Columbus and Hernán Cortés. The frontier is the foundational myth of modernity; it is our creation myth. The modern world is constructed by forging and conquering new frontiers: "The first ideal of the pioneer was that of conquest."[3]

In what has been called "the most influential piece of writing in the history of American history"—his 1893 essay "The Significance of the Frontier in American History"—Frederick Jackson Turner set forth what came to be known as the frontier thesis:

> American social development has been continually beginning over again on the frontier. This perennial rebirth, this fluidity of American life, this expansion westward with its new opportunities, its continuous touch with the simplicity of primitive society, furnish the forces dominating American character. . . .
>
> In this advance, the frontier is the outer edge of the wave—the meeting point between savagery and civilization. . . .
>
> . . . And now, four centuries from the discovery of America, at the end of a hundred years of life under the Constitution, the frontier has gone."[4]

By the end of the nineteenth century, the western frontier "finally closed forever, with uncertain consequences for the American future."[5]

Yet myths do not easily die when historical conditions change; they may simply be adapted to the new context. Indeed, argued Turner, the values and worldview implicit in the frontier myth have become a part of U.S. culture: "Long after the frontier period of a particular region of the United States has passed away, the conception of society, the ideals and aspirations which it produced, persist in the minds of the people. . . . This experience has been wrought into the very warp and woof of American thought."[6] And Turner's very definition of the frontier myth (as quoted above) already suggests the particular conception of society underlying the myth. Herein lies the fundamental characteristic of the frontier myth, which gives it its power and rationale; the frontier is "the meeting point between savagery and civilization."

In the history and culture of the United States, the very drive to *extend* the frontier came to be seen as a constitutive feature of "civilization" itself: to be civilized *is* to extend the frontier, to expand, to seek new opportunities, to dominate, to conquer (in Tennyson's words, "How dull it is to pause, to make an end"). Conversely, then, to accept limits to this expansion is to undermine the very foundations of civilized society: "once free lands were exhausted . . . the whole moral fabric would collapse and the land descend into the state of depravity and tyranny that overcrowded Europe already knew."[7] Thus, implicit in the frontier myth is the assumption that the only alternative to expansion is decline, or degeneration. This begs the question, which Turner and other scholars were asking at the turn of the twentieth century: how will the United States react to the closing of the western frontier? Turner did not live to see the emergence of an answer during the remaining decades of the twentieth century.

As we stand at the beginning of the twenty-first century, however, I do think we can suggest an answer, an answer that lies not to the West but to the South. In retrospect, the turn of the twentieth century represented not so much the demise of the frontier as the replacement of the western frontier with a southern frontier. The westward territorial expansion, including the conquest of one-third of Mexico in the first half of the nineteenth century, was replaced by a southern expansion. Initially, this latter followed the pattern of military, geographical, and political expansion. Thus, in the first half of the twentieth century, the U.S. frontier became the Caribbean and Central America. Just as the western frontier had expanded into "virgin territory," so too would the southern frontier. After all, there is only one "America," only one "America the Beautiful." "America" *is* the United States.[8]

Thus, a new breed of pioneers rose up in the first decades of the new century, not only individual adventurers but also economic enterprises seeking to expand their markets, often in conjunction with U.S. political interests. The rapid growth of multinational corporations during this period provided possibilities for economic expansion unknown to earlier pioneers. When territorial expansion proved impracticable, more benign forms of economic expansion would take its place, even if sometimes with the aid of political and even military intervention. By the 1930s, contends historian Walter LaFeber, overt military intervention "had become too costly. Nor were such blatantly imperialist gestures any longer needed. The blunt instruments were replaced with the Good Neighbor's economic leverage."[9] Nevertheless, when the economic leverage weakened, for example, during the period between the Eisenhower and Reagan presidencies, they might require renewed political and military fortification.

Already in 1890, U.S. Secretary of State James G. Blaine had foreseen the form that the new frontier would take: "he pointedly observed, 'Our great demand is expansion,' but only in trade, for 'we are not seeking annexation of territory.' "[10] Between 1898 and 1901, the United States began to export capital to a degree previously unequalled and, by World War I, had erased its trade deficits.[11] As LaFeber has argued, "the dynamic new United States necessarily prepared itself to find fresh frontiers abroad to replace the closed frontier at home."[12] Moreover, U.S. activity on these fresh frontiers to the south would bear the marks of the earlier westward expansion, drawing on the same historical myth. U.S. attempts to extend its southern frontier "rested on views of history, the character of foreign peoples [i.e., 'savagery'], and politics that anticipated attitudes held by North Americans throughout much of the twentieth century. . . . North Americans seldom doubted that they could teach people to the south to act more civilized."[13]

If, as Frederick Jackson Turner averred, the frontier myth has been "wrought into the very warp and woof of American thought," the end of the nineteenth century did not signal the end of the frontier myth, only its relocation and reconceptualization. The persistence of that myth raises important questions for our society a century later. Standing at the threshhold of the twenty-first century, the United States is once again confronted with questions concerning the relationship between national identity and geographical boundaries. If the United States of the 1890s perceived national identity as linked to the western frontier, and thus feared a future with closed frontiers, contemporary political, military, and legislative attacks against immigrants suggest that the United States of the early twenty-first century perceives national identity as linked not to the frontier but to the "border," and fears a future with open borders.

If Turner's suggestion concerning the foundational character of the frontier myth is accurate, we should not assume that, simply because we now prefer the language of borders to the language of frontiers, the difference in terminology reflects a truly different understanding of history and identity. It may be that, today, the frontier myth still functions as the lens through which we as a society read the reality of our borders, especially the southern border, which, in the first decades of the twentieth century, became our new, "fresh frontier."

THE BORDER

In profound ways, the border defines the social existence and identity of U.S. Hispanics. Not surprisingly, then, it is a major theme in U.S. Latina/o literature, art, social theory, and theology.[14] In many of these writings, *the border* is revealed as much more than a geographical place. For Latinos and Latinas, the border is not only *where* we are located or *where* we come from, the border is *who* we are, people whose very identity and reality is *in between*.[15]

As *theologians* seeking to discover the presence of God in the ongoing life of our Latina/o communities, U.S. Hispanic theologians are today asking how the God of Jesus Christ may be encountered on the border. If the border is not merely a geographical category but is, more profoundly, an epistemological and anthropological category defining a *human* reality, a human community, is it possible to encounter God in the midst of that reality, that community? If so, how and where? If so, moreover, what is the role of the church in that reality?

At the same time, however, we must ask how the dominant culture's understanding of that border and the Latina/o understanding of the border may influence our reading of the border as a *locus theologicus*. Thus, before proceeding to the properly theological and ecclesiological arguments, we should ask how those arguments might be influenced by the frontier myth—and how they might be influenced by a Latina/o understanding of the border.[16]

The Latina/o perception of the border is rooted in the distinctive history of Latin America itself. While the modern drive for territorial expansion and domination is at the heart of both the Iberian and British colonization of the Americas, the processes of expansion developed differently in the North and South:

> The difference was that in the north it was possible and convenient to push back the native inhabitants rather than to conquer and subdue them. What northern colonialists wanted was land [rather than slave labor]. The original inhabitants were a hindrance. So, instead of subjugating the Indians, they set about to push them off their lands, and eventually to exterminate them. If the myth in the Spanish colonies was that the Indians were like children who needed someone to govern them, the myth in the English colonies was that the Indians were non-people; they didn't exist, their lands were a vacuum. In north Georgia, in the middle of Cherokee County, there is a monument to a white man who was, so the monument says, "the first man to settle in these parts." And this, in a county that is still called "Cherokee"!
>
> This contrast in the colonizing process led to a "border" mentality in Mexico and much of Latin America, and a "frontier" mentality in the United States. Because the Spanish colonizers were forced to live with the original inhabitants of the land, a *mestizo* population and culture developed. . . . In contrast, in the lands to the north, the process and the myth were of a constantly moving frontier, pushing back the native inhabitants of the land, interacting with them as little as possible. There was civilization this side of the frontier; and a void at the other side. The West was to be "won." The western line, the frontier, was seen as the growing edge; but it was expected to produce growth by mere expansion rather than by interaction.[17]

Justo González suggests that this historical difference has given rise to different conceptions of the border. In the North, the border is perceived as moving in only one direction: outward; in the South, the border is perceived as allowing for movement in both directions. In the North, any movement back across the border is thus perceived as "an incursion of the forces of evil and backwardness into the realm of light and progress."[18] If, as Frederick Jackson Turner so explicitly declared, what lies on the other side of the border is mere "savagery," then any movement back toward the North must be prohibited as a threat to *civilization,* a threat to national identity, a threat to national security. Above all, however, any movement north forces civilized society to confront its barbaric *alter ego.*

In other words, Turner was right: on the frontier Western civilization *does* encounter savagery. What he failed to see was that the savagery Western civilization encounters is *its own.* And that is why the U.S. fears any movement back across the border toward the north: not, ultimately, because this country wants to deny the existence of "those" savages south of the border, but because, for its own sense of national identity, the United States—like all Western societies— *must* deny the existence of *its own* savagery. The faces of those "savages" are the mirrors of this nation's soul; they are the *dangerous memory* that is never quite fully repressed. The faces of the *savages* are what the German theologian Johann Baptist Metz has called "dangerous memories, memories which make demands on us."[19] But an acknowledgment of this fact would necessarily call into question the United States' very identity as the "New Jerusalem" (in the words of Ronald Reagan) or a bridge to the twenty-first century (in the words of Bill Clinton). Collective denial is a much more palatable alternative.

"It is precisely in that willful innocence," warns Justo González, "that guilt lies. . . . The reason why this country has refused to hear the truth in its own history," he continues,

> is that as long as it is innocent of such truth, it does not have to deal with the injustices that lie at the heart of its power and its social order. . . . In our country, such guilty innocence is the handmaiden of injustice. Injustice thrives on the myth that the present order is somehow the result of pure intentions and a guiltless history. . . . Perhaps once we are agreed that we are all *ladrones* [thieves], it will be easier for all of us to see more clearly into issues of justice.[20]

The reason why the myth of innocence, the frontier myth, must be exposed is not to ascribe blame to some while exonerating others. The reason is that only when we are honest about our present and past reality will we be able to more effectively bring our future reality into harmony with our national ideals. (After all, repressed memories live on under the surface and will continue to resurface in barbaric ways, such as attacks against immigrants and anyone whose existence recalls those dangerous memories.) To serve as just such a reminder is, according to González, "one of our functions as a Hispanic minority in this country. It is not a pleasant function, for few love those who destroy the myths by which they live. But it is a necessary function that we must courageously fulfill."[21] Perhaps our country will treat its Latinos and Latinas differently when it acknowledges that the Hispanic presence here, in U.S. cities and towns, is a direct result of this country's progress. Can this society admit that that progress, however extraordinary, has nevertheless come at great cost, a cost that our entire nation is currently paying, whether in the physical poverty of our blighted inner cities or the spiritual poverty of our gated suburbs?[22]

The possibility that "every great work of civilization" may indeed also be "a work of barbarism" is inconceivable in the light of the frontier myth, which gave birth to our nation; an impenetrable border (i.e., the southern frontier) remains the last hope for maintaining our identity as the greatest country in the world, an example of unimpeded progress in an otherwise barbaric world. "The quest for human purity," contends Virgilio Elizondo, "defines boundaries and very quickly excludes those who have been the product of territorial transgression. There seems to be an inner fear that the children of territorial transgression pose the deepest threat to the existence of the group and to the survival of its purity."[23]

Yet a border need not function as a frontier that only expands and excludes; it need not function as a safeguard for the illusory purity of one side. Even if too-often denied in practice, an alternative understanding of the border is implicit in the *mestizo* history of Latin America:

> A border is the place at which two realities, two worldviews, two cultures, meet and interact. . . . at the border growth takes place by encounter, by mutual enrichment. A true border, a true place of encounter, is by nature permeable. It is not like medieval armor, but rather like skin. Our skin does set a limit to where our body begins and where it ends. Our skin also sets certain limits to our give-and-take with our environment, keeping out certain germs, helping us to select that in our environment which we are ready to absorb. But if we ever close up our skin, we die."[24]

A border may function to affirm differences while, at the same time, allowing for an interaction that will be mutually enriching. Such a border, however, would presuppose a mutual recognition that "we are all *ladrones* [thieves]," with the humility entailed in such an admission. None of us are innocent, Euro-American or Latino-American:

> Hispanics . . . always knew that our ancestors were not guiltless. Our Spanish ancestors took the lands of our Indian ancestors. Some of our Indian ancestors practiced human sacrifice and cannibalism. Some of our Spanish forefathers raped our Indian foremothers. Some of our Indian foremothers betrayed their people in favor of the invaders. It is not a pretty story. But it is more real than the story that white settlers came to this land with pure motivations, and that any abuse of its inhabitants was the exception rather than the rule. It is also a story resulting in a painful identity."[25]

To be Hispanic is not merely to live *on* the border; it is to *be* a border, to live *in between* the rapist and the violated woman, to experience the pain of that ambiguity. But, to be Hispanic is also to know that that ambiguity can be the seedbed of new life; the border can be the birthplace of a new human community unafraid of *impurities* because it knows that none of us are *pure*. Such a recognition of the ambiguity of *all* human histories is a necessary precondition for an understanding of the difference between a frontier and a border.[26] It is a precondition for understanding the difference between *America* and the United States, between an *American* and an *estadounidense*.[27]

CHAPTER 15

TOWARD A POSTCOLONIAL HOMILETIC

JUSTO L. GONZÁLEZ'S CONTRIBUTION TO HISPANIC PREACHING

Pablo A. Jiménez

INTRODUCTION

The beginning of the twenty-first century finds the Western world in the midst of a paradigm shift. Almost all philosophers, sociologists, anthropologists, and theologians agree that the profound cultural changes we have been experiencing since the 1950s announce the birth of a new "era" in human history. However, the consensus ends there. Several competing movements and models are trying to explain the sudden, rapid, and constant changes our cultures are going through.

For some, we are witnessing the death of modernity and the birth of a postmodern world.[1] For others, these changes evidence a crisis in modernity. For still others, we are experiencing the acceleration of modernity, dubbed "hypermodernity" (or, in French, *surmodernité*).[2]

While the so-called First World is busy debating if the postmodern era is dawning or not, Third-World scholars have been studying the history, impact, and consequences of Anglo-European colonial rule in their respective continents, subcontinents, and nations.[3] These "postcolonial" approaches were originally developed as models for literary criticism. Their aim was to study the literature produced in the former colonies, particularly the one written in English in the former British colonies. In time, scholars began to apply the new "postcolonial" critical theory to all kind of cultural and historical "texts," not just to literary ventures. Thus, "postcolonial studies" emerged as a new discipline of study, fueled by the political theory developed by the movements that fought for the liberation of the Anglo-European colonies and by French critical theory.

Today, the word *postcolonial* is used in mainly three different contexts.[4] First, *postcolonial state* describes a nation that attained independence from Anglo-European colonial rule. Second, *postcolonial criticism* studies the literature produced by authors from such nations, even if they live and write in Europe or the United States. Third, *postcolonial theory* considers the effects of and reactions to colonial ideology upon those communities that were under Anglo-European hegemony.

The affirmation of cultural identity is one of the characteristics of these post-modern/postcolonial times. In the Unites States, different ethnic groups have been trying to affirm a distinct cultural identity. During the last forty years, African Americans, Asian Americans, Native Americans, and Hispanics have claimed a place in the larger American society. At the same time, they have been trying to "construct" an identity that may bind peoples who, although sharing some cultural traits, actually descend from different nations. In the case of Hispanics, the Spanish language serves as the cultural "glue" that bonds people who trace their ancestry to more than twenty different countries. The Hispanic or Latina/o "movement" has focused on issues such as civil rights, immigration, trade, bilingualism, and military interventions in Latin America and the Caribbean, among others.

The search for identity has made an impact in the field of religious studies, where scholars from different ethnic backgrounds are developing theologies from their particular social locations. Hispanic theology, in its different expressions, is one of those new contextual theologies. I believe that—given that the United States has exerted colonial and neocolonial hegemony over Latin America and the Caribbean—Hispanic theology should see postcolonial theory as a dialogue partner. As a matter of fact, some Latino and Latina theologians have been doing so at different levels. In particular, Justo L. González offers us throughout his extensive bibliography several concepts that shadow, parallel, and, sometimes, stem from postcolonial studies.

In this chapter, I will explore González's contribution to Hispanic preaching. It is my contention that his reflections on the subject pave the way for the development of a Hispanic homiletic. The first section expands the definition of *postcolonial*, identifying concepts that may further the dialogue with Hispanic theology. The second section surveys González's writings on colonialism, hermeneutics, and homiletics. The final section suggests guidelines for the development of a postcolonial approach to homiletics based on González's contributions to the field.

POSTCOLONIAL STUDIES

As stated earlier, "postcolonial studies"[5] is a vast field usually divided in two different disciplines: postcolonial literary criticism and postcolonial theory. A common presupposition to both disciplines is that identity is a social construct, shaped by ideological forces. These disciplines see colonial discourse as a powerful ideology that fostered and supported Anglo-European hegemony over different nations in Asia, Africa, Indonesia, and Latin America. Colonial ideology also shaped the identity of different ethnic groups. Postcolonial studies, thus, analyzes the way in which Anglo-European colonialism defined, changed, and redefined the cultural identity of the colonized peoples. It also analyzes the way in which the objectification of the colonized as "the other," defined Anglo-European cultures.

An example may help us better understand this basic tenet of postcolonial critique. In order to conquer America, Europeans defined the Amerindians as "savages" in need of tutelage. After a bitter debate on the humanity of the newly "discovered" peoples, European scholars concluded that although they were indeed human the Amerindian's intellectual abilities were hopelessly impaired. This determination allowed Europeans to cast themselves in the role of "masters" with a moral responsibility to care for the Amerindians. It also marked the beginning of racism, the ideology that gave pseudoscientific and even theological sanction to the inferiority of "people of color." Therefore, in defining Amerindians as an inferior race of savages in need of tutelage, colonial ideology also defined Anglo-Europeans as a superior race of civilized people ideally fit to rule the world.[6]

Most postcolonial critics use the ideas of Antonio Gramsci as the choice tools for economic, social, and political analysis.[7] Gramsci made important contributions to Marxist thought, affirming that the economic structure supports an ideological superstructure. Although economy and ideology are inextricably linked, the idea of a "superstructure" facilitates the analysis of ideologies that foster social problems such as racism and sexism. Gramsci also affirmed that the ruling oligarchies exerted "hegemony" over the masses. Even though hegemony is an oppressive power, the masses usually accept it. They have been convinced by ideological propaganda that the hegemony of the ruling classes is unavoidable. It is either the best option or the only option. In acquiescing to the hegemony of the dominant classes, the masses become "subalterns" to them.

Of course, there is much more to Gramsci's thought. He also spoke of "historical blocks," "organic intellectuals," and "anti-hegemonic" movements. However, even this brief and incomplete summary offers us a glimpse of how his brand of Marxist analysis informs postcolonial thought. "Hegemony" is a key concept, used to describe the political and economic power that Anglo-European nations exerted over the rest of the world. Colonial discourse and racism were the ideologies that validated the hegemony of Europe and the United States over colonial subjects. These powerful ideologies shaped the self-image and identity of the colonial "subalterns," who were acculturated to see Anglo-European hegemony as logical, natural, or even divinely foreordained. In brief, Gramsci's thought is a valuable tool for postcolonial thought.

Hispanic Theology as a Postcolonial Endeavor

By now, the points of contact between Hispanic theology and postcolonial thought must be evident. Hispanic theology is a contextual theology that explores how colonial and neocolonial Anglo-European hegemony shaped this conglomerate of people that we have come to call "Hispanic/Latina/o." The analysis and deconstruction of colonial discourse is key for understanding Hispanic identity and for the development of anti-hegemonic action/reflection. Hispanic theology seeks to unmask the racist ideological superstructure that inflicts so much pain on Latinos and Latinas. It also seeks to give a voice to the previously silent Hispanic "subalterns" who, victimized by a racist school system, were taught to acquiesce and even contribute to their own oppression.

Several Hispanic religious scholars have used postcolonial thought as a tool for the development of their theological thought. We can see the influence of postcolonial thought even in the early work of Virgilio Elizondo.[8] As we know, Elizondo proposed the metaphor of *mestizaje* as a key concept for the analysis of the Hispanic condition. This metaphor embodies the social processes that produced what we now call "Hispanic American" subculture. For Elizondo, Hispanics are the end result of a process of cultural hybridization, of the miscegenation of Spaniards, Amerindians, and Anglo-Europeans.

The use of the word *mestizaje* by Elizondo was certainly influenced by French thought. As we know, during the mid-twentieth century, France waged several wars in Africa, trying to retain hegemony over its former colonies. This tense situation fostered a lively academic debate on colonialism, evidenced in the work of Aimé Cesaire,[9] Léopold Sédar Senghor,[10] Albert Memmi,[11] and Frantz Fanon,[12] among others. One of the images used in these debates to depict cultural hybridization[13] was precisely *métis*, the French word for *mestizo*. In this sense, we can affirm that Elizondo borrowed the concept of *métissage* from the early postcolonial debates. We can also affirm that he correctly adapted it and employed it in the development of what we now call "Hispanic theology."

Besides Elizondo, two other important Catholic theologians have used postcolonial thought as a tool for social analysis. First, Fernando F. Segovia has consistently used concepts as "the other," "hegemony," and "alterity" in his many writings.[14] Second, Ada María Isasi-Díaz also uses postcolonial concepts in her keen analysis of the Hispanic condition.[15] By the same token, postcolonial thought is becoming the critical tool of choice of the younger generation of Hispanic scholars, particularly of those who have been mentored by Segovia and Isasi-Díaz.[16]

Postcolonial Clues in González's Theology

As stated earlier, it is our contention that the Hispanic theology developed by Justo L. González in his many writings shadows, parallels, and, on occasion, uses postcolonial concepts. In this section, I will try to detect postcolonial clues in his historical, anthropological, theological, hermeneutical, and homiletic writings.

HISTORICAL WRITINGS

First and foremost, Justo L. González is a historian of theology. His early publications included a *Historia de las misiones* (History of the Christian Mission) in one volume, a comprehensive *History of Christian Thought* in three volumes, and a shorter volume entitled *The Development of Christianity in the Latin Caribbean.*[17] The first part of the latter describes Christianity under the colonial regime. It details the methods, the theory, and the establishment of Spanish hegemony in the Americas. In this book González lays the foundation for the comprehensive critique of colonial discourse that he developed in his later writings.

González revisited the topic of Spanish colonial rule in his comprehensive *History of the Church.*[18] This book began as a "novelized" approach to church history, aimed at laypeople and licensed preachers. That is why this book was originally published in ten short volumes. In time, the book proved useful in academic circles, becoming the textbook of choice in many seminaries. Finally, it was edited in its present two-volume format.

In any case, the second volume of this book begins in a startling fashion. The section on the Reformation begins with an analysis of the role of the Spanish crown in the events that set it in motion. In this way, González places the colonial enterprise at the center of the Renaissance, and of the Reformation. This is a departure from the traditional approaches that viewed these movements as purely European events. It is also in agreement with the postcolonial assertion that the colonial enterprise shaped European identity.

González's church history revisits and expands the analysis of the ideological justification of Spanish hegemony in America. He pays particular attention to the anti-hegemonic response of clerics like Fray Bartolomé de las Casas, who opposed the theological ideas that legitimized the exploitation of the Amerindians in the Caribbean basin.

Ever the historian, González dedicates several sections of his book *Mañana*— a systematic theology from a Hispanic perspective—to historical issues.[19] In this book, González revisits some of the historical issues he explored in his previous writings. However, here his tone is more militant. This is also the case in his essays published in *Desde el reverso.*[20] In his latter writings, his critique of the colonial enterprise and its consequences is more acerbic and direct.

ANTHROPOLOGICAL WRITINGS

Even González himself would be surprised at the title of this subsection. Nonetheless, the fact is that he has published several essays on Hispanic identity. For lack of a better term, I am classifying such essays as "anthropological."

Here we must go back to *Mañana*, which begins with an extensive exploration of Hispanic identity. The first chapters of the book analyze topics such as what is a minority perspective and what are the religious and ethnic implications of such a perspective. It also describes the phenomenal growth of the Hispanic community. It even studies the Hispanic Catholic background and the Protestant experience, announcing the dawning of a "New Reformation."

"Hispanics in the United States" is another essay on the subject in González's bibliography.[21] It argues that Hispanics are emerging as a "new" subculture in the nation. González explains that the fledgling Hispanic culture includes linguistic, cultural, and even culinary elements from different Latin American ethnic traditions. People from a wide array of cultural backgrounds are coming together to forge a new "Hispanic/Latina/o" identity. He highlights the role of the Christian churches as fulcrums of this process of hybridization or *mestizaje*.

THEOLOGICAL WRITINGS

González's writings on systematic theology are too numerous to summarize here. For this reason, I will only comment on four: *Christian Thought Revisited, Mañana, Out of Every Tribe and Nation*, and the essay "Metamodern Aliens in Postmodern Jerusalem."

In *Christian Thought Revisited*,[22] González classifies the early church theologies in three types labeled "a, b, and c." The latter one is portrayed as a pastoral theology whose main exponent in the ancient world was Irenaeus. This type of theology is akin to the contemporary contextual theologies that use an action/reflection model. Therefore, this book empowers contemporary ethnic theologies to reappropriate the church's theological tradition.

If *Christian Thought Revisited* lays the foundation for the development of contextual theologies, *Mañana* presents a comprehensive Hispanic one. In its methodology, the book is close to Latin American liberation theology, given that it begins with the comprehensive social analysis described above. *Mañana* is a theological manifest that declares the emergence of a "Hispanic/Latina/o" identity and, then, develops a systematic theology from that social location.

For its part, *Out of Every Tribe and Nation*[23] is an effort to develop a multi-ethnic and multicultural systematic theology. Its importance for our study is that it brings together insights from other minority groups that have also suffered the consequences of colonial hegemony. African Americans, Native Americans, and even Asian Americans share a crucial common trait with Hispanics: their cultural identity has been forged in dialogue with Anglo-European colonial discourse.

Finally, González wrote an essay on postmodernity titled "Metamodern Aliens in Postmodern Jerusalem."[24] One of the key features of the article is its suspicious attitude toward postmodern thought. González deconstructs the postmodern assertion that there are no master narratives. He fears that the "new metanarrative is that there is no metanarrative, that all narratives are partial, contingent to such a degree that they have no power to demand allegiance."[25] Then, González proposes what he calls a "metamodern" approach to history. However, he explicitly states that "what I mean by 'metamodern' is similar to what Stephen Slemon means by 'post-colonial.' "[26] The similarity consists in the claim that there are authoritative cultural texts that former colonial subjects can use to "pry open the structures of power created by modernity and allowed to continue standing unchallenged by postmodernity."[27]

HERMENEUTICAL WRITINGS

While my generation knows González mainly as a historian, younger generations know him for his writings on theological and biblical hermeneutics. For example, maybe the best-known chapter of *Mañana* is the one titled "Reading the Bible in Spanish." Here, González proposes a hermeneutic methodology that empowers the reader to read the Bible from a Hispanic/Latina/o perspective (even if such reader is not fluent in Spanish).

Later on, González expanded his contribution to hermeneutic theory in *Santa Biblia*.[28] In this book González explores seven metaphors that are used in Hispanic theology to embody, summarize, and analyze the Hispanic condition. *Marginalization* and *poverty* evoke the struggle against colonial and neocolonial oppression that causes so much suffering among our people. *Mestizaje* and *mulatez* describe the hybridization processes that shape the Hispanic community. *Exile* and *alien* speak of the consequences of neocolonial rule and military intervention in Latin America. *Solidarity* is the metaphor that calls us to unite in an anti-hegemonic historical block against the deadly forces that oppress our people.

Besides hermeneutic theory, González has also published several biblical commentaries. In many ways, his commentary on the book of Acts is programmatic,[29] given that it describes how the early Christian community forged a new social identity. In many ways, that is the task at hand for the contemporary Hispanic Christian community.

González has also published three books on Revelation (two of them cowritten with Catherine G. González).[30] The latest one is titled *For the Healing of the Nations.*[31] In this volume González compares current cultural conflicts with the ones that rocked the Mediterranean basin in the first centuries of the Christian era. The book of Revelation is seen, then, as an account of how some early Christian communities addressed such cultural conflicts. Among González's writings, this is the one that comes closer to using postcolonial concepts for social analysis. González affirms that one of the results of Roman hegemony was a growing "multiculturalism" that posed serious challenges to Roman social identity. As was the case with Acts, González suggests that there is a clear parallel between the cultural conflicts in the biblical world and the challenges that multiculturalism poses to the former Anglo-European colonial rulers.

HOMILETIC WRITINGS

Justo L. and Catherine G. González cowrote *Liberation Preaching,*[32] an influential textbook on how Latin American liberation theology can inform contemporary preaching. One of the many virtues of the book is its call to take into consideration the social location of the preacher and of the congregation. Justo provides several examples of how his ethnicity shapes his interpretation of the Bible and his reading of the church's tradition. Catherine reads the same Bible and tradition from her particular social location.

The Gonzálezes expanded their views on the impact of identity and social location in preaching in an essay titled "The Larger Context."[33] Here they explored the sacramental, social, political, and economic contexts of North American preaching. They followed these contributions with the publication of *The Liberating Pulpit,* a revised and expanded edition of *Liberation Preaching.*[34]

TOWARD A POSTCOLONIAL HOMILETIC

As we have seen, the work of Justo L. González offers several points of contact with postcolonial thought. Throughout his many writings in different theological fields, González reiterates the importance of identity, social location, and ideological critique for the development of contextual theologies.

In the case of Hispanic Americans, such topics lead us to a confrontation with the colonial discourse that legitimized the Anglo-European hegemony over Latin America and the Caribbean. It is impossible to construct a theology with, from, and for the Hispanic/Latina/o people without addressing the way in which colonial discourse shaped our identity as "colonial subalterns."

It is precisely this "subaltern" identity that presents the toughest challenge to the postcolonial condition to the Hispanic community. If indeed we have been acculturated to think ill of ourselves by a socialization system that teaches us in myriad ways that we are inferior to people of Anglo-European ascendancy, how can we find a "voice" to speak against such an oppressive system? If indeed we have internalized our positions as social and economic "subalterns," how can the "subaltern" speak?[35]

The options are few. First, the subaltern may never speak for him or herself (given that it would be impossible to escape the identity as a "colonized" person). Second, an intellectual elite may be able to voice the wants and needs of the colonial subaltern (although we may ask how the academic prevailed over his or her "subaltern" identity). A third option would affirm that subaltern groups maintain cultural practices and "texts" that empower them to deconstruct the false identity imposed by colonial rule. This means that the "subaltern" has always been able to speak and that he or she has been constantly speaking (even though the colonial rulers disregarded or actively suppressed his or her voice).

Mutatis mutandis, I ask: can the subaltern *preach*? In other words, can the Hispanic Christian community deconstruct the false identities fostered by the colonial theologies that defined us as "subaltern"? Can the Latino people develop counterhegemonic religious practices and "texts"? Can we find a "voice" to preach a contextualized gospel that reads the Bible and the tradition from our social location? I repeat, can the (Hispanic) subaltern *preach*?

My response is that yes, we can indeed preach. However, in order to preach the liberating gospel in a relevant fashion the Hispanic community needs to construct a postcolonial homiletic. Such homiletic theory, informed by Hispanic theology and hermeneutics, will denounce and unmask the colonial ideologies that undermined our people. Such homiletic theory will empower Hispanic preachers to be poets, prophets, and pastors of the communities they serve.

In his many writings, Justo L. González laid a foundation upon which the younger generations of Hispanic theologians will be able to construct a postcolonial homiletics that will give a "voice" to the previously "voiceless." González has given us valuable historical, anthropological, theological, hermeneutical, and homiletic tools. Let us use them wisely in the construction of a homiletic theory and practice that announces boldly the liberating gospel to "el pueblo de Dios."

Doing Theology in Spanish

Hispanic Theological Methodology, Dialogue, and Rationality

Luis G. Pedraja

Theology is more than thinking about God; theology is something we do, incorporating various aspects of human existence, thought, and practice as they relate to God. Traditionally, we equate the discipline of theology with the areas of theology that involve critical reflection, philosophical theology, and Western European philosophical traditions that incorporate rationalist tendencies and other vestiges of modernism. Even postmodernism with its multiverse retains a theoretical-reflective paradigm that is defined by Western European standards.[1] However, while critical reflection is an important part of theology, it is not its sole component. Our praxis, faith, language, and culture affect our theology and play a crucial role in our theological reflection and its ultimate outcome. If we limit our reflection to the critical-theoretical and fail to explore how our culture, economy, and social location affect our theology, the result is a truncated and stilted theology.

Latina/o theologians are quite capable of engaging in critical and theoretical theological reflection à la Western European theoretical-rationalistic style that permeates current theological discussion. Most of us did it for our dissertations, and many of us still continue to make significant contributions in the fields of philosophical and systematic theology.[2] However, most of us recognize the need to go beyond Western European philosophical paradigms of theologizing and theorizing. Hence, Hispanic-Latina/o theology incorporates other aspects of theological reflection and other non-Western European forms of rationality that are nevertheless essential components of theological reflections.

In a sense, the notion that the dominant Western European models for doing theology are superior and more scholarly is actually incorrect and ultimately detrimental to theology. Even more, I will argue, these models, with their emphasis on detached, individualistic, theoretical reflection, are actually truncated and triumphalistic ways of doing theology. This does not mean that they are unimportant. All forms of theological reflection are necessary, and abstract critical theological reflection, as encountered in the Western European philosophical traditions, allows us to analyze in depth certain theological dimensions of our faith and beliefs by reducing complex elements into more manageable concepts. However, if we allow theological reflection to be reduced to only one form of theologizing by placing it above other forms, we develop a false and truncated understanding of the complexity of God and human experience.[3] Hence, it is necessary to examine our faith and beliefs in a more overarching manner, which is what Hispanic theologians strive to do.

DOING THEOLOGY IN SPANISH

The legacy of Justo L. González, along with other leading Hispanic American theologians, provides us with alternative paradigms for theologizing in more holistic ways. In *Mañana: Christian Theology from a Hispanic Perspective*, González suggests the provocative idea that we should read the Bible in Spanish.[4] In asserting that we need to read the Bible in Spanish, González does not intend for everyone to learn the Spanish language. Rather, what González advocates is a noninnocent reading of Scriptures that includes an exploration of the issues of power, politics, and nondominant readings from our own perspective.[5] González's suggestion and outline for reading the Bible in Spanish provides us with one of several paradigms for developing an understanding of Hispanic methodologies.

In several of my own writings, I propose that we expand to theology the hermeneutics that González applies to the Scriptures.[6] In doing so, I propose that we will find the key to understanding the unique characteristics that define Hispanic theological methodology—a methodology already being used by our theologians. Hence, doing theology in Spanish means that we need to examine the influence that power, politics, dominance, culture, and economic perspectives have in our theological work, just as González suggests we do with Scripture.[7] In doing so, we accomplish the following. First, we can do theology with integrity and humility.[8] By *integrity*, I mean that we are honest in examining the particular cultural, social, and economic perspectives that we assume and presuppose in engaging in our theological reflection, as well as acknowledging our particular agendas, biases, and intentionality. By *humility*, I mean our recognition of the limitations inherent in engaging in theology—limitations born out of our narrow vision, entrenchment in our culture and language, finite perspectives, and human limitations. Second, because we acknowledge our limitations, we are also able to entertain the notion that our theology is by no means exhaustive or systematic in nature but rather inescapably limited by our finite standpoint in a particular history, society, and ethos. Thus, we are both motivated and able to engage in an honest dialogue with others, a dialogue that does not seek to subsume the other's views under our own. This inevitably leads us to a greater furthering of our theological inquiry and understanding.

Doing theology in "Spanish," to continue using González's phrase, requires us to go beyond abstractions and focus on the concrete, lived experience of our people, acknowledging the historicity and particularity of all theology.[9] Theology, I propose, is not about universals but about particulars. In accepting the incarnation and the biblical understanding of God, we need to acknowledge that God is not an abstract universal but a concrete reality that we encounter in concrete events and enfleshed in actual persons. In such a setting, the theological questions are no longer about God and culture, as if they exist in a dichotomous relationship, but about God's presence as encountered through culture, history, and human flesh. Such an understanding does not promote an identity between God and culture, but it does acknowledge the impossibility of encountering God outside of it.[10] Furthermore, if theology is particular, then it must have an impact on the particular—it must create a concrete reality, not merely state it. Theology should not merely reflect but also affect faith and action.

PRAXIS AND LIBERATION

Doing theology in Spanish requires us to move beyond theological reflection toward praxis. Like Latin American liberation theologies, Hispanic theologians not only provide a new theological content (*theoria*) but also engage in a new way of doing theology (*praxis*).[11] The criteria that González provides for reading the Bible in Spanish, which I am applying to theological methodology, demonstrates the existing affinity between Latina/o theology and liberation theology. Indeed, Latina/o theology is indebted to Latin American liberation theologies, as well as other liberation theologies, for their theological development. Like other theologians of liberation, Hispanic theologians pay attention to the concrete reality of the people as a locus of theological reflection and as an impetus for action. Hence, Hispanic theologians are not merely satisfied with presenting new theoretical interpretations of doctrine or describing the theological content of Hispanic faith and beliefs. They also engage in a theological hermeneutics that respects diversity and examines the influence of power, oppression, and culture on the living faith of a people—the same types of requirements advocated by González for reading the Bible. In addition, they also prescribe new directions for action and seek to move the church into an active praxis that foreshadows the hope of God's rule.

Hispanic theologians often follow a schema not unlike that of the threefold pastoral method of seeing, judging, and acting used by Latin American liberation theologians. This method involves a socioanalytic examination of the particularity of the situation (seeing), a hermeneutical approach to the Scriptures that takes oppression and the perspectives of the oppressed seriously (hearing), and a practical application dictated by the preceding meditations.[12] However, unlike South American liberation theologies, Hispanic Americans employ additional or different tools in their analysis and hermeneutics due to their different geographical and socioeconomic locations.

Due primarily to their location in the United States, Hispanic theologies must confront a broader and more complex set of issues beyond the sinful oppressive structures that promulgate poverty. Hispanics must also address issues of acculturation, discrimination, racism, hybridity, and a complex socioeconomic situation that often makes us both oppressors and oppressed. While poverty and oppression still play a crucial role in our theological reflections, issues such as ethnic and racial identity, marginalization, sexism, culture, language, and popular religion are also central to our theologies. While some of these issues might be present in Latin America, they are not always addressed to the same extent as they are in our North American setting. Thus, it is crucial to note that while Hispanic American theologians share in the common legacy of Latin American liberation theologies and have been deeply influenced by their methodology, the two are not identical nor can they be subsumed into each other.

LIVED EXPERIENCE AND ETHNOGRAPHIC ANALYSIS

A key component of reading the Bible in Spanish for González is the necessity of attending to the hermeneutical voice of the little ones of society: the poor, the marginalized, the excluded, the "unsophisticated."[13] This finds a correlate expression in our theology as we incorporate the voices of those who are commonly excluded from theological dialogue and as we examine the reality of our people. To accomplish this objective, the theological methodologies of Latina/o theologians use diverse tools, which often go beyond the traditional boundaries of theology and philosophy. Hispanic American theologians often use methodological tools from other disciplines, such as anthropology and sociology, to engage in a more thorough reflection of the situation of the people and an analysis of the particularity of the people's embodied faith. In a sense, our theological hermeneutics and theological method are our way of both "seeing" and "hearing" our people, acknowledging them and their lived experience as a true *locus theologicus*.

A methodology that exemplifies this dimension of our theological reflection comes from our *mujerista* theologians, who have led the way in using ethnographic analysis to do theology from the perspective of Latinas in the United States. Building upon the work of the social psychologist Harold Garfinkel, *mujerista* theologians, such as Ada María Isasi-Díaz, recognize the "practical rationality," reflective nature, and contextual reality of everyday life, as well as the value of social interaction and life-creating activity in developing a real picture of the community described.[14] Building upon this principle, and ensuring the accuracy of the description through the feedback of the community, *mujerista* theologians engage in ethnographic analysis to acknowledge the culture and faith of their community and accurately describe the distinctive characteristics and traits of these communities' faith.[15] Rather than theorizing and extrapolating abstract notions that might seek to subsume the particularity of the women's lived experience, these analyses allow the women to elaborate upon their own understanding of their experience and faith.

By doing theology with an ethnographic methodology, *mujerista* theologians are able to reflect on the particularity of lived experience and on the historicity of the women engaged in dialogue.[16] Hence, they enhance theological reflection and effect a concrete change by advocating for an embodied theology, a theology that emerges out of life and experience rather than out of conjectures and mere rational maneuvering. In this sense, theology is fully a part of life and faith, not apart from life and a living faith. Yet, in doing so, *mujerista* theologians do not take an irrational or antirational theological stance. Rather, they expand the notion of rationality to encompass something other than abstract philosophical thought, thus, making their theology more encompassing, and more human, than others.[17]

Using the methods derived from the social sciences (enhanced by individual observations, the examination of beliefs, and the incorporation of other theological tools) augments the theological reflection of *mujerista* theologians.[18] Because these tools and methods take place within a gathered group of women from the community, the process preserves a concrete locus and a lived reality that would be impossible in a detached academic exercise. Other sociological models and philosophical methodologies produce an abstract, and supposedly a universal, compendium of traits, often organized into a schema that fits into the intentionality and theoretical biases of the researcher. *Mujerista* theologians, on the other hand, go beyond philosophical abstraction by employing ethnographic analysis, thus seeking to accurately reflect the reality of a concrete community, as well as their emergent and communal beliefs. The result is a less truncated and more holistic theology than that of theologies influenced by Western European methodologies that emphasize detachment and abstraction.

Latina/o theology cannot be merely detached reflections or abstract studies of our communities. On the contrary, it should emerge from our respective communities and should strive to acknowledge the influences and biases that our communities impart upon our theological reflection. In doing so, we acknowledge the value of including the voices and theological reflections of our people, especially those among them who are marginalized and oppressed, as essential to our theology. The result is a comprehensive theology that includes more than philosophical, abstract, and technical reflections, while adhering to the criterion of including the hermeneutics of the disenfranchised. Our theological reflection, while including theory, goes beyond it, connecting to the concrete reality of the Hispanic people, drawing upon them as a source of theology, and empowering them to both reflection and action. Thus, unlike the detachment and isolation that often mark the theological reflection of Eurocentric theologies, Hispanic theologies are and should continue to be more collaborative in nature.

TEOLOGÍA EN CONJUNTO:
A COLLABORATIVE METHODOLOGY

In *Mañana,* González both highlights and proposes a model for doing theology that distinguishes the methodology of Hispanic theologians from that of the most common ways in which academic theologians approach their subject. He calls this model *Fuenteovejuna theology.*[19] The name González offers for this model comes from a town immortalized in a play by Lope de Vega in which the people rebel against the tyrannical rule of the town's commander, killing him. Their battle cry and their later defense against the inquisitor investigating the commander's death is "Fuenteovejuna, *todos a una*" (Fuenteovejuna, all at one).[20] According to González, the collaborative process of doing Hispanic theology reflects a collaborative methodology, much like the battle cry of the townspeople.[21] In addition, this collaborative manner for doing theology also parallels the second rule in his outline for reading the Bible in "Spanish" that requires understanding the Bible as addressing a community of faith.[22] Hence, in doing theology in "Spanish," the demand calls for it to be a communal exercise.

This collaborative methodology, first identified by González and which would later be more obviously termed *teología en conjunto* (collaborative theology), differentiates itself from standard theological models for doing theology in the detached, abstract, competitive, and individualistic manner that tends to prevail in the academy.[23] González even suggests that this is a contribution that Hispanics can bring to a theological enterprise fraught with individualism and competitiveness and thus better reflect the role of theology as a task of the church as a whole, which is by definition, according to González, a community.[24]

What González accomplishes in advocating a collaborative approach is not a departure from theological tradition. Rather, it is a recovery of the church's theological heritage.[25] Instead of developing theology from a philosophical model feigning objectivity and a Cartesian detachment, theology emerges from an ecclesial model that engages in an ongoing communal dialogue, thus locating theology as a domain of the church. By its very nature, this approach also minimizes the impact of individual perspectives and agendas on theology.

Such a communal model for doing theology can only develop through an ongoing dialogue that engages different people who share perspectives that are different from our own. The dialogue itself is not so much a method, per se in the traditional way, but a way of doing theology in community—a community that includes the people, as well as other theologians. However, Hispanic theologians, like many other marginalized theologians, often use a dialogic approach to their theological endeavor, making the dialogue itself a methodology that accepts diversity and engages other perspective as subjects rather than objects of analysis. Dialogic methodologies of this fashion will still use the more common methods of reflection, such as the dialectic, analytic, synthetic, and correlative methods.[26] But they use them in a process of dialogue that engages the subject of reflection fully, not attempting to subsume the other in a preconceived paradigm but empowering the subject's own self-definition.

Dialogic methodology can easily be confused with dialectic, synthetic, and correlative methods—all of which tend to be confused with each other by people unfamiliar with them. Yet, it is different from them in several ways. First, it does not necessarily assume the opposition of two ideas (perspectives) nor strive for a resolution of the tension as tends to be the case in dialectic methods. Second, it does not merge concepts to create a new notion that blends or overarches the two, as might be the case in synthetic methods. Third, while it does correlate similar perspectives to discover common themes and trends in the process, like the method of correlation, it does not presuppose a philosophical or theological paradigm that needs to be placed in correspondence with each other.

Dialogic methodologies are based in the presupposition that we all bring different perspectives to a discussion and that by engaging each other in mutual respect, we can enhance one another's perspective and disclose one another's biases. Furthermore, it is not a closed system that strives for a resolution of difference, but an open system that expands through the acceptance and incorporation of differences. Even when using analysis in trying to define the elements of dialogue, the analysis takes a more holistic approach, as in the *mujerista* theologian's use of ethnographic analysis.

Using dialogue as the primary methodological paradigm for doing theology brings difference and particularity to the forefront. Rather than seeking the reduction of the subject of dialogue to preset paradigms that eradicate differences, the subject remains concretely real and participates fully in a process of mutual definitions and redefinition in the dynamics of the relationship itself as both seek to understand each other. Hence, the concreteness and particularity of theology remain intact, but not in isolation from each other.[27]

GOING BEYOND TRADITIONAL MODELS

Generally, we tend to speak of reason in its primary critical functions, equated for the most part with theoretical dimensions. To these, we can also add two other forms of reason that we encounter in philosophical discourse: moral (praxis) and aesthetic. These forms are not always associated with theology per se, but they are part of theological and philosophical discourse, incorporating their own technical and critical forms of reflection. In volume one of his *Systematic Theology*, Paul Tillich outlines a fourth form of reason that he calls ecstatic (existential) reason, which is different from the type of critical-cognitive work in which academic theologians engage but which is part of all belief.[28] The technical, formal forms of reason, usually equated with the theoretical, are the ones we most often equate with rationality. Thus, when we think of theology, we most often equate it with that part of it that engages in theoretical reason, or at least, formal technical reason. At another level, liberation theology and moral theology expand our understanding of theology to include the realm of practical reason by helping us understand that theory cannot be separated from praxis. Latina/o theologians, along with a few European theologians like von Balthazar, have expanded this notion even further. In their work, they engage in reflection that incorporates aesthetic reason, such as in the works of Roberto S. Goizueta and Alex García-Rivera. In addition, they also engage in reflection that incorporates faith and the concrete particularity of experience that reflects elements of ecstatic reason.

While Tillich might not have envisioned such a broadening of his outline of ecstatic reason, he does recognize the interconnectedness of all the forms of reason and their importance to theology, specially in moving beyond the technical-theoretical dimensions of theology. If we limit the process of doing theology to the formal, technical, theoretical, and Eurocentric forms of reasoning, we ultimately produce a truncated and triumphalistic theology. What Justo González and other Hispanic theologians provide us is an alternative that merits consideration and that broadens theology to include the voices of the marginalized in the ever-growing dialogue that is part of doing theology. Ultimately, they point to the need of broadening theology to include its ecstatic dimensions of reason, what we refer to as the faith of the people. Latina/o theology is by far a more comprehensive approach to theology than those that solely explore detached, abstract, rationalistic, critical-theoretical dimensions of faith and the church while ignoring other dimensions of reason, culture, and faith.

CHAPTER 17

SPIRIT WITHOUT BORDERS: PENTECOSTALISM IN THE AMERICAS

A PROFILE AND PARADIGM OF "CRIOLLO" PENTECOSTALISM

Eldin Villafañe

It's a big word that emerged in the last decades of the twentieth century and dominates the Wall Streets, Madison Avenues, and media institutions of our world: *globalization*.

Most people perceive *globalization* in economic or market terms, although we are fully aware that it also points to the electronic superhighway; the many people movements; and the cultural, religious, and social transactions across many borders. Indeed, global mobility of people, resources, ideas, faith, and systems define our contemporary world.

For me, one of the most significant areas of the globalization phenomenon is stated well in a current book entitled, *The Globalization of Pentecostalism: A Religion Made to Travel.*[1] I represent this faith tradition that is quintessentially a global religion—truly imbued with a Spirit without borders.

If we are to believe Christian demographer David Barrett or Vinson Synan, Pentecostals and charismatics have grown from a handful of believers at the beginning of the last century to a worldwide estimate of 530 million (1999) and growing![2]

C. Peter Wagner, speaking about this global religion, states: "My research has led me to make this bold statement: 'In all human history, no other non-political, non-militaristic, voluntary human movement has grown as rapidly as the Pentecostal-Charismatic movement in the last 25 years.'"[3] Notwithstanding the possible hyperbole in this remark, we must, to say the least, make some sense of this tremendous growth of Pentecostalism—a religion made to travel.

Two major questions about Pentecostalism inform my thinking, they constitute the double foci of my remarks: first, what are some of the distinguishing characteristics of Pentecostal religiosity? and second, what factors account for its phenomenal growth?

Before I respond to the above, I need to make the following clarifications: Pentecostalism is not just, as some would narrowly define, a "tongues movement"—referring to its glossolalic cultic expressions. Rather, as I would broadly define it, Pentecostalism is that branch of Christianity that emphasizes the power and presence of the person, work, and gifts of the Spirit. And adding Killiam MacDonell's mission and trinitarian note, it is "directed toward the proclamation that Jesus Christ is Lord to the Glory of God."[4]

Furthermore, world Pentecostalism is not a monolithic religious reality. Far from it, Pentecostalism, like many world religions, has taken the native garb of its historical and cultural context. It is a kaleidoscope of diverse national and local experiences.

Yet, as André Corten and Ruth Marshall-Fratani would remind us:

> Despite the enormous differences which separate these countries and the individual societies within them, the Pentecostal manifestations in these diverse cultures have many similarities. Contemporary Pentecostalism provides a striking example of the paradox of difference and uniformity that seems to be at the heart of processes of transnationalism and globalization.[5]

What follows will provide a profile of Pentecostalism by highlighting certain of its salient characteristics and will seek to account for its growth by offering a paradigm of its proliferation. It is a somewhat bold attempt to get to the universal of global Pentecostalism by way of the particular. The particular being the "Criollo" (native or indigenous) Pentecostalism of Latin/Hispanic America.

Juan Sepúlveda provides a succinct definition of "Criollo" Pentecostalism, "as a form of popular religiosity, that is, as a religious experience strongly rooted in the popular culture and identity."[6] Moreover, Carmelo Alvarez would add that it is "economically and structurally independent of any foreign mission, with an autonomous (native) pastoral ministry."[7] "Criollo" Pentecostalism will serve as a microcosm of global Pentecostalism.

Three categories will be used to present elements of this profile and paradigm of "Criollo" Pentecostalism. In my study of Pentecostalism they represent key elements that both describe "Criollo" Pentecostalism and account for its proliferation. These elements cut across psychological, sociopolitical, cultural, religious, and theological lines. Furthermore, they represent my belief that multiple and cumulative social-spiritual causations best define or explain Pentecostal growth.

The three elements, or three "P"s, are: Presence, Popular Classes, and Primal Spirituality.

PRESENCE: PENTECOSTALISM AS AN URBAN PHENOMENON

Several years ago while on a trip to Brazil I was impressed, time and again, by two common scenes in the *favelas* (slums) of Rio de Janeiro. One was the presence of many children flying kites and the other was the many *Assembléia de Deus* (Assemblies of God) churches. To me they both spoke loudly of hope amid an urban context defined by marginality and poverty. It also spoke to me about the important role Pentecostalism has played and is playing in many urban centers of the Americas, particularly its *barrios, favelas,* or ghettos. Pentecostalism is mostly an urban phenomenon. It was born among poor urban workers.

Historically, there has been an ongoing debate as to the genesis of Pentecostalism as a modern religious movement. Some scholars look back to Charles Fox Parham, Topeka, Kansas (1902), others to William Joseph Seymour, the one-eye black pastor of the Apostolic Faith Mission in Los Angeles, California (1906). While still other scholars would emphasize a polycentric development with common roots in the Wesleyan-Holiness and Keswickian revivals of the late nineteenth century. Yet all would agree that as a *movement*, Pentecostalism owes its *worldwide* impetus to the Azusa Street revival (1906–1909) under Seymour in urban Los Angeles.

It is important to note that the Azusa Street revival drew a significant number of Hispanics living in the Los Angeles area. The names of Luis López and Juan Navarro are noted as early participants of the Azusa Street revival, thus among the first Pentecostals. As early as 1912, Hispanics were organizing their own independent Pentecostal churches throughout the major cities in California, Texas, and Hawaii.[8]

In Latin America—from its beginning in the pioneering work of Willis C. Hoover in Valparaiso and Santiago, Chile (1906–1909), or Luigi Francescon in São Paulo, Brazil (1909), to Francisco Olazábal in Victoria, Texas (1923), and Juan Lugo in Ponce, Puerto Rico (1916), and both in New York City in the 1920s—the *locus* of Pentecostalism has been in the urban centers of the Americas.

Pentecostalism's growth has paralleled the phenomenon of urbanization throughout the Americas. Its growth reflects the growth of many of its cities. Mark Searing's research data paint the following portrait:

> Between 1950 and 1990, the urban population (in Latin America) increased from 59 million to 306 million. . . . During the same 1950-1985 periods its urban community moved from 40 percent to 67.4 percent, and the percentage of those living in cities of a million people or more escalated from 23 to 31 percent. . . . The greatest growth has been in the very large cities. . . . [though] forty-nine percent of Latin America's population lives in cities of over 100,000."[9]

Brazil is a fascinating example of Pentecostal urban growth. R. Andrew Chesnut, in his excellent work, *Born Again in Brazil: The Pentecostal Boom and the Pathogens of Poverty,* notes that among Protestants, "in Brazil's second largest city, Rio de Janeiro, *crentes* [believers], the great majority of whom (91 percent) are Pentecostal, have founded an average of one church per workday since the beginning of the decade."[10]

It's interesting to note here that the 30 million Pentecostals in Brazil represent 80 percent of all the Pentecostals in Latin America. And, Brazil has the largest population of Catholics in the world (150 million), while at the same time counting the largest Pentecostal population in the world.[11] Latin America accounts for 35 percent of all the Pentecostals in the world.[12]

At present "Criollo" Pentecostalism represents the fastest-growing segment of Pentecostalism, due in no small measure to the fact that it is the movement most open to the contextual, cultural, and religious experiences of its urban locality.

While all Pentecostal growth is not limited to its cities, the urban metropolis is the primary *locus* of Pentecostal vitality in the Americas.

POPULAR CLASSES: PENTECOSTALISM AS HEALER OF THE PATHOGENS OF POVERTY

From its beginning Pentecostalism has been the "haven of the masses."[13] It has thrived among societies' "disinherited."[14]

Competing paradigms have been offered to explain this attraction of the masses to Pentecostalism. Among the earliest scholarly works one finds Renato Pobleto and Thomas F. O'Dea's study, "Anomie and the 'Quest for Community': The Formation of Sects Among the Puerto Ricans of New York" published in 1960.[15] This was a seminal study of Puerto Rican Pentecostal growth in the *barrio,* focusing on Emile Durkheim's anomie theory. Pobleto and O'Dea's study preceded the better-known and developed works on anomie theory and Pentecostalism by Emilio Willems, *Followers of the New Faith,*[16] and Christian Lalive d'Epinay, *Haven of the Masses.*

The anomie thesis posits that Pentecostal growth is due to the dislocation of poor migrants to the city by forces of industrialization, urbanization, and capitalist development and that the Pentecostal community provides a comprehensive resolution to this anomie state of normlessness or value dissonance in modern society.

Recently, David Stoll[17] and David Martin[18] have added to the anomie thesis citing political oppression, personal religious identity, the revision of consciousness, and the creation of free social space as critical factors propelling Pentecostal growth in Latin America.

I believe that while all the above-noted theses are insightful, even necessary for the understanding of "Criollo" Pentecostalism, they are, nevertheless, not sufficient. I reiterate my earlier statement that a better understanding of Pentecostalism is to be found in multiple and commutative causations. In this regard I find promising Chesnut's thesis on Pentecostals' growth among the poor.

Chesnut posits "that the dialectic between poverty-related illness and faith healing provides the key to understanding the appeal of Pentecostalism in Brazil and much of Latin America."[19] He wisely enlarges his concept of illness to include not just somatic maladies but also social expressions of distress. He thus classifies illness into these categories: physical, social, and supernatural.

Time and space does not permit an elaboration and/or a critique of Chesnut's nuanced ethnographic work, but let me just note a few of his important findings:

1. Pentecostalism thrives among the poor because it offers healing to those experiencing the health crisis of poverty.
2. The search for healing is central to the conversion process.
3. Health is maintained through the spiritual and ideological force of their new faith.

Let me quote Chesnut here:

> With the instruments of spiritual ecstasy, mutual aid, ideological dualism, and moral asceticism at their disposal, Pentecostals inoculate themselves against many of the diseases of poverty. . . . Spiritual ecstasy, experienced through the gifts of the Spirit, baptism in the Holy Spirit, and music, allows believers to transcend the material deprivation of their everyday lives. Filled with the power of the Spirit, believers exorcise the demons of poverty.[20]

Chesnut's remarks concerning the "maintenance of health" strategies provided by Pentecostals coheres well with that interpretive understanding that while conditions of deprivation and disorganization may be causal or "facilitating conditions" in the genesis of a movement, its development and growth must be sought in the dynamics of the movement itself.[21]

We now turn to Harvey Cox's notion of primal spirituality, which I believe moves us further in that direction.

PRIMAL SPIRITUALITY: PENTECOSTALISM AS A PRIMAL AND POSTMODERN SPIRITUALITY

It is Harvey Cox's thesis that the heart of Pentecostalism, and the key to its growth, lies in what he calls "primal spirituality." For him primal spirituality responds to the profound spiritual emptiness of our times, and it does so by going beyond the levels of creed and ceremony to touch the core of human religiousness.[22]

He defines primal spirituality as "that largely unprocessed nucleus of the psyche in which the unending struggle for a sense of purpose and significance goes on. . . . [it is] the "imago dei," the image of God in every person."[23]

He posits that Pentecostalism enables a recovery, on a personal and communal level, three dimensions of this elemental spirituality. These three dimensions, which touch the heart of what it is to be a *homo religiosus*, are primal speech, primal piety, and primal hope.

Primal Speech

Primal speech underlines the glossolalic, or "ecstatic utterance," or the praying in the Spirit that speaks *from* and *to* the language of the heart. Cox, referring to his teacher Paul Tillich's writings, defines this ecstasy as "not an irrational state," but as "a way of knowing that transcends everyday awareness, one in which 'deep speaks to deep.' "[24]

In my own study of this primal speech I call it the "Salsa of the Spirit."[25] I agree with Frank Macchia that, "*glossolalia* is a hidden protest against any attempt to define, manipulate or oppress humanity. *Glossolalia* is an unclassifiable, free speech in response to an unclassifiable, free God, that is according to Kasemann, 'a cry for freedom.' "[26] Furthermore, I see tongues (*glossolalia*) theologically as a sigh and sign of liberation, witnessing in the Latino *barrios* the cry for liberation and justice. As such, I suggest seven ways in which tongues are signs of liberation in the poverty-stricken *barrios* of the Bronx or of Latin America.

Tongues are:

1. Signs of confirmation that *God is present* with the poor and oppressed.
2. Signs of *divine value* of the person—no matter who he or she is.
3. Signs of *divine affirmation* of women, children, youth, and the elderly. As Acts 2:17 reminds us,
   > I will pour out my Spirit upon all flesh,
   >> and your sons and your daughters shall prophesy,
   > and your young men shall see visions,
   >> and your old men shall dream dreams.
4. Signs of the *voice of the voiceless* in society.
5. Signs of *equality/egalitarianism* that should exist among God's people. Because of the leveling of the *glossolalic* experience, all can receive a "word" from the Lord; "calling," "ministry," "leadership," as well as "theology" is not the province of an elite.
6. Signs of the *prophetic* and *priestly* role of the people of God.
7. Signs of *eschatological hope*.[27]

Primal Piety

By primal piety Cox notes the archetypal religious expressions that have emerged in Pentecostalism, such as healing, dreams, visions, trance, and dance.

These are seen as primeval modes of praise and supplication manifested in Pentecostal worship services.

This primal piety is strikingly expressed in the *culto* (worship service) of "Criollo" Pentecostalism, which is a highly participatory *fiesta* (celebration). As Orlando Costas notes, "the Pentecostal *culto* is spontaneous, creative, and intensely participatory."[28]

In the Pentecostal *culto* indigenous musical instruments are used, autochthonous "coritos" are sung, and time is subject to the "event" of the *culto* and not necessarily to a timetable. It is a spirituality whose creedal statement is not to be found written and read in the *culto,* but one that is verbally given in *testimonios* (testimonies, given its repetitive structure) and in sermon. Both are, in essence, authentic creeds and theological confessions of faith.

Although, a significant theological paradigm informing most "Criollo" Pentecostal churches is to be found in the "full gospel" or fourfold theological pattern: Jesus saves, baptizes in the Holy Spirit, heals, and will come again. These four christological themes define a basic gestalt of Pentecostal thought and ethos.[29] Nevertheless, I contend that the *culto* is the central expression of "Criollo" spirituality and implicit theology, thus the *locus theologicus* of any would be Pentecostal theology.[30]

To Cox's noted archetypal religious expressions one needs to add those that Steven Land calls the *psychomotor activities* manifested in the Pentecostal *culto.* These reflect spirit-body correspondence present as: (1) *raising hands* in praise, clapping to the glory of God, and extending the right hand of fellowship or joining hands to pray; (2) *dancing in the Spirit* or swaying in the "wind" of the Spirit—a form of liturgical dancing; (3) *slain in the Spirit*, that is to be prostrated on one's back, overcome by the holy presence of God, called euphemistically by charismatics, "resting in the Spirit"; (4) spontaneous *Jericho march*, that is marching around—usually inside—the church, symbolizing the falling of walls of oppression or resistance; and (5) *divine healing*, through the laying on of hands, and anointing with oil.[31]

And of course, one needs to add what Russell Spittler calls *sacred expletives*—joyful exclamations, such as "Gloria a Dios," "Cristo Vive," "Alelujah," "Amén," and so on.

Pentecostal spirituality not only touches deeply the primal piety of the person but also, by its very nature—its emphasis on the affections, *testimonios* (stories), and transrational or suprarational—appeals powerfully to the postmodern mind-set.

Primal Hope

Primal hope points to the future. It is Pentecostalism's eschatological hope—a mostly millennial outlook that insists "that a radically new world age is about to dawn."[32]

It is also a hope that informs the quest for a world delivered from racism, sexism, violence, poverty, and oppression. One, though, that in most Pentecostal cultural logic gets resolved—some would say dissipated—in the exuberant *culto* and its emotional catharsis. Although, there are signs of a significant number of leaders and thinkers who see the eschatological hope as a powerful critique of all absolutist sociopolitical structures that dehumanize.

It is important to also note that this primal hope imbues each *culto* with the expectation of the presence of the Spirit to manifest itself in a real and powerful way.

As Richard Shaull so eloquently puts it:

> People for whom the world has been a prison, many of whom are living, in a sense, on their own "death row," facing total deprivation and abandonment, enter, through the Spirit, into another realm. They find themselves in another world, an open world, in which the gates of their prison have been unlocked. It is a world in which the sick are being healed, broken families restored, broken lives put together again, and desperate economic situations often changed. . . . [This is a] concrete indication that the reign of God is already breaking into the present.[33]

I conclude with some commentary, on what could be called a fourth "P" for "Perils"; although, in reality they are challenges. At the dawn of a new millennium, "Criollo" Pentecostalism faces many challenges. Chief among these are: (1) the role of women in ministry; (2) the place of "tongues" (the debate about the initial sign of the Spirit's baptism); (3) eschatology (the challenge to dispensational theologies' hegemony); (4) ecumenism (level of participation and charges of proselytism); (5) legalism and the second *mestizaje* (the second and third generations' lifestyle/holiness); (6) a movement from a community ethic to a social ethic (one consistent with the understanding of the "liberating spirit"and justice, which raises the question of the level of political participation and the development of an "Espiritualidad Política"[34]); (7) seduction by a "prosperity gospel" and materialism; and (8) leadership development (developing a Pentecostal theology and ethic that is biblical coheres with its best traditional expressions, and is consistent with its experience of the Spirit). This means the need to develop a new cadre of theologically educated leaders with solid Pentecostal identity, ecumenical spirit, and a readiness to meet the challenges of a postmodern world.

LIBERATING PRAXIS

Religious Education in an Immigrant Community

A Case Study

Elizabeth Conde-Frazier

THE PROCESS OF IMMIGRATION

In the early arrival stage of immigration, which is the first week to six months, persons begin the process of familiarizing themselves with their new environment and they remain involved with their homeland and meet fellow immigrants. They move on to acquire new tools, learn the language, understand the customs, and, possibly, develop more flexible gender roles. They start to organize themselves in support groups. This can take up to three years.

The next several years are for continuing this adjustment in the different dimensions of their lives, and they remain linked with fellow immigrants. The following part of this journey is harder, for it involves maintaining cultural flexibility and accommodation, developing realistic expectations of the new generation, developing a positive identity, and realizing that they should expect lasting personality changes.

Last, survival needs are met, there is a reentry into the new culture, and persons are able to connect past, present, and future. This process of restabilization takes at least one generation.

During this entire process, we see a community that perhaps begins the process of entry into a new culture by maintaining a tension between trying to contain the chaos of the destabilization of all patterns of life and restabilization, a restabilization that entails the incorporation of many new elements into the remaking of new patterns of meaning-making in order to be able to accommodate their new realities. Eventually, a new cultural pattern emerges that richly combines the old and the new. Each new generation will mix the two in new and different ways so that there is both a continuity and discontinuity with the culture as it was in its country of origin.

Notice that in the process, perspective keeps changing. There is new information obtained every day. It must be incorporated in some way. This calls us to continuous re-creation of the environment or the reality we live. New skills and data must be acquired to survive. Experience and opportunities help make new information and skills accessible or inaccessible. For example, in the 1960s and 1970s, immigrants coming to New York City were being trained for manufacturing jobs, which were moving out of the city. The schools were knowingly training the young people for vocations that were being phased out as the economy was shifting to a service economy. This created great unemployment in those communities. and set in motion a myriad of problems that plague communities where unemployment is high. In this case, the experiences and opportunities made new data and skills unavailable to this immigrant community.

The type of interaction that the community has with the dominant culture is also important in this process. For example, whether a new group experiences racism and to what degree will affect their sense of self-esteem and identity or their sense of understanding of themselves in this new world, which ultimately affects their ability to progress and reestablish their lives.

Another factor that will introduce new pieces for the consideration and redefinition of the entire community is the interaction of the second generation with the new culture. How this next generation will incorporate new elements and mix them into the formation of the community may create tensions, adaptations, substitutions, and new things. All of these encounters, interactions, and incorporations involve a process of creating new knowledge in the community at a very rapid pace. To survive this, one learns to think in a conjunctive manner. In other words, we bring element A and element B, which are in tension with or contradict each other and which no one else would even think of blending, and we'll make them into a new interwoven tapestry. We're not an either-or people but a both-and community.

IMPLICATIONS FOR RELIGIOUS EDUCATION

So, how should we approach theological construction from the point of view of the Latina community in this process? What are the implications that this dynamic has for religious educators, for the understanding of God and God's action in the world, of God's call to these communities, and of how they understand their relationship with God and others in their new world? Where might one begin to look to answer this? How might our approach take place?

As religious educators, considering these questions and our own awareness of how we enter the community for dialogue about these matters helps us to consider issues related to the *voice* of the community. Mary Belenky and her associates point out that " 'voice' [is] more than an academic shorthand for a person's point of view. . . . It is a metaphor that can apply to many aspects of [a person's] experience and development. . . . The development of a sense of voice, mind, and self [are] intricately intertwined."[1]

Voice has to do with the ways in which we are connected or disconnected to the world. So let's look at something. The church is in the midst of this community. How does it relate to the schools, immigration, commerce, social agencies, transportation, and others? What tools does it need to interact?

The language barrier will affect the voice of the church in the community. The breadth of the voice of the church shapes it into a more attentive, dialogical, and caring body in relationship to its mission and in its task to relate to the needs of the world in which they now minister. Theology has to do with worldview. The connections or lack thereof with its new world will influence the theological construction of the church.

In order to play a key role in the new community, the church must construct a theology that takes seriously issues of social justice as central in its responses to the realities of these diasporic communities and for the development of a ministerial practice that addresses the issues. In order for this to take place, theological positions may need to be expanded and deepened.

DEEPENING AND EXPANDING THE THEOLOGY

It is possible for a theological position to be expanded or redefined by a change in the way one relates to the world. When one's reflection of the structural relationships in one's world is not included in the theological conversation for the formation of the leadership, this expansion cannot occur. This happens when theological education does not pose or answer questions pertaining to the context of the people and when there is no analysis of that context. Instead, theological education then becomes the accumulation and memorization of doctrinal truths that have already been formulated by those outside of our community. The educational process asks and answers questions that the people are not asking. As stated by theologian Samuel Solivan at a conference for ministry and theological reflection where Hispanic ministers and laypersons attended: "They have given us a canned theology of yesterday to be refried for today."[2] This implies that the missiology of the Hispanic church is being shaped by those outside of the Hispanic community who do not take into consideration the full context of the community where the church is located.

This results in a missiology that does not really speak to the context and a dialogue between church and community that will be undercut as will be the church's commitment to that context. This is not to say that there does not exist a relationship between the church and its context but that the relationship is affected by the limitations in the church's view of that context.

The educational resources of the Hispanic community have been informed by an evangelical tradition that has separated the church from the affairs of the world. Thus, the church can only view its mission as it relates to personal behaviors. Pietism and sin are defined in privatistic terms alone. Critical thinking, which includes a broader understanding of one's reality, is curtailed.

One way to change this concept of mission and to foster critical thinking is through the theological training of the local pastors. Any critical reflection in the local church requires the support and leadership of the pastor at some level. Soliván describes the teaching role of the pastor as emanating from his or her spiritual leadership.

> The pastor is the spiritual leader of the community, the interpretive link between God, the people, and the world. . . . The pastor as a source for theological construction and critique may function as the embodiment of a dependent model of ministry that serves to maintain the ecclesial and secular structures of oppression or as a source of support and action for overcoming the forces of injustice and dependence.
>
> The pastor . . . constitutes a most strategic venue for influencing the worldview of the community. . . . The pastor can serve as a critical hermeneutical key in redefining the questions, the tools, and the sources to be used in reconstructing a liberating response to the needs of our people.[3]

THE ROLE OF THEOLOGICAL EDUCATION IN EFFECTING CHANGE

Theological education may begin to effect a change in the missiological conception of the pastors by using the experience of persons as a theological source. Soliván places experience as a source that helps pastors to venture out from the tradition with the purpose of seeing and feeling what God sees and feels in the lives of the marginalized and neglected rather than becoming accustomed to the devastation in the communities where they live and minister. It has been the female pastoral leadership that has played a crucial role in providing a different point of view from that held traditionally by the male pastorate. For these women, the authority of their call to ministry has come through their attentiveness to their experience with the Holy Spirit in light of the Scriptures and the context of their communities. This has led them into a different truth that has stood in contrast to the tradition and, therefore, is asking new questions of the tradition.

Women have allowed this new truth to guide not only their understanding of their call to ministry but also the shape they have given to their ministries. They have provided another "entry point to new sources and insights for constructing a theological perspective that can better serve our Hispanic community."[4]

Our passion in prayer is informed by meditation and Bible study. This has been the way that women have dared to hold beliefs that differ from some of the traditions of their communities of faith about their call and about the forms of ministry. When theology has dichotomized the religious and the secular, the world and the church, women's experiences have led them to understand the scriptures in a way that prophetically moves us to go beyond those boundaries. We have sat on boards and organized the community; in short, we have taken political action. We do not articulate it that way because we are not always conscious of what we are in fact doing. We are impelled by the scriptures and by a deep love for others that comes to us in prayer.[5]

THE SOURCE OF EXPERIENCE IN THEOLOGICAL CONSTRUCTION

The role of the source of experience in theological construction emerges as an entry point for reinforming the worldview of pastors, teachers, and preachers in the church, all of whom are an important resource for informing the church's worldview and mission. This discussion recognizes experience not as a sole or more weighty source for theological construction but as one of four sources, the others being: the Scriptures, tradition, and reason. These four are in a dialogical relationship with one another.

The historical and geographical locus of the Protestant Hispanic people has changed. This change must be considered in the theological construction of the Hispanic church. The truth of the incarnation requires that the church's mission also be incarnational. Experience as a source is reappropriated for this theological task. Jürgen Moltmann reminds us that, "as the Christian church, the church must remind theology of God's people and insist on a theology which has relevance for that people."[6]

It is for these reasons that the training of Hispanic church leaders is key to transforming the missiological understanding of the Hispanic church into one that relates to all of the dimensions of the life of the community. The most accessible and influential vehicle for theological training in the Hispanic community is the Bible institute.

A major study about Hispanics and theological education, commissioned by The Fund for Theological Education,[7] showed how, in New York City alone, there are approximately six thousand Hispanics studying in about forty Bible institutes. How does this compare with other forms of theological education used by the dominant population? In the entire Mid-Atlantic area, which includes New York, there are only one hundred Hispanic students at graduate schools accredited by the Association of Theological Schools.[8] Formal theological education in its present form is not viewed as accessible by Hispanics. One of the reasons for this is reflected in the report by the President's Hispanic Education Commission, which showed that the national portion of Hispanics with bachelor degrees is 4.9 percent and that those with master's degrees is only slightly more than 2 percent.[9] The cost of traditional forms of theological education is another reason why Hispanics seek alternative options. All these factors make Bible institutes the form most used for the preparation of Hispanic church leadership.

THE BIBLE INSTITUTE TODAY

The Bible institute is an adult education model where one works full-time during the day at a secular job and studies in the evening. Classes are structured to accommodate the needs of its participants, many of whom are bivocational pastors pursuing a secular job for financial stability while serving as part-time, oftentimes unpaid, ministers in a church.[10] In this setting persons are educated while in the context of their ministry. This model provides theological training for pastors without a college education. It does so in Spanish, the first language of the participants. Each of these characteristics make the institute the most accessible theological education institution to Hispanic pastors and lay leaders.[11] Courses are designed for both the clergy and the laity, although sometimes there are courses specifically geared toward the pastors' needs. This is why the institute model is used by the Hispanic mainline churches as well.

Over the last several years I have had the honor of working with Bible institutes and together we did a study. I used grounded theory as my method of research.[12] During the study, the Bible institutes named several categories that described the nature of the dynamics of their training centers. I have selected a few of these as a way of discussing the educational approaches and epistemological principles that could be helpful for our task as religious educators in immigrant communities. Further on, I will also comment on how these centers point to directions in religious education that may be helpful to dominant culture communities as well.

MINISTRY AND INTUITIVE REFLECTION

In every time and culture, Christians are faced with how to make the message of the gospel relevant. When a people immigrate, this becomes an even more pressing task for the church, and it becomes part of how persons begin to form a worldview in their new environment. This process involves contextualization. The theological definition of contextualization refers to taking the unchanging message of the gospel and translating or relating it into a particular human situation or context. One asks and answers the questions related to what it means to be a Christian in a present time and place. The truth of the gospel then speaks into a specific context in a way that brings life to it.

Many institutes are providing the opportunity for the type of reflection about ministry and how it relates to the context indirectly. This type of reflection is taking place intuitively and serendipitously as persons raise questions about their personal and ministerial experiences in the light of the Scriptures. This usually gives way to a sharing of other experiences that reflect several solutions to the problem. Each solution may serve to raise questions from yet another perspective and so on. In the process, persons are exploring solutions to the problems in light of what they are studying. It results in a creative process of coming to ministerial action. This action is tested in one's ministry. It may reemerge in a different class discussion at which time the cycle begins once more. Persons are reflecting on how what is being learned affects what they are doing. In this sense, it is transformational learning. The only problem with this intuitive reflection is that it is not an intentional part of the curricula. Students are not tested on this emerging knowledge. It is treated as a temporary, out-of-curriculum discussion. Another dimension of the learning/teaching environment is what the Bible institutes have named discernment and what we might call *critical thinking*.

DISCERNMENT: CRITICAL THINKING

Critical thinking is integral to this type of intuitive reflection.[13] It is also an exercise in which the people are already involved every day. The evidence of this is in their survival. Every day they ask critically: "How do we survive?" At the same time that they are asking these questions in the intuitive reflection process, the texts that Bible institutes use present doctrinal data as facts with no opportunity for interaction or discussion.

If the present texts and curricula do not provide for people the chance to think critically and theologically, nor to ask their own questions, how do we intentionally prepare the leadership to propose an alternative model to the orthodox one that would affirm some of the basic doctrines of the faith while also providing theological/biblical resources for incorporating social action and justice?

AN ORTHODOX STARTING POINT

The Scriptures and the affirmation of pneumatology are an orthodox starting point in these communities.[14] The Holy Spirit is given to the church for its work and function. It gives the church the capacity for knowledge since it leads us into all truth (John 16:13). This provides the foundation for us to allow the Spirit to lead us in truth. It frees us to examine the faith. This also implies that we don't yet have all truth. It suggests an open-ended dialogical pedagogy. The truth of doctrine is not closed. Revelation, therefore, continues through the role of the Holy Spirit and the discernment of the community. The Spirit leading us into all truth requires that the truth continue to unfold before us and brings prophecy and hope. Why does the Spirit have to lead us? Why not just read doctrine? The answers to these questions come out of our very understanding of Scriptures.

The Scriptures call us to "always be ready to make . . . an accounting for the hope that is in you" (1 Pet 3:15) or to give a responsible articulation of the reasons for our faith and trust in Christ. Therefore, it is the source of the Scriptures that frees us to critique and to question. In light of this, we must take contextualization seriously. Who we are and the world of which we are a part become a fundamental departure for critical theological thinking. The exercise of asking these questions starts to model this process, for we are asking: Why? What does this mean?

CACIQUISMO/ISSUES OF AUTHORITY

Critical thinking poses problems of authority. In the Hispanic Protestant church, authority is built first on the authority residing in God, in God's revelation, the Scriptures, and then on the secondary authority, which is the tradition and our daily experiences with God through the work of the Holy Spirit. All of these factors assume that the issue of authority is placed within the community of faith. This authority is transmitted and expressed through the ministry of teaching and preaching so that the person of the preacher and/or teacher is the one vested with spiritual authority for the exercise of these gifts in the interest of the edification of the community[15] (1 Cor 12:7-11; Eph 4:11-12).

When looking at authority issues, we must consider not only the theological dimension but also the cultural and sociopolitical reality that informs these. The expression and exercise of authority in the church have been informed by a sociopolitical context of dictatorship and colonialism. This is a cultural anthropology that mitigates against asking questions. The *why* question is an unacceptable question in a culture that does not question authority and where God's authority is a received orthodoxy. We cannot simply flip over therefore and start asking questions all of a sudden.

Caciquismo and *caudillismo* are the words used by the participants to describe the model of authority that has existed in the church. The word *cacique* was the name used by the Tainos to refer to a prince, a noble, or any leading inhabitant of a small town or village.[16] *Caciquismo* refers to the tendency to have chiefs or persons in whom resides authority and therefore everyone yields to their authority, and no one questions. *Caudillismo* refers to the practice of having *caudillos* or commanders of an armed troop to whom one responds with the faithfulness of a soldier taking orders.[17]

One institute sought to handle this issue by redefining the authority of the teacher. To do this they emphasized the communal authority Paul describes in the Letter to the Corinthians. Authority is a gift of the Holy Spirit with the purpose of fulfilling God's mission. Those with the responsibility of teaching in the church must see their authority as a corporate authority. This makes the teaching/learning setting the place where the community of faith together discerns the will of God throughout the Scriptures, the tradition, and one's daily experience with the Holy Spirit in order to carry out God's will. Teachers and students become learners together in this process. The role of the teacher in this setting is no longer that of sole interpreter or keeper of the doctrine or the tradition, but of one with the responsibility for reflecting on the illumination of the Spirit. The teacher's role is now to be a model and facilitator of critical thinking; as such, the teacher models and nurtures questioning in the classroom. The truth can then be tested against the wisdom of the gathered community. This allows a nonhierarchical and communitarian epistemology to emerge.

DINÁMICA DE LA SENSIBILIDAD/SENSITIVITY

Moving toward critical thinking is a transformational experience and demands from the teacher particular sensitivity. A teacher must deal responsibly when bringing students from a place of no questioning into a place of questioning; from a place of authoritarian authority to a place of communal authority. Critical thinking and exposing persons to different perspectives can be transformational and one must process the experience itself as well as the integration of the new and the old. The very foundations of a person's life are being changed and redefined, so the teacher must be sensitive to the pace at which this takes place and to the places of disjuncture. Helping the students integrate their new perspectives with their previous ones and helping them to take action in accordance with their new understandings is part of the responsibility of leading persons into critical thinking. Jesus was sensitive to what his hearers were able to receive. Teachers in this context must therefore exercise a pastoral dimension in their teaching.

MULTIPLE CONSTRUCTIONS OF KNOWING

The student body at Bible institutes represents a wide range of educational backgrounds that extends from persons with no formal education to persons with doctoral degrees. Knowledge, or in this case knowledge of the Word, comes through gathering of the community's life together and its worship. Worship here signifies not only the liturgy but the spiritual worship referred to in Romans 12:1, which means one's lived faith. Knowledge of the Word, therefore, comes through one's everyday walk of faith as well as the liturgy and formal teaching. This knowledge does not depend on literacy alone, since it may come through the illumination of the Word in the oral interpretation, which takes multiple forms including the hymnody, *coritos* or spiritual songs, testimonies, and poetry. The Spirit gives insight not preconditioned by literacy. Recognition of this leaves open the possibility that those who have not previously received a high level of formal education may nonetheless be chosen by the Spirit to have knowledge and wisdom, and those with degrees understand that there is a source of knowledge beyond that represented by their degree.[18] This makes them open to receiving this "knowledge beyond" in the learning dynamic. This openness to a "knowledge beyond" is a door to working with the tradition in order to expand it.

In Bible institute communities, it is the leading of the Holy Spirit that takes the present beliefs and leads one into questions about the existing truths, pointing to their limits. This is the work of critiquing the tradition.

DISCONTINUITY WITH THE TRADITION

This dynamic involves both a continuity and a discontinuity with the tradition. Mary Boys indicates that the tradition exists to make transformation possible.[19] In an immigrant community, tradition is needed for grounding one in one's history, values, and beliefs. It is necessary for identity and for creating a community consensus. In the church, it honors the living faith of those who are no longer with us. Upon coming to a new context, it gives us a base from where we ask: How shall we live and express our faith in this new land? It is important to come to understand ourselves and our new situations.

Boys also gives a helpful distinction for defining tradition. She makes a distinction between the content of the tradition that she calls *traditium* and the process of handing it down which is a *traditio*. The *traditium* has shaped our faith and needs to be a part of the curricula at Bible institutes. It is the *traditio* that, I suggest, needs to be expanded to include a critical thinking dimension in order that the teaching may be more liberating and so that the tradition is not simply quoted but critiqued.[20]

To simply quote the tradition leads to legalism and the idolizing of the tradition. To critique it leads to affirmation or preservation of those elements in it that continue to be life-giving in our new situation and to change and extend its limits so that it can address the new situation. Boys borrows from Gerhard von Rad to describe this process as a reactualizing process. The prophets selected, combined, or rejected particular components of the tradition and used them in different times to bring a message to the people. To reactualize is to use the ancient traditions not to invoke the past but to see what they reveal about the present and the future. The tradition then interprets present experience and "the past speaks to the present for the sake of the future,"[21] thus creating a dialectic among the three. The tradition then becomes a living tradition that fosters liberation.

How did Jesus deal with the tradition? To look at this is to ask how Jesus as teacher approached this task. One way he did this was through the parables. The parable takes the tradition and the familiar or the consensus of the people and uses it to bring out the unfamiliar. It turns the tradition upside down. The tradition is then seen as unfinished and therefore opens up the possibility of transformation. This leaves room for exploration. It is this type of understanding that is needed for transforming the tradition. The very realities of immigration, for example, confront us with the limits of our traditions continuously. They also confront us with the traditions of a new land. As we examine these against our values, we may find that they also are in need of transformation. The traditions are reactualized in order to help us live our relationship with God, neighbor, and the creation. It is for the edification or, in the literal sense, for the building up of the community. The religious educator must maintain a tension between the continuity and discontinuity of the tradition. The continuity entails handing on or transmitting the tradition. At the same time, the very nature of the tradition requires that we critique it in order to reactualize it; hence, we teach to create a new world.

Earlier I spoke of the dynamic of intuitive reflection. I want to use that dynamic of the theological reflection of the people to introduce new elements that can serve as sources for doing theology. I am indebted to Hispanic theologian Samuel Soliván for his work in this area.[22] Allow me to briefly define the term *orthopathos*.

Orthopathos makes use of the two terms *ortho* and *pathos*. *Pathos*, in the classical Greek understanding, refers to self-alienation. Generally it refers to the experience of suffering or anguish that can result in self-alienation. In the early Christian tradition, the understanding of *pathos* was self-empowering, particularly as presented in the climax of the Christian message where God is the one who loves to the point of suffering. The term *orthopathos* makes the distinction between suffering that results in self-alienation and suffering that becomes a source for liberation and social transformation. It is looking for a way to transform human suffering into a resource for liberation.[23] *Orthopathos* is doing theology by engaging with those who suffer. Soliván names this as a conjunctive theological method. It bridges the truth claims of orthodoxy and the liberating engagement sought by orthopraxis. As such, Soliván presents *orthopathos* as a way to appropriate pathos as an epistemological resource.[24]

The pathos of the Bible institute community is found in the sharing of their journeys. These journeys represent "la queja, el grito, el dolor, el clamor de la gente."[25] People speak of their experiences of suffering and the personal and emotional dimensions of these journeys; however, when it comes to the political dimensions of the suffering or the *pathos*, these are spiritualized. This is because our Protestant missionary legacy did not permit us to speak of the political elements in relationship to our theology. Politics were separated from the sacred. Anything, therefore, that has the sense of the political is allegorized.[26] Our action is also spiritualized. We say, "Let's pray," instead of "Let's go to a march." We need therefore an intermediary language or a theological scaffold for bridging the reflection of the people and their theology. The language would integrate the political realm with the theological and would therefore help the Bible institute to make meaning out of the interplay between the religious experience and the political dimensions of their lives. When politics becomes part of the theology and the sacred it can become a legitimate Christian activity.[27]

The Bible institutes are the community of the poor engaging their and their neighbor's suffering through their ministries. In their learning process they seek to integrate correct doctrine with correct action. However, as a first-generation immigrant community, they lack an understanding of the sociopolitical and economic structures as well as critical theological tools for questioning and reinterpreting the Scriptures in light of their own experiences and insights. This prevents them from becoming orthopathic communities.

JOURNEYS OF SUFFERING AS HERMENEUTICAL INSIGHT

In order to use these journeys of suffering as hermeneutical insight, teachers at Bible institutes need to become aware of the spiritualizing dynamic so that they can point to it and help students unpack it. The Scriptures, especially the Old Testament, are a rich resource for helping us to unpack spiritualized journeys and for recapturing the sociopolitical dimensions of our lives. The stories of Moses, Daniel, Nehemiah, and Esther are just some of the passages that would be helpful toward this end.[28] Lifting up the political dimensions of these passages would stimulate discussion of parallel issues today. Another way that the institutes could lead the way in developing a communal language is to widen the language of love to neighbor.

The testimonies or faith stories and the preaching of the gospel are the people's attempts in Hispanic congregations to share a journey from alienation to wholeness. When the journey includes only the spiritual or psychological dimensions, it points to only a part of that wholeness. For example, a recovering addict may share his journey to wholeness by referring to his addiction as sin and showing how Jesus, through salvation and the power of the Word, guided him to breaking his addiction. However, he has not mentioned what drew him to the addiction in the first place. This is where issues of oppression and marginalization are found. Educators need to draw out this discussion.

This understanding promotes the next phase to which intuitive reflection needs to be moved, and that is pastoral action or praxis. Community action ministries are already present through after-school centers, AIDS ministries, drug rehabilitation programs, counseling centers, and others. Some churches are becoming involved in faith-based community organizing. Sharing the experiences and journeys as well as reflecting critically on this action will move ministerial practice to orthopraxis. It is the leading of the Spirit, characterized as orthopathic, that can move these communities from practice to praxis because it is this leading that can empower them to question and reinterpret the Scriptures in light of their own experiences and insights. Therefore, the Holy Spirit is a prerequisite for a hermeneutical shift that births a ministerial shift in Bible institute communities.[29]

SUMMARY

These represent some of the main issues of religious education in the Hispanic immigrant community and a humble offering of some suggestions for those of us engaged in the education of the church. I have shown the importance of taking seriously the historical and cultural location of persons in order to facilitate their own theologizing out of that context. I have explored a basis for a culturally responsible theological pedagogy that engages the educator and the participant in a self-conscious partnership in a process of intuitive reflection and new ministerial action.[30]

CONCLUSION

Perhaps this has been a bit interesting, but what does this have to do with non-Hispanic communities or with those who are not involved in any manner with Bible institutes? Religious education today is about how we speak about the eternal nature of the gospel and God's love in a culture that is characterized as constantly and rapidly changing. This rapid and continuous change characterizes the dynamic of immigrant as well as nonimmigrant communities. Looking at the problems of religious education in the Hispanic community serves as a case study for helping us consider educational approaches in similar contexts. How so?

We've given consideration to how to appropriate and expand the sources of authority, how to discern the context of postmodern life, and how to encourage the use of critical thinking skills. We have discussed issues pertaining to the continuity and discontinuity of the tradition and how to process new elements. As a part of this, we explored the epistemological issues raised by feminists,[31] such as the influences that shape our assumptions about who participates in the creation of theology or knowledge by discussing what the role and authority of the educator is in this learning process, the social-historical context of the knower, and the multiple ways of knowledge that function in a singular context. We have looked at how to travel from the biblical text to the text of persons' lives, and we have identified wherein lie the epistemological insights of the people in order to draw out a transformative hermeneutic. All of these offer religious educators from any community ways of understanding and carrying out their tasks.

There is another reason for presenting this discussion. Orlando Costas, dean and professor, said that the mission of theological institutions should be to prepare women and men to "lead the church in its ministry to, with and among the 'sinned-against'—the victims, the vulnerable, the poor, the oppressed, and the powerless—bringing the promise of liberation, justice, and God's Kingdom to them in word and deed."[32] Theological education is about partnerships. Religious educator Robert Pazmiño lays out a framework of a paradigm that embraces multicultural and multicontextual realities.[33] The new paradigm is a "multicultural model that assumes each contributing ethnic group can equally share their heritage with that of others in a climate of mutual respect."[34] This affirms both one's God-given ethnic and cultural identity and the identity of the other.

Last, the paradigm challenges us to take risks in exploring partnerships that will build ways to make available theological education to those who have not participated in the past. In this essay, I have presented a case study and the possibilities of new models and paradigms for religious education in communities experiencing change. I have represented their struggles and questions alongside suggested theoretical frameworks. Strong theoretical statements may be temporarily inspirational and provocative; however, the prophetic for me is in the people's striving and questioning. The very act of looking at this together is the transformative piece. Imagine for a moment that you are holding a piece of a puzzle in your hand but do not have any of the other pieces to the puzzle. Imagine yourself in a room with many others, each of whom holds one piece of the same puzzle. Like the others in this imaginary room, I have but one piece of the puzzle of a vision for religious education. You each have another piece and it is only when we come together that the full vision can emerge.

THE MANTLE OF MENTORSHIP

Ester Diaz-Bolet

Mentors are guides. They lead us along the journey of our lives. We trust them because they have been there before. They embody our hopes, cast light on the way ahead, interpret arcane signs, warn us of lurking dangers, and point out unexpected delights along the way.[1]

Mentoring, one of the oldest forms of human development, may be traced to the Stone Age when specially talented individuals instructed younger people in the arts and knowledge required to perpetuate their skills, "thus laying the foundations of the earliest civilization."[2] Emphasizing the importance and relevance of mentoring for all times, Shea asserts that "mentoring cannot be considered a fad or an inconsequential activity."[3]

The term *mentor* had its inception in Homer's epic *The Odyssey*. Odysseus, a Greek king and warrior preparing for a ten-year journey, entrusted the care of his household and the oversight of his only heir, Telemachus, to Mentor, an old trusted friend. Mentor, a caring and beneficent individual, guided, urged, protected, educated, and counseled young Telemachus in his growth from boyhood to manhood.[4]

Chip R. Bell cites two reasons why the history of the term *mentor* is instructive. "First, it underscores the legacy nature of mentoring. . . . Second, Mentor . . . combined the wisdom of experience with the sensitivity of a fawn in his attempts to convey kingship skills to young Telemachus."[5]

As people identified the special characteristics of Mentor in other persons, the word *mentor* came to refer to a person who was a trusted friend, adviser, guide, teacher, and helper.[6]

Mentoring also had a transcendental basis for the ancient Jewish nation, which regarded the mentoring function as divinely ordained and believed its effectiveness to be crucial.[7] The Hebrew word *rabbi*, meaning "my teacher" or "my mentor," serves to illustrate the importance that was placed on mentoring as the vehicle through which biblical instruction, customs, and culture would be perpetuated throughout the generations.[8]

Mentoring dyads may be found in the earliest literature from Genesis to the present. Moses and Joshua, Elijah and Elisha, as well as Ruth and Naomi are three of several examples of mentoring relationships evident in the Old Testament. Jeffrey A. Fager suggests that the mentoring relationship of Moses and Joshua seems to portray an apprenticeship model, whereas the relationship between Elijah and Elisha is a father-son model. Regardless of the model, both relationships are between a superior and an inferior. Most important, Fager underlines the utilitarian aspect present in both cases.[9]

The exploration of Canaan marked the beginning of the teacher-student relationship between Moses and Joshua. Moses gave Hoshea a new name, Joshua—"The Lord saves"—before sending him on the expedition. This was the first step in Joshua's preparation as future leader of the people. During the forty years of wilderness wandering, Moses guided Joshua. Under Moses' leadership, Joshua fought the Amalekites, and he continued to acquire the military know-how that years later he used to become the conqueror of Canaan. Joshua also served at Sinai under the direction of Moses and, ultimately, was chosen to succeed Moses. Three insightful observations are gleaned from Jim Ryan's comments on this mentoring relationship: (1) Joshua's loyalty to Moses was an important ingredient in his training as successor; (2) Joshua's faith in God was increasing and being strengthened through the mentoring of Moses; and (3) "God confirmed the benefits of mentoring when Joshua was chosen to succeed Moses."[10]

González refers to the duo of Elijah and Elisha to emphasize the awesome responsibility and privilege in being a mentor called by God. González considers Elijah's noted miracles and strong actions against injustice and idolatry as secondary in importance to the "appointment and training of his successor, under God's guidance."[11]

Ruth and Naomi portray a woman-to-woman mentoring relationship. Naomi became Ruth's mentor in the ways of Naomi's God and of her people when Ruth decidedly chose to stay with Naomi and to follow her unconditionally. Naomi's mentor role is evident again when she interprets and guides Ruth's activity in Boaz's fields; thus "Ruth acts and Naomi becomes her mentor."[12] Francisco Garcia-Treto depicts Naomi as emblematic of the "successful mentor, whose double commitment to the advancement of her protégée and to the continuation of the family tradition which contained both of them has resulted in her own needs being bountifully served."[13]

The pages of the New Testament give testimony of the Master Mentor, Jesus Christ, who used mentoring as the main method to propagate the faith he founded. Although he preached to the masses, Jesus gave himself to the Twelve. He exemplified mentoring as he lived among them, taught them by word and example, challenged and encouraged them. Jesus was their guide, mentor, counselor, companion, and friend. Jesus provided instruction and practice in many aspects of ministry through this close association. Christ also mentored Mary, Martha, and Nicodemus. It was through the multiplication of this transfer of life that Jesus sought to transform the world.[14]

A female mentoring dyad depicted in the New Testament is Mary and Elizabeth. Jean-Pierre Ruiz proposes that the lack of clarity regarding whether Mary went to visit Elizabeth to seek advice about her own predicament or to help Elizabeth during the final months of her pregnancy suggests in some ways, that "both women are mentors and both are protégés."[15]

Paul participated in a myriad of mentoring experiences during his Christian life. González points out that Paul had several mentors and identifies Ananias, Barnabas, and a group of Christian church leaders in Antioch as three that stand out. Ananias, the first Christian Paul met after his Damascus Road experience, not only introduced Paul to the Christian faith and to baptism but also was the first to speak to Paul of his call from God to tell others what he had seen and heard. Another was Barnabas who mentored, sponsored, and guided Paul at various times in Paul's life. One salient example was when Barnabas provided legitimacy for Paul at a time when many in the Jerusalem church were skeptical and afraid of Paul. Last, some of the Christian leaders in Antioch mentored Paul in coming to understand his call more fully.[16]

Efrain Agosto identifies additional instances of mentoring when Paul, the mentor, gives instructions to his protégé, Timothy, invoking "the formalities of public worship and a kind of ordination."[17] Another example of mentoring, perhaps more informal, is found in the letter to Philemon, Paul's protégé of sorts, concerning the appropriate manner to receive Paul's envoy, Onesimus. Agosto contrasts the relationship of father to son, or elder to younger mentoree seen in Paul and Timothy with the mentoring approach in Philemon as one of "brother to brother, and partner to partner."[18]

God's multiplication process may be seen at work as Barnabas mentored Paul, who mentored Timothy. Timothy mentored the church elders who, in turn, invested themselves in others. Paul mentored Priscilla and Aquila, who mentored Apollos. Paul also served as mentor to Titus, who was to mentor the church elders in Crete.[19] The principle was succinctly expressed by Paul in 2 Timothy 2:2, "And what you have heard from me through many witnesses entrust to faithful people who will be able to teach others as well."

Ron Lee Davis illustrates the biblical model of mentoring this way:

Step 1:   "I minister, you watch."
Step 2:   "We minister together."
Step 3:   "You minister, and I watch."
Step 4:   "You find another to minister with you and to mentor."[20]

Rooted in biblical principles within a solid theological framework, mentoring offers Christians the opportunity to enter "a relational experience in which one person empowers another by sharing God-given resources."[21] Mentoring involves a transfer of wisdom, information, experience, confidence, and insight from a mentor to a mentoree, facilitating development or empowerment.[22]

Sondra Higgins Matthaei, Bobb Biehl, and Justo L. González shed additional light on the role of mentoring for Christians. Matthaei introduces the phrase *faith-mentor*, which she defines as "a cocreator with God who, as a living representative of God's grace, participates in the relational, vocational, and spiritual growth of other persons.[23]

Biehl describes mentoring as a "lifelong relationship, in which a mentor helps a protégé reach her or his God-given potential."[24] He clarifies that mentoring is mostly an informal phenomenon where two people who like each other and desire to see each other succeed, help each other in a context of friendship, companionship, and correction.[25]

González specifies that mentors are individuals whom God uses to help us clarify God's call. He explains that, for Christians, the reason for having a mentor should not be to seek help in climbing the ladder of prestige or power. Therefore, González advises that it is not necessary to find an outstanding mentor, "but rather one who, even in spite of personal shortcomings, is willing to listen with us for the Word of God, and to be obedient to God's will."[26]

Reflecting further on mentoring, one realizes that the concept of mentoring was first conceptualized in the mind of God and that God made provisions for it through the indwelling Holy Spirit. The spiritual and practical dimensions of the life of the believer of Christ are guided by the Holy Spirit of God, not for a while but until the day of redemption.

Regardless of the circumstances that the believer may face, the Counselor is ever present to guide and direct the believer's decisions and actions. When the believer does not know what to do, the Holy Spirit provides the wisdom. When the believer knows not what to say, the Holy Spirit provides the words. When the believer's memory fails, the Holy Spirit engages the recall mechanism. When the believer is overtaken by weakness, the Holy Spirit ministers accordingly by praying for and interceding on behalf of the believer.

As the body of Christ, gifted and indwelled by the Holy Spirit, the believers are one in the Spirit, free to give and receive as mentors, protégés, or both, regardless of gender, ethnicity, education, or social status. Believers are called to assist in the empowerment of others along the journey. As God's Spirit mentors the believers according to their needs with the ultimate purpose of shaping the believers into the likeness of Christ, believers must answer the call to help others to decipher, clarify, and obey God's call in every aspect of their lives.

Inherent in the words of the Master, "Follow me," is the divine strategy for preparing servant leaders and followers. As imitators of Jesus Christ, Christian men and women are called to be mentors and to pour their lives into the lives of others while never ceasing to learn at the feet of the Master Mentor.[27]

Standing alongside others and sharing with them godly principles of personal growth and professional development are at the core of the mentoring experience. The call is clear; the need is evident.

The mantle of mentorship rests upon our shoulders. The Lord beckons us to follow his steps as we lead those entrusted to our care.[28]

THE VOICES OF HIS STUDENTS

Edwin I. Hernández, Kenneth G. Davis, Philip E. Lampe

INTRODUCTION

Anyone who is a successful spouse, parent, minister, colleague, and friend is a blessing. Justo L. González, however, is all that and also teacher, administrator, author, lecturer, mentor, exegete, historian, and editor. But the most apt description for him may be "educator." With pen and pulpit, through books and bureaucracy, he has been more influential in the education of more Hispanic students of theology and ministry than perhaps anyone else in the United States. Especially through his crucial work with the Hispanic Summer Program and the Hispanic Theological Initiative, he has made possible the educated opinions expressed below of the next generation of Hispanic scholars and ministers.

We gathered the following opinions through a nationwide series of interviews conducted through the generosity of the Pew Charitable Trust. This was part of the National Survey of Hispanic/Latino Theological Education. Its quantitative data and analysis is forthcoming.[1] However, the interviews generated about seventy pages of transcripts describing the qualitative experience behind that data. Although we can only present a summary of that latter information here, we hope that the generous number of direct quotations will allow these students to speak for themselves because that indeed is what the influence of Justo L. González the educator has meant, that is, Hispanics in theology can speak their own truth. These voices are gathered under the headings "Vocation," "Education," and "Recommendations."

VOCATION

From the interviews, it appears that to be most effective, a person needs support from a trusted other to discern a call from God. Most students said that a priest, minister, or teacher was instrumental in their entry into the seminary or religious studies program. In almost every case, an important person in their lives helped them decide to follow their calling and helped make them feel that they could succeed in their vocation.

> [My pastor] was a very enthusiastic person who motivated a lot of youth, and he didn't care if you [were] sixteen or seventeen. If he saw that you may have some talent for ministry, he would come up to you and say, 'You need to continue, finish high school, and then you can go to university or to seminary.' All this encouragement sparked a light in me and a desire to do just that. (Female from Dallas)

A common experience among discerning future ministers was that they were given some position of importance that made them feel trusted and capable of exercising leadership. This was often in school or in their church. Exercising responsibility helped them follow their calling to ministry.

It also appears helpful if the seed of ministry is planted early. Children should learn at an early age that it is important to aid others. Family, school, and church can plant that seed.

> I'll have to say that my influence came from an early pastor in my . . . small town in Texas. . . . this priest, through his influence, encouraged me to consider the divine work, and gave me a desire to look at the ministry. . . . it was through different people like the priests, the bishops, and especially the Hispanics that I met. . . . they encouraged me to stay in the seminary. (Male from Dallas)

If it takes a village to raise a child, one might say it takes a church to raise up a minister. Moreover, it is important to have role models, especially those who are Hispanic. It is often necessary for prospective ministers to see Hispanics in ministry before they actually consider such a future for themselves. Females say they also need female role models. Several Hispanic women stated that they needed to have other Latinas as role models. Otherwise, they sometimes feel that women are somehow less gifted than men and cannot succeed. Males seem to benefit from seeing both female and male role models.

> I don't see women [in theology schools]; there is very little women involvement there. . . . I feel I had two strikes against me: that I am Hispanic and that I [am] a woman. (Female from San Antonio)

While encouragement from others is important, it seems to be less forthcoming for those considering a celibate, priestly vocation. Families sometimes oppose such a decision because priests can't get married, have children, and carry on the family name. Vocation, a call to minister, is primary for our interviewees. Education is only a means to that ultimate goal. Many expressed the opinion that it is necessary to know more in order to help or serve better. However, education is also perceived as important in order to gain respect and to qualify for certain positions. The more education one has, the more possibilities are open to one. Paradoxically, therefore, education does not narrow the vocational choice but tends to broaden its scope.

Despite familial and church support, and role models, often whether a person enters the ministry or seminary depends on financial aid. Education is expensive, and it is difficult to work and study at the same time, especially if a person is married. When students incur debts in order to receive the required education, it is extremely difficult to pay back the loans because ministers are so poorly paid. Therefore financial considerations may keep many Latinas and Latinos from following their calling.

> The experience within the Pentecostal churches [is that] . . . students that were going to [a] school of theology . . . invest money . . . and half of the churches will not reimburse them for the money they invest in education. (Male from Chicago)

Institutions need to address the financial need of Hispanic students. One possibility mentioned is that perhaps a particular Hispanic community could pay for the education of a student with the promise that after graduation that recipient would work for that same community. Moreover, many interviewees do not know of all of the scholarships available to them. Better dissemination of such information is necessary.

> When I decided to study, we had to begin to save money wherever we could to pay for this investment. But it wasn't enough, so we had to borrow money from credit cards and from banks. (Male from Chicago)

Even overcoming these difficulties and actually arriving in seminary is not always the final obstacle. Sometimes a Hispanic student feels alone in seminary when surrounded by non-Hispanics, who often do not understand or accept him or her. In some institutions, Hispanics do not feel welcomed. Several expressed a fear that too much education may actually distance them from the people they want to serve, namely those who are frequently uneducated or poorly educated. At the same time, the realization dawns that if they did not receive sufficient education, that lack itself could hinder them from serving their community properly or to the best of their ability. Our interviewees then sometimes face a dilemma: too little education may mean they cannot serve to their full potential, but too much education may remove them from a position of solidarity with the people they most want to serve.

> The education here is out of touch with the cultural reality and the everyday church of the people by which one was motivated to study at the beginning of the educational journey. . . . they do not take into consideration my cultural, historical, and linguistic development. . . . I find myself in a contradiction because I went out of my community motivated by them to go and prepare to be their pastor, but what that means is to put myself in the hands of a denomination that wants me to prepare for a membership which is mostly white American. (Male from New York City)

Finally it was mentioned repeatedly that students need instruction and training in how to serve the Hispanic community specifically, rather than some abstract community in general. Such training must recognize that the Hispanic community is very diverse.

> I had a situation where I had to do a paper about my family of origin. I suppose that if it's my family of origin, I am going to talk about Puerto Rico. But the curriculum did not contain anything about Puerto Ricans. The books recommended for class had outdated material [about Hispanics] from the 60s. (Female from Boston)

Many students expressed a desire to serve their own community, but they may be sent or asked to serve other communities. In fact, once ordained, Hispanics minister in both ecclesial and nonecclesial situations and to Hispanics as well as to others. Wherever and with whomever they end up working, it is helpful if there is a community to give them support and encouragement.

EDUCATION

There are special difficulties for Hispanics studying in the United States if they were born elsewhere. There are differences between the educational systems in their countries and those in the United States. Our society is also different. Therefore, they have to learn new material not only in a foreign language but also in a different society and school system, both of which are sometimes perceived as hostile.

> With some of the professors I was told at one point by that I was too emotional [and] that I shouldn't be. . . . it was almost like saying you don't quite meet what we want you to be. . . . I wasn't as Americanized as well as they would have like for me to be. (Female from San Antonio)

U.S. schools tend to focus solely on mainstream society and often do not include material that Hispanic students may find relevant for their ministry to fellow Latinas and Latinos. This can be frustrating. Several students felt that students, teachers, and administrators in such schools had discriminated against them.

> I have taken classes from professors who don't integrate any crosscultural concern in their courses; the history of the church is the history of the European church and that's all. They never talk to you about your culture, or if they do they just do it in one day or half of an hour. (Male from Berkeley)

The vast majority of seminary professors are not Hispanic. Such teachers are not always open to the concerns of Hispanic students, or they may not know

Hispanic cultures well enough to answer their questions or address their concerns. They often do not show how to apply studies to everyday life and the apostolate of their Latino and Latina students. Some non-Hispanic teachers give poor grades to Hispanic students if the students have ideas or concerns at odds with those of the teacher.

> There was this incident that I still don't understand where a professor told us [not to] read this particular book. . . . I wanted to read it to see what the book said. . . . so when I wrote my research paper at the end of the course on that very same book. . . . he said, 'I am not giving you an "A" because you didn't do what you were supposed to do.' How could [he] possibly tell us about this book and then tell us not to read it? (Anonymous)

And some Hispanic students were concerned that many classes on Latinos and Latinas are taught by non-Hispanics. This is compounded by the fact that there are not enough Hispanic teachers or administrators. Without such cultural brokers, many schools are not sympathetic enough to the challenges to Hispanics (language, culture, finances, isolation).

> How can somebody be teaching what it is to be a Hispanic . . . who is not even a Hispanic? . . . [A] professor once told me he knew where [I was] coming from because he spoke Spanish. Just because you know the language does not mean you know how I live, think, or feel . . . just because you read it in a book doesn't tell you how we live. (Female from San Antonio)

Again, even successfully negotiating all these concerns and actually arriving on campus is often not enough to insure that Hispanics can reflect theologically on the experience of their own community. Schools in the U.S. often have a very limited number of books or other resources available to anyone who wants to do research on Hispanics. Libraries are inadequate.

> It's most frustrating to look at the syllabus of an ecclesiology course which mentions every other group under the sun, and not even one section on the Hispanic church in the U.S. (Female from New York City)

Since seminaries were founded for non-Hispanic seminarians and are still mainly devoted to them, Latina/o students may get lost. And because the number of Hispanic students studying in individual seminaries and schools of theology is often very small, they frequently feel quite isolated. Females are still a new phenomenon in many of those institutions, and sometimes they are still seen as threats to vocations and treated as people who should be avoided.

> The church is afraid of women, and the educational system also in general. But I think that as we sit and dialogue with these seminarians, they begin to see a dif-

ferent side of us: not as women who are hungry for men, but as women who are hungry for the love of God and for justice in our world. (Female from San Antonio)

Schools need more night classes for students who work days in order to pay for their education. And with married students, decisions about school, work, and finances must be made together with their spouses. Family responsibilities also affect work, class, and study time. Consequently some students who leave school before ordination do not even think about the possibility of other professional ministry, although they still feel a desire to serve. That is why, after graduation, there is a temptation to leave the ministry for a better salary elsewhere in order to pay accumulated bills.

Several interviewees complained that they were expected to assimilate and become Anglicized. Perhaps it would be helpful if past and present Hispanic students would get together to network: talk, support, encourage, and give suggestions. This kind of gathering could help make practical applications of theological and philosophical studies.

We are entering areas that are new territory for most of us. We need avenues for Latinos out there to support each other by dialogue about our struggles, to know that there are other Latinos who know what I'm going through. (Male from Chicago)

RECOMMENDATIONS

Hispanics have high dropout rates (in the year 2000, 88 percent of white Anglos completed high school but only 56 percent of Latinos and Latinas). There are many reasons for this, including the need to work in order to help the family. This makes it extremely difficult for almost half of Hispanic youth to think seriously about higher education for ministry. They must be encouraged to stay in school, be persuaded that they can succeed academically, and demonstrate that goal through appropriate role models and creative financial incentives. More specific recommendations from interviewees follow.

It would seem desirable to encourage (in public schools) or require (in denominational schools) public service activities. Some denominational schools (high schools and colleges) already require a specified number of service hours each year for graduation. This allows individuals a sense of responsibility, leadership, and the satisfaction of being able to help others. It gives them a taste of ministry.

Develop a program for lay ministries. I bet they would see thousands of people going for something like that. . . . There may be a point in which these individuals may be captured and want to go on to the next level. (Male from Berkeley)

Try to have at least one Hispanic mentor available at each institution that educates Hispanic students. At each school, form a Hispanic club, which could be part of a larger organization of all area schools. These could meet periodically to talk, interact, support, and so on. Alumni could be invited to join and participate. This would give Hispanic students the networking they desire.

> You need a support agency along the way. . . . when you enter Seminary, all of the sudden you're forgotten and you have no contact; there is not a friend there. . . . this will provide somebody to look to get guidance. . . like a consultant. (Female from Boston)

> A group of people that has helped me is the Hispanic caucus, a nonofficial group. . . . it's the only group that doesn't have a lot of preambles to talk about [our] problems and the realities. (Male from Chicago)

Seek sources of special funding for scholarships for Hispanic students in ministry, possibly from the Hispanic community itself.

> I'm a working man who goes to school, I'm not a student who works. That is the way it is for me in [applying for] scholarships. . . . it's very difficult to compete and to do the research that will categorize you as a scholar [with] a full time job. . . . If I want to go to school, I've got to support my family first, and that's where I'm at right now and that is one of my biggest obstacles. (Male from Chicago)

Encourage teachers to give practical applications to their subject matter, especially in reference to Hispanic communities. If this is not possible, or practical during class, a special time and place (maybe field trips) could be arranged to answer practical questions and give suggestions. Maybe a person in ministry from the Hispanic community could do this if teachers cannot.

> I [became] very close to the visiting professors who came to teach. . . . These professors were speaking to my heart . . . motivated me on a personal level. . . . Those classes that I took with those professors made all the difference to my experience. (Male from Berkeley)

Perhaps some classes could be offered in a bilingual/bicultural format. This would benefit both Hispanic and Anglo students who are not very knowledgeable about each other's respective culture and yet must interact with each other.

> I think that we need a more aggressive approach at the MA level to have courses contextualized. . . . we've had some courses that have been bilingual and interesting. . . . but we've not done it intentionally. (Male from Dallas)

Encourage and promote more personal and social interactions between Hispanic and Anglo students. Gordon Allport shows that such authority—sanctioned interaction with common goals and equal status—promotes acceptance and reduces prejudice and discrimination.

CONCLUSION

In 1988, Justo L. González published *The Theological Education of Hispanics* through The Fund for Theological Education. It was at that time that his influence really began to be felt outside the classroom and administrative offices he had so ably occupied before. The progress of U.S. Hispanics in theological education at the end of the last century was due in large part to this educator par excellence. It was largely because of his influence that we could honor him by including the voices of these students he has directly or indirectly touched.

Some of the interviewees may be considered negative. Their remarks, unfortunately, reflect the quantitative data. However, much has been done and continues do be done to ameliorate those negative experiences through the work of Justo L. González and his colleagues. Interviewees recognized this also.

> One of the things that theological education has done is challenge my faith. Because you tend to build this simplistic faith . . . but God is a mystery, and how can you simplify a mystery? . . . my education became my prayer. . . . it was an exciting adventure in faith. Every day new doors were being opened and new questions sought answers. . . . at the same time it affirmed a lot of the popular religion that I learned as a Hispanic. . . . it has taken me full circle. . . . education calls us to look beyond the beads of a rosary. (Female from San Antonio)

> [My school] is getting a good start in being sensitive to the people that are coming. . . . they took care of me. . . . I didn't know the language when I got there and they were so careful to get me a tutor, to get people to work with me. They helped all the way through so I could learn this language and I could finish my career. (Female from Dallas)

And this may be among the noblest attribute of this educator we honor. Although he himself experienced situations quite like those described by his students, one almost never hears him complain. Excellence, example, hard work, the details of administration and building coalitions, the drudgery of fundraising, these are the ways he has spent his energy. And as a consequence, the seminaries of the United States are better for all of us.

HISPANIC PROTESTANT CONVERSIONS

David Maldonado Jr.

H ispanic Protestants seem to have two questions that are inevitably asked of them: Where are you from? and When did you convert? These are questions of ethnicity and religion. What is really being asked is, Why is it that you, a Hispanic, are Protestant? Conventional wisdom has told us that Hispanics are Catholic, and if you are not Catholic there must be some explanation. The conversion question is always there.

I used to consider the question annoying and coming from ignorant or prejudiced persons. Thus, I ignored the question and denied its importance. Recently, I have had the opportunity of getting back to this question so irritating to me in the past. I no longer believe that it is irrelevant, coming from ignorant people, or unworthy of a response. On the contrary, I have come to recognize that responding to the question of Hispanic Protestantism is an important task, long postponed by many of us. The religious reality in Latin America and in this country is one in which Hispanic Protestantism demands a helpful understanding.

Although I did not convert from Catholicism (I am a fourth-generation Methodist), I am intrigued by the question of beginnings at the personal and familial levels. This involves the question of conversion. How and why did Latinos convert to Protestantism? What is their story? How do they describe it? What was the process and what were the consequences? How can these stories help us understand Hispanic Protestantism today and implications for the future? In my current research, I have had the privilege of interviewing Hispanic Protestants and have come across many stories of conversion. I did not set out to study Hispanic conversions, but I could not avoid them. They are important stories recorded in the religious memory of individuals, families, and the church. They are personal stories kept alive through *testimonios* and thus are part of the life of the church.

The question of Hispanic Protestantism has a historical response. This includes the marginal status of the northern Mexican settlements and the thin presence of Mexican Catholic pastoral leadership in the north. It includes the impact of liberalism in Mexico and the search by Mexicans for alternatives within the context of anticlericalism. But it also involves the story of Manifest Destiny, Celtic religious expression, Anglo domination, Protestant missionary activity, and the "home mission activity" of Protestant denominations. These help to understand the context and dynamics during the first conversions.

Hispanic conversions to Protestantism also call for insights to the current situation. This requires not only an analysis of the impact of history but also reflection on how the current social context defines and shapes the conversion experiences. How does the Hispanic cultural and traditional religious context shape religious life and facilitate or discourage conversion? How do socialization, social change, and acculturation influence religious conversion among Hispanics? In addition, there is the question of the individual and her or his personal life situation. What particular religious and life experiences help us understand conversion? Conversion occurs within a social-historical context, but it is also a personal experience.

Such inquiries are important, for they provide an appreciation of the social-historical context and dynamics that facilitate and shape religious conversion. They help us understand the broader social situation as more than a passive background but rather as an active environment influencing and shaping human experience and action. Factors such as contact between culturally different peoples and religious traditions, social structures and social dynamics that define status, mobility, and access, and activities of religious bodies that lead to religious contact and exposure contribute to shaping religious life, including conversion among Hispanics. But the question is still there: how was it that these individual Latinas/os became Protestant? What was the specific situation that made conversion possible? How do they describe and explain the process? Who was involved? What personal, religious, social, or other factors contributed to conversion? What were the consequences of converting to Protestantism?

In reviewing some of the current conversion and Hispanic literature, several terms presented a challenge: *denominational switching, recruitment,* and *proselytism.* The first, *denominational switching,* has been a popular term referring to changing denominational membership, especially within a family of denominations. For example, to transfer from one denomination to another within evangelical denominations or between mainline denominations can de described as denominational switching. Switching denominations is usually initiated by the individual and might involve convenience, access, or personal preferences at the time. Denominational switching may involve movement back and forth among similar denominations depending on particular situations. It does not involve a major change of religious belief, liturgy, or culture. Continuity is a major factor that facilitates switching. When applied to Hispanics converting to Protestantism, the notion of denominational switching was not very helpful. For Hispanics to join a Protestant church, the step involves major changes in religious belief systems, liturgy, and culture, in addition to religious identity. A common response to why they converted to Protestantism was the Catholic system of religious beliefs, that is, the veneration of Mary, saints, confession, the pope, and so on. Hispanic converts view the differences between Catholic and

Protestant belief systems as major. Joining a Protestant church means taking on a very different theological and religious perspective. It is not simply a matter of attending a different church.

In addition, participation in Protestant religious worship involves a very different liturgy. Converts speak of the dramatic difference between the mass and Protestant worship, especially the role of congregational singing, Bible study, and the centrality of preaching. Another common description is the difference that Hispanic converts perceive in the life of the church. They describe the intimacy and caring nature of Protestant congregations and the role of the laity. This was described as a very different congregational culture. For those converting before Vatican II, the use of Spanish was a significant difference. In general, changing from the Catholic Church to a Protestant church involved major change in religious belief systems, liturgy, and culture. This is described as a definite break from previously held beliefs and practices. It is not simply a matter of switching denominations but changing religious traditions and expressions.

The two other terms were *recruitment* and *proselytism*. The first term is popularly used in reference to the work of religious cults in the "recruitment" of members. Some literature refers to the term *brainwashing*. New members are often referred to as recruits. Although some Catholic material still refers to Protestants as "cults," this term is not helpful in understanding Hispanic Protestantism, especially among mainline traditions. *Proselytism* refers to the intentional efforts of converting persons from one tradition to another. It is an active strategy to convince persons of leaving their religious home or tradition and joining the new religious perspective and community (one denomination or tradition raiding the flock of another). These two terms connote concepts that are not always helpful. These terms suggest that converts are passive actors in the conversion experience and process. They suggest that aggressive religious advocates somehow do a "sell job" on some poor gullible persons.

Conversations with Hispanic converts suggest that many of these converts played a more active role in their conversions. They were already engaged in a process of questioning and were open to or searching for answers to various religious, spiritual, or life questions. Some had already distanced themselves from the church with a certain level of dissatisfaction and were open to other possibilities. Such situations suggest not just a predisposition or a receptive state for conversion but one in which the potential convert is searching. In some cases, converting to Protestantism was an act against a specific action by the Catholic Church or a priest.

In addition, converts speak of their acts of accepting the Protestant faith and making a decision to accept the experience of conversion. It involved an intentional decision to complete the process. They were aware of the religious, familial, personal, and social consequences. Conversion involved a struggle and required an intentional step. It was not an easy decision and was one that only they could make. To become Protestant was not a passive decision made for them. Rather, it was one with which they wrestled and for which they ultimately took responsibility.

But what is conversion anyway? What are we talking about? Conversion means many things to all of us. Its usage has included brainwashing, sudden and emotional religious experiences, salvation, rebirth, as well as rational choice, religious formation, and socialization. Although conversion is actually quite a complex psychological, sociological, and theological phenomenon, in simple terms, conversion refers to a change or transformation in a person's life, religious orientation and practice, as well as religious identity.[1] It involves private or personal aspects as well as social or public aspects. Personal aspects of conversion include matters such as personal awareness of the divine and personal religious beliefs. The individual's relationship with God is central to the conversion experience. The personal side of conversion also refers to changes in the individual such as self-understanding and the meaning that conversion and faith have for the person.

Social aspects of conversion relate to more public matters. These include changes in the person's public lifestyle. A newly converted person may change daily life behavior such as smoking, drinking, language, and other personal habits and activities. The individual may change friendships, social circles, and social activities. Another public aspect of conversion is joining a new religious community and participating in their religious activities, rituals, and life. For the convert, the public aspect of religious life may be just as important as the private aspects. The public manifestation may well be understood as the affirmation of the private experience.

Lewis Rambo, in *Understanding Religious Conversion*, suggests that conversion includes taking on a religious dimension in life when none was held, turning from one religious tradition to a new tradition and claiming a new religious belief system, and embracing a new way of relating to God.[2] It also can refer to the intensification experience or conversion within the faith.

Although his book is not specifically focused on Hispanic conversion, it is quite useful in analyzing religious change among Hispanics who have converted to Protestantism. The usefulness of Rambo's approach is his understanding of conversion as a process dynamically connected to the social-cultural context. He offers a contextual model of conversion. Within such a model, conversion occurs not in a vacuum but rather in a social context and mediated through people, institutions, communities, and groups. Such an approach opens the possibility that conversion involves a variety of factors including cultural, social, personal, and religious. A contextual understanding of conversion suggests that the context is not simply a passive setting or background for such a religious drama. Rather, the context becomes an active factor in facilitating, defining, and shaping the conversion experience. The environment creates expectations for the convert, and conversion is judged by that environment. Conversion becomes a phenomenon that is to be more fully understood as a transformation occurring within a dynamic context involving factors beyond the immediate religious setting or event. The change may be sudden, but many times it is a matter of gradual change or a dynamic process.

According to Rambo, as a process, conversion involves several stages or arenas. Although each stage may be defined as distinct in a sequential pattern, stages are interactive and may reflect more of a spiral pattern than linear. Persons may move back and forth between stages as they wrestle with the whole issue of conversion. Rambo suggests seven stages or factors: context, crisis, quest, encounter, interaction, commitment, and consequences. He also insists that any study of conversion must include the consideration of cultural, social, personal, religious, and historical factors. I will take liberties with Rambo's model to reflect with you on conversion experiences among Hispanics who have turned to Protestantism.

I want to share the conversion experiences of some Hispanic Protestant converts taking liberties in summarizing almost eighty in-depth conversations. My intent is not to provide specific cases, although that is forthcoming, but rather to share an overview of what I have heard and how these can be understood within the framework offered by Rambo's contextual model of conversion as a process of change.

HISPANIC CONVERSIONS:
FROM CATHOLIC TO PROTESTANT

Context

A. Catholic upbringing. The Hispanic converts were born into Catholic families. Their formative environments were culturally Catholic by identity, tradition, and practice. Although church attendance was not a high priority, identification with the Catholic Church and tradition was clear, though varying in intensity. They knew themselves to be Catholic. They were baptized in the Catholic Church, and many went through catechism. Attendance tended to be highest as children and dropped as they entered their teenage years. The Catholic mass did not seem to make a strong impact on most of these individuals. To be Catholic was more a matter of tradition and culture.

The family was an important context. However, the family did not seem to be a place of religious instruction or practice such as prayer, Bible study, or meditation. There were some cases where home altars were present, but these were identified as belonging to mothers or grandmothers. None of the converts reported that they participated in home religious practices. Nonetheless, they all shared a respect for their mothers and grandmothers for their religious practices. Very few could remember seeing a Bible at home. Whatever religious instruction they received was through and in the church.

When questioned on their religious instruction, many reported frustration with the content and method of instruction. It was remembered as simplistic, narrow, and unbending. Most went through catechism untouched and unchallenged. A sense of questioning and rebellion was common. In addition, priests and nuns were described as impersonal. There were some exceptional cases where parents were the instructors.

In summary, most converts describe their upbringing and religious context as Catholic, though nominal in nature. They do not see themselves as having been strong and active members of the church. On the contrary, they describe themselves as marginal to the Catholic Church. They describe themselves as Catholic by identity and culture, but marginally Catholic by practice.

B. *Social Marginality: ethnic and social context.* The vast majority of the converts interviewed were born and reared in Hispanic communities. Their social environment was culturally segregated and thus Hispanic. This is especially true of small towns and villages today and of large cities before the civil rights era. This reflects the historical context of racial and ethnic segregation and housing discrimination. In addition, most converts recall ethnic tension between Anglos and Hispanics. Such descriptions suggest social and economic marginality. The question is, how might a social context of marginality influence conversion? An old suggestion is that Hispanics seek conversion to Protestantism out of economic self-interest—that by becoming Protestant, they will have greater accessibility to economic and social mobility. There might also be the suggestion that some actively seek acculturation in order to reduce their marginality. Not one of my interviewees mentioned any economic or social benefit by becoming Protestant. On the contrary, ethnic lines and divisions continued beyond the conversion experience.

C. *Catholic-Protestant dynamics.* As residents of Hispanic *barrios*, these converts lived in communities that were not only Hispanic but also Catholic. The dominant religious tradition was and is Catholic. This means that life in the Hispanic community is shaped by the historic role that Catholicism has played in shaping the culture in those communities. Many community events, cultural activities, and interpersonal relationships revolve around the church and religious events. The social system of the community is Catholic by tradition, identity, and practice. The connection between the Catholic Church and community life is assumed as a natural relationship. To be Hispanic means to be Catholic.

In such a socioreligious context, Protestants were perceived as different, mainly insignificant, and on the margins of social life. In fact, Protestants were defined as traitors to the Catholic faith and Hispanic community. Because of their lifestyles they were viewed as hypocrites and pietistic. Protestants were to be avoided and certainly not to be seriously considered for courting purposes. To be Protestant was not a popular thing. Several persons shared stories of physical fights and rock-throwing incidents between Catholics and Protestants. In essence, the Hispanic community was split along religious traditions with a wide and antagonistic gap between Catholics and Protestants. The Protestant-Catholic dynamic was a significant environmental factor that shaped the social context in the past as well as in many locations today.

The question is, how might such a social context influence conversion? How could a Hispanic living in such a traditional Catholic community with anti-Protestant attitudes openly expressed become Protestant? One possible response is that the Protestant faith and church may have been so vilified that when persons came to see it more closely, they found that Protestantism, instead of being the evil it was described as was actually quite liberating and positive. Converts report their impressions of how the Protestant church was friendly, warm, and caring.

Another significance for conversion of such a social context is the recognition of the social and religious barriers that need to be overcome for conversion to occur, as well as the social consequences of having converted. To attend a Protestant church or religious activity, to marry a Protestant, or to allow oneself to be exposed to Protestantism in some other way, is highly unusual and unlikely. In addition, having heard the attitudes toward Protestants and observed their social status and role in the local community, becoming Protestant can be quite difficult. In addition, within a family context that has been Catholic for generations, to leave the Catholic Church may mean to lose your family. Such a social context may well discourage conversion; and if conversion does occur, it may well hold dramatic personal and social consequences.

In summary, the social context, especially with regard to ethnic and religious factors suggests a situation in which conversion to Protestantism was highly unlikely and many barriers had to be overcome. And if conversion did occur, dramatic social consequences could be expected.

Awareness of and Exposure to Protestantism

Awareness of Protestants and exposure to Protestantism can be a significant factor in conversion. Positive experiences with persons of the Protestant faith and positive contact with Protestantism can provide a receptive predisposition for conversion. This is especially true in a social context described above. Such seems to be the experience of those who have converted. For example, several individuals shared that they lived near a Protestant church and that they enjoyed listening to the music and accepted invitations to attend vacation Bible school and then Sunday school classes. These initial contacts provided positive experiences that countered the negative social context. Once an initial experience was had, attitudes changed and more contact was possible.

For many Hispanics who have converted to Protestantism, awareness of and contact with Protestants did not happen until they entered public schools. It was in this context that they met Protestant children, but this was not an issue for them at that point in their lives. Several remember Protestants coming to their homes and remember seeing their parents interact with them. Significant contact was more common during teenage years. This involved dating and friendships. Although dating across the Catholic-Protestant divide was not encouraged, personal attraction overcame established barriers. Interestingly, many attended youth church activities and found these to be positive experiences and a foundation for conversion.

Several cases involved having parents from both traditions—one parent Catholic and the other Protestant. In most of these cases they were baptized and reared as Catholics. This experience was reported as neither positive nor negative; it was just the nature of the situation. They simply went to church with one parent. Nonetheless, they report a respect for the Protestant parent for not giving up his or her religious faith.

A most interesting finding is the significant number of Hispanic Protestants whose first contact with Protestantism was through marriage. Many of these converts had unpleasant experiences with the Catholic Church because the priest would not perform their wedding ceremony. Feeling rejected by their church, they turned to the Protestant church of their partner for the wedding. Being married to Protestant partners was a means of contact with Protestantism. Alternating churches or attending both churches was tried, as well as going their separate ways on Sunday mornings. Dissatisfaction with the family being divided on Sundays led to the visitation of the Protestant church on a more consistent basis. In addition, the religious loyalty of the Protestant partner and his or her lifestyle was an attraction that led to examining Protestantism.

Most converts remember hearing the common attitudes and rumors about Protestants and observed the social treatment. They remember calling Protestants *aleluyas* and recall parental advice to find a good Catholic for a mate. Awareness of the anti-Catholic and anti-Protestant reality was part of their social context.

Sudden Conversions

Yet, conversion occurred. I begin by reflecting on some of the most dramatic stories of conversion. These are normally described as sudden conversions. Such conversions are usually remembered as having occurred at a particular time, space, and situation. The convert can tell where he or she was, the situation, and the specific feelings during and after the event. Many of these conversion events are reported to be highly charged experiences involving emotional expression that may be public. Yet, some are described as quiet private experiences. In most of these cases, conversion involves a total and instantaneous transformation. The change is immediate, and the convert becomes aware of the transformation at the very moment of conversion.

Hispanic converts have experienced their conversions in church and revival settings, in private homes, in Bible study sessions, in the hospital, during the birth of a child, because of a car accident, or while driving down the highway. Most indicated that they had no idea that they were about to experience conversion. Conversion was totally unanticipated and for many still unexplainable. The conversion experiences remain a mystery as to why, especially why them. Nonetheless, the experiences are vivid in their minds and can be described in detail. Some report feeling strange and uncertain as to what was happening to them. It was a feeling they had never known. Sudden conversions are described as a sense of being overwhelmed by God's presence and grace and leading to feelings of relief, joy, freedom, and peace. Some dropped to their knees; others cried; and some were in quiet peace.

That Hispanics also experience sudden conversion is not a mystery or the question. Our question is to understand it within a contextual model rather than strictly a psychological framework that is popular in studying sudden conversions. The contextual model does not eliminate the person or personal issues and dynamics. Rather, the person is understood within the context. Likewise, a contextual model suggests that environmental factors are important in understanding human experience and behavior. The individual is always interacting with the environment. Thus, could it be that given the depth and intensity of the religious issue within the Hispanic community, especially with regard to Protestantism, that individuals struggle with the question of accepting a different religious orientation and that the final outcome can be an explosive experience of feelings and religious breakthrough?

Gradual Conversions

Another type of religious conversion is popularly called gradual conversion. This refers to conversion as a process over a longer period of time that may take months and even years. Gradual conversion usually involves a process of rational thought and decision-making. It may involve examination, reflection, study, dialogue, and consideration of various matters. A key to gradual conversion is the active involvement of the converting person. It is not a spontaneous event that overwhelms the individual; rather, gradual conversion is a process in which the converting person may engage in the consideration of various aspects of converting including factors beyond the religious. Thus conversion is not something that happens to an individual. It is a process through which an individual works through various stages of a transformation that involves religious, personal, social, and even cultural aspects.

The stories of Hispanic conversion included many cases of gradual conversion. As mentioned above, many of the gradual conversions were associated with marriages with Protestant mates. Marriage with a Protestant provided a daily contact with a Protestant person and opportunities to explore the Protestant faith with the spouse. Likewise, it provided the opportunity to observe a Protestant lifestyle and experience the broader Protestant family and friendship circles. In the cases where the couple agreed to visit each other's churches, such agreements provided direct exposure to Protestant religious life and worship.

There were some cases in which conversion was a rational decision to unify the family in their religious life. Dissatisfaction with alternating between churches, going separately each to their own church, or not attending a church at all resulted in some Catholics deciding to join the Protestant church. Several converts indicated that they converted to the Protestant church for the sake of the family and the children. Although this may sound somewhat like denominational switching for the sake of family unity, converts shared that making the decision was not easy and that it involved much struggle and thought. The decision was life-changing.

Other cases of gradual conversion involved individuals who for various reasons attended Protestant schools such as the Presbyterian schools in New Mexico or Methodist schools in Texas. These individuals were seeking basic education, English instruction, or simply a good private education. Attending Protestant schools involved chapel attendance where they experienced Protestant worship and heard Protestant preaching. Some schools required Bible study as well. In addition, these students came into direct contact with Protestant teachers and students and were influenced through friendships.

There were some interesting cases of converts who had broken away from the Catholic Church for various reasons such as disputes or negative experiences with the priests. For example, there are many cases of Hispanics who were threatened by their priest for sending their children to Protestant schools. In some cases, a priest would not allow them to participate in baptism because their children attended Protestant schools. Disputes with priests also related to their unwillingness to perform wedding ceremonies because of a Protestant mate. Such disputes and negative experiences led many to distance themselves from the Catholic Church and to begin to question church practices and religious faith. The option was to attend the Protestant church, which eventually led to the conversion to Protestantism.

There were also cases of converts who had been exposed to the Protestant faith through long-term attendance of vacation Bible school, Sunday school, youth groups, and even worship services. Some attended Protestant churches for years before deciding to convert. These converts shared that it was difficult for them to determine exactly when they converted to Protestantism. Rather that it was a process that gradually led them to know themselves as Protestants.

In most of the above types of gradual conversion, conversion to the Protestant church involved an extended exposure to the Protestant faith and religious community. This allowed the converts to have direct contact and interaction with Protestants and, thus, make their own assessment and decision. They were able to compare religious beliefs, assess congregational life, and consider whether Protestantism was for them. In essence, conversion was up to them to decide. They could have stopped the process and returned to the Catholic faith and community. Instead, they chose to continue the process to completion. These cases also illustrate that conversion involved conscious decisions and that the convert was an active agent in the process.

Consequences Conversion

Conversion from Catholicism to Protestantism within the Hispanic context involves personal transformations as well as changes in the social life of the individual. Some of these changes or consequences are intentional and sought by the convert. Others, especially in the social realm include unintended consequences that may be quite painful. The first changes are personal transformations. These can include dramatic changes in personal habits and lifestyles. For example, many converts, especially those who experienced sudden conversions share that, at the moment they converted, they stopped smoking, drinking, and using foul language. Such habits became distasteful and undesirable. Their transformation also included an intense interest in Bible study and prayer. They began personal spiritual habits in their daily lives, a pietistic lifestyle, and a renewed commitment to the family.

Another form of personal transformation was in the realm of self-understanding and identity. They took on a theological worldview defining themselves as "saved" or as "Christian." They perceived their preconversion days as "unchristian," as being "nonbelievers, sinners, or lost in the world." Some could identify with the term *evangélico*, a Spanish term equivalent to "Protestant." Few used the term *Protestante*. Most referred to themselves as *Cristianos*, or Christian.

A second form of change occurred in the converts' relationship with their social environment. The most immediate change was with their families, most of whom remained Catholic. The initial reaction to conversion was of family shock, displeasure, and distancing. In some cases a total break occurred. Converts were cut off from their families. Family members refused to speak to or receive visits from the converts. Certainly, family members would not visit the new Protestant home. However, some indicated that, over time, relations were reestablished. However, family conversations avoided any discussion of religion or the conversion experience.

Conversion also had an impact on relations with the broader social network and context. This was especially true of friendship circles and work settings. Friends and coworkers noted the new lifestyle of the convert and responded in a variety of ways. There was some teasing especially about personal habits that were shared with the groups such as drinking. But there was also a respect for the new person. Such lifestyle changes meant many friends also distanced themselves and social contacts with the old crowd lessened.

An important change in the public life of converts occurred in the level of their participation in the life and work of a Protestant congregation. Converts became active members of the church with much interest in prayer meetings, Bible studies, and almost any activity occurring in the church. Church membership and participation became an important element in their lives. Their newly found faith, "Christian lives," and church activity became highly visible and public.

Converts are an important element within the Hispanic Protestant church. They remind the current church of its beginnings as a church founded by converts. The Hispanic Protestant church had its origins in conversion. Yet, many second- and third-generation Hispanic Protestants may not have heard the stories of conversion and the price paid by those who took this step. Converts bring new energy and high levels of commitment to the church and its ministry. They connect the current church to its religious and social history.

In today's commitment to ecumenical interests, conversion can be a disputed topic. This is true if conversion is defined simply as "denominational switching" or "proselytism." However, conversion also involves the exciting discovery of religious faith and the transformation of people. Hispanic conversion to the Protestant church does not have to be anti-Catholic. On the contrary, conversion is the experience of people who have found the power of religious faith and its ability to transform their lives. This is not an exclusive message of the Protestant church but one shared by all Christian churches.

LATINA/O THEOLOGY: SHIBBOLETH OR SIBBOLETH?

A NEW ACCENT IN THEOLOGY

Jesse Miranda

The February 8, 1999, issue of *Christianity Today* contained an article about five young theologians who represent the dawn of a new era. These new theologians, one of whom was a woman, were considered "new" because they bring to the theological discourse new issues and paradigms and refuse to work within the paradigms inherited from their academic progenitors. Their fresh approach to old issues, the article goes on to indicate, is "[signaling] a discernible and surprising shift within the fields of biblical studies and theology."[1]

What is not mentioned in the article is that the boundaries of this "shift" are now beyond the borders of North America. The shift in theological discussions is considered a "new reformation." The traditional Eurocentric camp is no longer the dominant voice of the theological discourse. According to Justo González in his book *Mañana*, "This reformation is arising, like that of the sixteenth century, in the periphery of Christendom—in the Third World and among minorities in the traditional centers of Christianity."[2]

In essence what is being said is that Third World theology is now likely to be the representative Christian theology. The voices that formerly were excluded are now being included in the theological discussion. And the accent of theology is likely to move from an exegesis of the text to a "cultural exegesis." This, says Bill Dyrness, dean of the School of Theology at Fuller Theological Seminary, means that "the center of gravity of Christianity has shifted from the Western world to the Third World."[3]

There is a story in the book of Judges (12:1-7) where the men of Ephraim and the men of Gilead, even though they were brothers, go to battle against each other. It accentuates the division of community, the creation of new boundaries, and the use of language for political expediency. It is a case of failure to communicate with each other. It is also a reminder of the new challenges that face the Christian church in the new millennium, in particular, in the area of theology where the language and content of theological discussion is changing.

The purpose of this chapter is to explore the dimensions and implications of these new theological discussions from a Latina/o perspective and interpret its meaning to the Hispanic community in the United States. Justo González is among the leading voices from the religious and ethnic minority perspective that bring *the new accent* and nuances to the theological discussion.

Of the many contributions González makes to a theological discussion in the global arena, two contributions are especially significant. The first is the reminder that "the church is by definition a community. . . . the best theology is . . . communal."[4] The second is to dissect the main foci of the Hispanic American identity and reality into the social focus and the cultural focus.[5]

THEOLOGY AS CONVERSATION

Theology is the orderly presentation of the experience, belief, and understanding of God. And if the best theology is communal, as González states, then the theological discussion is at its best as a conversation of the community. The *Diccionario de Sinónimos Castellanos* explains "La conversación es la palabra de la familia y de la sociedad" (conversation is the word and property of the community).

In modern times the theological task and presentation has been a unilateral conversation among a homogeneous and elite group of intellectuals of Eurocentric, white male orientation. But the dynamic growth of Christianity in the Third World has given its scholars a voice, which offers an opportunity of a more coherent theology with a global and relevant thrust.

Globalization, as this challenge has come to be known, is the issue at hand, and the call to globalize theological conversation is an important goal. Hispanics are now coming to a position to contribute to a constructive theological conversation and toward the creation of a more coherent global theology. The challenge is in the creation of a common theological vocabulary and the articulation of our deepest experiences of the gospel story.

The suggestion I am making is to use the story form to understand and communicate our story. Story is the primary way that God chose to give us God's revelation and the primary literary form for receiving that revelation. From beginning to end, the Scriptures are primarily written in the form of story. The reason that story is so basic to our human nature is that life itself has a narrative shape—a beginning and end, plot and characters, conflict and resolution.

Here are two such stories that relate to the two salient issues of Latina/o Christians: exclusion and inclusion, oppression and liberation. More important, both of these stories serve as the content for the discourse analysis of the theological task and for a conversation with the global community.

THE STORY ABOUT A
CONVERSATION AT THE WALL

A dramatic encounter between the Assyrians and Judah as described in 2 Kings 18 is the story of the conversation at the wall of the city about the terms of surrender of the community behind the wall. In the story the common people speak a different language from that of the ruling powers and dominant people at the wall. In this text the Hebrew, not Aramaic, is the public language of international diplomacy. It is the language of the wall. When that language is spoken to the community behind the wall, it not only is a foreign language but also serves as an act of intimidation. Ultimately, the saving of the city takes place as Yahweh intervened in the mismatch between a ruling power and a tiny kingdom without the communication skills and visible resources to succeed.

Language, like walls, serves to include or exclude people, oppress or liberate, as this story reveals. By *language* is meant the cultural focus and the values and standards associated with a people's identity. Language becomes symbolic of the issues of power and position of the people.

The deeper issue is regarding the worldview, the basic philosophy of life. A conquest imposes not only the institutions of the conqueror but a new worldview. The ideas, logic, art, customs, language, and religion of the conqueror are forced into the life of the conquered, which results in a total conquest. There is an old saying: Those who tell the stories rule the world.

The language of Western theology has had the dominant and ruling power in the theological enterprise. Its preferred tools for theological inquiry have been the scientific method. It values a reasonable Christianity, a sure knowledge explained with precision and descriptive certainty.

On the other hand, Latin Americans, and to a lesser degree U.S. Latinas/os, have been talking with each other, developing a local theology. Because of their situation in a more diverse and complex world they have learned to use the tools of description and analysis of social scientists. For this reason they tend to reflect more on the actual social and even the economic situation of people when doing theology.

Here are some of the dimensions and the distinctions of each of the languages of the competing voices in the theological conversation. Divided into the old and new, this is how they differ.

An Old Language	A New Accent
Traditional	Periphery
Western	Third World
Emphasis is on knowing	Emphasis is on doing
Influenced by Greek philosophy	Influenced by the social sciences
Critical and analytical	Descriptive and interpretive
Observer's point of view	Actor's point of view
Cognitive and reflective	Practical and symbolic
Propositional	Narrative
Reflection precedes practice	Practice precedes reflection
Critical	Situational

This is not to say that the propositional form for expressing theological truth in the tradition of Western theology will cease to exist. Neither is it to say that critical skills will be replaced by more descriptive ones. But it does mean that Western theology, as it is known today, will change. It is likely to become more descriptive and less normative, more practical and less academic. More important, the theological imperialism—a product of the exaggerated individualism that González mentions[6]—will be replaced by a more coherent theology with a global and relevant thrust.

THE STORY ABOUT A CONVERSATION AT THE WELL

One day Jesus left the Judean countryside and went back to Galilee. But to get there, he had to pass through Samaria. He came to Sychar, a Samaritan village. The fourth chapter of John narrates the story of Jesus' conversation with the Samaritan woman at the well. This is a story that is as dramatic as it is deep. Especially if it's read with a historical-cultural lens, in which case Samaria becomes a paradigmatic community.

First, Samaria is a story that is a symbol-image of a new creation. Abraham, Jacob's well, and Mount Gerizim, which are in the content of the conversation, were the symbolic institutions of the Samaritan identity. This historical-cultural symbolism was an authentic basis for dialogue and exchange and opened up a new possibility of ending the centuries of silence. The commonness of a single human family out of Abraham and the underlying theme of the unity of the human race becomes a connecting tissue. The synthesis of the religious symbolism of the Samaritans and those of the Jews into a single coherent symbol-image ushered in a new, shared experience. In the end, Jesus touched the deepest recesses of this woman, and she became a new person.

In a Quaker meeting one man broke the silence of the meeting to speak of the great experience of meeting across language, racial, and religious boundaries and of the wonder of being able to reach across the barriers and touch another human being, the turning of strangers into friends.

Then Martin Buber, a Jewish scholar, stood up. Buber said that meeting another person was a great thing, but not the greatest thing. "The greatest thing any person can do for another is to confirm the deepest thing in him, in her— to take the time and have the discernment to see what's most deeply there, most fully that person, and then confirm it by recognizing and encouraging it."[7] Thus, because of the Samaritan woman and the good Samaritan stories, Samaria is symbolic of the threshold of a new encounter and new possibilities in biblical history.

Second, Samaria is the story of the tragedy of exclusion and the thrill of inclusion. The Samaritan story is symbolic of the historical rift between people because of their differences, be they because of race, ethnicity, politics, or religion. Samaria is that frontier region of human discord whose people became the historical agents of a new unity, God's new society. The pain of having been excluded by others and the joy of having been included into the kingdom was what was most deeply felt by the Samaritan woman when she was delivered from religious and cultural captivity.

The problem of ethnic and cultural conflicts is part of a larger problem of *identity and otherness*, which merits a central place in theological reflection on social realities. Richard J. Mouw, writes in his book, *Uncommon Decency*, the cultural diversity "is not so much diverse *views* of reality as diverse *viewings* of the world. . . . Our outlooks are shaped by such factors as ethnicity, race, geography, . . . economic status and gender."[8]

Finally, it is a story of liberation and transformation that begins with a conversation. Samaria represents the discovery of the liberating gospel over and above the social and cultural identities of its people. As González reminds us, although the process of cultural awakening is a positive development, such awakening of culture is to be equated with the liberation of God.

The conversation at the well introduces us to the fluidity of identities and the reversal of the thought categories between Jews and Samaritans. It represented a reversal from Jewish religion to God's spirituality and a reversal from a provincial identity to a global community. It was in essence a missiological shift. Jesus' visit to Samaria symbolized the shift of attention from the mission to Israel to the global mission as it was to be carried out later according to the book of Acts.

The progression of the gospel is a story that crosses from Jerusalem, Judea, Samaria, and to the ends of the earth (Acts 1:8). Jerusalem was the place of law and religion and the sphere of judgment (righteousness), the place of right knowledge and proper order. Judea and Galilee were the places of identity and racial variety, the places of revelation and compassion.

Samaria, however, was the place of engagement with cultural diversity, the intersection of thought and action, theory to practice. Here is the place for *doing* the right thing. This not the place where description of what is wrong and saying the right thing is the standard of excellence; but rather Samaria is a place for improving, in a very intentional way, the human condition regardless of gender, class, citizenship, and ideology.

The ideas about identity have changed for some Hispanic Americans. Although identity is still a salient theme, there is a move to go beyond identity issues to dignity, productivity, and unity issues in their theological journey. The generation of Latina/o students in seminary today is four decades removed from the civil rights movement and has different views on social issues. This generation of Latinas/os is also two decades removed from the "christening" or naming of their raza. "What took you so long?" they ask. And, "you are still not certain what we should call ourselves?" "Am I Hispanic or Latino?" "Am I Latina/o or Chicana/o?" The answer goes something like: "Whatever, mija." "Solo Dios sabe, mijo." "What's in a name after all?"

David Abalos, a young scholar, says "names and concepts belong to us as a people and as individuals. . . . We choose to rename ourselves or to change its significance, because we have come to a different and better understanding of who we are."[9] Abalos continues,

> For example, *la comunidad Chicana* has as one of its battle cries, *Que Viva la Raza*. But the meaning has dramatically changed. In the 1960s and 1970s, it was a defiant cry that emphasized our nation, culture, and history in an exclusive manner. But we have matured politically, and so now we can go beyond the confrontational to the inclusive, wider, and deeper meaning of our humanity by asserting that anybody from whatever background who cares deeply about our people and all people is a member of *La raza*.[10] (Excerpts reprinted with permission of *The Hispanic Outlook in Higher Education Magazine*, no. 9, vol. 17, 1999.)

Why this progression? Is it because of a better understanding of who they are, as Abalos points out? Is it a case of what González calls "innocent history,"[11] that is, the selective forgetfulness used by Euro-Americans to avoid the consequences of a more realistic memory?

Let me introduce the idea that this new generation is dichotomizing that one single entity of Hispanic identity and disembodying our *mestizaje* to view its social-cultural facets more fully and distinctly.

GALILEE TODAY, SAMARIA MAÑANA

The Galilean journey is a well-known topic among Hispanic Americans. Writers such as Orlando Costas, Virgilio Elizondo, and Justo González have taken us through Galilean landscape and as Hispanic Americans have had a déjà vu experience of our social and cultural reality. As marginalized people we Hispanics have in the concept of *mestizaje* the substance of our identity.

Without changing the substance it is possible to cut facets of our *mestizaje*. González helps us dissect this reality when he draws a distinction between the social focus and cultural focus of Hispanic identity. He says the social focus is something we share with many others, while the cultural focus of Hispanic identity is exclusively our own.[12] The cultural focus of our identity is Spanish language and its set of values, while associated with the social focus is education, employment, politics, and so on, with which we participate with those outside our community. Another example he gives for this dissection is when he states, "the soul and the body are not two different parts of a person but rather the same person as seen from different perspectives."[13]

In the same manner, Galilee and Samaria are not two different experiences of our Hispanic identity but are rather "differing viewings" of our reality, to use Mouw's term. Moreover, Galilee and Samaria are two distinct localities on the underside of theology that help us to articulate the dialectics of a social-cultural identity seeking to be whole and heard.

The following chart outlines the theological dialectics of Galilee and Samaria and a constructive symbolism for theological conversation.

Discourse of Analysis	
<u>Galilee</u>	<u>Samaria</u>
Nature	
Theological	Missiological
The faith of Abraham	The family of Abraham
Monotheism	A universal race
Historical Significance	
Jesus begins ministry to the Jews	Jesus begins mission to the world
The hotbed of nationalism and revolution	The launch site of global outreach
Geography	
In Palestine: farthest point north	South of Galilee
Open fertile land	Forbidden wilderness
Lakeside and mountain ranges	Dry and arid land
Wealthy province	Poor province
Populated by foreigners	Prohibited land
Crossroads of the world	Off the beaten path
Encircled by non-Jewish nations	Surrounded by the Jews
People Characteristics	
Jews	Gentiles
Chosen People	Outcast people
Circumcised	Uncircumcised
Open to new ideas and influence	Defensive and hostile
Highlanders	Low life
Inhabited by foreigners	Rejected as foreigners
Mixed population	Mixed bloodlines
Essence	
Reflection	Action
Repose	Motion
Distinctives	
Legitimization	Authentication
Category or class status	Ancestry or bloodline
Provincial	Universal
Sterile	Reproductive
Rhetoric	
Rank and order	Caste and pedigree
Group	Race
Grade	Line
Division	Descent

The U.S. Hispanic story, as the Samaritan story, is a narrative that needs to be told by the whole church and not just a part of that community. It was the Samaritan factor that a complacent early church needed to meet the challenge of a competitive and pluralistic society. It may well be that the contribution of U.S. Hispanics to the theological conversation can change the script of the present theological conversation to help create a more coherent global theology for future generations.

Liberative Educational Practice

Reassessing Educational Configurations

Robert W. Pazmiño

Back in 1988, I wrote an article, which Dr. Justo González graciously accepted for publication in *Apuntes*, that explored the realities of multicultural education from the perspective of the North American Hispanic community. The article was entitled "Double Dutch" in relation to the rope game that involves the tandem interaction of two ropes.[1] These ropes were suggestive of the balancing of two cultures required of Hispanic persons in the United States navigating between diverse cultures in the formation of one's identity. Hispanics seek to affirm both Latina/o culture and North American culture that can be creatively balanced to form a distinctive blend. Implicit in that earlier analysis was an assessment of educational configurations that Hispanics confront in terms of exclusion, devaluation, and perceived deficiency in relation to the differences from the dominant culture of the United States. With the passage of time reassessment is required. Have the educational dynamics for North American Hispanics changed? Has the landscape shifted significantly? Has the notoriety of such Latina/o entertainers as Ricky Martin and Jennifer Lopez in popular culture signaled a shift in the educational culture of schools, communities, and churches to allow for liberative practice among Hispanic persons, among all persons?

Before assessing an educational configuration, one needs to know what one is. An educational configuration is a cluster or network of agencies that pass on a culture or educational content to persons. This concept was fully developed in the pioneering work of the educational historian Lawrence Cremin. Cremin's creative recounting of educational history in the United States in the colonial (1607–1783), national (1783–1876), and metropolitan (1876–1980) periods provide perspective for the task of reassessment.[2] From the work of Bernard Bailyn in *Education in the Forming American Society*, Cremin identified the four educational agencies or axles in colonial settings to include the home, the church, the community, and the society.[3] In the national period, the additional educational agencies or institutions that emerged included the schools and a host of voluntary associations like libraries, museums, and child advocacy or support groups like the YMCA and YWCA. During the metropolitan period, the rise of the body politic and the media is noteworthy. The media include newspapers, radio, film, books and periodical literature, television, and computers with a host of multimedia combinations such as the Internet. The relationships and interactions of these various agencies or institutions represent an educational configuration. Cremin's shorthand for describing these relationships is that the agencies confirm, complement, and/or contradict one another and have varied impacts upon individuals in particular communities dependent in some ways upon their distinctive learning styles and personal histories. While this calls for the recounting of personal educational histories, educators can assess the shifts in the larger educational plates of a society just as geologists study the shifts in tectonic strata and substrata of the earth. The relationship between education and culture with specific reference to Latina/o culture is warranted in that education can be defined, as Bernard Bailyn suggested, as "the entire process by which a culture transmits itself across the generations."[4] This process of education is described in both Deuteronomy 6 and Psalm 78 where children and youth receive the educational heritage from their families. For Hispanic persons this process of transmission becomes particularly challenging when the dominant culture demeans or devalues Latina/o culture and has done so systematically over time with the dominance of Northern European American values and perspectives. The response to this history of oppression is to seek for a liberative praxis that fosters hope. Hope is imagined in teaching and learning encounters where the identity of Hispanic persons is affirmed and their contributions to the wider public life is welcomed. Educators have identified this hope in relation to the need for educational equity in practice. I define this equity in terms of access to educational resources, respect of difference, space to be heard, the presence of appropriate ethnic role models, and shared power and authority.[5] It is with these particulars that an assessment of the educational configuration of Hispanic persons is undertaken. These same criteria can be considered in assessing the educational experience of other identifiable cultural groups in the United States and other nations globally.

Before reassessing the educational configuration for Hispanic persons in the United States, educators can identify distinctive values we embrace. Ones that I would affirm include a stress on relationships, passion, and a cultural mix that emerges from the blending of cultures and persons in familial and communal life. From the educational experience of living on the margins, Hispanics may also embrace posing questions, seeking alternatives, and searching for a common table that will accommodate all in educational practice. These emphases naturally emerge from the experiences of oppression and injustice shared with other marginated peoples globally. The Puerto Rican missiologist Orlando Costas described these experiences of marginalization in *Christ Outside the Gate*, where Jesus himself in his earthly ministry identified with those forced to remain outside society's acceptable circles.[6] In addition, Hispanic persons in comparative studies as cited by Norman Wilson tend to be identified as "field dependent," which means they "rely to a great degree on their peers and surrounding environment to help them make sense of their experiences." Hispanic persons also "tend to be more emotionally responsive and empathetic to others, as opposed to detached, aloof, and reflective. . . . Field dependency also is generally accompanied by a more holistic and visual approach to reality as opposed to an analytical and verbal orientation."[7] This field dependency notes general tendencies and cannot be used to assess all individuals denying their personal qualities and differences. Nevertheless, field dependency implies the need to allow for the formation of a sense of community and dialogue in liberative educational practice. Such practice would also allow for emotional expression or intelligence and avoid a celebrative reluctance that can typify too many educational experiences devoid of joy and enthusiasm. With these values, educators can assess the various educational agencies of contemporary configurations that include the media, schools, families, communities, churches, the economy, the body politic, and various voluntary associations that include a host of organizations that have emerged in the last twelve years. In any particular local community the nature and interaction of these various educational agencies or institutions will vary. Each agency or institution has a curriculum that operates either in explicit or implicit ways. The attempt here is to assess in broad generalities what shifts have occurred, if any, since 1988. My particular context of New England, with roots from New York City, have an impact upon my perceptions along with my own cultural heritage. My heritage is Ecuadorian from my father's heritage and Puerto Rican through marriage to my wife and adoption into her home community and congregation of East Harlem during my formative young adult years.

MEDIA

Beginning with an assessment of the media indicates the importance that various media play in the educational experience of children and youth today. As compared with the number of hours the average person spends in elementary and secondary schooling, media viewing generally surpasses those numbers significantly with no vacation time from their influence. In relation to the media, one notes the significant increase in the availability of Spanish language television programming and periodical literature designed for the Hispanic population. When my father's family first arrived from Ecuador in New York City in 1900, their business ventures included a pictorial magazine and radio station in Spanish. There was not a sufficient Spanish-speaking population in those years to sustain such ventures. Today my sixteen-year-old daughter is able to affirm her identity through monthly viewing of *Latina* and *Hispanic* magazines and to celebrate the contributions of Hispanic persons featured at the national ALMA

(American Latino Media Arts) Awards. The National Council of La Raza presents these awards, which celebrate the positive portrayal of Latinas/os in film and television. For the generation of my son, there is the new publication of *Generation Ñ* that parallels interest in Generation X from the wider culture. All of these developments can be affirmed in bringing before the public awareness the realities of the North American Hispanic community. The most visible impacts have occurred through the emergence of Hispanic artists in the fields of music and the arts. When the heroes and heroines of the wider culture can be persons like oneself, hope for honoring one's gifts and talents is fostered. The rise of Hispanic entertainers is significant if one considers the public educational advocacy of persons like Edward James Olmos beyond his portrayal of Jaime Escalante. But challenges remain to foster greater positive portrayal of Hispanics and greater representation in various media.

SCHOOLS

In the case of the schools, the situation is more problematic as compared with the media with the high drop-out rates for Hispanic youth and significant gaps in the academic achievements of Hispanic children. Whereas the percentage of Hispanic children in elementary schools has increased, a corresponding increase in the quality of the schooling and the presence of Latina/o teaching staff to serve as role models has not kept pace. The gaps require coordinated efforts at the public policy level along with community participation sustained over a number of years to make a difference, especially in urban settings. Creative leadership that sees beyond the current trend of stressing outcomes and competencies to realize transformative educational experiences for all children and youth is required. Education needs to become a national, regional, state, and local priority, and the political support may not sustain such when increasing numbers of children are Hispanic and other "persons of color." The need for educational equity continues to be an issue as the Hispanic population enters communities outside of urban concentrations and rises through the middle class. This rise of some cannot be at the expense of the vast host of working-class Hispanic families. These families struggle each day for survival and a sense of dignity. Education has historically provided a vehicle for a better life; and the elementary, secondary, and higher educational systems need to become user friendly for increasing numbers of Hispanic students.

FAMILIES

Hispanic persons highly value their family connections and nurture others beyond the nuclear family preoccupation prevalent in the dominant culture of the United States. Family connections support persons struggling for survival in what can be an alien culture for first-generation immigrants. The realities confronting second-generation Hispanics force them to contend with the need to retain one's primary identity amid pressures for assimilation in the dominant culture. Historically the dominant culture assumed that Hispanic persons would no longer embrace their cultural distinctives. Fortunately, Hispanic culture has fostered a sense of being both-and persons who can be both Hispanic and North American. Family connections make possible and nurture Hispanic cultural ties that serve to sustain persons. The challenge for the third and subsequent generations is to remember what some second-generation folk may have forgotten. The pressures to forget cultural distinctives come with the effort to make it economically and to be accepted socially and culturally in various communities of the United States. The extended family roots provide the necessary corrective. However, the health of families in terms of economic, social, and spiritual viability requires the support of both public and private sectors in policy and programs that honor Hispanic distinctives.

COMMUNITIES

The health of communities where Hispanics live, work, and contribute is related to the dynamics I name as huddling and mixing. In huddling, Hispanic persons themselves gather as a community by choice or for survival to foster a sense of identity and solidarity. In huddling, common bonds and causes are identified, and persons organize to address corporate needs and demands. In mixing, Hispanic persons form bridges and alliances with non-Hispanics to address broader communal and societal issues. Life in a multicultural setting calls for both processes of huddling and mixing. With the diversity across the Hispanic community, huddling has brought challenges for leadership and the identification of a broad agenda that honors the variety of voices and perspectives. Despite the differences among Hispanic groups and persons, joint efforts have been forged in the last several years. The complexion of mixing has also taken new directions as the numbers of Hispanics in the general population have increased with projections of being the largest minority group within the next several years. The health of the communities where Hispanics live varies greatly at the local level; and the task still remains of forming alliances across communities on the state, regional, and national levels. One dimension of mixing that calls for attention by Hispanics is communication among various generations themselves. However, the value of extended family finds broader expression as the community is embraced as a gathering of extended families seeking a common good.

CHURCHES

Hispanic persons are noted for their countercultural spiritual and religious affinities in an age of disbelief.[8] The vitality of churches that honor the use of the Spanish language and/or affirm Hispanic cultural distinctives is a testimony to their religious roots. In relation to the emergence of Hispanics on the national level in the United States, a new challenge for Hispanic churches, congregations, and parishes is in the area of public theology and advocacy. This challenge is related to the dynamics of huddling and mixing. The prior huddling is essential to form a sense of identity and solidarity, but a wider public role calls for a mixing that brings Hispanic distinctives to the multicultural table set in the public arena. The Hispanic church in the life of the public calls for a broader agenda in addition to the tasks of survival. Survival requires the perspective of hope, but also of courage in engaging public encounters. Such public encounters will require the expression of outrage for what many of our people confront each day of their lives in trying to survive with dignity.

THE ECONOMY

Economic realities impinge upon the access to educational opportunities and the ability of folk to thrive with the opportunities made available to them. When Hispanic families hover at the lowest levels of the economy, questions must be asked regarding the complex of forces that work against their improvement. The relation of economic realities to education along with health and other basic services points up the contradictions of the system intended to serve all. The periodical *Hispanic Business* appropriately celebrates the contributions of Hispanic businesses and persons within the wider economy. Next steps require the economic empowerment of those marginated from advances up to this point in an expanding national and global economy.

THE BODY POLITIC

Political life has direct impacts upon educational policies, programs, and practices. The aims of education in some settings have embraced the hopes and distinctives of the Hispanic community because of political action. Whereas multicultural emphases have expanded some horizons, the impact of "English only" initiatives have squelched an openness to the difference that Hispanics offer at a common table. Some political efforts have brought increased representation of Hispanics among teachers and educational administrators, however much more remains to be accomplished to gain equity. The future may not hold too much promise with the movement away from affirmative action as a way to sustain diversity. Further assessment remains to be completed regarding the impacts.

VOLUNTARY ASSOCIATIONS

One very positive note to celebrate has been the rise of associations and organizations that have served to link Hispanics in various fields and the advocacy made possible by these efforts. In the religious area, this has included cooperative efforts among Catholic, mainline Protestant, and various Pentecostal groups. The legacy of Justo González includes his leadership among theological educators in forging several of these associations that continue to make a difference, including the Hispanic Summer Program, AETH, and the Hispanic Theological Initiative.

CONCLUSION

This chapter has explored liberative educational practice in relation to a reassessment of the educational configuration experienced by Hispanics in the United States. Such assessment is required by each faith community globally in working toward the fulfillment of the values of God's kingdom expressed in relation to educational equity for all persons created in God's image and worthy of care and respect. Liberative educational practice requires that attention be given to all the dimensions of educational configurations. This perspective affirms all of educational life as a concern to God and those who seek to serve God through their teaching ministries. This has been exemplified in the life and ministry of Dr. Justo González.

THE PUBLISHED WORKS OF
JUSTO L. GONZÁLEZ

Compiled by Catherine Gunsalus González

I. BOOKS AND MONOGRAPHS

Translations of González's works are included as separate items only when done by González himself. A number of these are also adaptations by the author to a different audience.

1. *Revolución y encarnación*. Río Piedras, P.R.: La Reforma, 1965; second edition, 1966.
2. *Desde los orígenes hasta el Concilio de Calcedonia*. Vol. 1 of *Historia del pensamiento cristiano*. Buenos Aires: Methopress, 1965; second edition: Miami: Caribe, 1992.
3. ed., *Por la renovación del entendimiento*. Río Piedras, P.R.: La Reforma, 1965.
4. *The Development of Christianity in the Latin Caribbean*. Grand Rapids: Eerdmans, 1969.
5. *From the Beginnings to the Council of Chalcedon*. Vol. 1 of *A History of Christian Thought*. Nashville: Abingdon, 1970. A translation and updating of number 2 above. Ten printings to 1984. Second edition, 1987. Korean translation, Seoul, 1988; Chinese translation, Nanjing, 2002; Portuguese translation in process.
6. *Historia de las misiones*. Buenos Aires: Methopress, 1970.
7. *Ambrosio de Milán*. San José, Costa Rica: Centro de Publicaciones Cristianas, 1970.
8. *From Saint Augustine to the Eve of the Reformation*. Vol. 2 of *A History of Christian Thought*. Nashville: Abingdon, 1971. Nine printings to 1985. Second edition, 1987. Korean translation, Seoul, 1988; Chinese translation, Nanjing, 2002; Portuguese translation in process.
9. *Desde San Agustín hasta las vísperas de la Reforma*. Vol. 2 of *Historia del pensamiento cristiano*. Buenos Aires: Methopress, 1972; second edition: Miami: Caribe, 1992. Same as number 8 above.
10. *Jesucristo es el Señor*. San José, Costa Rica: Caribe, 1975. Reprint: Miami: Unilit, 1999.
11. *Itinerario de la teología cristiana*. San José, Costa Rica: Caribe, 1975. Reprint, 1979.
12. *From the Reformation to the Present*. Vol. 3 of *A History of Christian Thought*. Nashville: Abingdon, 1979. Six printings to 1984. Second edition, 1987. Korean translation, Seoul, 1988; Chinese translation, Nanjing, 2002; Portuguese translation in process.
13. with Catherine Gunsalus González. *Their Souls Did Magnify the Lord: Studies on Biblical Women*. Atlanta: John Knox, 1977.
14. with Catherine Gunsalus González. *Sus almas engrandecieron al Señor*. Miami: Caribe, 1977. A translation and adaptation of number 13.
15. *Luces bajo el almud*. San José, Costa Rica: Caribe, 1977.
16. with Catherine Gunsalus González. *Vision at Patmos: Studies in the Book of Revelation*. New York: Friendship, 1978; second edition: Nashville: Abingdon, 1990.
17. *La era de los mártires*. Vol. 1 of *Y hasta lo último de la tierra*. Miami: Caribe, 1978. Portuguese translation, São Paulo, Brazil.

18. *La era de los gigantes.* Vol. 2 of *Y hasta lo último de la tierra.* Miami: Caribe, 1978. Portuguese translation, São Paulo, Brazil.
19. *La era de las Tinieblas.* Vol. 3 of *Y hasta lo último de la tierra.* Miami: Caribe, 1978. Portuguese translation, São Paulo, Brazil.
20. *La era de los altos ideales.* Vol. 4 of *Y hasta lo último de la tierra.* Miami: Caribe, 1979. Portuguese translation, São Paulo, Brazil.
21. with Catherine Gunsalus González. *Rejoice in Your Savior: A Study for Lent-Easter.* Nashville: Graded Press, 1979.
22. *La era de los sueños frustrados.* Vol. 5 of *Y hasta lo último de la tierra.* Miami: Caribe, 1979. Portuguese translation, São Paulo, Brazil.
23. *La era de los reformadores.* Vol. 6 of *Y hasta lo último de la tierra.* Miami: Caribe, 1980. Portuguese translation, São Paulo, Brazil.
24. *La era de los conquistadores.* Vol. 7 of *Y hasta lo último de la tierra.* Miami: Caribe, 1980. Portuguese translation, São Paulo, Brazil.
25. with Catherine Gunsalus González. *Liberation Preaching: The Pulpit and the Oppressed.* Nashville: Abingdon, 1980.
26. with Catherine Gunsalus González. *In Accord: Let Us Worship.* New York: Friendship, 1981.
27. ed., *Proclaiming the Acceptable Year: Sermons from a Perspective of Liberation.* Valley Forge: Judson, 1982.
28. *La era de los dogmas y las dudas.* Vol. 8 of *Y hasta lo último de la tierra.* Miami: Caribe, 1983. Portuguese translation, São Paulo, Brazil.
29. *Early and Medieval Christianity.* Vol. 1 of *The Story of Christianity.* New York: Harper & Row, 1984. A translation and adaptation of the vols. 1-5 and 7 of *Y hasta lo último de la tierra.* Korean translation, Seoul; Russian translation, St. Petersburg; Japanese translation, Tokyo.
30. *From the Reformation to the Present.* Vol. 2 of *The Story of Christianity.* New York: Harper & Row, 1985. A translation and adaptation of the vols. 8-10 of *Y hasta lo último de la tierra.* Korean translation, Seoul; Russian translation, St. Petersburg; Japanese translation in progress.
31. *Juntamente con Cristo: Un comentario sobre los textos de Cuaresma y Semana Santa.* Nashville: Ediciones Discipulado, 1985.
32. *La era de los nuevos horizontes.* Vol. 9 of *Y hasta lo último de la tierra.* Miami: Caribe, 1987. Portuguese translation, São Paulo, Brazil.
33. *La era inconclusa.* Vol. 10 of *Y hasta lo último de la tierra.* Miami: Caribe, 1988. Portuguese translation, São Paulo, Brazil, in press.
34. *Probad los espíritus: Un comentario sobre los textos de Adviento y Navidad.* Nashville: Ediciones Discipulado, 1987.
35. with Catherine Gunsalus González. *Paul: His Impact on Christianity.* Nashville: Graded Press, 1987. Leader's Guide also available.
36. *The Crusades: Piety Misguided.* Nashville, Graded Press, 1988.
37. *Monasticism: Patterns of Piety.* Nashville, Graded Press, 1988.
38. *The Theological Education of Hispanics.* New York: Fund for Theological Education, 1988.
39. *Christian Thought Revisited: Three Types of Theology.* Nashville: Abingdon, 1989. Rev. ed. Maryknoll, N.Y.: Orbis, 1999. Korean translation, Seoul.
40. with Catherine Gunsalus González. *A Faith More Precious Than Gold: A Study of 1 Peter.* Louisville: Horizons, 1989. Korean and Spanish translations. Spanish version also by González.
41. *Faith and Wealth: A History of Early Christian Ideas on the Origin, Significance, and Use of Money.* San Francisco: Harper & Row, 1990. Chinese translation, Taipei, 2000.

42. *Mañana: Christian Theology from a Hispanic Perspective.* Nashville: Abingdon, 1990. German translation: Göttingen: Vandenhoek & Ruprecht.
43. ed., *Each in Our Own Tongue: A History of Hispanic United Methodism.* Nashville: Abingdon, 1991.
44. ed., *En nuestra propia lengua.* Nashville: Abingdon, 1991. A translation of number 43.
45. ed., *Voces: Voices from the Hispanic Church.* Nashville: Abingdon, 1992.
46. *Out of Every Tribe and Nation: Christian Theology at the Ethnic Roundtable.* Nashville: Abingdon, 1992.
47. *Hechos.* Comentario Bíblico Hispanoamericano. Miami: Caribe, 1992.
48. *Mentors as Instruments of God's Call* (a booklet). Nashville: General Board of Higher Education and Ministry, 1992.
49. *Desde la Reforma hasta nuestros días.* Vol. 3 of *Historia del pensamiento cristiano.* Miami: Caribe, 1979; second edition: Miami: Caribe, 1992.
50. with Catherine G. González. *The Liberating Pulpit.* Nashville: Abingdon, 1994.
51. *Luke.* Vol. 11 of *Journey Through the Bible.* Nashville: Cokesbury, 1994. Leader's Guide also available.
52. *Bosquejo de historia de la iglesia.* Decatur, Ga.: AETH, 1995. Portuguese and Korean translations.
53. *Acts of the Apostles.* Vol. 13 of *Journey Through the Bible.* Nashville: Cokesbury, 1995. Leader's Guide also available.
54. *When Christ Lives in Us.* Nashville: Abingdon, 1995. With separate study guide.
55. ed., *¡Alabadle! Hispanic Christian Worship.* Nashville: Abingdon, 1996.
56. *Tres meses en la escuela de Mateo.* Nashville: Abingdon, 1996.
57. *Santa Biblia: The Bible through Hispanic Eyes.* Nashville: Abingdon, 1996.
58. *Church History: An Essential Guide.* Nashville: Abingdon, 1996.
59. *Tres meses en la escuela del Espíritu.* Nashville: Abingdon, 1997.
60. with Catherine G. González. *Revelation.* Louisville: Westminster/John Knox, 1997.
61. *Tres meses en la escuela de la prisión.* Nashville: Abingdon, 1997.
62. *Tres meses en la escuela de Patmos.* Nashville: Abingdon, 1997.
63. *Desde el siglo y hasta el siglo: Esbozos teológicos para el siglo XXI.* Mexico City: Seminario Teológico Presbiteriano, 1997.
64. *Tres meses en la escuela de Juan.* Nashville: Abingdon, 1998.
65. *Juan Wesley: Herencia y Promesa.* San Juan, P.R.: Seminario Evangélico, 1998.
66. ed., *Obras de Wesley.* 14 vols. Franklin, Tenn.: Providence House, 1996–1998.
67. *For the Healing of the Nations: The Book of Revelation in an Age of Cultural Conflict.* Maryknoll, N.Y.: Orbis, 1999.
68. *Mark's Message for the New Millennium.* Nashville: Abingdon, 2000.
69. *Jonás.* Buenos Aires: Kairós, 2000.
70. *Acts: The Gospel of the Spirit.* Maryknoll, N.Y.: Orbis, 2001.
71. *La historia también tiene su historia.* Buenos Aires: Kairós, 2001.
72. *Mapas para la historia futura de la iglesia.* Buenos Aires: Kairós, 2001.
73. *Three Months with Matthew.* Nashville: Abingdon, 2002.
74. with Zaida Maldonado-Pérez. *An Introduction to Christian Theology.* Nashville: Abingdon, 2002.
75. *The Changing Shape of Church History.* St. Louis: Chalice, 2002.
76. *La historia como ventana al futuro: Ensayos sobre la historia de la iglesia.* Buenos Aires: Kairós, 2002.

77. *Perseverantes en la esperanza.* San Juan, P.R.: Iglesia Cristiana, Discípulos de Cristo, 2003.
78. *Three Months with the Spirit.* Nashville: Abingdon, 2003.
79. with Zaida Maldonado-Pérez. *Introducción a la teología cristiana.* Nashville: Abingdon and AETH, 2003.
80. *Wesley para a América Latina hoje.* São Paulo, Brazil: Editeo, 2003. An adaptation and translation of number 65.
81. *Three Months with Revelation.* Nashville: Abingdon, 2004.
82. *Diccionario ilustrado de intérpretes de la fe.* Barcelona: CLIA, 2004.
83. *Jesus Calls.* Nashville: Abingdon, 2004.

II. ARTICLES AND LESSONS IN LECCIONES CRISTIANAS

Lecciones Cristianas is a United Methodist publication for weekly adult Bible study. Also published by the American Baptists under the title of *Verdad y vida*.

1968

"La Reforma en el Siglo XVI y en el XX," Año 1, Septiembre–Noviembre, No. 1, pp. 1-5.

1971

4 de julio: "Libres Para Servir," Año 3, Junio–Agosto, No. 4, pp. 27-30.
11 de julio: "Dios, el Cristiano, y el Gobierno," Año 3, Junio–Agosto, No. 4, pp. 31-35.
18 de julio: "Dios, el Cristiano, y el Código Civil," Año 3, Junio–Agosto, No. 4, pp. 36-40.

1972

5 de marzo: "El Fundamento de la Iglesia," Año 4, Marzo–Mayo, No. 3, pp. 13-17.
12 de marzo: "El Poder del Espíritu en la Iglesia," Año 4, Marzo–Mayo, No. 3, pp. 18-21.
19 de marzo: "La Comunidad de los Redimidos," Año 4, Marzo–Mayo, No. 3, pp. 22-25.
26 de marzo: "Un Solo Cuerpo en Cristo," Año 4, Marzo–Mayo, No. 3, pp. 26-29.
2 de abril: "La Iglesia del Señor Resucitado," Año 4, Marzo–Mayo, No. 3, pp. 30-34.
9 de abril: "La Iglesia: Comunidad que Adora," Año 4, Marzo–Mayo, No. 3, pp. 35-38.
16 de abril: "La Iglesia se Organiza Para Realizar su Misión," Año 4, Marzo–Mayo, No. 3, pp. 39-42.
23 de abril: "La Iglesia: Comunidad que Testifica," Año 4, Marzo–Mayo, No. 3, pp. 43-46.
30 de abril: "El Mandato Misionero de la Iglesia," Año 4, Marzo–Mayo, No. 3, pp. 47-50.
7 de mayo: "La Iglesia Responde a la Necesidad Humana," Año 4, Marzo–Mayo, No. 3, pp. 51-54.
14 de mayo: "La Iglesia Proclama el Evangelio," Año 4, Marzo–Mayo, No. 3, pp. 55-58.
21 de mayo: "El Ministerio Docente de la Iglesia," Año 4, Marzo–Mayo, No. 3, pp. 59-62.
28 de mayo: "La Iglesia Necesita Renovarse," Año 4, Marzo–Mayo, No. 3, pp. 63-66.
"El Aumento de la Población y La Responsabilidad Cristiana," Año 5, Septiembre–Noviembre, No. 1, pp. 1-3.

1973

"Los Diez Mandamientos y el Mundo Moderno," Año 5, Junio–Agosto, No. 4, pp. 1-3.
1 de julio: "La Respuesta a la Herencia," Año 5, Junio–Agosto, No. 4, pp. 31-36.
8 de julio: "Reverencia Para la Vida Humana," Año 5, Junio–Agosto, No. 4, pp. 36-41.
15 de julio: "El Concepto Cristiano del Sexo," Año 5, Junio–Agosto, No. 4, pp. 42-47.
22 de julio: "Los Derechos y Responsabilidades del Propietario," Año 5, Junio–Agosto, No. 4, pp. 47-52.
29 de julio: "Vive la Verdad," Año 5, Junio–Agosto, No. 4, pp. 53-58.

1974

3 de marzo: "Poder Para Crecer," Año 6, Marzo–Mayo, No. 3, pp. 9-14, 63.
10 de marzo: "Cuando el Espíritu Llena la Vida," Año 6, Marzo–Mayo, No. 3, pp. 15-19.
17 de marzo: "Venciendo Obstáculos," Año 6, Marzo–Mayo, No. 3, pp. 21-25.
24 de marzo: "La Aventura de la Fe," Año 6, Marzo–Mayo, No. 3, pp. 25-30.
31 de marzo: "Venciendo Barreras Humanas," Año 6, Marzo–Mayo, No. 3, pp. 31-35.
7 de abril: "Sirviendo Humildemente," Año 6, Marzo–Mayo, No. 3, pp. 36-40.
14 de abril: "El Pacto y la Resurrección," Año 6, Marzo–Mayo, No. 3, pp. 41-46.
21 de abril: "El Espíritu Trasciende las Instituciones," Año 6, Marzo–Mayo, No. 3, pp. 47-52.
28 de abril: "Una Estrategia Misionera," Año 6, Marzo–Mayo, No. 3, pp. 52-57.
5 de mayo: "Diferentes Reacciones al Evangelio," Año 6, Marzo–Mayo, No. 3, pp. 58-63.
12 de mayo: "El Evangelio se Enfrenta a la Cultura," Año 6, Marzo–Mayo, No. 3, pp. 64-69.
19 de mayo: "Un Testimonio Audaz Provoca Controversia," Año 6, Marzo–Mayo, No. 3, pp. 70-75.
26 de mayo: "¿Cuándo Es una Persona Realmente Libre?" Año 6, Marzo–Mayo, No. 3, pp. 75-80.
"¿Qué Significa la Consagración Hoy?" Año 7, Diciembre–Febrero, No. 2, pp. 5-7.

1975

6 de abril: "La Gloria de Dios en la Creación," Año 7, Marzo–Mayo, No. 3, pp. 36-41.
13 de abril: "La Responsabilidad del Hombre Para la Creación," Año 7, Marzo–Mayo, No. 3, pp. 41-47.
20 de abril: "El Pacto Entre Dios y el Hombre," Año 7, Marzo–Mayo, No. 3, pp. 47-52.
27 de abril: "El Constante Amor de Dios," Año 7, Marzo–Mayo, No. 3, pp. 52-57.
4 de mayo: "La Presencia de Dios con el Hombre," Año 7, Marzo–Mayo, No. 3, pp. 57-63.
11 de mayo: "Imperativos Eticos," Año 7, Marzo–Mayo, No. 3, pp. 63-68.
18 de mayo: "Responsabilidad Personal," Año 7, Marzo–Mayo, No. 3, pp. 69-75.
25 de mayo "¿Dónde Está Nuestra Seguridad?" Año 7, Marzo–Mayo, No. 3, pp. 75-80.

1976

7 de marzo: with Catherine Gunsalus González, "La Consagración Total de Jesús," Año 8, Marzo–Mayo, No. 3, pp. 9-13.
14 de marzo: with Catherine Gunsalus González, "La Necesidad del Arrepentimiento," Año 8, Marzo–Mayo, No. 3, pp. 14-19.

21 de marzo: with Catherine Gunsalus González, "Una Acusación de Hipocresía," Año 8, Marzo–Mayo, No. 3, pp. 20-25.

28 de marzo: with Catherine Gunsalus González, "La Preparación Para el Regreso del Señor," Año 8, Marzo–Mayo, No. 3, pp. 26-31.

4 de abril: with Catherine Gunsalus González, "El Ser Humano Bajo Juicio," Año 8, Marzo–Mayo, No. 3, pp. 32-37.

11 de abril: with Catherine Gunsalus González, "El Rey Rechazado," Año 8, Marzo–Mayo, No. 3, pp. 38-42.

18 de abril: with Catherine Gunsalus González, "Rechazo y Resurrección," Año 8, Marzo–Mayo, No. 3, pp. 43-47.

"El Reto de un Sueño," Año 8, Junio–Agosto, No. 4, pp. 1-4.

3 de octubre: with Catherine Gunsalus González, "Nuestra Necesidad de Reconciliación," Año 9, Septiembre–Noviembre, pp. 33-37.

10 de octubre: with Catherine Gunsalus González, "Reconciliados por Cristo," Año 9, Septiembre–Noviembre, pp. 38-42.

17 de octubre: with Catherine Gunsalus González, "Vivos en Cristo," Año 9, Septiembre–Noviembre, pp. 43-48.

24 de octubre: with Catherine Gunsalus González, "Libres en Cristo," Año 9, Septiembre–Noviembre, pp. 49-53.

31 de octubre: with Catherine Gunsalus González, "Seguros en el Amor de Dios," Año 9, Septiembre–Noviembre, pp. 54-59.

7 de noviembre: with Catherine Gunsalus González, "Unidos Bajo Dios," Año 9, Septiembre–Noviembre, pp. 60-64.

"Cristo, el Eterno Contemporáneo," Año 9, Diciembre–Febrero, No. 2, pp. 1-4.

1977

"El Libro del Exodo y la Libertad Cristiana," Año 9, Junio–Agosto, No. 4, pp. 1-4.

18 de diciembre: "Dios llama a una vida recta," Año 10, Diciembre–Febrero, No. 2, pp. 21-25.

25 de diciembre: "La Esperanza de un Día Mejor," Año 10, Diciembre–Febrero, No. 2, pp. 26-37.

1978

16 de abril: "El Precio de la Convicción," Año 10, Marzo–Mayo, No. 3, pp. 43-47.

23 de abril: "Ensanchando el Círculo," Año 10, Marzo–Mayo, No. 3, pp. 48-53.

30 de abril: "Una Nueva Dirección," Año 10, Marzo–Mayo, No. 3, pp. 54-58.

7 de mayo: "Poniendo el Evangelio a Trabajar," Año 10, Marzo–Mayo, No. 3, pp. 59-63.

4 de junio: "Extendiendo las Buenas Nuevas," Año 10, Junio–Agosto, No. 4, pp. 9-14.

11 de junio: "Resolviendo Conflictos," Año 10, Junio–Agosto, No. 4, pp. 15-19.

18 de junio: "Respondiendo a las Buenas Nuevas," Año 10, Junio–Agosto, No. 4, pp. 20-25.

25 de junio: "Enderezando el Mundo," Año 10, Junio–Agosto, No. 4, pp. 26-30.

23 de julio: "El Reto Cristiano a los Valores," Año 10, Junio–Agosto, No. 4, pp. 47-52.

30 de julio: "Dedicados al Crecimiento Cristiano," Año 10, Junio–Agosto, No. 4, pp. 53-57.

6 de agosto: "Ciudadanos de Dos Mundos," Año 10, Junio–Agosto, No. 4, pp. 58-63.

13 de agosto: "Listo a Testificar," Año 10, Junio–Agosto, No. 4, pp. 64-69.

20 de agosto: "Fe en Tiempos Peligrosos," Año 10, Junio–Agosto, No. 4, pp. 70-74.

27 de agosto: "Un Evangelio sin Trabas," Año 10, Junio–Agosto, No. 4, pp. 75-80.

3 de diciembre: "Dios te Extiende su Mano," Año 11, Diciembre–Febrero, No. 2, pp. 12-18.

10 de diciembre: "Dios te Habla," Año 11, Diciembre–Febrero, No. 2, pp. 19-25.

17 de diciembre: "Dios te Juzga y Perdona," Año 11, Diciembre–Febrero, No. 2, pp. 26-31.

24 de diciembre: "Dios con Nosotros," Año 11, Diciembre–Febrero, No. 2, pp. 32-37.

31 de diciembre: "El Amor Redentor de Dios," Año 11, Diciembre–Febrero, No. 2, pp. 38-44.

1979

1 de julio: "Viviendo con Nuestras Decisiones," Año 11, Junio–Agosto, No. 4, pp. 38-43.

8 de julio: "Escogiendo tu Dios," Año 11, Junio–Agosto, No. 4, pp. 44-50.

15 de julio: "Valor Para Decir la Verdad," Año 11, Junio–Agosto, No. 4, pp. 51-57.

22 de julio: "Cómo Tratar a los Enemigos," Año 11, Junio–Agosto, No. 4, pp. 58-64.

29 de julio: "La Fe Exige Acción Moral," Año 11, Junio–Agosto, No. 4, pp. 64-70.

"La Autoridad de la Palabra de Dios," Año 12, Septiembre–Noviembre, No. 1, pp. 1-4.

23 de diciembre: "La Palabra Encarnada," Año 12, Diciembre–Febrero, No. 2, pp. 33-38.

30 de diciembre: "Un Testigo de la Palabra Viviente," Año 12, Diciembre–Febrero, No. 2, pp. 39-45.

1980

6 de enero: "La Familia de Jesús," Año 12, Diciembre–Febrero, No. 2, pp. 46-51.

13 de enero: "Cuestión de Vida o Muerte," Año 12, Diciembre–Febrero, No. 2, pp. 52-58.

20 de enero: "Dos que Trajeron Otros," Año 12, Diciembre–Febrero, No. 2, pp. 59-65.

27 de enero: "Una Nueva Oportunidad Para la Consagración," Año 12, Diciembre–Febrero, No. 2, pp. 66-71.

3 de febrero: "Compartiendo el Agua de Vida," Año 12, Diciembre–Febrero, No. 2, pp. 72-78.

10 de febrero: "Ayudando y Sanando," Año 12, Diciembre–Febrero, No. 2, pp. 79-84.

17 de febrero: "Sabiendo que Hay Alguien que se Preocupa," Año 12, Diciembre–Febrero, No. 2, pp. 85-90.

24 de febrero: "¿Quién es Ciego?" Año 12, Diciembre–Febrero, No. 2, pp. 91-96.

2 de marzo: "Uno que Escuchó," Año 12, Marzo–Mayo, No. 3, pp. 12-17.

9 de marzo: "Tentaciones que Traicionar," Año 12, Marzo–Mayo, No. 3, pp. 18-23.

16 de marzo: "Los Peligros de la Conveniencia," Año 12, Marzo–Mayo, No. 3, pp. 24-29.

23 de marzo: "El Uso del Poder," Año 12, Marzo–Mayo, No. 3, pp. 30-36.

30 de marzo: "Madurando el la Fe," Año 12, Marzo–Mayo, No. 3, pp. 37-42.

6 de abril: "De la Tristeza al Gozo," Año 12, Marzo–Mayo, No. 3, pp. 43-49.

"El Evangelio de Mateo," Año 13, Diciembre 1980–Febrero, No. 2, pp. 1-4.

1981

1 de febrero: "¡Confía en la Victoria de Dios!" Año 13, Diciembre–Febrero, No. 2, pp. 69-75.

8 de febrero: "Ten Compasión," Año 13, Diciembre–Febrero, No. 2, pp. 76-82.

15 de febrero: "Vive tu Fe," Año 13, Diciembre–Febrero, No. 2, pp. 83-89.

22 de febrero: "Amaos Los Unos a Los Otros," Año 13, Diciembre–Febrero, No. 2, pp. 90-96.

3 de mayo: "La Palabra Final de Dios," Año 13, Marzo–Mayo, No. 3, pp. 66-72.

10 de mayo: "El Autor de Nuestra Salvación," Año 13, Marzo–Mayo, No. 3, pp. 73-78.

17 de mayo: "Nuestro Gran Sumo Sacerdote," Año 13, Marzo–Mayo, No. 3, pp. 79-84.

24 de mayo: "Entre Tú y Dios," Año 13, Marzo–Mayo, No. 3, pp. 85-90.

31 de mayo: "Autor y Consumador de Nuestra Fe," Año 13, Marzo–Mayo, No. 3, pp. 91-96.

"Jesús, Hombre de Compasión," Año 14, Diciembre–Febrero, No. 2, pp. 5-7.

6 de diciembre: "El Hijo de Dios," Año 14, Diciembre–Febrero, No. 2, pp. 12-18.

13 de diciembre: "El Hijo del Hombre," Año 14, Diciembre–Febrero, No. 2, pp. 19-25.

20 de diciembre: "Nos Ha Nacido un Salvador," Año 14, Diciembre–Febrero, No. 2, pp. 26-31.

27 de diciembre: "Hemos Encontrado al Mesías," Año 14, Diciembre–Febrero, No. 2, pp. 32-37.

1982

3 de enero: "Jesús el Señor," Año 14, Diciembre–Febrero, No. 2, pp. 38-44.

10 de enero: "Como Siervo," Año 14, Diciembre–Febrero, No. 2, pp. 45-51.

25 de abril: "Seguridad en Momentos de Tensión," Año 14, Marzo–Mayo, No. 3, pp. 61-66.

2 de mayo: "Dios Enjuicia a sus Iglesias," Año 14, Marzo–Mayo, No. 3, pp. 67-72.

9 de mayo: "Una Visión de Adoración," Año 14, Marzo–Mayo, No. 3, pp. 73-78.

16 de mayo: "Perseguidos Pero Victoriosos," Año 14, Marzo–Mayo, No. 3, pp. 79-84.

23 de mayo: "Cristo: Juez Justo," Año 14, Marzo–Mayo, No. 3, pp. 85-90.

29 de mayo: "Todas las Cosas Hechas Nuevas," Año 14, Marzo–Mayo, No. 3, pp. 91-96.

"El Pentateuco," Año 15, Septiembre–Noviembre, No. 1, pp. 5-7.

5 de diciembre: "El Carácter del Evangelio de San Lucas," Año 15, Diciembre–Febrero, No. 2, pp. 13-18.

12 de diciembre: "Anunciando el Nacimiento de Jesús," Año 15, Diciembre–Febrero, No. 2, pp. 19-25.

19 de diciembre: "Los Primeros Años de Jesús," Año 15, Diciembre–Febrero, No. 2, pp. 26-32.

25 de diciembre: "Jesús Comienza su Ministerio," Año 15, Diciembre–Febrero, No. 2, pp. 33-38.

1983

"La Reforma Protestante del Siglo Decimosexto en España," Año 15, Marzo–Mayo, No. 3, pp. 1-4.

3 de julio: "Jefté: Celo sin Sabiduría," Año 15, Julio–Agosto, No. 4, pp. 39-44.

10 de julio: "Sansón: Destino Fallido," Año 15, Julio–Agosto, No. 4, pp. 45-51.

17 de julio: "Ana: Promesa Cumplida," Año 15, Julio–Agosto, No. 4, pp. 52-58.

24 de julio: "Naamán: Seguidor Vacilante," Año 15, Julio–Agosto, No. 4, pp. 59-64.

31 de julio: "Joás: Rey Extraviado," Año 15, Julio–Agosto, No. 4, pp. 65-70.

1984

1 de enero: "Dios Contra su Pueblo," Año 16, Diciembre–Febrero, No. 2, pp. 39-44.
8 de enero: "El Canto de la Viña," Año 16, Diciembre–Febrero, No. 2, pp. 45-51.
15 de enero: "Visión y Misión," Año 16, Diciembre–Febrero, No. 2, pp. 52-57.
22 de enero: "¡Volveos al Señor!" Año 16, Diciembre–Febrero, No. 2, pp. 58-63.
29 de enero: "Un Día de Gozo y Felicidad," Año 16, Diciembre–Febrero, No. 2, pp. 64-70.
5 de febrero: "Yo Soy el Señor," Año 16, Diciembre–Febrero, No. 2, pp. 71-76.
12 de febrero: "El Siervo del Señor," Año 16, Diciembre–Febrero, No. 2, pp. 77-83.
19 de febrero: "¡Venid a la Fiesta!" Año 16, Diciembre–Febrero, No. 2, pp. 84-89.
26 de febrero: "El Culto que Dios Busca," Año 16, Diciembre–Febrero, No. 2, pp. 90-96.

1985

21 de abril: "La Fe se Encuentra con el Sufrimiento," Año 17, Marzo–Mayo, No. 3, pp. 53-58.
28 de abril: "La Fe Lucha con el Sufrimiento," Año 17, Marzo–Mayo, No. 3, pp. 59-65.
5 de mayo: "La Fe a pesar del Sufrimiento," Año 17, Marzo–Mayo, No. 3, pp. 66-72.
12 de mayo: "Enfrentando la Futilidad de la Vida," Año 17, Marzo–Mayo, No. 3, pp. 73-80.
19 de mayo: "El Valor de la Sabiduría," Año 17, Marzo–Mayo, No. 3, pp. 81-86.
26 de mayo: "Dos Formas de Vida," Año 17, Marzo–Mayo, No. 3, pp. 87-93.

1987

6 de diciembre: "Es tiempo de cambiar," Año 20, Diciembre–Febrero, No. 2, pp. 8-11.
13 de diciembre: "Un nuevo comienzo," Año 20, Diciembre–Febrero, No. 2, pp. 13-16.
20 de diciembre: "Experimentando gran gozo," Año 20, Diciembre–Febrero, No. 2, pp. 17-20.
27 de diciembre: "Compartiendo en el ministerio," Año 20, Diciembre–Febrero, No. 2, pp. 21-24.

1988

3 de enero: "Encontrando la verdadera felicidad," Año 20, Diciembre–Febrero, No. 2, pp. 26-29.
10 de enero: "Amando a los que no nos agradan," Año 20, Diciembre–Febrero, No. 2, pp. 30-33.
17 de enero: "Relacionándonos con Dios y con los demás," Año 20, Diciembre–Febrero, No. 2, pp. 34-37.
24 de enero: "Una salvación completa," Año 20, Diciembre–Febrero, No. 2, pp. 39-42.
31 de enero: "Continuando la obra de Jesús," Año 20, Diciembre–Febrero, No. 2, pp. 43-46.
7 de febrero: "La grandeza del reino," Año 20, Diciembre–Febrero, No. 2, pp. 48-51.
14 de febrero: "Reclamar o renunciar," Año 20, Diciembre–Febrero, No. 2, pp. 52-55.
21 de febrero: "La vida en la comunidad cristiana," Año 20, Diciembre–Febrero, No. 2, pp. 56-59.
28 de febrero: "El camino de la grandeza," Año 20, Diciembre–Febrero, No. 2, pp. 60-63.
6 de marzo: "El futuro de los discípulos," Año 20, Marzo–Mayo, No. 3, pp. 7-10.
13 de marzo: "Fortaleza para el futuro," Año 20, Marzo–Mayo, No. 3, pp. 11-14.

20 de marzo: "En lucha con el futuro," Año 20, Marzo–Mayo, No. 3, pp. 15-18.

27 de marzo: "El reto de la cruz," Año 20, Marzo–Mayo, No. 3, pp. 19-23.

3 de abril: "La victoria sobre la muerte," Año 20, Marzo–Mayo, No. 3, pp. 24-27.

10 de abril: "La comisión de los discípulos," Año 20, Marzo–Mayo, No. 3, pp. 28-31.

4 de diciembre: "La promesa de Dios puesta en duda," Año 21, Diciembre–Febrero, No. 2, pp. 7-10.

11 de diciembre: "La promesa de Dios aceptada," Año 21, Diciembre–Febrero, No. 2, pp. 11-14.

18 de diciembre: "Regocijo ante la grandeza de Dios," Año 21, Diciembre–Febrero, No. 2, pp. 15-18.

25 de diciembre: "La celebración del nacimiento del Salvador," Año 21, Diciembre–Febrero, No. 2, pp. 19-22.

1989

1 de enero: "Ungido para anunciar las buenas nuevas," Año 21, Diciembre–Febrero, No. 2, pp. 25-28.

8 de enero: "La misión es nuestra," Año 21, Diciembre–Febrero, No. 2, pp. 29-32.

15 de enero: "La salud y el perdón," Año 21, Diciembre–Febrero, No. 2, pp. 33-36.

22 de enero: "El perdón como medida del amor," Año 21, Diciembre–Febrero, No. 2, pp. 37-40.

29 de enero: "Un paso hacia la sanidad," Año 21, Diciembre–Febrero, No. 2, pp. 41-44.

5 de febrero: "En busca del reino de Dios," Año 21, Diciembre–Febrero, No. 2, pp. 47-50.

12 de febrero: "Señales de gratitud," Año 21, Diciembre–Febrero, No. 2, pp. 51-54.

19 de febrero: "La respuesta al llamado de Dios," Año 21, Diciembre–Febrero, No. 2, pp. 55-58.

26 de febrero: "Cómo hacerse discípulo," Año 21, Diciembre–Febrero, No. 2, pp. 59-62.

3 de diciembre: "Señal que apunta a Jesús," Año 22, Diciembre–Febrero, No. 2, pp. 9-12.

10 de diciembre: "La vida puede comenzar de nuevo," Año 22, Diciembre–Febrero, No. 2, pp. 13-16.

17 de diciembre: "Nunca más tener sed," Año 22, Diciembre–Febrero, No. 2, pp. 17-20.

24 de diciembre: "El significado de la venida de Cristo," Año 22, Diciembre–Febrero, No. 2, pp. 21-24.

31 de diciembre: "Salud completa," Año 22, Diciembre–Febrero, No. 2, pp. 26-29.

1990

7 de enero: "Testimonio ineludible," Año 22, Diciembre–Febrero, No. 2, pp. 30-33.

14 de enero: "Hambre satisfecha," Año 22, Diciembre–Febrero, No. 2, pp. 34-37.

21 de enero: "Libres estamos," Año 22, Diciembre–Febrero, No. 2, pp. 38-41.

28 de enero: "En pos de la luz," Año 22, Diciembre–Febrero, No. 2, pp. 42-45.

4 de febrero: "Escoged la luz," Año 22, Diciembre–Febrero, No. 2, pp. 47-50.

11 de febrero: "La decisión de servir," Año 22, Diciembre–Febrero, No. 2, pp. 51-54.

18 de febrero: "Seguir el camino," Año 22, Diciembre–Febrero, No. 2, pp. 55-58.

25 de febrero: "El poder del Espíritu," Año 22, Diciembre–Febrero, No. 2, pp. 59-62.

4 de marzo: "Donde hay amor," Año 22, Marzo–Mayo, No. 3, pp. 4-7.

11 de marzo: "Bajo la dirección del Espíritu," Año 22, Marzo–Mayo, No. 3, pp. 8-11.

18 de marzo: "Frente a decisiones cruciales," Año 22, Marzo–Mayo, No. 3, pp. 12-16.

25 de marzo: "Negar a Jesús," Año 22, Marzo–Mayo, No. 3, pp. 17-21.

1 de abril: "Ante la verdad," Año 22, Marzo–Mayo, No. 3, pp. 22-25.

8 de abril: "Ante la muerte," Año 22, Marzo–Mayo, No. 3, pp. 26-30.
15 de abril: "La Resurrección y la fe," Año 22, Marzo–Mayo, No. 3, pp. 31-34.

1991

1 de septiembre: "Escogido para servir," Año 24, Septiembre–Noviembre, No. 1, pp. 6-10.
8 de septiembre: "Trabajo en conjunto," Año 24, Septiembre–Noviembre, No. 1, pp. 11-15.
15 de septiembre: "Proclamar las buenas nuevas," Año 24, Septiembre–Noviembre, No. 1, pp. 16-20.
22 de septiembre: "Salud completa," Año 24, Septiembre–Noviembre, No. 1, pp. 21-24.
29 de septiembre: "En medio de las diferencias," Año 24, Septiembre–Noviembre, No. 1, pp. 25-29.
6 de octubre: "En respuesta a las necesidades," Año 24, Septiembre–Noviembre, No. 1, pp. 30-34.
13 de octubre: "Valor para escoger," Año 24, Septiembre–Noviembre, No. 1, pp. 35-38.
20 de octubre: "En busca del Dios verdadero," Año 24, Septiembre–Noviembre, No. 1, pp. 39-42.
27 de octubre: "Aprender unos de otros," Año 24, Septiembre–Noviembre, No. 1, pp. 43-47.
3 de noviembre: "Al servicio de la iglesia," Año 24, Septiembre–Noviembre, No. 1, pp. 48-51.
10 de noviembre: "Frente a las crisis," Año 24, Septiembre–Noviembre, No. 1, pp. 52-56.
17 de noviembre: "Defender tu fe," Año 24, Septiembre–Noviembre, No. 1, pp. 57-60.
24 de noviembre: "La proclamación del evangelio," Año 24, Septiembre–Noviembre, No. 1, pp. 61-64.

1993

6 de junio: "Una vida digna," Año 25, Junio–Agosto, No. 4, pp. 6-9.
13 de junio: "Cristo, nuestro modelo," Año 25, Junio–Agosto, No. 4, pp. 10-13.
20 de junio: "Llamamiento supremo," Año 25, Junio–Agosto, No. 4, pp. 14-17.
27 de junio: "Regocijaos en el Señor," Año 25, Junio–Agosto, No. 4, pp. 18-21.
4 de julio: "Cristo por encima de todo," Año 25, Junio–Agosto, No. 4, pp. 24-27.
11 de julio: "Cristo lo es todo," Año 25, Junio–Agosto, No. 4, pp. 28-31.
18 de julio: "La vida en Cristo," Año 25, Junio–Agosto, No. 4, pp. 32-35.
25 de julio: "La reconciliación en Cristo," Año 25, Junio–Agosto, No. 4, pp. 38-41.
1 de agosto: "Nueva vida," Año 25, Junio–Agosto, No. 4, pp. 45-48.
8 de agosto: "Nueva comunión," Año 25, Junio–Agosto, No. 4, pp. 49-52.
15 de agosto: "Nueva conducta," Año 25, Junio–Agosto, No. 4, pp. 53-56.
22 de agosto: "Un nuevo orden familiar," Año 25, Junio–Agosto, No. 4, pp. 57-60.
29 de agosto: "Nuevas fuerzas," Año 25, Junio–Agosto, No. 4, pp. 61-64.

1994

5 de junio: "Dios se preocupa," Año 26, Junio–Agosto, No. 4, pp. 7-10.
12 de junio: "El llamado de Dios y nuestra respuesta," Año 26, Junio–Agosto, No. 4, pp. 11-14.

19 de junio: "Dios libera," Año 26, Junio–Agosto, No. 4, pp. 15-18.

26 de junio: "Dios nos da la victoria," Año 26, Junio–Agosto, No. 4, pp. 19-23.

3 de julio: "Dios provee," Año 26, Junio–Agosto, No. 4, pp. 24-27.

10 de julio: "Dios provee dirección," Año 26, Junio–Agosto, No. 4, pp. 28-31.

17 de julio: "Dios busca la obediencia," Año 26, Junio–Agosto, No. 4, pp. 32-35.

24 de julio: "Dios perdona," Año 26, Junio–Agosto, No. 4, pp. 36-39.

31 de julio: "Dios está en medio nuestro," Año 26, Junio–Agosto, No. 4, pp. 40-43.

7 de agosto: "Alégrate por la propiedad de Dios," Año 26, Junio–Agosto, No. 4, pp. 46-49.

14 de agosto: "Acepta la dirección de Dios," Año 26, Junio–Agosto, No. 4, pp. 50-53.

21 de agosto: "Amarás al Señor tu Dios," Año 26, Junio–Agosto, No. 4, pp. 56-59.

28 de agosto: "Decide tú obedecer," Año 26, Junio–Agosto, No. 4, pp. 60-63.

1995

3 de septiembre: "La promesa de un nuevo poder," Año 28, Septiembre–Noviembre, No. 1, pp. 14-18.

10 de septiembre: "La dádiva de un nuevo poder," Año 28, Septiembre–Noviembre, No. 1, pp. 19-23.

17 de septiembre: "El poder salvador de Cristo," Año 28, Septiembre–Noviembre, No. 1, pp. 24-28.

24 de septiembre: "Valor para obedecer," Año 28, Septiembre–Noviembre, No. 1, pp. 29-33.

1 de octubre: "¿Cómo servir?" Año 28, Septiembre–Noviembre, No. 1, pp. 35-39.

8 de octubre: "El valor de la persona," Año 28, Septiembre–Noviembre, No. 1, pp. 40-44.

15 de octubre: "Frente a Jesús," Año 28, Septiembre–Noviembre, No. 1, pp. 45-49.

22 de octubre: "Sin acepción de personas," Año 28, Septiembre–Noviembre, No. 1, pp. 50-54.

29 de octubre: "La vida con propósito," Año 28, Septiembre–Noviembre, No. 1, pp. 55-59.

5 de noviembre: "Un evangelio para todos," Año 28, Septiembre–Noviembre, No. 1, pp. 61-65.

12 de noviembre: "La gracia puesta a prueba," Año 28, Septiembre–Noviembre, No. 1, pp. 66-70.

19 de noviembre: "Se solicita ayuda," Año 28, Septiembre–Noviembre, No. 1, pp. 71-75.

26 de noviembre: "El poder vencedor del Evangelio," Año 28, Septiembre–Noviembre, No. 1, pp. 76-80.

1996

1 de diciembre: "Alegrémonos en Dios," Año 29, Diciembre–Febrero, pp. 14-18.

8 de diciembre: "Rindémonos a la voluntad de Dios," Año 29, Diciembre–Febrero, pp. 19-23.

15 de diciembre: "Recibamos el mensaje de Dios," Año 29, Diciembre–Febrero, pp. 24-28.

22 de diciembre: "Respondamos al Hijo de Dios," Año 29, Diciembre–Febrero, pp. 29-33.

29 de diciembre: "Creamos las promesas de Dios," Año 29, Diciembre–Febrero, pp. 34-39.

1997

5 de enero: "Demos testimonio de Cristo," Año 29, Diciembre–Febrero, pp. 40-44.

12 de enero: "Sepamos escoger," Año 29, Diciembre–Febrero, pp. 45-49.

19 de enero: "Confesemos a Cristo," Año 29, Diciembre–Febrero, pp. 50-54.

26 de enero: "Seamos fieles a Cristo," Año 29, Diciembre–Febrero, pp. 55-60.

2 de febrero: "Comprometámonos a estimular a los demás," Año 29, Diciembre–Febrero, pp. 61-65

9 de febrero: "Seamos fieles testigos," Año 29, Diciembre–Febrero, pp. 66-70.

16 de febrero: "Prestémonos apoyo mutuo," Año 29, Diciembre–Febrero, pp. 71-75.

23 de febrero: "Seamos obreros fieles," Año 29, Diciembre–Febrero, pp. 76-79.

1998

1 de marzo: "Buenas nuevas para hoy," Año 30, Marzo–Mayo, pp. 6-10.

8 de marzo: "La compasión en acción," Año 30, Marzo–Mayo, pp. 11-15.

15 de marzo: "Autorizado para servir," Año 30, Marzo–Mayo, pp. 16-21.

22 de marzo: "Esperanza ante la muerte," Año 30, Marzo–Mayo, pp. 22-28.

29 de marzo: "El precio de las convicciones," Año 30, Marzo–Mayo, pp. 29-33.

5 de abril: "Un nuevo modo de dirigir," Año 30, Marzo–Mayo, pp. 34-39.

12 de abril: "El misterio de la muerte y la resurrección," Año 30, Marzo–Mayo, pp. 40-44.

19 de abril: "El precio de la irresponsabilidad," Año 30, Marzo–Mayo, pp. 45-49.

26 de abril: "Tristeza en medio de la celebración," Año 30, Marzo–Mayo, pp. 50-55.

3 de mayo: "Apertura ante la verdad," Año 30, Marzo–Mayo, pp. 56-60.

10 de mayo: "Obstáculos a la verdad," Año 30, Marzo–Mayo, pp. 61-65.

17 de mayo: "El matrimonio y el divorcio," Año 30, Marzo–Mayo, pp. 66-70.

24 de mayo: "¿Qué es la verdadera grandeza?" Año 30, Marzo–Mayo, pp. 71-75.

31 de mayo: "Una fe para tiempos difíciles," Año 30, Marzo–Mayo, pp. 76-80.

1999

6 de junio: "Aceptemos lo que Dios provee," Año 31, Junio–Agosto, pp. 11-18.

13 de junio: "Los orígenes," Año 31, Junio–Agosto, pp. 19-23.

20 de junio: "Relaciones quebrantadas," Año 31, Junio–Agosto, pp. 24-28.

27 de junio: "De la tragedia a la esperanza," Año 31, Junio–Agosto, pp 29-33.

4 de julio: "La aventura de la fe," Año 31, Junio–Agosto, pp. 35-39.

11 de julio: "Promesas sorprendentes," Año 31, Junio–Agosto, pp. 40-44.

18 de julio: "Darlo todo," Año 31, Junio–Agosto, pp. 45-49.

25 de julio: "El engaño y la bendición," Año 31, Junio–Agosto, pp. 50-54.

1 de agosto: "Huir de las dificultades," Año 31, Junio–Agosto, pp. 56-60.

8 de agosto: "Ante el temor y el peligro," Año 31, Junio–Agosto, pp. 61-65.

15 de agosto: "Dificultades familiares," Año 31, Junio–Agosto, pp. 66-70.

22 de agosto: "Oportunidades de servicio," Año 31, Junio–Agosto, pp. 71-75.

29 de agosto: "Relaciones restauradas," Año 31, Junio–Agosto, pp. 76-80.

5 de diciembre: "Tiempo de preparación," Año 32, Diciembre–Febrero, pp. 14-18.

12 de diciembre: "Tiempo de prueba," Año 32, Diciembre–Febrero, pp. 19-23.

19 de diciembre: "Tiempo de adoración," Año 32, Diciembre–Febrero, pp. 24-28.

26 de diciembre: "Tiempo de regocijo," Año 32, Diciembre–Febrero, pp. 29-33.

2000

2 de enero: "El compromiso," Año 32, Diciembre–Febrero, pp. 35-39.

9 de enero: "La oración," Año 32, Diciembre–Febrero, pp. 40-44.

16 de enero: "La salvación integral," Año 32, Diciembre–Febrero, pp. 45-49.

23 de enero: "El poder," Año 32, Diciembre–Febrero, pp. 50-54.

30 de enero: "Las recompensas," Año 32, Diciembre–Febrero, pp. 55-59.

6 de febrero: "La dirección de la Palabra," Año 32, Diciembre–Febrero, pp. 61-65.

13 de febrero: "El gozo de estar listos," Año 32, Diciembre–Febrero, pp. 66-70.

20 de febrero: "La muerte en beneficio nuestro," Año 32, Diciembre–Febrero, pp. 71-75.

27 de febrero: "El fundamento de nuestra autoridad," Año 32, Diciembre–Febrero, pp. 76-80.

3 de diciembre: "Preparación para el nacimiento del Salvador," Año 33, Diciembre–Febrero, pp. 14-18.

10 de diciembre: "La obediencia al llamado de Dios," Año 33, Diciembre–Febrero, pp. 19-23.

17 de diciembre: "La alabanza a Dios," Año 33, Diciembre–Febrero, pp. 24-28.

24 de diciembre: "Dé la bienvenida al Salvador," Año 33, Diciembre–Febrero, pp. 29-33.

31 de diciembre: "Reconocer a Cristo," Año 33, Diciembre–Febrero, pp. 34-38.

2001

7 de enero: "Descubramos nuestra misión," Año 33, Diciembre–Febrero, pp. 40-44.

14 de enero: "El costo del discipulado," Año 33, Diciembre–Febrero, pp. 45-49.

21 de enero: "Celebramos la reconciliación," Año 33, Diciembre–Febrero, pp. 50-54.

28 de enero: "Preparación para el futuro," Año 33, Diciembre–Febrero, pp. 55-59.

4 de febrero: "Salvación para los perdidos," Año 33, Diciembre–Febrero, pp. 61-65.

11 de febrero: "El servicio como camino hacia la grandeza," Año 33, Diciembre–Febrero, pp. 66-70.

18 de febrero: "El cumplimiento de la misión," Año 33, Diciembre–Febrero, pp. 71-75.

25 de febrero: "¡Eres testigo!" Año 33, Diciembre–Febrero, pp. 76-80.

2002

3 de marzo: "Restaurar la relación con Dios," Año 34, Marzo–Mayo, pp. 14-18.

10 de marzo: "Restaurar la relación con Dios," Año 34, Marzo–Mayo, pp. 19-24.

17 de marzo: "Un ejemplo de fe," Año 34, Marzo–Mayo, pp. 25-29.

24 de marzo: "Los frutos de la justificación," Año 34, Marzo–Mayo, pp. 30-34.

31 de marzo: "Una nueva vida," Año 34, Marzo–Mayo, pp. 35-39.

7 de abril: "¿Habrá esperanza?" Año 34, Marzo–Mayo, pp. 40-45.

14 de abril: "¿Cómo van a oír?" Año 34, Marzo–Mayo, pp. 46-51.

21 de abril: "¿Cómo hemos de vivir?" Año 34, Marzo–Mayo, pp. 52-56.

28 de abril: "¿Quién podrá juzgar?" Año 34, Marzo–Mayo, pp. 57-61.

5 de mayo: "Vivir según la verdad," Año 34, Marzo–Mayo, pp. 62-66.

12 de mayo: "La familia de Dios," Año 34, Marzo–Mayo, pp. 67-71.

19 de mayo: "El valor de la libertad," Año 34, Marzo–Mayo, pp. 72-76.

26 de mayo: "Decisiones y consecuencias," Año 34, Marzo–Mayo, pp. 77-81.

2003

2 de marzo: "El principio del evangelio," Año 35, Marzo–Mayo, pp. 4-9.

9 de marzo: "Jesús llama a los pecadores," Año 35, Marzo–Mayo, pp. 10-15.

16 de marzo: "El poder de Jesús," Año 35, Marzo–Mayo, pp. 16-21.

23 de marzo: "Misión cumplida," Año 35, Marzo–Mayo, pp. 22-27.

30 de marzo: "La impureza surge de adentro," Año 35, Marzo–Mayo, pp. 28-33.

6 de abril: "La purificación de la comunidad que adora," Año 35, Marzo–Mayo, pp. 34-39.

13 de abril: "Las viejas tradiciones cobran nuevo sentido," Año 35, Marzo–Mayo, pp. 40-46.

20 de abril: "El triunfo sobre la adversidad," Año 35, Marzo–Mayo, pp. 47-51.

27 de abril: "La fe conquista el temor" Año 35, Marzo–Mayo, pp. 52-57.

4 de mayo: "La fe que se atreve," Año 35, Marzo–Mayo, pp. 58-63.

11 de mayo: "La fe es seguimiento," Año 35, Marzo–Mayo, pp. 64-69.

18 de mayo: "Enfrentando la incredulidad," Año 35, Marzo–Mayo, pp. 70-75.

25 de mayo: "¿Cuán atrevida es tu fe?" Año 35, Marzo–Mayo, pp. 76-81.

Notas para el maestro (in Lecciones Cristianas)

Año 3, Junio–Agosto 1971, No. 4, pp. 72-74.

Año 4, Marzo–Mayo 1972, No. 3, pp. 67-80.

Año 17, Marzo–Mayo 1985, No. 3, p. 94.

Año 20, Diciembre 1987–Febrero 1988, No. 2, pp. 6-63.

"La Navidad y la cultura," Año 21, Diciembre 1988–Febrero 1989, No. 2, pp. 20-22. Previously published in *Probad los Espíritus*, no. 34.

Año 21, Diciembre 1988–Febrero 1989, No. 2, pp. 4-64.

Año 21, Marzo–Mayo 1988, No. 3, pp. 2-28.

"La Navidad y la Encarnación," Año 22, Diciembre 1989–Febrero 1990, No. 2, pp. 4-5. Adapted from *Probad los Espíritus*, no. 34.

Año 4, Diciembre 1989–Febrero 1990, No. 2, pp. 7-78.

Año 4, Marzo–Mayo 1990, No. 3, pp. 2-38.

Año 6, Septiembre–Noviembre 1991, No. 1, pp. 3-80.

Año 7, Junio–Agosto 1993, No. 4, pp. 7-80.

Año 8, Junio–Agosto 1994, No. 4, pp. 16-80.

Año 10, Septiembre–Noviembre 1995, No. 1, pp. 14-80.

Año 11, Diciembre 1996–Febrero 1997, No. 2, pp. 12-80.

Año 12, Marzo–Mayo 1998, No. 3, pp. 3-80.

Año 13, Julio–Agosto 1998, No. 4, pp. 15-80.

Año 13, Diciembre 1999–Febrero 2000, No. 2, pp. 15-80.

Año 14, Diciembre 2000–Febrero 2001, No. 2, pp. 15-80.

Año 16, Marzo–Mayo 2002, No. 3, pp. 10-81.

Año 17, Marzo–Mayo 2003, No. 3, pp. 5-80.

III. UPPER ROOM DISCIPLINES

with Catherine Gunsalus González. "For Everything There Is a Season" (January 1-7, 1978): 13-19.

"The Stern Grace of God" (October 23-29, 1983): 308-14.
"Between Wisdom and Folly" (September 12-18, 1988): 268-74.
"Of Sheep and Shepherds" (April 30–May 6, 1990): 132-38. Reprinted in 1993, pp. 128-34.
"Back to Basics" (December 30-31, 1996): 379-80.
"Back to Basics" (January 1-5, 1997): 13-15
"Challenge and Change" (August 16-22, 1999): 240-46.

IV. OTHER BIBLE STUDY MATERIALS

with Catherine Gunsalus González. "Preparing for His Coming: A Study of Gospel Texts for Advent and Christmas." *Christmas Packet: Alternatives*, n.d.

with Catherine Gunsalus González. "The Person of Jesus." *The Adult Leader* 14, no. 2 (December–February 1981–1982): 28-55.

with Catherine Gunsalus González. "A Christian Approach to Family Issues." *The Adult Leader* 8, no. 3 (December–February 1981–1982): 56-79.

with Catherine Gunsalus González. "Completion of Matthew." *The Adult Leader* 8, no. 3 (March–May 1976): 28-55.

with Catherine Gunsalus González. "Not Many Were Powerful." *United Church of Christ A.D. 1978* 7, no. 7 (August 1978): 38-39. Also published in *United Presbyterian A.D. 1978* 7, no. 7 (August 1978): 38-39.

with Catherine Gunsalus González. "Not Many Were Powerful: Considering Our Call." *United Church of Christ A.D. 1978* 7, no. 8 (September 1978): 40-41. Also published in *United Presbyterian A.D. 1978* 7, no. 8 (September 1978): 40-41.

with Catherine Gunsalus González. "Not Many Were Powerful: A Vision of Urban Renewal." *United Church of Christ A.D. 1978* 7, no. 10 (November 1978): 43-44. Also published in *United Presbyterian A.D. 1978* 7, no. 10 (November 1978): 43-44.

with Catherine Gunsalus González. "Not Many Were Powerful: Mary, Martha, and the Good Samaritan." *United Church of Christ A.D. 1978* 7, no. 11 (December 1978): 40-41. Also published in *United Presbyterian A.D. 1978* 7, no. 11 (December 1978): 40-41.

with Catherine Gunsalus González. "Not Many Were Powerful: Star-gazing Religion." *United Church of Christ A.D. 1978* 8, no. 1 (January 1979): 42-43. Also published in *United Presbyterian A.D. 1978* 8, no. 1 (January 1979): 42-43.

with Catherine Gunsalus González. "Not Many Were Powerful: When God's Power Failed." *United Church of Christ A.D. 1979* 8, no. 2 (February 1979): 24-25. Also published in *United Presbyterian A.D. 1979* 8, no. 2 (February 1979): 24-25.

with Catherine Gunsalus González. "Not Many Were Powerful: What Is to Prevent Us?" *United Church of Christ A.D. 1979* 8, no. 3 (March 1979): 36-37. Also published in *United Presbyterian A.D. 1979* 8, no. 3 (March 1979): 36-37.

with Catherine Gunsalus González. "Not Many Were Powerful: The Unconvincing Resurrection." *United Church of Christ A.D. 1979* 8, no. 4 (April 1979): 10-11, 50. Also published in *United Presbyterian A.D. 1979* 8, no. 4 (April 1979): 10-11, 50.

with Catherine Gunsalus González. "We Are They and They Are We." In *The Bible and Christian Values*. Nashville: Graded Press, 1980. Leader's guide pp. 28-41. Student's book pp. 34-49.

"The Sign of Jonah." In *Racism: The Church's Unfinished Agenda*, A Journal of the National United Methodist Convocation on Racism (September 13-16, 1987): 35-40.

"The Story of Jesus." Teaching Helps in *Adult Bible Studies Teacher* 10, no. 2 (December 1993–February 1994): 16-80.

Leader's Guide. Luke. Vol. 11 of *Journey Through the Bible*. Nashville: Cokesbury, 1994.

Leader's Guide. Acts. Vol. 13 of *Journey Through the Bible*. Nashville: Cokesbury, 1995.

"The Story of Christian Beginnings." Teaching Helps in *Adult Bible Studies Teacher* 4, no. 1 (September–November 1995): 16-80.

Lent, Easter 1996: Scriptures for the Church Seasons. Nashville: Cokesbury, 1995.

"Wisdom for Living (Ecclesiastes, Job, Proverbs)." *Adult Bible Studies*, Teacher 6, no. 4 (June–August 1998): 16-80.

with Catherine Gunsalus González. *El Discípulo: Libro del maestro* (March/August 1999): 13-152.

El Discípulo: Libro del Maestro (Marzo/Agosto 2003): 13-146.

El Discípulo: Libro del Alumno (Marzo/Agosto 2003): 13-139.

V. ARTICLES IN JOURNALS AND PERIODICALS

"Crisis y Promesa de la Misión Mundial." *El Boletín* (Seminario Evangélico de Puerto Rico) (Abril–Junio 1967): 13-18.

"El Principio de la Reforma y la Reforma Como Principio." *El Boletín* (Seminario Evangélico de Puerto Rico) 32, no. 3 (Julio–Septiembre 1967): 4-7.

"El cristiano en la historia." *El Boletín* (Seminario Evangélico de Puerto Rico) 34, no. 2 (Abril–Junio 1969): 3-15.

"Today's Mission in the Land of Mañana." *Encounter* 33, no. 3 (Summer 1972): 278-86.

"Como Escogidos de Dios." *Diversos Dones, Un Espíritu* (División Femenil, Junta de Ministerios Globales, La Iglesia Metodista Unida) (1974): 3-4.

"Un Cuerpo—Diferentes Funciones." *Diversos Dones, Un Espíritu* (División Femenil, Junta de Ministerios Globales, La Iglesia Metodista Unida) (1974): 13-14.

"Ni Frío Ni Caliente." *Diversos Dones, Un Espíritu* (División Femenil, Junta de Ministerios Globales, La Iglesia Metodista Unida) (1974): 31-32.

"Cuida de Mis Ovejas." *Diversos Dones, Un Espíritu* (División Femenil, Junta de Ministerios Globales, La Iglesia Metodista Unida) (1974): 45-46.

"Los Ministerios en la Iglesia Protestante." *Ministerios Eclesiales en América Latina* (Bogotá, Colombia: CELAM, 1974): 106-20.

"Athens and Jerusalem Revisited: Reason and Authority in Tertullian." *Church History* 43, no. 1 (March 1974): 17-25. Reprinted in *Studies in Early Christianity*. Vol. 8. Edited by Everett Ferguson, David Scholer, and Paul Corby Finney. Hamden, Conn.: Garland Publishing, 1993).

"Liturgy and Politics: A Latin American Perspective." *Missiology: An International Review* 2, no. 2 (April 1974): 175-81.

"Inner and Outer Authority in St. Teresa of Avila." *CELEP Occasional Essays* 4, no. 3 (October 1977): 29-39.

"Searching for a Liberating Anthropology." *Theology Today* 34, no. 4 (January 1978): 386-94.

"Theology 'From Below,'" *Directions in Hispanic American Theology* (Joint Strategy and Action Committee) 10, no. 7 (February 1979).

"The Church's Hispanic Presence." *The Interpreter* 23, no. 5 (June 1979): 31.

"Liberation Theology: Is It Scriptural?" *Presbyterian Survey* 69, no. 10 (November 1979): 14-17.

"Wanted: Minority Ministers: How can the church expect to reach the whole world when almost all its ministers are alike?" *Presbyterian Survey* 70, no. 2 (February 1980): 43-44.

"Guía para el pastor hispano." *El Intérprete*, Año 19, Enero–Marzo 1981, No. 1, pp. 18-23.

"Celebrating Our Unity in Cultural Diversity." *The Interpreter* 25, no. 3 (March 1981): 8-10.

"Biblical Handles on Hunger." *Handles for Action* 4, no. 2 (Spring 1984): 5-20.

"The Things That Make for Peace." *Handles for Action* 4, no. 3 (1984): 3-14.

"El Espíritu Santo en el Nuevo Testamento." *El Intérprete*, Año 22, Abril–Junio 1984, No. 2, pp. 4-6.

"A Heritage of Hunger." *Presbyterian Survey* 75, no. 2 (March 1985): 18-21.

"Sanctuary: Some Historical, Legal, and Theological Considerations." *Exodus* (Presbyterian Church [U.S.A.] Refugee Concerns Network) 3, no. 3 (Spring 1985).

"Sanctuary: Historical, Legal, and Biblical Considerations." *elsa* 14, no. 1 (January 1986): 12-20.

"I Believe . . . In Sanctuary." *Alternatives* 12, no. 2 (Summer 1986): 14-20.

"Why Sponsor? A Biblical and Theological Basis for Sponsorship." *Exodus* (Presbyterian Church [U.S.A.] Refugee Concerns Network) 4, no. 3 (Summer 1986).

"The Two Faces of Hispanic Christianity." *The Judson Bulletin* 6, no. 1 (New Series 1987): 17-26.

"Of fishes and wishes: Confronting a hunger Myth!" *Vanguard* (March/April 1987): 4.

"Hacia un redescubrimiento de nuestra misión." *Apuntes* 7, no. 3 (Fall/Otoño 1987): 51-60. Reprinted in *El Intérprete*, Año 26, Enero–Febrero 1989, No. 1, pp. 5-7.

"Sanctuary: Part of Our Heritage." *Response Ability*, no. 29 (Winter 1987): 12-13.

"Para que el mundo crea." *El Intérprete*, Año 26, Enero–Febrero 1988, No. 1, pp. 5.

"Testifiquemos." *El Intérprete*, Año 27, Marzo–Abril 1989, No. 2, pp. 18-19.

"Reading the Bible in Spanish." *Apuntes* 9 (Summer 1989): 39-46.

"Faith and Wealth in the Early Church." *Biblical Literacy Today* 4, no. 2 (Winter 1989–1990): 14.

"Pluralismo, justicia y misión: un estudio bíblico sobre Hechos." *Apuntes* 10 (Spring 1990): 3-8.

"Piety and Mercy: Working with Christ." *Covenant Discipleship Quarterly* 5, no. 2 (January 1990): 1, 24. Also published in Spanish under the title "Piedad y Misericordia: Colaborando con Cristo." *Discípulos Responsables*, Tomo Tres, Número Dos, Enero 1990, pp. 1, 24.

"Where Frontiers End . . . And Borders Begin." *Basta!* (February 1990): 19-22.

"El pluralismo en la iglesia." *El Intérprete*, Año 28, Julio/Agosto 1990, No. 4, pp. 12-13.

"The Next Ten Years." *Apuntes* 10 (Winter/Invierno 1990): 84-86.

"Lights in the Darkness." *Christian History* 35 (Vol. 11, no. 3, 1992): 32-34.

"The Christ of Colonialism." *Church & Society* (January/February 1992): 5-36.

"Hispanics in the United States." *Listening: Journal of Religion and Culture* 27, no. 1 (Winter 1992): 7-16.

"Voices of Compassion." *Missiology: An International Review* 20, no. 2 (April 1992): 163-73.

"Loving the Enemy I Can't Forgive." *The Living Pulpit* 1, no. 3 (July–September 1992): 20-21.

with Catherine Gunsalus González. "Babel and Empire: Pentecost and Empire." *Journal for Preachers* 16, no. 4 (Pentecost 1993): 22-26.

"Espiritualidad Política." *El Faro*, Año 108, Marzo/Abril 1993, pp. 55-57.

"St. Francis Was Right after All." *The Living Pulpit* 2, no. 2 (April–June 1993): 21.

"Globalization in the Teaching of Church History." *ATS Theological Education* 29, no.2 (Spring 1993): 49-71.

"Reading the Bible in Spanish." *Unidad Cristiana/Christian Unity* 1, no. 1 (August 1993): 5-9.

"View from the Crossroads." *Perspectives* (McCormick Theological Seminary) (Fall 1993): 1-3.

"¡Levantemos nuestro monumento!" *Punto de Apoyo* (McCormick Theological Seminary) 2, Nos. 6-7, Noviembre/Diciembre 1994.

"La otra cara de la Navidad." *El Intérprete*, Año 32, Noviembre/Diciembre 1994, No. 6, p. 5.

"Hispanic Theological Education." *Ministerial Formation* (Geneva, World Council of Churches) no. 70 (July 1995): 27-28.

"A Letter From Outer Space." *The Living Pulpit* 4, no. 4 (October–December 1995): 36-37.

"The Year 2016: Where Will We Be by Then?" *Apuntes* (Summer 1996): 40-50.

"Finding the Truth." *Christian History* 51 (Vol. 15, no. 3, 1996). (Excerpts from *The Story of Christianity*.)

"The Great Family of God." *Circuit Rider* 20, no. 9 (November 1996): 12-13.

"The Church and Changing Societies: A View from the United States." *Chinese Theological Review* (1997): 14-35.

"Reading Ourselves in Spanish." *Apuntes* (Spring 1997): 12-15.

"Faith and Wealth: The Early Church and Ours." *The Living Pulpit* (July–September 1997).

"A Concluding Word: Good Shoulders for Our Mantle." *Theology Today* (1998): 516-19. (Issue edited jointly by González and Kenneth Davis.)

"Thinking about God." *Circuit Rider* 22, no. 2 (1998): 21.

"Algunas indicaciones sobre traducciones del inglés." *El Intérprete*, Año 37, Marzo/Abril 1999, No. 2, p. 11.

"The Family in Historical Perspectives." *The Living Pulpit* (July–September 1999): 11-12.

"The Reformation of the Twenty-First Century: A Reformation of Unity." *Mid-Stream* 38, no. 4 (October 1999): 3-10.

"The Whole Truth: Minority Scholars, the Academic Community, and the Church." *Apuntes* 20, no. 4 (Winter 2000): 144-49.

"The Hispanic Summer Program: Vision and History." *Apuntes* 20, no. 1 (Spring 2000): 4-8.

"Placing the M.A.P. within the Larger Map of Seminary, Church, and Community." *Perspective* (Southern Methodist University) (Fall/Winter 2000–2001): 5-8. Also published in *Apuntes* 20, no. 2 (Summer 2000): 57-65.

"Interpreting Hispanic Population Growth: Moving from Fear to Joy." *Newsletter of the Committee in Hispanic Ministries* 7, no. 6 (June 2001): 1-2. (Excerpt from paper written for the Board of Higher Education and Ministry.)

"Devolver lo recibido: La biblioteca de Jorge y Ondina." *Cuba teológica*, No. 1, 2001, pp. 2-9.

"Where There Is a Will, There Is a Way." *Journal for Preachers* 25, no. 4 (Pentecost 2002): 32-34.

with Catherine G. González. "The Ins and Outs of Pentecost." *Journal for Preachers* 26, no. 4 (Pentecost 2003): 9-14.

"Would Wesley Be Surprised?" *Circuit Rider* 27, no. 3 (May–June 2003): 6-7. Spanish version: "Wesley, estaría sorprendido?" *El Estandarte Evangélico* 120, no. 2 (Junio 2003): 6-7.

"¡Ojalá! Relectura del 10 de setiembre hacia un nuevo 12 de setiembre." *Revista Evangélica de Teología* (Buenos Aires), Vol. 1, 2003, pp. 45-68.

VI. CHAPTERS AND SECTIONS IN OTHER BOOKS

"A Parable of Grace." Pages 95-96 in Marion Van Horne, *Write the Vision: A Manual for Writers*. New York: Committee on World Literacy and Christian Literature, 1963.

"Encarnación e historia." Pages 151-67 in *Fe cristiana y Latinoamérica hoy*. Edited by C. René Padilla. Buenos Aires: Ediciones Certeza, 1974.

"The Work of Christ in Saint Bonaventure's Systematic Works." Pages 371-85 in vol. 4 of *S. Bonaventura 1274–1974*. Edited by J. G. Bougerol. Grottaferrata (Rome): Collegio S. Bonaventura, 1974.

"Un Cuerpo—Diferentes Funciones." Pages 13-14 in *Diversos Dones, Un Espíritu*. División Femenil, Junta de Ministerios Globales, La Iglesia Metodista Unida, 1974.

"The Forgiveness of Sins: A Theological Brief." Pages 221-24 in *Christian Theology: A Case Study Approach*. Edited by Robert A. Evans and Thomas D. Parker. New York: Harper & Row, 1976.

"Los ministerios en la iglesia protestante." (Primer Encuentro Latinoamericano Teología y Pastoral de los Ministerios, CELAM, Quito, Ecuador 16-24 de Agosto de 1974). Pages 106-20 in *Ministerios eclesiales en América Latina*. Bogotá, Colombia: Consejo Episcopal Latinoamericano, 1976.

with Catherine G. González. "Life at the Dawn of the Kingdom: The Readings from Acts for the Easter Season." Pages 183-88 in *Social Themes of the Christian Year: A Commentary on the Lectionary*. Edited by Dieter T. Hessel. Philadelphia: Geneva, 1983).

Prologue. Pages 9-12 in Marcos Antonio Ramos. *Panorama del protestantismo en Cuba*. Miami: Caribe, 1986.

with Catherine Gunsalus González. "The Larger Context." Pages 29-54 in *Preaching as a Social Act: Theology and Practice*. Edited by Arthur Van Seters. Nashville: Abingdon, 1988.

Prologue. Pages 11-16 in David White. *Jesús y los de abajo*. Mexico City: CUPSA, 1990.

"Setting the Context: The Option for the Poor in Latin American Liberation Theology." Pages 9-26 in *Poverty and Ecclesiology: Nineteenth-Century Evangelicals in the Light of Liberation Theology*. Edited by Anthony L. Dunnavant. Collegeville, Minn.: Liturgical Press, 1992.

Foreword. Pages ix-xi in Luis N. Rivera. *A Violent Evangelism: The Political and Religious Conquest of the Americas*. Louisville: Westminster/John Knox, 1992.

Foreword. Pages 7-12 in Bernard E. Quick, *A Vision Transformed*. Ocean City, Md.: Skipjack, 1992.

"La enseñanza de la historia de la iglesia desde una perspectiva global." Pages 13-46 in *Desde el reverso: Materiales para la historia de la iglesia*. Mexico City: El Faro, 1993.

"América Latina en perspectiva histórica." Pages 129-41 in *Desde el reverso: Materiales para la historia de la iglesia*. Mexico City: El Faro, 1993.

with Catherine G. González. "An Historical Survey." Pages 13-32 in *The Globalization of Theological Education*. Edited by Alice Frazer Evans, Robert A. Evans, and David A. Roozen. Maryknoll, N.Y.: Orbis, 1993.

"Voices of Compassion Yesterday and Today." Pages 3-12 in *New Face of the Church in Latin America*. Edited by Guillermo Cook. Maryknoll, N.Y.: Orbis, 1994.

"In Remembrance of Me: Present, Past, and Future." Pages 159-65 in *Hidden Stories: Unveiling the History of the Latino Church*. Edited by Daniel R. Rodríguez Díaz and David Cortés-Fuentes. Decatur, Ga.: AETH, 1994.

"The Religious World of Hispanic Americans." Pages 111-30 in *World Religions in America: An Introduction*. Edited by Jacob Neusner. Louisville: Westminster/John Knox, 1994.

"Confusion at Pentecost." Pages 146-49 in *The Bible in Theology and Preaching*. Edited by Donald K. McKim. Nashville: Abingdon, 1994.

"Historia de la interpretación bíblica." Pages 79-118 in *Lumbrera a nuestro camino*. Edited by Pablo A. Jiménez. Miami: Editorial Caribe, 1994.

"How the Bible Has Been Interpreted in Christian Tradition." Pages 83-106 in vol. 1 of *The New Interpreter's Bible*. Nashville: Abingdon, 1994.

"Predicación bíblica y justicia social." Pages 13-25 in *Púlpito cristiano y justicia social*. Edited by Daniel Rodríguez and Rodolfo Espinosa. Coyoacán, Mexico: Publicaciones El Faro, n.d.; San Juan, P.R.: Ediciones Borinquen, 1994.

"Reading from My Bicultural Place: Acts 6: 1-7." Pages 139-47 in *Reading from This Place*, vol. 1. Edited by Fernando F. Segovia and Mary Ann Tolbert. Minneapolis: Fortress, 1995.

with Catherine Gunsalus González. "Liberation Preaching." Pages 307-8 in *Concise Encyclopedia of Preaching*. Edited by William H. Willimon and Richard Lischer. Louisville: Westminster John Knox, 1995.

"Hispanics in the New Reformation." Pages 238-59 in *Mestizo Christianity: Theology from the Latino Perspective*. Edited by Arturo J. Bañuelas. Maryknoll, N.Y.: Orbis, 1995.

"Minority Preaching in a Postmodern Age." Pages 183-90 in *Sharing Heaven's Music: The Heart of Christian Preaching*. Edited by Barry L. Callen. Nashville: Abingdon, 1995.

"Experiences at the Interface." Pages 26-28 in *Philanthropy and Religion in a Civil Society: Experiences at the Interface*. Washington, D.C.: Council on Foundations, 1995.

Foreword. Pages ix-xiii in *Telling the Churches' Stories*. Edited by Timothy J. Wengert and Charles W. Brockwell Jr. Grand Rapids: Eerdmans, 1995.

"Metamodern Aliens in Postmodern Jerusalem." Pages 340-50 in *Hispanic/Latino Theology: Challenges and Promises*. Edited by Ada María Isasi-Díaz and Fernando F. Segovia. Minneapolis: Fortress, 1996.

"A Hymn That Will not Let Me Go." Pages 107-13 in *Desiring Charity in All Things: Unity, Liberty and Charity*. Edited by Donald E. Messer and William J. Abraham. Nashville: Abingdon, 1996.

"In Quest of a Protestant Hispanic Ecclesiology." Pages 80-97 in *Teología en Conjunto: A Collaborative Hispanic Protestant Theology*. Edited by José David Rodríguez and Loida I. Martell-Otero. Louisville: Westminster John Knox, 1997.

Foreword. Pages ix-xi in *Teología en Conjunto: A Collaborative Hispanic Protestant Theology*. Edited by José David Rodríguez and Loida I. Martell-Otero. Louisville: Westminster John Knox, 1997.

Foreword. Pages ix-xiii in *Fe en busqueda de nuevos conocimientos: Una introducción al estudio de la religión cristiana*. Edited by Guillermo Ramírez Muñoz, et al. Mexico City: International Thomson Editores, 1997.

Foreword. Pages vii-ix in Pedro Sandín Fremaint. *Consejos del Tío Pedro y otros ensayos sermoneros*. San Juan, P.R.: Seminario Evangélico de Puerto Rico, 1998).

"For the Healing of the Nations: The Book of Revelation and Our Multicultural Calling." Pages 1-7 in *The One and the Many: Christian Identity in a Multicultural World*. Edited by Thomas R. Thompson. New York: University Press of America, 1998.

"Can Wesley Be Read in Spanish?" Pages 161-68 in *Rethinking Wesley's Theology for Contemporary Methodism*. Edited by Randy L. Maddox. Nashville: Kingswood Books, 1998.

"A Hispanic Perspective: By the Rivers of Babylon." Pages 80-97 in *Preaching Justice: Ethnic and Cultural Perspectives*. Edited by Christine Marie Smith. Cleveland: United Church Press, 1998.

Foreword. Pages 9-11 in Hiram Almirudis. *Comentario de la carta del apóstol Pablo a Filemón*. Barcelona: CLIE, 1998.

"Postscript: Hanging on an Empty Cross: The Hispanic Mainline Experience." Pages 293-303 in *Protestantes / Protestants: Hispanic Christianity within Mainline Traditions*. Edited by David Maldonado Jr. Nashville: Abingdon, 1999.

"Aportes de cubanos fuera de Cuba a la teología: Una visión protestante." Pages 180-89 in *Filosofía, Teología, Literatura: Aportes cubanos en los últimos 50 años*. Edited by Raúl Fornet-Betancourt. Vol. 25 of *Monographien del Internationale Zeitschrift für Philosophie*. Aachen, Germany: Wissenschafts Verlag, 1999.

"The Changing Geography of Church History." In *Theology and the New Histories*. Edited by Gary Macy. Maryknoll, N.Y.: Orbis, 1999.

Foreword. Pages 5-8 in Inés J. Figueroa. *El proceso administrativo en la iglesia*. Miami: Caribe, 1999.

Foreword. In Eduardo Guerra. *La parábola del buen samaritano: Un ensayo de los conceptos de santidad y compasión*. Barcelona: CLIE, 1999.

"Reinventing Dogmatics: A Footnote from a Reinvented Protestant." Pages 217-29 in *From the Heart of Our People: Latino/a Explorations in Catholic Systematic Theology*. Edited by Orlando O. Espín and Miguel H. Díaz. Maryknoll, N.Y.: Orbis, 1999.

"Sin, Forgiveness, and the Experience of God." Pages 199-207 in *Beyond Borders: Writings of Virgilio Elizondo and Friends*. Edited by Timothy Matovina. Maryknoll, N.Y.: Orbis, 2000.

A personal note. Pages 116-18 in *Theologie im III. Millenium: Quo vadis? Antworten der Theologen*. Edited by Raúl Fornet-Betancourt. Frankfurt: Die Deutsche Bibliothek, 2000).

"Scripture, Tradition, Experience, and Imagination: A Redefinition." Pages 61-73 in *The Ties that Bind: African American and Hispanic American / Latino/a Theologies in Dialogue*. Edited by Anthony B. Pinn and Benjamín Valentín. New York: Continuum, 2001. Also "Response," on pages 94-96.

"The Alienation of Alienation." Pages 61-70 in *The Other Side of Sin: Woundedness from the Perspective of the Sinned-Against*. Edited by Andrew Sung Park and Susan L. Nelson. Albany: State University of New York Press, 2001.

"Acts of the Apostles." Pages 103-21 in *The New Testament: Introducing the Way of Discipleship*. Edited by Wes Howard-Brook and Sharon H. Ringe. Maryknoll, N.Y.: Orbis, 2002.

Foreword. Pages 13-16 in Juan Varela. *El culto cristiano: Origen, evolución, actualidad*. Barcelona: CLIE, 2002.

Foreword. Pages 9-14 in Alberto Radhamés Arias. *Los mejores días de tu vida*. Chicago: Alas de Aguila, 2002.

"Sembrador al voleo." In *Camino a Emaús: Compartiendo el ministerio de Jesús*. Edited by Ada María Isasi-Díaz, Timoteo Matovina, and Nina M. Torres-Vidal. Minneapolis: Fortress, 2002.

Foreword. In José David Rodríguez. *Justicia en nombre de Dios: Confesando la fe desde la perspectiva hispano/latina*. Mexico City: El Faro, 2002.

Foreword. In Pablo A. Jiménez. *Principios de predicación*. Nashville: Abingdon, 2003.

Foreword. In Carlos F. Cardoza-Orlandi. *Una introducción a la misión*. Nashville: Abingdon, 2003.

Foreword. In Guillermo Ramírez Muñoz. *Introducción al Antiguo Testamento*. Nashville: Abingdon, 2003.

Foreword. In Ismael García. *Introducción a la ética cristiana.* Nashville: Abingdon, 2003.

Foreword. In C. Michael Hawn. *One Bread, One Body: Exploring Cultural Diversity in Worship.* Bethesda, Md.: Alban Institute, 2003.

"Por qué y para qué escribo." Pages 43-55 in *La aventura de escribir.* Lima: Ediciones Puma, 2003.

Foreword. In Johnny Ramírez-Johnson, Edwin I. Hernández, et al. *Avance: A Vision for a New Mañana.* Loma Linda, Calif.: Loma Linda University Press, 2003.

Foreword. In Joel N. Martínez and Raquel M. Martínez. *Fiesta Cristiana: Recursos para la adoración / Resources for Worship.* Nashville: Abingdon, 2003.

"Una iglesia vocacionada para ejercer sus ministerios." Pages 9-24 in *Una iglesia vocacionada para ejercer sus ministerios.* San Juan, P.R.: Iglesia Cristiana Discípulos de Cristo de Puerto Rico, 2004.

Foreword. In Jorge E. Maldonado. *Introducción al asosoramiento pastoral.* Nashville: Abingdon, 2004.

Foreword. In Stephen B. Bevans and Roger P. Schroeder. *Constants in Context: A Theology of Mission for Today.* Maryknoll, N.Y.: Orbis, 2004.

VII. BOOK REVIEWS

Sergio Torres and John Eagleston, *Theology in the Americas* (Maryknoll, N.Y.: Orbis, 1976). Reviewed in *Occasional Bulletin* (April 1977): 35-36.

Robert M. Grant, *Early Christianity and Society* (New York: Harper & Row, 1977). Reviewed in *Religion in Life* 47, no. 2 (Summer 1978): 248-49.

Winston D. Persaud, *The Theology of the Cross and Marx's Anthropology: A View from the Caribbean* (New York: Peter Lang, 1991). Reviewed in *Missiology: An International Review* 22, no. 2 (April 1994): 252.

Mark Kline Taylor, *Remembering Esperanza: A Cultural-Political Theology for North American Praxis* (Maryknoll, N.Y.: Orbis, 1990). Reviewed in *Interpretation: A Journal of Bible & Theology* (April 1994): 222-24.

Lewin W. Williams, *The Caribbean Theology* (New York: Peter Lang, 1994). Reviewed in *Missiology: An International Review* 25, no. 2 (April 1997).

David Chidester, *Christianity: A Global History* (San Francisco: HarperSanFrancisco, 2000). Reviewed in *The Washington Post*, December 24, 2000.

VIII. OTHER MATERIALS

"Los Reformistas Españoles." Separata of *El Boletín* of the Evangelical Seminary of Puerto Rico, n.d. Also published in English as "The Spanish Reformers."

"La historia de occidente: Bosquejo de una concepción bibliófila." Instituto Internacional de Estudios Superiores (Comunidad Teológica de México), 24 de octubre de 1972. [7 pages].

with Catherine Gunsalus González. "How Total Is 'Total'?" Committee on Women's Concerns, Office of the General Assembly, The Presbyterian Church in the United States, October 1975. Also published in *Learning with 5*, no. 1 (January 1977): 18-21.

with Catherine Gunsalus González. "The Many Faces of United Methodists." *Broadly Graded Elective.* Nashville: Graded Press, 1983.

The Hispanic Ministry of the Episcopal Church in the Metropolitan Area of New York and Environs. New York: Trinity Grants Board, 1985.

"U.S. Basic Communities." *Seeds* 9, no. 4 (April 1986): 3.

"Of Fishes and Wishes." *Seeds: Sprouts Edition* (November 1986).

"Of Figs and Grapes." *Bread for the World in Louisiana* 6, no. 3 (November 1987).

By Raúl Quintanilla as told to Justo L. González. "My Best Christmas Gift." Page 13 in "A Christmas Reader." *Alternatives* 13, no. 4 (Winter 1987): 13. Reprint: *Mennonite Brethren Herald* 30, no. 23 (December 6, 1991): 6.

"Beyond 'Pocketbook' Voting." *Alternatives* 14, no. 3 (Fall 1988): 4.

"The Crusades: Piety Misguided." Pages 61-75 in *Cloud of Witnesses: Leader's Guide.* Nashville: Graded Press, 1988.

"Monasticism: Patterns of Piety." Pages 45-59 in *Cloud of Witnesses. Leader's Guide.* Nashville: Graded Press, 1988.

"Why Do Some Suffer and Others Not?" *Seeds* 11, no. 2 (February 1988): 32.

"Some Reflections on Faith and Wealth." *The Ellul Studies Forum,* Issue 6 (November 1990): 5-6.

"The Future Is God's." *Whose Birthday Is It, Anyway? Alternatives* (Christmas 1993):10.

"Comfort In God's Promise." *Whose Birthday Is It, Anyway?* Alternatives (Christmas 1993): 12.

"Finding Joy in Christmas." *Whose Birthday Is It, Anyway? Alternatives* (Christmas 1993): 14.

"The Supreme Surprise." *Whose Birthday Is It, Anyway? Alternatives* (Christmas 1993): 16.

"He Came to His Own." *Whose Birthday Is It, Anyway? Alternatives* (Christmas 1993): 18.

"God's Holy Family." *Whose Birthday Is It, Anyway? Alternatives* (Christmas 1993): 20.

"Which King Will We Follow?" *Whose Birthday Is It, Anyway? Alternatives* (Christmas 1993): 22.

"A Theology for Generation X." Companion booklet to *Generation X Training Video,* n.d., 69-72.

"Credo hispano / Hispanic Creed." *Mil voces para celebrar: Himnario metodista* (Nashville: The United Methodist Publishing House, 1996), 69-70.

"De los cuatro rincones del mundo." *Mil voces para celebrar: Himnario Metodista* (Nashville: The United Methodist Publishing House, 1994), no. 378.

"Gracias, Dios vivo." *Mil voces para celebrar: Himnario Metodista* (Nashville: The United Methodist Publishing House, 1994), no. 386.

"Toward a Theology for a Hispanic Pastoral Praxis / Teología para una pastoral hispana." Board of Higher Education and Ministry, The United Methodist Church, *Occasional Papers,* no. 95 (March 1999).

IX. INTERVIEWS AND VIDEOS

"Justo González al habla: La historia se enseña y se escribe a partir del futuro." By Eliseo Pérez Alvarez. *El Faro,* Julio–Agosto 1992, pp. 124-27.

Generation X Training Video. Nashville: General Board of Discipleship, United Methodist Church, 1993.

"Interview with Justo L. González." By Neil M. Alexander. *Cokesbury's Good Books Catalog* (Fall/Winter 1993–1994): 2-3.

"Hispanic Writer Challenges Denomination." *Committee on Hispanic Ministries Newsletter* 3, no. 1 (December 1995): 1-2.

Wesley en Puerto Rico: Implicaciones teológicas y pastorales del ministerio de Juan Wesley. 7 vídeos. San Juan, P.R.: Seminario Evangélico de Puerto Rico, 1997.

"General Synod [of the R.C.A.] Keynote Address." First Reformed Church, June 15, 1997.

Host for "Christian Believer." The United Methodist Publishing House, 30 segments.

Several videos in the United Methodist DISCIPLE series.

Four videos on Church History and Introduction to Theology, in Spanish, for the Christian Church (Disciples of Christ).

X. ARTICLES IN DICCIONARIO ILUSTRADO DE LA BIBLIA (MIAMI: EDITORIAL CARIBE, 1974)

Ahava
Alejandría
Alejandro, El Grande
Alfabeto
Amrafel
Antíoco
Arvad
Babilonia (Ciudad)
Babilonia (Región e Imperio)
Belsasar
Cabul
Caldeos, Caldea
Carquemis
Dura
Egipto
Elam
Escitas
Escriba
Escritura
Escrituras
Et-Baal
Faraón
Fenicia
Gnosticismo
Hamurabi
Hechicería
Hena
Hiram
Idolatría (con R.F.B.)
India
Javán

Jezabel
Libertos
Libro
Lugares altos
Merolac-Baladán
Mizraím
Nabucodonosor
Necao
Nergal-Sarezer
Partia, Partos
Patros
Peregrino
Pibiset
Ptolomeo
Quedorlaomer
Rab-Mag
Ramesés
Sarepta
Sefarad
Seleuco
Sidón
Sinagoga (con R.F.B.)
Sisac
Suquienos
Tafnes
Tarsis
Tel-Abib
Tirhaca
Tiro
Ur (con J.M.Br.)

XI. ARTICLES IN THE DICTIONARY OF BIBLE AND RELIGION (NASHVILLE: ABINGDON, 1986)

Abelard
Adoptionism
Alban
Albertus Magnus
Albigenses
Alcuin
Alexandrian Theology
Ambrose of Milan
Anchorite
Anselm
Ante-Nicene Fathers
Anthony of Egypt
Anthony of Padua
Antiochene Theology
Apollinarians/Apollinarius
Apologists (Greek)
Apostles' Creed
Apostolic Fathers
Aquinas, Thomas
Arianism/Arius
Athanasian Creed
Athanasius
Athenagoras
Augustine/Augustinianism
Augustine of Canterbury
Averroes
Avignon
Barnabas, Epistle of
Basel, Council of
Basil the Great
Bede, the Venerable
Berenger of Tours
Boethius
Bonaventure
Boniface VIII, Pope
Caesaropapism
Cappadocian Fathers
Capuchins
Carmelites
Carthusians
Catacombs
Catechumen
Cathars/Cathari
Catherine of Alexandria
Catherine of Siena
Celsus
Cerinthus

Chalcedon, Council of
Charlemagne
Charles V
China Inland Mission
Christendom
Christopher
Christotokos
Chrysostom, John
Church Expectant/Militant/Triumphant
Church Fathers
Cistercians
Clement XI, Pope
Clement XIV, Pope
Clement of Alexandria
Clement of Rome
Cloud of Unknowing, The
Cluny
Coke, Thomas
Confessions of Augustine
Constance, Council of
Constantine, Emperor
Constantinople, Councils and Creed of
Coptic Church
Crusades
Cure of Souls
Cyprian of Carthage
Cyril of Alexandria
Cyril of Jerusalem
Dark Night of the Soul
Defrock
Desert Fathers
Diatessaron
Didache
Diognetus, Epistle of
Dionysius the Great
Dionysius the Pseudo-Areopagite
Docetists
Doctors of the Church
Dominic/Dominicans
Donation of Constantine
Donatists
Double Procession of the Holy Spirit
Duns Scotus, John
Early Church, History of Christianity in
    the
Ecce Homo
Ecumenical Councils

Edict of Milan
Ephesus, Council of
Established Church
Eusebius of Caesarea
Excommunication
Flagellation
Glossa Ordinaria
Gothic
Gottschalk
Grail, Holy
Gratian
Great Schism
Gregory I, the Great
Gregory VII, Pope
Gregory of Nazianzus
Gregory of Nyssa
Hadrian I
Hagiography
Hermit

Herodotus
Hilary of Poitiers
Hildegard
Hippolytus
History of Christian Doctrine
Holy Roman Empire
Homoousion/Homoiousion
Hugh of St. Victor
Hypostatic Union/Hypostasis
Icon/Iconography
Iconoclastic Controversy
Ignatius of Antioch, Epistles of
Innocent III
Investiture Controversy
Irenaeus of Lyon
Isidore of Seville
Middle Ages, Christianity in the
Pietism

XII. ARTICLES IN DICCIONARIO DE HISTORIA DE LA IGLESIA (MIAMI: EDITORIAL CARIBE, 1989)

Anglicanismo y Episcopalismo en América Latina
Anselmo de Canterbury
Bainton, Roland Herbert
Bernabé, Epístola de
Bismarck, Otto Von
Conferencias Misioneras Protestantes
Haití
Iglesia y Estado en América Latina
Juana Inés de la Cruz
Mackay, John A.
Mártires
Mozárabe, Liturgia
Neill, Stephen Charles
Padres Apostólicos
Salmerón Alfonso
Suso, Enrique
Teresa de Avila
Toynbee, Arnold
Valdés, Juan y Alfonso
Vodu en América Latina

XIII. ARTICLES IN DICCIONARIO ILUSTRADO DE INTÉRPRETES DE LA FE (BARCELONA: CLIE, 2004)

Abaudo
Abbot, Edwin
Abbot, George
Abdías de Babilonia
Abelardo
Abgaro, Epístola de Jesús a
Abraham Ecchellensis
Acacio de Berea
Acacio de Cesarea
Acacio de Constantinopla
Acta sanctorum
Actas de los mártires
Acton, Barón
Adam, Karl
Adamancio
Adán de Marsh
Adán de San Víctor
Adelardo de Bath
Adelmano
Adsón de Luxeuil
Aecio
Agobardo de Lyón
Agustín de Hipona
Alano de Lille
Alberto el Grande
Alejandro de Afrodisias
Alejandro de Alejandría
Alejandro de Hales
Amalrico de Bena
Ambrosio
Amolo de Lyón
Amyraut, Moise
Anchieta, J. de
Anfiloquio de Iconio
Aniceto
Anorio
Anselmo de Laón
Antonio de Padua
Apeles
Apolinario de Hierápolis
Apolinario de Laodicea
Araquel de Tauriz
Arístides
Aristón de Pela
Aristoteles
Arnauld, A.
Arnobio

Arrio
Artemón
Asterio el Sofista
Atanasio
Atón de Verceil
Babai el Grande
Bacon, Rogerio
Báñez, Domingo
Bar Berika, Ebedjesu
Bar Hebreo, Gregorio
Bar Isho'dad de Merv, Teod.
Bar Nun, Isho
Bar Senaja, Elías
Bar Sushan, I.
Bardesanes
Barlaam
Baronio, César
Barsumas
Basilio de Anquira
Basilio de Cesarea
Beato de Liébana
Belarmino, R.
Bellamy, Joseph
Berengario
Blandrata, G.
Boecio
Boecio de Dacia
Bonifacio VIII
Bossuet, Jacques
Boston, Thomas
Bradwardino
Bruno, Eusebio
Budé, Guillermo
Buenaventura
Bulgaris, Eugenio
Butler, Joseph
Cabasilas, Nicolás
Cabasilas, Nilo
Cadbury, Henry Joel
Calcedonia, Concilio de
Calixto
Calvino
Camerario, Bartolomé
Camerario, Joaquin
Cameron, John
Cameron, Richard
Canisio, Pedro

Cano, Melchor
Capadocios
Cartwright, Thomas
Case, Shirley Jackson
Casiodoro
Catalina de Génova
Catarino, Ambrosio
Cayetano, Tomás de Vio
Celestio
Centurias de Magdeburgo
Cerulario, Miguel
Cesáreo de Arlés
Chandler, Samuel
Chauncy, Charles
Cipriano
Cirilo de Alejandría
Cirilo de Jerusalén
Cirilo de Turov
Clarembaud de Arras
Clarke, William Newton
Claudiano Mamerto
Clemente de Alejandría
Clemente de Smolensk
Concilios
Constantinopla, Conc. 381
Constantinopla, Conc. 553
Constantinopla, Conc. 681
Constantinopla, Conc. 869-70
Constanza, Concilio de
Cornelio
Cranmer, Tomás
Cuadrato
D'Ailly, Pierre
Dámaso I
David de Dinant
De Maistre, Joseph Marie
Demetrio de Cizico
Demetrio de Lampe
Denk, Hans
Derrida, Jacques
Deusdedit
Dídimo el Ciego
Dietrich de Niem
Diodoro de Tarso
Diogneto, Discurso a
Dionisio de Alejandría
Dionisio de Roma
Dionisio el Areopagita
Dióscoro
Doctores de la Iglesia
Donato

Dort, Sínodo de
Dositeo de Jerusalén
Durand de Troarn
Ebedjesus Bar Berika
Economos, Constantino
Efeso, Concilio de
Efrén Sirio
Egidio de Lessines
Egidio de Roma
Egidio de Viterbo
Elias Bar Senaya
Elipando de Toledo
Elxai
Encratitas
Encyclion
Eneas de Gaza
Eneas de París
Enrique de Gante
Epifanio
Esteban de Niobe
Esteban de Tournai
Eudes de Stella
Eudoxio
Eunomio
Eusebio de Cesarea
Eusebio de Dorilea
Eusebio de Emesa
Eusebio de Nicodemia
Eustacio de Antioquía
Eustacio de Sebaste
Eutiques
Farmaquides, Teocleto
Fausto de Milevis
Fausto de Riez
Félix de Urgel
Ferrara-Florencia, Concilio
Firmiliano de Cesarea
Fishacre, Ricardo
Flaviano de Constantinopla
Floro de Lyón
Focio
Fredegiso de Tours
Frolando de Senlis
Fulberto de Chartres
Fulgencio de Ruspe
Gadamer
Garnerio de Rochefort
Gaunilo
Gautier de San Víctor
Gelasio
Genadio de Marsella

Genadio de Novgorod
Gerardo de Abbeville
Gerardo de Borgo San Donino
Gerberto de Aurillac
Gerhoch de Reichersberg
Germán de Constantinopla
Germinio de Sirmio
Gezo de Tortona
Gilberto de la Porrée
Girard, Rene
Godofredo de Fontaines
Godofredo de la Vendome
Godofredo de San Víctor
González, Domingo
Gotescalco de Orbais
Gregorio Acindino
Gregorio de Catino
Gregorio de Datev
Gregorio de Elvira
Gregorio el Grande
Gregorio de Nacianzo
Gregorio de Neocesarea
Gregorio de Nisa
Gregorio de Rimini
Gregorio del Sinaí
Grosseteste, Roberto
Guido de Osnaburgo
Guillermo de Auvergne
Guillermo de Auxerre
Guillermo de Champeaux
Guillermo de Conches
Guillermo de La Mare
Guillermo de Saint Amour
Güitmundo de Aversa
Habermas
Hadrumento, monjes de
Harris, George
Harris, J. R.
Haymón de Halberstadt
Hegesipo
Heidegger, Martin
Heirico de Auxerre
Heleno de Tarso
Heraclas
Hermias
Hesshusen, Teillmann
Hilario de Arlés
Hilario de Poitiers
Hilarión de Kiev
Hincmaro
Holov, Juan

Honorio (papa)
Honorio de Augsburgo
Hormisdas
Hosio de Córdoba
Hugo de Chartres
Hugo de Estrasburgo
Hugo de Fleury
Hugo de San Víctor
Humberto (Cardenal)
Hut, Hans
Hutter, Jacobo
Ibas de Edesa
Ildefonso de Toledo
Ireneo
Isho Bar Nun
Isidoro de Pelusio
Isidoro de Sevilla
Jacobo de Edesa
Jacopone de Todi
Jerónimo
Jeroteo
Joaquín de Fiore
Jorge de Arabia
Juan Itálico
Juan de Antioquía
Juan de Avila
Juan de Cournailles
Juan de Damasco
Juan de España
Juan de Jando
Juan de la Rochelle
Juan de Parma
Juan de Saint Giles
Juan de Salisbury
Juan el Diácono
Juan el Gramático
Juan el Teutón
Juan Filopón
Juan Peckham
Julián de Eclano
Julián de Halicarnaso
Juliano Pomaro
Justiniano
Justino
Killwardby, Roberto
Lactancio
Lanfranco
Langton, Esteban
León el Grande
Leon de Ocrida
Leoncio de Antioquía

Severo de Antioquía
Sexto Julio Africano
Sigerio de Brabante
Simeón de Polock
Simeón Neoteólogo
Simón de Tournai
Sócrates (historiador)
Sofronio de Jerusalén
Sorbón, Roberto
Sotérico Panteugenos
Soto, Domingo de
Sozómeno
Stancaro, Francesco
Strigel, Victorino
Suidas, Nicetas
Sulpicio Severo
Suso, Enrique
Taciano
Tanquelmo
Tempier, Esteban
Teodoreto
Teodoro Bar Koni
Teodoro de Mopsuestia
Teodoro de Raithu
Teodulfo de Orleans

Teognis de Nicea
Teognosto
Tertuliano
Thierry de Chartres
Timoteo Aelluro
Trento, Concilio de
Turretin, Benedict
Turretin, François
Turretin, Jean-Alphonse
Ulrico de Estrasburgo
Ursacio
Valente (obispo)
Verona, Concilio de (1184)
Vicente de Lerins
Vicente de Paúl
Víctor, obispo de Roma
Vitalis
Vives, Luis
Wilgardo de Ravena
Wolfelm de Brauweiler
Yahya Ben Adi
Zacarías de Mitilene
Zanchi, Jerónimo
Zósimo

CONTRIBUTORS

Efrain Agosto is Professor of New Testament and Director of Programa de Ministerios Hispanos at Hartford Seminary.

Carmelo E. Alvarez is Affiliate Professor of Church History and Theology at Christian Theological Seminary in Indianapolis, Indiana.

Edwin David Aponte is Director of Advanced Studies and Associate Professor of Christianity and Culture at Perkins School of Theology, Southern Methodist University, Dallas, Texas.

Elizabeth Conde-Frazier is Associate Professor of Religious Education at Claremont School of Theology in Claremont, California.

Kenneth G. Davis is Associate Professor of Pastoral Studies at the St. Meinrad School of Theology in St. Meinrad, Indiana.

Ester Diaz-Bolet is Assistant Professor of Administration, School of Educational Ministries, Southwestern Baptist Theological Seminary, Fort Worth, Texas, and former president of Asociación para la Educación Teológica Hispana (AETH).

Virgilio Elizondo is the former rector of San Fernando Cathedral; Distinguished Visiting Professor of Theology, University of Notre Dame, Indiana; and founder and first president of the Mexican American Cultural Center, San Antonio, Texas.

Orlando O. Espín is Professor of Systematic Theology and Director of the Center for the Study of Latino/a Catholicism at the University of San Diego, California.

Ismael García is Professor of Ethics at Austin Presbyterian Theological Seminary in Austin, Texas.

Francisco O. Garcia-Treto is J. F. R. King Professor of Religion at Trinity University, San Antonio, Texas.

Roberto S. Goizueta is Professor of Theology at Boston College, President of the Catholic Theological Society of America, and past President of the Academy of Catholic Hispanic Theologians of the United States.

Edwin I. Hernández is Director of the Center for the Study of Latino Religion, University of Notre Dame, Indiana.

Pablo A. Jiménez is Director of www.predicar.org, a Web site dedicated to homiletics, and National Pastor for Hispanic Ministries of the Christian Church (Disciples of Christ) in the United States and Canada.

Philip E. Lampe is Professor of Sociology at University of the Incarnate Word in San Antonio, Texas.

Daisy L. Machado is Associate Professor of History of Christianity and Hispanic Church Studies at Brite Divinity School in Fort Worth, Texas.

David Maldonado Jr. is President Emeritus at Iliff School of Theology, Denver, Colorado.

Zaida Maldonado Pérez is Associate Professor of Theological Studies at Asbury Theological Seminary, Florida campus.

Jesse Miranda is Distinguished Professor and Director of Center for Urban Studies and Ethnic Leadership (CUSEL) at Vanguard University, Costa Mesa, California, and founding and current president of the *Alianza de Ministerios Evangélicos Nacionales* (AMEN).

Alvin Padilla is Dean of Gordon-Conwell Theological Seminary, Boston, and Associate Professor of New Testament.

Samuel Pagán is President Emeritus, and Catedrático, at Seminario Evangélico de Puerto Rico, Rio Piedras.

Robert W. Pazmiño is Valeria Stone Professor of Christian Education at Andover Newton Theological School in Newton Centre, Massachusetts.

Luis G. Pedraja is Executive Associate Director at Middle States Association Commission on Higher Education.

Guillermo Ramírez-Muñoz is Academic Dean and Professor of Old Testament and Hebrew at Evangelical Seminary of Puerto Rico, San Juan.

Luis N. Rivera-Pagán is Henry Winters Luce Professor of Ecumenics at Princeton Theological Seminary.

Fernando F. Segovia is Oberlin Graduate Professor of New Testament and Early Christianity at Vanderbilt University, Nashville, Tennessee.

Aida Besançon Spencer is Professor of New Testament at Gordon-Conwell Theological Seminary, Hamilton, Massachusetts.

Eldin Villafañe is Ricardo Tañon Distinguished Professor of Hispanic Christianity, Ethics, and Urban Ministry at Gordon-Conwell Theological Seminary; Founding Director of Gordon-Conwell's Boston campus, Center for Urban Ministerial Education (CUME); and past president of Asociación para la Educación Teológica Hispana (AETH).

Notes

INTRODUCTION

1. James Joyce, *A Portrait of the Artist as a Young Man* (New York: B. W. Huebsch, 1916).

2. Isabel Allende, *The Stories of Eva Luna* (New York: Macmillan, 1991), 150.

1. MARGINALITY AND SOLIDARITY IN 1 CORINTHIANS

1. See Justo L. González, *Santa Biblia: The Bible through Hispanic Eyes* (Nashville: Abingdon, 1996).

2. See ibid., 41-42, for examples of this with regard to Acts 13.

3. See ibid., 58.

4. Ibid., 78-79, cites Mexican-American theologian Virgilio Elizondo and his seminal work on Hispanic theology, *Galilean Journey: The Mexican-American Promise* (Maryknoll, N.Y.: Orbis, 1983).

5. González, *Santa Biblia*, 80.

6. See ibid., 80-84, for detailed development of Paul's *mestizaje*.

7. Ibid., 91.

8. Ibid., 93-95, citing the work of Francisco Garcia-Treto, "El Señor guarda a los emigrantes," *Apuntes* 1, no. 4 (Winter 1981): 4-7.

9. González, *Santa Biblia*, 95-98.

10. Ibid., 104, citing a sermon by Pablo Jiménez.

11. John Elliot, *A Home for the Homeless: A Social-Scientific Criticism of First Peter, Its Situation and Strategy* (Minneapolis: Augsburg Fortress, 1990).

12. See González, *Santa Biblia*, 107-8, for this description and its implications for biblical hermeneutics by Hispanics today.

13. Ibid., 108-10, 113.

14. Ibid., 110-11.

15. Ibid., 111-12.

16. Ibid., 112-13.

17. So argues Margaret M. Mitchell, *Paul and the Rhetoric of Reconciliation: An Exegetical Investigation of the Language and Composition of 1 Corinthians* (Louisville: Westminster John Knox, 1991), 68-70.

18. As depicted by ibid., 198-200.

19. See Gerd Theissen, *The Social Setting of Pauline Christianity: Essays on Corinth* (Philadelphia: Fortress, 1982), 145-74, for this interpretation of 1 Cor 11:17-34.

20. For more on the collection for the Jerusalem church and Paul's efforts to exact gifts from his Greek churches, see Dieter Georgi, *Remembering the Poor: The History of Paul's Collection for Jerusalem* (Nashville: Abingdon, 1992).

21. L. L. Welborn, *Politics and Rhetoric in the Corinthian Epistles* (Macon, Ga.: Mercer University Press, 1997), 3.

22. See ibid., 3-5, for a discussion of these and other political terms used by Paul here in 1 Cor 1–4.

23. See Richard Horsley, *1 Corinthians* (Abingdon New Testament Commentaries; Nashville: Abingdon, 1998), 44-45.

24. Welborn, *Politics and Rhetoric*, 8-16.

25. Ibid., 5.

26. In particular see Stephen Pogoloff, *Logos and Sophia: The Rhetorical Situation of 1 Corinthians* (Atlanta: Scholars, 1992), who demonstrates the problem of ornamental rhetoric as a means of social status enhancement versus Paul's concentration on pre-senting the content of the gospel, without the need for ornament, but spiritual "power."

27. See Peter Marshall, *Enmity in Corinth: Social Conventions in Paul's Relations with the Corinthians* (Tübingen: Mohr, 1987), for how patronage affected Paul's relationships with certain elite members of the Corinthian community's leadership.

28. See, for example, Horsley, *1 Corinthians*, 33, 47-56.

29. Perhaps they were what Wayne Meeks called "status inconsistents," those with newfound wealth, for example, but still not at the center of power in Corinth because of other criteria such as family ties or political positions. See Meeks, *The First Urban Christians: The Social World of the Apostle Paul* (New Haven: Yale University Press, 1983), 51-73. Nonetheless, they were well-off compared to other members of the Corinthian community and acted in ways that humiliated the poorer members.

30. For an extensive study of Paul's use of slave language as a metaphor for Christian living, including leadership, see Dale Martin, *Slavery as Salvation: The Metaphor of Slavery in Pauline Christianity* (New Haven: Yale University Press, 1990).

31. For an extensive discussion of Paul's approach to leadership in 1 Corinthians, see Andrew D. Clarke, *Secular and Christian Leadership in Corinth: A Socio-Historical & Exegetical Study of 1 Corinthians 1-6* (Leiden: E. J. Brill, 1993).

32. See John T. Fitzgerald, *Cracks in an Earthen Vessel: An Examination of the Catalogues of Hardships in the Corinthian Correspondence* (Atlanta: Scholars, 1988), for a study of how Paul used the practice of Greco-Roman hardship catalogs to describe the sacrifice inherent in his apostleship.

33. As suggested by Horsley, *1 Corinthians*, 63-67, among others.

34. See Marshall, *Enmity in Corinth*, 203-5, who shows the connection between being "puffed up" and the elite social status of Paul's opponents in Corinth.

35. For a detailed study of these connections of the problems in 1 Corinthians to a group of patrons who oppose Paul at every turn, see John K. Chow, *Patronage and Power: A Study of Social Networks in Corinth* (Sheffield: Sheffield Academic Press, 1992).

2. GENESIS 1:1–2:4

1. See for example Barbara Green, *Mikhail Bakhtin and Biblical Scholarship: An Introduction* (Semeia Studies 38, ed. Danna Nolan Fewell; Atlanta: Society of Biblical Literature, 2000); and Walter L. Reed, *Dialogues of the Word: The Bible as Literature according to Bakhtin* (Oxford: Oxford University Press, 1993).

2. Mark G. Brett, *Genesis: Procreation and the Politics of Identity* (London and New York: Routledge, 2000).

3. Ibid., 22.

4. M. M. Bakhtin, *The Dialogic Imagination: Four Essays* (ed. Michael Holquist; trans. Caryl Emerson and Michael Holquist; Austin: University of Texas Press, 1981), 358.

5. Green, *Mikhail Bakhtin*, 58.

6. Bakhtin, *Dialogic Imagination*, 358.

7. Ibid.

8. Ibid., 279. See also Ruth Coates, *Christianity in Bakhtin* (Cambridge: Cambridge University Press, 1998), 108; Alexandar Mihailovic, *Corporeal Words: Mikhail Bakhtin's Theology of Discourse* (Evanston, Ill.: Northwestern University Press, 1997), 27; and Homi K. Bhabha, *The Location of Culture* (London; New York: Routledge, 1994), 188.

9. Brett, *Genesis*, 23. Brett furnishes a fuller statement of the "intentional hybridity" of the final editing of Genesis at the beginning of his book's concluding chapter ("Whose Genesis? Which Orthodoxy?") on page 137.

10. Bakhtin, *Dialogic Imagination*, 84

11. Green, *Mikhail Bakhtin*, 62.

12. Gary Saul Morson and Caryl Emerson, *Mikhail Bakhtin: Creation of a Prosaic* (Stanford: Stanford University Press, 1990), 429; quoted in Green, *Mikhail Bakhtin*, 63-64.

13. Roberto S. Goizueta, "Fiesta: Life in the Subjunctive," in *From the Heart of Our People: Latino/a Explorations in Catholic Systematic Theology* (ed. Orlando O. Espín and Miguel H. Díaz; Maryknoll, N.Y.: Orbis, 1999), 84-99.

14. Richard Blanco, "Havanasis" in his *City of a Hundred Fires* (Pittsburgh: University of Pittsburgh Press, 1998), 37-38.

15. Brett, *Genesis*, 24.

16. Ibid., 24.

17. Ibid., 25.

18. Ibid.

19. Ibid.

20. Ibid., 25-26

21. Ibid., 26

22. Ibid.

23. Ibid., 27.

24. Ibid., 28.

25. Ibid.

26. Ibid., 29.

27. Ibid., 27.

28. Hermann Gunkel, *Genesis* (trans. Mark E. Biddle; Mercer Library of Biblical Studies, ed. Joseph Blenkinsopp, et al.; Macon, Ga.: Mercer University Press, 1997), lxxx.

29. Ibid.

30. Ibid., 122.

31. Claus Westermann, *Genesis 1–11: A Continental Commentary* (trans. John J. Scullion; Minneapolis: Augsburg Fortress, 1994), 170.

32. Gerhard von Rad, *Genesis: A Commentary* (rev. ed.; The Old Testament Library, ed. Peter Ackroyd, et al.; Philadelphia: Westminster, 1973), 62-63.

33. Westermann, *Genesis 1–11*, 171.

34. Ibid.

35. Ibid.

36. Ibid., 172.

37. Goizueta, "Fiesta," 84-99.

38. Ibid., 90

39. Ibid. Goizueta says: "to celebrate life as gift in the midst of a culture that views life as an object to be controlled is a prophetic act; to 'waste' time celebrating in the midst of a culture where time is a priceless commodity ('time is money') is a subversive act."

40. Ibid., 91.

41. Ibid., 96.

42. Blanco, *City of a Hundred Fires*, 37-38.

43. Ibid., 37.

44. African drums used in the dance rituals of Santeria.

45. Blanco, *City of a Hundred Fires*, 37.

46. Ibid.

47. Ibid.

48. Ibid., 38.

3. SONGS OF THE SERVANT OF THE LORD

1. This essay is dedicated to my colleague and friend Justo González. During his long and fruitful ministry he has demonstrated a sincere commitment to the causes and concerns described and affirmed in the Songs of the Suffering Servant of the Lord. In addition to his studies on the Servant of the Lord, we should identify the following: C. R. North, *The Suffering Servant in Deutero-Isaiah: An Historical and Critical Study* (2nd ed.; London: Oxford, 1956), 192-219; H. H. Rowley, *The Servant of the Lord and Other Essays on the Old Testament* (London: Lutterworth, 1952), 49-53; H. L. Ginsberg, "The Oldest Interpretation of the Suffering Servant," *VT* 3 (1953): 400-404).

The book by B. Duhm, *Das Buch Jesaia* (Gottingen: Vandenhoeck & Ruprecht, 1892) was a pioneer and fundamental in the identification and study of the Songs of the Servant as independent components within the book of Isaiah. With the passing of time, the conclusions of Duhm have been revived and actualized in light of new understandings of Isaiah; see Tryggve Mettinger, *A Farewell to the Servant Songs: A Critical Examination of an Exegetical Axiom* (Lund: Gleerup, 1983).

The history of the Jewish interpretations of Isaiah 53 is found in *The Fifty-Third Chapter of Isaiah According to Jewish Interpreters* (ed. S. R. Driver and A. Neubauer; New York: Ktav, 1969).

My analysis of the relationship between the Songs of the Servant and the "Daughter of Zion" follows the recent and important study of John F. A. Sawyer, "Daughter of Zion and Servant of the Lord in Isaiah: A Comparison," *JSOT* 44 (1989): 89-107. For a study on the history of the interpretation of the Songs, see the insightful book by Sawyer himself, *The Fifth Gospel* (Cambridge: Cambridge University Press, 1996), 83-99.

2. See the commentaries on Isaiah cited throughout this essay.

3. The word *servant* appears twenty times in Deutero-Isaiah (one time in plural form); thirteen times it is related with the people of Israel; and the other seven are included in the Songs of the Servant of the Lord and related passages. See 41:8, 9; 42:1, 19; 43:10; 44:1, 2, 21, 26; 45:4; 48:20; 49:5, 6; 50:10; 52:13; 53:11; 54:17. Richard J. Clifford, "Book of (Second) Isaiah," *The Anchor Bible Dictionary* (New York: Doubleday, 1992), 3:499-500.

4. The intimate relationship between the poems of the Servant and the expiatory mission of Christ is initially found, in all likelihood, in the words of Jesus himself; afterward

the Christian church followed and elaborated on this perception of his ministry. Referring to this theme, see the important work of J. Jeremias, *The Servant of God* (London: SCM, 1965), 99-106; also very important are the books by C. H. Dodd, *According to the Scriptures: The Substructure of New Testament Theology* (London: James Nisbet, 1952) and Oscar Cullmann, *The Christology of the New Testament* (Philadelphia: Westminster, 1975.)

5. Augustine, *Sermons on the Liturgical Seasons* (trans. Mary Sarah Muldowney; *The Fathers of the Church* 38, ed. Roy Joseph Deferrari; New York: Fathers of the Church, 1959), 80-81.

6. From the studies of Duhm, *Das Buch,* the discussions regarding the poems of the Servant of the Lord have been affected by two basic methodological propositions: (1) each poem is independent, and (2) the Songs have a literary prehistory that does not necessarily relate with the Isaiah literature.

In the analysis of the diverse possibilities of the interpretation of the Songs of the Servant, we follow J. McKenzie, *Second Isaiah* (AB 20; Garden City, N.Y.: Doubleday, 1967), xxxviii-xliv). See also North, *Suffering Servant,* whose study is fundamental to understand the history and the hermeneutical alternatives of the Songs.

7. Some studies, advancing the theories of Duhm, identify five (42:5-9) or seven poems of the Servant (42:5-9; 49:7, 8-13) in Deutero-Isaiah; and others see more Songs in Trito-Isaiah (for example, 61:1-4; 62:1-12; 63:7-14; 66:1-11). See E. Dussel, "Universalismo y misión en los poemas del Siervo de Yahveh," *Ciencia y Fe* 20 (1964): 419-64; and A. Ricciardi, "Los Cantos del Siervo de Yavé," *Cuadernos de Teología* 4 (1976): 123-28.

8. In regard to the description of the story of the Servant, see the systematic work, previously cited, of McKenzie, *Second Isaiah,* xxix.

9. Clifford, "The Book of (Second) Isaiah," AB 3:500.

10. McKenzie, *Second Isaiah,* xxxix-xl; see also the article of P. Wilcox and D. Paton-Williams, "The Servant-Songs in Deutero-Isaiah," JSOT (1988): 79-102.

11. The early church saw in the figure of the Servant a reference to Jesus of Nazareth.

12. See McKenzie, *Second Isaiah,* xliv.

13. To respond to this argument some authors have indicated that the Servant is not all the people but a select remnant of Israel; Ginsberg, "Oldest Interpretation."

14. McKenzie, *Second Isaiah,* xliv-xlv.

15. S. Mowinckel initially defended this interpretation, although later in his academic career he abandoned this theory; see McKenzie, *Second Isaiah,* xlvi.

According to North, scholars have identified at least fifteen persons whom they can relate to the figure of the Servant of the Lord, among whom are the following: Isaias, Uzziah, Josiah, Ezekiel, Job, Moses, Joaquim, Cyrus, Sesbazar, Zorobabel, Nehemiah, Eleazar (*Suffering Servant,* 192-93). With the passing of time, and also with the development and deepening of studies of the Songs, several of these theories have been exegetically and theologically abandoned.

16. The important discussion for the church that evaluates the relation of the Songs of the Servant with Jesus of Nazareth can be found in the work of F. F. Bruce, *The New Testament Development of Old Testament Themes* (Grand Rapids: Eerdmans, 1969).

17. North, *Suffering Servant,* 192-219.

18. See particularly I. Engnell, "The Ebed-Yahweh Songs and the Suffering Messiah in 'Deutero-Isaiah,'" BJRL 31 (1948): 54-93; McKenzie, *Second Isaiah,* l-liii.

19. McKenzie, *Second Isaiah,* li.

20. In reference to the theory of "cooperative personality" in the Bible, the study of H. Wheeler Robinson, "The Hebrew Conception of Corporate Personality," is very important (BZAW 66 [1936], 49-62); see also the relevant and important works of Rowley, *Servant of the Lord;* McKenzie, *Second Isaiah,* lii-lv; Cullmann, *Christology of the New Testament,* 51-53.

21. McKenzie, *Second Isaiah*, lii.

22. In respect to the promise of the dynasty of David and its theological implications, see the articles of David M. Howard, Jr., "David," *The Anchor Bible Dictionary* (New York: Doubleday, 1992), 2:41-49; and Michael D. Guinan, "Davidic Covenants," *The Anchor Bible Dictionary* (New York: Doubleday, 1992), 2:69-72.

23. McKenzie, *Second Isaiah*, liii-liv.

24. In the study of the relationship between the Songs of the Servant and Jesus we should take into consideration the following additional factors: the most important texts for Jesus were the fourth Song of the Servant and other passages in Isaiah (43:4; 44:26; 50:10; 59:21; 61:1-3); Jesus himself related some ideas of the second and third Song with his disciples (Matt 5:14, 16, 39; cf. Isa 49:3, 6; 50:6); and although the church saw in Jesus the optimal fulfillment of the poems of the Servant, it continued relating them with all of the people of Israel (Luke 1:54).

The relation of the Servant of the Lord and the Messiah in Judaism is complex and intimate; see Cullmann, *Christology of the New Testament*, 55-58.

25. In this comparative analysis, we follow the study of Sawyer, "Daughter of Zion."

26. Ibid., 250-51.

27. In the evaluation of the biblical interpretations of the images of the Servant, we follow Bruce, *New Testament Development*, 83-99; see also Rowley, *Servant of the Lord*, and Cullmann, *Christology of the New Testament*, 60-69.

28. See particularly the important work of F. F. Bruce, *Biblical Exegesis in the Qumran Texts* (Grand Rapids: Eerdmans, 1959).

29. It is very important to note that the direct references to the Songs of the Servant are essentially found in the Hymns of Thanksgiving, in which one can clearly identify the third Song; see Bruce, *Biblical Exegesis*, 92-93.

30. In reference to the Greek translation of Isaiah and the interpretation of the Songs of the Servant, see Cullmann, *Christology of the New Testament*, 73, and, particularly I. L. Seeligmann, *The Septuagint Version of Isaiah: A Discussion of Its Problems* (Leiden: Brill, 1948). It is important to note that in four texts of the Acts of the Apostles, Jesus is given the Greek title that the Septuagint translated of the Servant of the Lord in Isaiah; Acts 3:13, 26; 4:27, 30.

31. The Targum of the prophets is a free translation of the Hebrew text to the Aramaic; see the presentations in J. F. Stenning, *The Targum of Isaiah* (Oxford: Clarendon, 1949); and Josep Rivera Florit, *El Targum de Isaías: Versión Crítica, Introducción y notas* (Valencia: Biblioteca Midrashica 6 Institución de San Jerónimo), 1988. A particularly good study of the Targum of Isaiah is the following: E. R. Rowland, "The Targum and the Peshita Version of the Book of Isaiah," *VT* (1959): 178-91.

32. That reference in the Second Epistle to the Corinthians is possibly an allusion to Isaiah 53:10-11; see Bruce, *New Testament Development*, 96; and also Cullmann, *Christology of the New Testament*, 55.

33. Bruce, *New Testament Development*, 98-99; Cullmann, *Christology of the New Testament*, 60-69.

4. "IT IS THESE YOU OUGHT TO HAVE PRACTICED, WITHOUT NEGLECTING THE OTHERS"

1. I employ the terms *Hispanic/Latina, Caribbean,* and *Latin American* in order to reflect the diversity and plurality among our people.

2. See for example, among his works, ch. 2 in *Mañana* (Nashville: Abingdon, 1990), 31-42; *La Santa Biblia* (Nashville: Abingdon, 1996); *¡Alabadle!* (Nashville: Abingdon, 1996), 9-27; *Juan Wesley: herencia y promesa* (Rio Piedras: Seminario Evangélico, 1998); *Christian Thought Revisited: Three Types of Theology* (Maryknoll, N.Y.: Orbis Books, 1999).

3. For the purpose of teaching, I make a distinction between ritualism(s) and rite or rituals. The former has a negative connotation, but the latter aims to describe their positive social functions.

4. Fred B. Craddock, *Luke* (Louisville: Westminster John Knox, 1990), 158-59; Douglas R. A. Hare, *Matthew* (Louisville: Westminster John Knox, 1993), 267-69. The fact that this text appears in Luke as well as in Matthew suggests that both were drawn from source Q, but they use them creatively according to their particular theological interests.

5. Una muestra de la extensa bibliografía que podríamos citar para apoyar esta afirmación la podemos encontrar en la revista *Revista de Interpretación Bíbloica Latinoamericana (RIBLA)* #10 con el título *Misericordia Quiero, no Sacrificios*.

6. Bruce J. Malina and Richard L. Rohrbaugh, *Social-Science Commentary on the Synoptic Gospels* (Minneapolis: Augsburg Fortress, 1992), 357-59.

7. These laments are a type of literary genre that we also find in the Old Testament prophets. See Isa 5:8-23; Amos 5:18, H. W. Wolff, *A Commentary on the Books of Joel and Amos* (Philadelphia: Fortress, 1977), 242-45.

8. P. Bonnard, *Evangelio según San Mateo* (Madrid: Ediciones Cristiandad, 1976), 507-8. Mark Allan Powell, *God with Us* (Minneapolis: Augsburg Fortress, 1995), 13, 47, 66, 118. Especially read Leviticus ch. 19.

9. This interpretation is mainly observed in Protestant exegesis, even though Catholic interpretations are not exempted from this trend.

10. Bruce J. Malina and Jerome H. Neyrey, "Conflict in Luke-Acts: Pivotal Values of the Mediterranean World," in *The Social World of Luke-Acts* (ed. Jerome H. Neyrey; Peabody, Mass.: Hendrickson, 1991), 25-65. Mark McVann, "Rituals of Status Transformation in Luke-Acts: The Case of Jesus the Prophet," in Neyrey, *Social World of Luke-Acts*, 333-58. Jerome H. Neyrey, "Ceremonies in Luke-Acts: The Case of Meals and Table-Fellowship," in Neyrey, *Social World of Luke-Acts*, 361-87. Jan Willem van Henten and Athalya Brenner, eds., *Food and Drink in the Biblical Worlds* (Semeia 86; Atlanta: Society for Biblical Literature, 1999); Ronald A. Simkins and Stephen L. Cook, eds., *The Social World of the Hebrew Bible: Twenty-Five Years of the Social Sciences in the Academy*, (Semeia 87; Atlanta: Society for Biblical Literature, 1999).

11. See Mark McVann, ed., *Transformations, Passages, and Processes: Ritual Approaches to Biblical Texts*, Semeia 67 (1995). The entire volume addresses this topic.

12. See, for example, Thomas W. Overholt, *Cultural Anthropology and the Old Testament* (Minneapolis: Augsburg Fortress, 1996); John H. Elliott, *What Is Social-Scientific Criticism?* (Minneapolis: Augsburg Fortress, 1993).

13. Frank H. Gorman Jr., "Ritual Studies and Biblical Studies: Assessment of the Past, Prospects for the Future," in *Semeia* 67 (1994): 13-36. David Hicks, *Ritual and Belief* (Boston: McGraw-Hill, 1999); Edmund R. Leach, "Ritual," in Hicks, *Ritual and Belief*, 176-83. Victor W. Turner, "Ritual Symbolism, Morality, and Social Structure Among the Ndemby," in Hicks, *Ritual and Belief*, 183-89.

14. Mary Douglas, "Justice as the Cornerstone: An Interpretation of Leviticus 18–20," *Interpretation* 53, no. 4 (1999): 341-50. This space is limited to cite the number of studies devoted to the subject of cultural anthropology. John K. Chance, "The Anthropology of Honor and Shame: Culture, Values, and Practice," *Semeia* 68 (1994): 139-51. Frank H. Gorman Jr., "Ritual Studies and Biblical Studies: Assessment of the Past, Prospects for the Future," *Semeia* 67 (1994): 13-36. John J. Pilch, "Response to Frank H. Gorman Jr., 'Ritual Studies and Biblical Studies,'" *Semeia* 67 (1994): 37-42.

15. McVann, "Rituals of Status Transformation," 333-58; Mark McVann, "Reading Mark Ritually: Honor-Shame and the Ritual of Baptism," *Semeia* 67 (1994): 179-98.

16. Mary Douglas, *In the Wilderness: The Doctrine of Defilement in the Book of Numbers* (Sheffield: Sheffield Academic Press, 1993); Daniel L. Smith, *The Religion of the Landless* (Bloomington, Ind.: Meyer-Stone, 1989), 8-13. See also Simkins and Cook, *Social World of the Hebrew Bible*.

17. Daniel L. Smith, *Religion of the Landless*, 8-13.

18. Ibid., 149.

5. TOWARD A HERMENEUTICS OF THE DIASPORA

1. It is amazing how resistant, sometimes bordering on the hysterical, male biblical critics from the world of the North Atlantic can be to any admission of contextuality in their own work, despite the fact that the concept of the *Sitz im Leben* ("the situation in life," or the social context) has been liberally applied from within the paradigm of historical criticism itself to the texts and authors in question. Such reactions, familiar to any individual not from that world or of minority status in that world, tend to be quite similar as well. The following stand out: (1) a reaffirmation of the hermeneutical model involving the retrieval of a meaning "back then" and its application "for today," not as a model, however, but as an unquestioned and unquestionable reality or modus operandi; (2) an ad hominem (or "ad feminam") argument to the effect that the proposed hermeneutical enterprise in effect abandons the realm of scientific and scholarly objectivity for that of subjective and political advocacy, without any critical analysis of the argument itself, that is, of the presuppositions involved in arguing that a particular hermeneutical stance is not politicized and, in effect, lacks any agenda of advocacy; and (3) an overall formulation of such argumentation in strong theological terms, derived either from the Protestant or the Catholic tradition (as the case may be), without any corresponding recognition of the undeniable and sometimes overriding theological foundations and agenda of their own critical work and hermeneutical stance. It should be noted that, for the most part, such reactions and arguments tend to lack a thorough and sophisticated theoretical foundation.

2. In this essay I shall be using the term "the other" in two ways: in a negative or pejorative way, when the definition of the other is imposed from the outside without taking the other into consideration; in a positive and constructive way, when the other is allowed to surface and describe itself as the other. While in the former case, a situation of overwhelming and overriding imposition, the term will be found in quotation marks, in the latter, a situation of respect and engagement, the term will appear without quotation marks.

3. I certainly do not mean to deny the presence of independence and uniqueness to individuals within such social groupings but rather to focus on those aspects that characterize individuals as members of specific social groupings. In any case such a relationship should never be conceived or formulated in terms of an either/or: individuals undergo a sustained, complex, and differentiated process of socialization; the process itself may be questioned, resisted, and altered by individuals. Likewise, I by no means wish to present such a framework as the sole and definitive framework for approaching and interpreting the biblical texts; it is but one strategy. For a number of other frameworks emerging out of the Hispanic American experience in the diaspora, see Fernando F. Segovia, "Hispanic American Theology and the Bible: Effective Weapon and Faithful Ally," in *We Are a People! Initiative in Hispanic American Theology* (ed. Roberto S. Goizueta; Minneapolis: Augsburg Fortress, 1992), 21-50.

4. On the political dynamics involved in such diasporas, see the excellent study by M. J. Esman, "The Political Fallout of International Migration," *Diaspora* 2 (1992): 3-41.

5. Just as I find myself "thrown" by birth into a discourse of colonialism and neocolonialism, I also find myself "thrown," as a result of such a discourse, into the further discourse of the "diaspora." In other words, the triple-layered colonial subject by birth becomes, through migration and exile, a minority subject within an alien and alienating culture; see the introduction to this book.

6. For descriptions of the social location of Hispanic Americans, see, for example, V. Elizondo, *Galilean Journey: The Mexican American Promise* (Maryknoll, N.Y.: Orbis Books, 1983), 5-46; A. Figueroa Deck, *The Second Wave: Hispanic Ministry and the Evangelization of Cultures* (New York: Paulist Press, 1989), 9-25; Justo L. González, *Mañana: Christian Theology from a Hispanic Perspective* (Nashville: Abingdon, 1990), 31-53; and idem, "Hispanics in the United States," *Listening: Journal of Religion and Culture* 27 (1992): 7-16.

7. The following working definition of *Hispanic Americans* is operative throughout: individuals of Hispanic descent, associated in one way or another with the Americas, who now live, for any number of reasons, on a permanent basis in the United States. For the rationale and attendant problems, see Segovia, "Hispanic American Theology," 25-30.

8. Fernando F. Segovia, "Two Places and No Place on Which to Stand: Mixture and Otherness in Hispanic American Theology," *Listening: Journal of Religion and Culture* 27 (1992): 26-40.

9. Again, though Hispanic Americans constitute a distinct and identifiable social configuration, the group does encompass a variety of similarly distinct and identifiable subgroups. To be sure, any description of the Hispanic American experience and reality will bear the imprint of the describer, even when the explicit aim of the description is to focus on the common characteristics rather than the distinguishing features. From a methodological point of view, therefore, it is important to describe this angle of vision, given the diversity that characterizes the group. The voice and perspective that follow are those of a first-generation immigrant of Caribbean descent, a naturalized citizen and original refugee from the Cuban experience of neocolonialism and colonialism, of political convulsion and exile.

10. Such an image is not at all surprising. It is a direct product of colonialism and neocolonialism. The colonized believe—and have been taught to believe—that the world of the colonizers is a superior world, where civilization, however conceived, has reached its zenith and now reaches out to the rest of the world. As a result, whatever is autochthonous or indigenous is regarded as ultimately inferior to what lies at the seat of the empire. This image has of course its counterpart among the colonizers: to lead and guide the inferior and the primitive to civilization, with contempt and derision going hand in hand with authoritarianism and paternalism. Given this bipolar view of the world on both sides, one can begin to understand the shock of the colonized within the womb of the colonizer: the exported image of civilization is very different from the everyday reality, especially with regard to their own perception within that civilization. On the contrast between colonizer and colonized, see the classic study by A. Memmi, *The Colonizer and the Colonized* (New York: Orion, 1965). For a sharp description of the relationship between the dominant and the subordinate from a feminist perspective, see J. Baker Miller, *Toward a New Psychology of Women* (2nd ed.; Boston: Beacon, 1986), 3-12; for a very interesting view of its relationship on the part of a Protestant Hispanic American, see González, *Mañana*, 21-30.

11. On this point, see the sharp remarks by González, "Hispanics in the United States," 11-14.

12. To do so does not imply a rejection of our tradition of mixture. Given our historical racial, cultural, and theological rejection by the mainstream or dominant culture, liberation becomes self-affirmation in the face of the mainstream—resisting colonization, so to speak. In a fundamentally segregationist culture, the very possibility of a continued mixture demands, for the mixture to be voluntary and not forced, sustained opposition and resistance, a decentering of the center, a valuation of the margin in the face of the center. Thus, quite ironically, self-affirmation becomes not at all a rejection of mixture but an option for proper and respectful mixture in the face of cultural annihilation.

13. I deliberately employ the term *mezcolanza* rather than *mezcla*, the proper translation for "mixture," to convey the highly indiscriminate—motley, unplanned, haphazard—character of the mixture; its meaning is best captured perhaps by the English terms *hodgepodge* or *jumble*.

14. The question is not, therefore, whether there should be historical criticism; it is a point I readily grant. The question rather is what kind of historical criticism should there be. What is rejected is historical criticism as traditionally practiced. On the fundamental questions involved, see Linda Hutcheon, *The Politics of Postmodernism* (New Accents; New York: Routledge, 1989), 62-92; and Hayden White, *Tropics of Discourse: Essays in Cultural Criticism* (Baltimore: Johns Hopkins University Press, 1978), 121-34.

15. On reader-response criticism, see Vincent B. Leitch, *American Literary Criticism from the Thirties to the Eighties* (New York: Columbia University Press, 1988), 210-37; Jane P. Tompkins, "An Introduction to Reader-Response Criticism," in *Reader-Response Criticism: From Formalism to Post-Structuralism* (ed. Jane P. Tompkins; Baltimore: Johns Hopkins University Press, 1980), ix-xxvi; S. Suleiman, "Introduction: Varieties of Audience-Oriented Criticism," in *The Reader in the Text: Essays on Audience and Interpretation* (ed. Susan Suleiman and Inge Crosman; Princeton, N.J.: Princeton University Press, 1980), 3-45. On reader-response criticism in biblical criticism, see R. S. Fowler, "Who Is the 'Reader' in Reader-Response Criticism?" in *Reader Response Approaches to Biblical and Secular Texts* (ed. R. Detweiler; Semeia 31; Decatur, Ga.: Scholars, 1985), 5-23; B. Lategan, "Introduction: Coming to Grips with the Reader in Biblical Literature," in *Reader Perspectives on the New Testament* (ed. E. V. McKnight; Semeia 49; Atlanta: Scholars, 1989), 3-20.

6. "EL HOGAR" AS MINISTRY TEAM

1. Saint Teresa of Avila, *The Way of Perfection* (trans. and ed. E. Allison Peers; Garden City, N.Y.: Doubleday, 1964), 46-47; Kieran Kavanaugh, *John of the Cross: Doctor of Light and Love* (New York: Crossroad, 1999), 44-45.

2. Justo L. González, *Mañana: Christian Theology from a Hispanic Perspective* (Nashville: Abingdon, 1990), 115, 136.

3. González, *Mañana*, 85. Others mention the importance of community in *Voces: Voices from the Hispanic Church* (ed. Justo L. González; Nashville: Abingdon, 1992), 24, 62-63, 122.

4. E. G. Robert and Julia Banks, *The Church Comes Home* (Peabody, Mass.: Hendrickson, 1998); Philip and Phoebe Anderson, *The House Church* (Nashville: Abingdon, 1975).

5. Scripture translations for this chapter are the author's.

6. Henry G. Liddell and Robert Scott, *A Greek-English Lexicon* (ed. H. S. Jones and R. McKenzie; 9th ed.; Oxford: Clarendon, 1940), 1203. See also Bruce W. Winter, *After Paul Left Corinth: The Influence of Secular Ethics and Social Change* (Grand Rapids: Eerdmans, 2001), 208.

7. Liddell and Scott, *Greek-English Lexicon*, 1203.

8. Peter Lampe, "The Family of New Testament Times," *Church and Society* LXXXIV, no. 2 (November/December 1993): 20. See also Gerd Theissen, *The Social Setting of Pauline Christianity: Essays on Corinth* (ed. and trans. J. H. Schuetz; Philadelphia: Fortress, 1982), 85-87, 92; L. L. Welborn, *Politics and Rhetoric in the Corinthian Epistles* (Macon, Ga.: Mercer University Press, 1997), 26; cf. Matt. 19:29. Halvor Moxnes, ed., *Constructing Early Christian Families: Family as Social Reality and Metaphor* (New York: Routledge, 1997); Carolyn Osiek and David L. Balch, *Families in the New Testament World: Households and House Churches* (The Family, Religion, and Culture; Louisville: Westminster John Knox, 1997).

9. Lampe, "Family of New Testament Times," 27. A household was comparable in importance to the city. Stephana(s)'s household could stand because it was not divided against itself (Matt 12:25). The quotations from Aristotle are from *Politics* (vol. 21 of Aristotle in 23 Volumes; trans. H. Rackham; Cambridge, Mass.: Harvard University Press, 1944).

10. 1 Cor 1:16 is even written as a unified concept: article, adjective, noun: "the Stephana(s)'s house."

11. See New American Standard Bible, Jerusalem Bible, New English Bible, New International Version, Good News Translation, and *The New Testament in Modern English* (Phillips).

12. For translations using inclusive words such as *people* and *leaders*, see New Revised Standard Version, New International Version Inclusive language edition, Contemporary English Version, Revised English Bible.

13. Guessing it is shortened from *Stephanēphoros* or *Stephanos*. Frederick Danker, *A Greek-English Lexicon of the New Testament* (Chicago: University of Chicago Press, 2000), 943; A. T. Robertson, *A Grammar of the Greek New Testament in the Light of Historical Research* (Nashville: Broadman, 1934), 254-55; F. Blass, A. Debrunner, R. W. Funk, *A Greek Grammar of the New Testament* (10th ed.; Chicago: University of Chicago Press, 1961), 68.

14. Charlotte Roueche, *Aphrodisias in Late Antiquity* (London: Society for the Promotion of Roman Studies, 1989), paragraph 137.

15. Henrico Stephano, *Thesaurus Graecae Linguae* (vol. 7; Paris: Institute Franciae Typographus, 1848–1854), 731. The only references to *Stephana* in the fall 1999 computerized *Thesaurus Graecae Linguae* were to 1 Cor 16. John Chrysostom in the fourth century A.D. assumed Stephana was a man in his homily on 1 Cor 16:15. P46 has no circumflex on the *a* of *Stephana*. *Stephanē* was found in a third-century A.D. inscription in Sicily; P. M. Fraser and E. Matthews, eds., *A Lexicon of Greek Personal Names* (vol. 3A; Oxford: Clarendon, 1997), 401.

16. Lampe, "Family of New Testament Times," 33n5. He also cites Chloe and Nympha as female heads of households (1 Cor 1:11; Col 4:15).

17. Nympha and Philemon also have a church in their house (Col 4:15; Phlm 1-2).

18. Lampe, "Family of New Testament Times," 21-26. Winter ably describes the ancient patron-client household. The *paterfamilias* would often make decisions for all, but Paul uses the plural verb, "they appointed themselves" (*After Paul Left Corinth*, ch. 9, esp. p. 196).

19. Joseph Henry Thayer, *Thayer's Greek-English Lexicon of the New Testament* (Marshallton, Del.: National Foundation for Christian Education, 1889), 41.

20. Theissen, *Social Setting*, 88. Welborn concludes from Theissen's comments that Stephana(s) apparently brought "material support" (*Politics and Rhetoric*, 23).

21. "The-of you (plural) - need / lack" is phrased as a unified concept (article, modifier, noun). If the lack were Paul's need for the Corinthians, how then was the Corinthians' spirit refreshed (v. 18)? Paul's need for the Corinthian church's presence would be fulfilled by some of its members (v. 17).

22. As early as Saint John Chrysostom in the fifth century, scholars have suggested Stephana(s), Fortunatus, and Achaicus brought Paul the Corinthian questions, which is possible, but then Paul, not these emissaries would have filled the void (1 Cor 16:17) (*Homilies* XLIV).

23. Andrew D. Clarke discovered that the use of the phrase "refresh spirit" is unique. It refers to "the resulting effect of an action" on one person's feelings or emotions by another person. "'Refresh the Hearts of the Saints': A Unique Pauline Context?" *Tyndale Bulletin* 47:2 (1996): 300.

24. Liddell and Scott, *Greek-English Lexicon*, 1897.

25. Aida Besançon Spencer, *Beyond the Curse: Women Called to Ministry* (Peabody, Mass.: Hendrickson, 1985), 118.

26. González, *Mañana*, 133.

27. Thayer, *Lexicon*, 237; Liddell and Scott, *Greek-English Lexicon*, 627. Gordon Fee aptly concludes: "for Paul the key to such respect or 'submission' is not sex or socioeconomic status but ministry." *The First Epistle to the Corinthians* (Grand Rapids: Eerdmans, 1987), 831.

28. Thayer, *Lexicon*, 118, 237.

29. See also María Pilar Aquino, "The Collective 'Dis-covery' of Our Own Power: Latina American Feminist Theology," and Ada María Isasi-Díaz, "*Un poquito de justicia—* a Little Bit of Justice: A *Mujerista* Account of Justice," in *Hispanic/Latino Theology: Challenge and Promise* (ed. Ada María Isasi-Díaz and Fernando F. Segovia; Minneapolis: Augsburg Fortress, 1996), 240-58, 329.

7. VOCACIÓN Y COMPROMISO

1. Kosuke Koyama, "American Church History from a Third World Perspective," in *Altered Landscapes: Christianity in America, 1935–1985* (ed. David W. Lotz, Donald W. Shriver Jr., and John F. Wilson; Grand Rapids: Eerdmans, 1989), 171-85.

2. Justo L. González, "Foreword," in *Telling the Churches' Stories: Ecumenical Perspectives on Writing Christian History* (ed. Timothy J. Wengert and Charles W. Brockwell Jr.; Grand Rapids: Eerdmans, 1995), ix.

3. Ibid.

4. Ibid.

5. González develops this concept of catholicity in all his writings. There are at least three places in which this concept is defined or used as an undergirding principle: *Mañana: Christian Theology from a Hispanic Perspective* (Nashville: Abingdon, 1990), *Out of Every Tribe and Nation* (Nashville: Abingdon, 1992), *Desde el Siglo y Hasta el Siglo: Esbozos Teológicos para el Siglo XXI* (Decatur, Ga., and Mexico City: AETH and STPM, 1997).

6. Wengert and Brockwell, *Telling the Churches' Stories*, xii-xiii.

7. *Historia del Pensamiento Cristiano* (vols. 1-2; Buenos Aires: Methopress, 1965–1972; vol. 3; Miami: Editorial Caribe, 1992. 2nd ed.; 3 vols.; Miami: Editorial Caribe, 1992–1993); *Historia de Las Misiones* (Buenos Aires: Methopress, 1970); *Revolución y*

Encarnación (Rio Piedras: Seminario Evangelico de Puerto Rico, 1965); *A History of Christian Thought* (Nashville: Abingdon, 1970–1975).

8. *Y Hasta Lo Ultimo de la Tierra* (10 vols.; Miami: Editorial Caribe, 1978–1988); *La Historia del Cristianismo* (Miami: Editorial UNILIT, 1994); *The Story of Christianity* (2 vols.; New York: HarperCollins, 1984–1985); *Bosquejo de Historia de la Iglesia* (Decatur, Ga.: AETH Books, 1995); *Church History: An Essential Guide* (Nashville: Abingdon, 1996; *Church History* is the English version of *Bosquejo de Historia de la Iglesia*); *Christian Thought Revisited: Three Types of Theology* (Nashville: Abingdon 1989; 2nd ed.; Maryknoll, N.Y.: Orbis Books, 1999)

9. Justo L. González, *Mentors as Instruments of God's Call* (Nashville: General Board of Higher Education and Ministry, 1992).

10. Justo L. González, *Christian Thought Revisited: Three Types of Theology* (Nashville: Abingdon, 1989).

11. Justo L. González, *Mañana: Christian Theology from a Hispanic Perspective* (Nashville; Abingdon, 1990).

12. Justo L. González, *Itinerario de la Teología Cristiana* (San José: Caribe, 1975).

13. Justo L. González, *¡Alabadle! Hispanic Christian Worship* (Nashville: Abingdon, 1996), 115.

8. VIEWS FROM THE MARGINS

1. The unnoted use of the terms *America* and *Americans* to refer to the United State and its citizens while a common practice of self-reference in the United States and used here for convenience nevertheless is extremely problematic. This especially is so when discussing the multicultural peoples who reside throughout the Western Hemisphere and therefore live in America (in the fullest sense) and are Americans, that is, residents of the Western Hemisphere. See Daisy L. Machado, "Latino Church History: A Haunting Memory," *Perspectivas: Hispanic Theological Initiative*, Occasional Papers 1 (Fall 1998): 25-28.

2. The allusions are to *Altered Landscapes: Christianity in America, 1935-1985* (ed. David W. Lotz, Donald W. Shriver Jr., and John F. Wilson; Grand Rapids: Eerdmans, 1989), Thomas A. Tweed, *Retelling U.S. Religious History* (Berkeley and Los Angeles: University of California Press, 1997), and to Robert Wuthnow, *The Restructuring of American Religion: Society and Faith Since World War II* (Princeton: Princeton University Press, 1988).

3. Bellah asserts that there exists a powerful dominant common U.S. culture characterized by utilitarian individualism working through the state and the market. See Robert N. Bellah, "Is There a Common American Culture?" *Journal of the American Academy of Religion* 66, no. 3 (Fall 1998): 613-25.

4. On the mythology of borderlands as solely a geographic construct of esoteric location, see Machado, "Latino Church History," 25-27.

5. See *Borders, Exiles, Diasporas* (ed. Elazar Barkan and Marie-Denise Shelton; Stanford: Stanford University Press, 1998).

6. See Thomas A. Tweed, "Introduction: Narrating U.S. Religious History," in Tweed, *Retelling U.S. Religious History*, 2-10.

7. See Clifford's "exhortations" on the need to study in a comparative way what is called here "margins" and "borderlands." James Clifford, *Routes: Travels and Translation in the Late Twentieth Century* (Cambridge, Mass.: Harvard University Press, 1997), 36-39. On the connections between diaspora peoples and religion and culture, see *Gatherings in*

Diaspora: Religious Communities and the New Immigration (ed. R. Stephen Warner and Judith G. Wittner; Philadelphia: Temple University Press, 1998).

8. The terms *Hispanic* and and the gender inclusive *Latina/o* are used to refer to those native-born or foreign-born inhabitants of the United States whose heritage is rooted in Latin America. *Latin American* is used here to refer to those who presently reside in one of the nations of Latin America, as distinguished from U.S. Latinas/os/Hispanics. The U.S. Census has recognized somewhat the complexity of these designations in its revision of the Hispanic/Latino category in the 2000 decennial census. This census also allowed for those identifying as Hispanic/Latino to indicate "subgroup" identities and identification with U.S. racial categories. This also makes it difficult to compare data from the 2000 Census with prior censuses. For further discussions on the terms *Hispanic* and *Latino* as sociopolitical constructs, see Mary Romero, "Introduction," in *Challenging Fronteras: Structuring Latina and Latino Lives in the U.S* (ed. Mary Romero, Pierrette Hondagreu-Sorels, and Vilma Ortiz; New York and London: Routledge, 1997), xiii-xvi; and Linda Martín Alcoff, "Is Latina/o Identity A Racial Identity?" in *Hispanics/Latinos in the United States: Ethnicity, Race, and Rights* (ed. Jorge J. E. Gracia and Pablo De Greiff; New York and London: Routledge, 2000), 23-44.

9. Elizabeth M. Grieco and Rachel C. Cassidy, *Overview of Race and Hispanic Origin* (C2KBR/01-1; Washington, D.C.: U.S. Department of Commerce, Economics and Statistics Administration, U.S. Census Bureau, 2001), 3.

10. The complexity of issues when speaking of nation-state entities and their diverse populations begins to become apparent in this context when questions such as the following are considered: "What are the boundaries of Latin America if, for instance we consider New York the largest Puerto Rican metropolis and Los Angeles the second-largest Mexican metropolis? Or, if we are dealing with the English-speaking Afro-Caribbeans of the Atlantic coast of Nicaragua who call themselves Creoles and whose cultural tastes include U.S. country music and Jamaican reggae?" Latin American Subaltern Studies Group, "Founding Statement," *boundary* 2 20, no. 3 (Fall 1993): 118.

11. Although starting in the 1990s there has been some change in attitude of dominant groups in U.S. society as consideration of different "faith-based initiatives" became part of political and public policy discussions. This is especially the case of the administration of President George W. Bush who in December 2002 signed an executive order to allow for federal funding for faith-based initiatives.

12. Justo L. González, *The Changing Shape of Church History* (St. Louis: Chalice, 2002), 7.

13. Ibid., 15.

14. Alex García-Rivera, *St. Martín de Porres: The "Little Stories" and the Semiotics of Culture* (Maryknoll, N.Y.: Orbis Books, 1995).

15. Ibid., 5. Moore offers a complementary corrective when he states that, "What was in conventional terms outside the American religious mainstream turned American religious history into an interesting story." R. Laurence Moore, *Religious Outsiders and the Making of Americans* (New York: Oxford University Press, 1986), 209.

16. Juan Flores, *Divided Borders: Essays on Puerto Rican Identity* (Houston: Arte Publico, 1993), 203. See also Daisy L. Machado, "Kingdom Building in the Borderlands: The Church and Manifest Destiny," in *Hispanic/Latino Theology: Challenge and Promise* (ed. Ada María Isasi-Díaz and Fernando F. Segovia; Minneapolis: Augsburg Fortress, 1996), 64-65.

17. See Justo L. González, "The Changing Geography of Church History," in *Theology and the New Histories* (ed. Gary Macy; Maryknoll, N.Y.: Orbis, 1999), 23.

18. Adams differentiates between postmodernity and postmodernism saying that "postmodernity is the condition in which late twentieth-century culture finds itself;

postmodernism is a reflection upon that condition and a response to it." Daniel J. Adams, "Toward a Theological Understanding of Postmodernism," *Cross Currents* 47, no. 4 (Winter 1997–1998): 519.

19. On the nature of the public sphere Habermas wrote that

> The bourgeois public sphere may be conceived above all as the sphere of private people come together as a public; they soon claimed the public sphere regulated from above against the public authorities themselves, to engage them in a debate over the general rules governing relations in the basically privatized but publicly relevant sphere of commodity exchange and social labor.

See Jürgen Habermas, *The Structural Transformation of the Public Sphere: An Inquiry into a Category of Bourgeois Society* (trans. Thomas Burger with Frederick Lawrence; Cambridge, Mass.: MIT Press, 1989), 27.

20. Over the years Habermas has refined but not abandoned this project of applying reason to public issues and concerns, thereby influencing social practice to attain the goal of human emancipation.

21. Mendieta comments on Habermas's connection to modernity, saying that

> Modernity is the self-immolation of God, where secularization is her calvary. Habermas, the great defender of Modernity continues this motif. For him, religion is liquified in its linguistifications. The great motifs of otherness, suffering, universal injustice, are, in Habermas's view, redeemed and rendered liquid, the same way an asset is turned into currency in discourse ethics.

Eduardo Mendieta, "From Christendom to Polycentric Oikonumé: Modernity, Postmodernity, and Liberation Theology," in *Liberation Theologies, Postmodernity, and the Americas* (ed. David Batstone, et al.; London and New York: Routledge, 1997), 258.

22. See Jean François Lyotard, *The Postmodern Condition: A Report on Knowledge* (trans. Geoff Bennington and Brian Massumi; Minneapolis: University of Minnesota Press, 1984), 60-67, 72-73.

23. See Nancy Fraser, "Rethinking the Public Sphere: A Contribution to the Critique of Actually Existing Democracy," in *Habermas and the Public Sphere* (ed. Craig Calhoun; Cambridge, Mass.: MIT Press, 1992).

24. Fraser, "Rethinking the Public Sphere," 123. The term *subaltern* is used "as a name for the general attribute of subordination in South Asian society whether this is expressed in terms of class, caste, age, gender and office or in any other way." Ranajit Guha, "Preface," in *Selected Subaltern Studies* (ed. Ranajit Guha and Gayatri Chakravorty Spivak; New York: Oxford University Press, 1988), 35.

25. Latin American Subaltern Studies Group, "Founding Statement," *boundary* 2 20, no. 3 (1993): 110-21.

26. The Latin American Subaltern Studies Group states that this restructured historiography can identify "the logic of the distortions in the representation of the subaltern in official or elite culture; and uncovering the social semiotics of the strategies and cultural practices of peasant insurgencies themselves." Latin American Subaltern Studies Group, "Founding Statement," 111. Cf. Ranajit Guha, "On Some Aspects of the Historiography of Colonial India," in Guha and Spivak, *Selected Subaltern Studies*, 37-43.

27. Latin American Subaltern Studies Group, "Founding Statement," 112.

28. Higginbotham focuses on the "public character and role of the black church" in distinction from those scholars who focus on civil/public religion. Evelyn Brooks Higginbotham, *Righteous Discontent: The Women's Movement in the Black Baptist Church*,

1880–1920 (Cambridge, Mass.: Harvard University Press, 1993), 7-13. On civil religion, see Robert N. Bellah and Phillip E. Hammond, *Varieties of Civil Religion* (San Francisco: Harper & Row, 1980), 3-23; Catherine Albanese, *America: Religions and Religion* (rev. ed.; Belmont, Calif.: Wadsworth, 1992), chs. 12-13.

29. Essentialist simplifications that may mask more than they reveal must be avoided. For what has become an important critique in this regard, see Gayatri Chakravorty Spivak, "Can the Subaltern Speak?" in *The Post-colonial Studies Reader* (ed. Bill Ashcroft, Gareth Griffths, and Helen Tiffin; London and New York: Routledge, 1995), 24-28.

30. While beyond the limits of this essay, it is important to be aware that part of the impetus for alternative identities is the imposed racial categories that individuals and communities deal with. Mendieta speaks to this when he states that, "Race, in short, has been part of an ideology of conquest, subjugation, and subalternization, of destruction and decimation." Eduardo Mendieta, "The Making of New Peoples: Hispanizing Race," in Gracia and Greiff, *Hispanics/Latinos in the United States*, 55.

31. García-Rivera states that

> hegemony is not an all-powerful arm of the state. It does serve the interests of the state, but hegemony is, in a sense, also an agreement between two classes. No regime can rely solely on direct coercion. It must find popular support by means of ideological control or hegemony. As such, hegemony is not so much a contrast but a two-edged sword, a process of accommodation and resistance by both dominant and subaltern classes through which a status quo is reached.

García-Rivera, *St. Martín de Porres*, 14-15. For a standard discussion on hegemony, see Eugene Genovese, *Roll, Jordan, Roll: The World the Slaves Made* (New York: Random House, 1976), 25-49, 147-49. See also Antonio Gramsci, *Selections from the Prison Notebooks of Antonio Gramsci* (ed. and trans. Quintin Hoare and Geoffrey Nowell Smith; New York: International Publishers, 1971), 195-96; 246-47.

32. Cf. Clifford, *Routes*, 261.

33. Help in avoiding reductionist readings while simultaneously maintaining an awareness of the power of religions in the subaltern community is found in the work of the philosopher and sociologist of religion Otto Maduro when he states that

> Las religiones no cumplen siempre ni solamente funciones conservadoras con respeto a las relaciones sociales conflictivas de dominación. Las religiones no necesariamente constituyen un obstáculo a la autonomía de las clases subalternas ni sus alianzas contra la dominación. Muchas religiones, en gran cantidad de procesos históricamente registrados, parecen haber jugado un claro papel en las luchas de dominados contra la dominación interna y/o externa.

Otto Maduro, *Religión y conflicto social* (Mexico City: Centro de Estudios Ecuménicos/ Estudios CRT, 1980), 190.

> Religions do not always perform purely conservative functions with respect to conflictive social relationships of dominance. Religions do not necessarily constitute an obstacle to the autonomy of subordinate classes, or to their alliances against domination.
> Many religions, in a great number of historically recorded cases, appear to have played a signal role in the struggle of dominated classes against internal or external domination.

The translation is from Otto Maduro, *Religion and Social Conflicts* (trans. Robert R. Barr; Maryknoll, N.Y.: Orbis, 1982), 136. I have cited the Spanish original because of the author's intentional use of "las clases subalternas," which loses some of its force in the translation "subordinate classes."

34. Otto Maduro, "Notes towards a Sociology of Latina/o Religious Empowerment," in Isasi-Díaz and Segovia, *Hispanic/Latino Theology*, 155.

35. Justo L. González, *Santa Biblia: The Bible Through Hispanic Eyes* (Nashville: Abingdon, 1996), 33-34.

36. Tracing the genealogy of both modernity and postmodernism is a study unto itself. Despite many pronouncements of its demise, modernity is still alive and well, although some now recognize that it may be more appropriate to speak of a plurality of modernities. See *Alternative Modernities* (ed. Dilip Parameshwar; Durham, N.C.: Duke University Press, 2001). Regarding postmodernity, some see a critique of modernity as early as the work of Friedrich Nietzsche, with the 1930s appearance of the term in the works of Federico de Onís (*Antología de la poesía española e hispanoamericana*, 1934) and Arnold Toynbee (*Study of History*). See Steven Connor, *Postmodernist Culture* (Oxford: Basil Blackwell, 1989); Stanley J. Grenz, *A Primer on Postmodernism* (Grand Rapids: Eerdmans, 1996); Charles Jencks, *What Is Post-Modernism?* (3rd ed.; New York: St. Martin's, 1989).

37. Justo L. González, "Metamodern Aliens in Postmodern Jerusalem," in Isasi-Díaz and Segovia, *Hispanic/Latino Theology*, 347. See also the critique of postmodernity found in Roberto Goizueta in *Caminemos con Jesús: Toward a Hispanic/Latino Theology of Accompaniment* (Maryknoll, N.Y.: Orbis, 1995), 132-72.

38. While not diminishing the extent of the horror of apartheid in South Africa, Philippe Bourgois makes a strong case for a type of apartheid in the United States. See Philippe Bourgois, *In Search of Respect: Selling Crack in El Barrio* (Cambridge: Cambridge University Press, 1995), 19-47.

39. By describing the Enlightenment as European-American, I recognize that it was an international phenomenon taking place both in Europe as well as in the Western Hemisphere, in the Spanish colonies as well as in British America.

40. See Enrique Dussel, *The Invention of the Americas: Eclipse of "the Other" and the Myth of Modernity* (trans. Michael D. Barber; New York: Continuum, 1995), 132, 138. While there are similarities in critique and approach, transmodernity and metamodernity should not be equated since it appears that transmodernity continues to share in the Enlightenment project, and it is not quite clear whether or not transmodernity has fully considered the perspectives of Latinas/os in the United States.

41. González, *Changing Shape of Church History*, 153.

42. See Adams, "Toward a Theological Understanding of Postmodernism," 518-30; Zygmunt Bauman, *Intimations of Postmodernity* (London: Routledge, 1992), 102; David F. Wells, *God in the Wasteland: The Reality of Truth in a World of Fading Dreams* (Grand Rapids: Eerdmans, 1994). Lakeland asserts that there really are several postmodernisms, each running concurrently as they comment on the modern from their particular perspective: poststructuralist intensification of modernist cultural impulses; eclectic reprise of premodern artistic themes and styles; appropriation of the Enlightenment spirit to move beyond the perceived inhumanity of late capitalist society; radical rejection of the white male Enlightenment master narrative; a nostalgic postmodernism, really a "countermodernism" in disguise, which seeks to undo the harm of the modern and—at least in it religious dress—build a series of New Jerusalems or Cities of God within the contemporary world. Paul Lakeland, *Postmodernity: Christian Identity in a Fragmented Age* (Minneapolis: Augsburg Fortress, 1997), xii.

43. While not a Latina/o voice, the statements of the evangelical theologian Grenz parallel González's concept of metamodernity on this point of metanarrative.

We might say that because of our faith in Christ, we cannot totally affirm the central tenet of postmodernism as defined by Lyotard—the rejection of the metanarrative. We may welcome Lyotard's conclusion when applied to the chief concern of his analysis—namely, the scientific enterprise. Indeed, we can live quite well without such myths as the progress of knowledge. But we cannot accede to the extension of Lyotard's thesis to reality as a whole.

Primer on Postmodernism, 164. See also Susan Brooks Thistlethwaite on the challenge of postmodernism to liberation theology in "On Becoming a Traitor: The Academic Liberation Theologian and the Future," in *Liberating the Future: God, Mammon, and Theology* (ed. Joerg Rieger; Minneapolis: Augsburg Fortress, 1998), 23-26.

44. For a discussion on meaning construction as the nexus of culture, social structure, and social action, see Anne Kane, "Reconstructing Culture in Historical Explanation: Narratives as Cultural Structure and Practice," *History and Theory* 39 (October 2000): 311-30.

45. In Mendieta's discussion of liberation theologies in Latin America, something akin to metamodernity is identified:

> The new theological paradigm that emerged from the suffering humanity of Latin America, and the Third World in general, has articulated a new vision of our planet and the human community that inhabits it. It is a vision in which we are always already in a here and now that is both the continuity of the past and the futurity of what is to come. In this sense, and to conclude these pautas, liberation theologies were postmodern before Europeans thought of postmodernism. At the same time liberation theologies are beyond postmodernism, or rather, to use Dussel's term, they are trans-modern insofar as they think the exhaustion and end of these mythologies from their simultaneity as well as their reverso, their underside.

Similar to what Mendieta says about liberation theologies, the religious realities of Hispanic/Latina/o Protestants in Philadelphia are in Dussel's sense "trans-modern," not a question of chronological succession but something beyond modernity, but also beyond postmodernity. See Mendieta, "From Christendom to Polycentric Oikonumé," in Batstone, et al., *Liberation Theologies,* 266-67. For an extended discussion on Dussel's concept of trans-modern perspective, see also Enrique Dussel, *1492: El encubrimiento del otro, hacia el origen del mito de la modernidad* (Madrid: Editorial Nueva Utopía, 1993).

46. See Hayden White, *Figural Realism: Studies in the Mimesis Effect* (Baltimore: Johns Hopkins University Press, 2000), 23.

47. See Aviezer Tucker, "The Future of Philosophy of Historiography," *History and Theory* 40 (February 2001): 37-56.

9. THE STATE OF U.S. LATINA/O THEOLOGY

1. I began my oral presentation expressing my sincere thanks to the Hispanic Theological Initiative and to its director, Dr. Zaida Maldonado Pérez, for this invitation to reflect on the past and future of U.S. Latina/o theology. At the oral presentation I also thanked Ms. Angela Schoepf (of HTI) and Dr. Luis Pedraja for their assistance in preparing the computerized visual part of my oral presentation. In this printed version I want to reiterate my gratitude to the colleagues mentioned in this note. Needless to say, I have chosen to keep, in this printed version, much of the oral style of the Princeton

lecture. This paper assumes that the reader is sufficiently familiar with U.S. Latina/o theology. This too was the assumption for the oral presentation of the present text. Consequently, this written version of the lecture is *not,* and must *not* be expected to be, a sufficient or adequate introduction to U.S. Latina/o theology. Much of what I discuss herein presupposes familiarity with our theological movement. For readers who desire introductory texts, I recommend the several collective works mentioned in these pages, although what follows might assist them in understanding or evaluating those introductory works.

2. Some scholars have begun to chart the history of U.S. Latina/o theology. Although the gathering and preservation of documentation is important and ongoing, it seems to me that there is not yet enough "distance" between the origins of our theological movement and its present. Nevertheless, some attempts have begun to appear, each addressing different historical concerns and using different methodological approaches. For example, see Eduardo Fernández, *La Cosecha: Harvesting Contemporary United States Hispanic Theology (1972–1998)* (Collegeville, Minn.: Liturgical Press, 2000); David Maldonado, ed., *Protestantes/Protestants: Hispanic Christianity within Mainline Traditions* (Nashville: Abingdon, 1999); and the thorough and excellent doctoral dissertation by Miguel H. Diaz, "A Study in U.S. Hispanic Theological Anthropology, 1972–1999" (PhD diss., University of Notre Dame, 2000). Needless to add, my concern over the lack of sufficient "distance" between the origins of and the present U.S. Latina/o theology must also be referred to the present paper.

3. One question, for example, that needs to be asked and thoroughly discussed is, what makes Latina/o theology distinctly "Latina/o"? Evidently, until a consensus emerges as a reply to this question I don't see how we could determine the exact origins of U.S. Latina/o theology. Needless to say, logically and methodologically, the ethnicity of the authors cannot be the main source of or justification for theological *latinidad.* There are some nineteenth-century U.S. Latina/o religious thinkers and pastors (e.g., Félix Varela and even Antonio José Martinez) who might very well qualify as forerunners (if perhaps not as founders), while a number of twentieth-century Latina/o writers could be arguably understood as part of the pastoral and theological shifts (in most denominations) that, in time, gave rise to U.S. Latina/o theology.

4. See Virgilio Elizondo, "Educación religiosa para el méxico-americano," *Catequesis latinoamericana* 4, no. 14 (1972): 83-86.

5. See Justo L. González, *The Development of Chrstianity in the Latin Caribbean* (Grand Rapids: Eerdmans, 1969).

6. It is simply impossible to offer here a complete bibliography of U.S. Latina/o theological works over the past two decades. There have been some attempts at organizing these bibliographies, but all such efforts have so far been partial because the published bibliographies have been organized either denominationally or along disciplinary lines (i.e., listings in systematics or in practical theology, etc.). Organizing and publishing a complete, ongoing, and annotated bibliography is perhaps a worthy (and very important) project, which the HTI or some of its awardees might consider as a service to the wider Latina/o theological community. The more comprehensive, but still partial, attempts so far have been: David Maldonado and Paul Barton, eds., *Hispanic Christianity within Mainline Protestant Traditions: A Bibliography* (Decatur, Ga.: AETH; Dallas: Perkins School of Theology, 1998); the bibliographic updates published periodically by Arturo Bañuelas (for example, in his *Mestizo Christianity* [Maryknoll, N.Y.: Orbis, 1995]); and in Orlando O. Espín and Miguel H. Díaz, eds., *From the Heart of Our People: Latino/a Explorations in Catholic Systematic Theology* (Maryknoll, N.Y.: Orbis, 1999).

7. It might be worth remembering that twenty years ago there was little sense of there being *one* Latina/o people in the United States. The diversity among the identifiably

Latina/o groups made such claim extremely difficulty—and yet, that is precisely what most Latina/o theologians did. We (because I was one of them) chose to build national and interdenominational alliances, given that most of our communities faced very similar problems and realities—politically, socially, and denominationally—across the country. It was then believed that if our own internal diversity were emphasized, it would make it much more difficult for Latinas/os to arrive at consensus of purpose and unity of action. So diversity was played down. I do not believe we ever wanted to ignore or erase our cultural and ethnic differences (indeed, we were and are very proud of our cultural and ethnic traditions); we did not want to let our internal diversity interfere with what was then viewed as a greater need or become a source for further internal fracture. Unity and consensus were very crucial. And I believe they still are; although I admit that—in great part due to the wisdom and success of this early strategy—we are *now* able to continue working together for common goals *and* cherish our internal diversity as richness and not as threat to unity. There is reason to believe, however, that even today we must still place consensus, unity, and alliance-building among the indispensable goals for all of our communities and theologies. Intra-Latina/o fracture is a realistic threat still. The wise balancing of commonalities and differences remains necessary in our present political, social, academic, and denominational contexts.

8. The first generation of Latina/o theologians were educated in either U.S., European, or Latin American universities. Evidently, not a single one of us had a Latina/o theological mentor or role model. There was no Latina/o theology per se, although a few articles and even fewer books had begun to appear suggesting this theology's needed birth. Consequently, the only scholarly tools and methods at our disposal were European, European American, or Latin American—and probably very denominationally bound. Our first task, then, was to commence construction of specifically Latina/o theological methods, categories, and other scholarly tools. This task (easy to mention but extremely difficult to carry out) required us to employ those elements we found in our earlier theological education and that we found useful for creating a U.S. Latina/o theology. Latin American liberation theologies, which by then had several decades of reflection and analysis behind them, proved to be the richest sources and the best of allies, but it was Latin American liberation theologies' foundational insight that made us realize, from the very start, that we could not adapt, translate, or somehow "bring over" their contributions into our U.S. contexts: we too had to start theologizing from *our* own peoples' realities. Although Latin American liberation theologies aided in the birth of a distinct U.S. Latina/o theology, our theological work was clearly ours and not an imitation of theirs. Anyone familiar with both sets of theologies will immediately notice the significant differences in methodological styles and, especially, in categories of analysis and topics. The same, *mutatis mutandis*, must be said in reference to European and European American theologies, although their influence was arguably less than Latin America's. I should also add that the social sciences were very important at the start of U.S. Latina/o theology (as they still are today). It would be unfair to list the theologians and social scientists who seem to have had the greater impact on the first generation of Latina/o theologians because some important names will inevitably be left out, so I will not attempt to compose such list here. Suffice it to say that our readings of these authors (some of whom were our teachers and/or dissertation advisors) were eclectic and selective; we reinterpreted them according to our theological needs. And, I think it wise to add, it is problematic to claim that all or most of the categories of analysis and methods, which have in time come to be identified with our Latina/o theology, can be traced solely and directly back to the genius of the four men I mentioned earlier (i.e, Elizondo, González, Costas, and Beltrán). No one can or will deny their extremely important roles in the birth of our theology, but this deserved recognition cannot be at the expense of ignoring or diminishing the early and equally crucial contributions of other very important colleagues.

9. The names of Gustavo Gutiérrez, Clodovis Boff, Leonardo Boff, Juan Luis Segundo, Hugo Assmann, Jon Sobrino, Rubem Alves, Enrique Dussel, Renato Ortiz, Otto Maduro, Pedro Ribeiro de Oliveira, and others, come to mind as some of the Latin American authors more frequently read by the first generation of Latina/o theologians.

10. See, for example, the first three collective works by Latina/o theologians, all published in the same year: Justo L. González, ed. *Voces: Voices from the Hispanic Church* (Nashville: Abingdon, 1992); Roberto S. Goizueta, ed., *We Are a People! Initiatives in Hispanic American Theology* (Minneapolis: Augsburg Fortress, 1992); and Allan Figueroa Deck, ed., *Frontiers of Hispanic Theology in the United States* (Maryknoll, N.Y.: Orbis, 1992). Also see the thematic index of *Apuntes* from this same period.

11. Virgilio Elizondo first suggested this category of analysis, which was accepted by many other Latina/o theologians and which has had a lasting impact on our theology (although today some have begun to move beyond it, looking to the Nahua notion of *nepantlah* as a richer category). On Elizondo's use and understanding of *mestizaje*, see, for example, his doctoral dissertation, "*Mestizaje*: The Dialectic of Cultural Birth and the Gospel; A Study in the Intercultural Dimension of Evangelization" (PhD diss., Mexican American Cultural Center, 1978); and also his *Christianity and Culture: An Introduction to Pastoral Theology and Ministry for the Bicultural Community* (Huntington, Ind.: Our Sunday Visitor Press, 1975), *Galilean Journey: The Mexican American Promise* (2nd ed.; Maryknoll, N.Y.: Orbis, 2000), and *The Future Is Mestizo: Life Where Cultures Meet* (Bloomington, Ind.: Meyer-Stone, 1988).

12. Latina/o theology has (very unfortunately) seldom dialogued with substantial issues raised by Black theology. However, there seems to be a growing interest on the part of some Black theologians to engage Latina/o theology's thought on *mestizaje*. See, for example, Zipporah G. Glass, "The Language of *Mestizaje* in a Renewed Rhetoric of Black Theology," in *Journal of Hispanic/Latino Theology* 7:2 (1999): 32-42. Perhaps Latina/o theology should pay closer attention to Black theologians' analyses of race and racism, as Latina/o theology delves deeper into its own race and class analysis (on this, see below: part 2, section 4).

13. A study on the limitations of *mestizaje* was Roberto S. Goizueta's article, "¿La Raza Cósmica? The Vision of José Vasconcelos," in *Journal of Hispanic/Latino Theology* 1, no. 2 (1994): 5-27. The fiercest and most thorough argument against the (uncritical) use of *mestizaje* as a category of analysis has been made by Dora María Téllez, based on her superbly researched historical study of a Nicaraguan case. See her ¡*Muera 'la Gobierna'! Colonización de Matagalpa y Jinotega, 1820–1890* (Managua, Nicaragua: Universidad de las Regiones Autónomas de la Costa Caribe Nicaragüense, 1999).

14. On the (early) search for the sources of a distinct Latina/o theology, see, as examples from a much broader body of literature: María Pilar Aquino, "Directions and Foundations of Hispanic/Latino Theology: Toward a *Mestiza* Theology of Liberation," in *Journal of Hispanic/Latino Theology* 1, no. 1 (1993): 5-21; and Sixto J. García's "Sources and Loci of Hispanic Theology," in idem, 22-42. And also see: Orlando O. Espín, "Grace and Humanness: A Hispanic Perspective," in Goizueta, *We are a People!* 133-64; idem, "Popular Religion as an Epistemology (of Suffering)," in *Journal of Hispanic/Latino Theology* 2, no. 2 (1994): 55-78; idem, "Tradition and Popular Religion: An Understanding of the Sensus Fidelium," in Deck, *Frontiers of Hispanic Theology,* 72-87; idem, "Grace and Humanness: A Hispanic Perspective," in Goizueta, *We Are a People!* 133-64; idem, "The Vanquished, Faithful Solidarity and the Marian Symbol: A Hispanic Perspective on Providence," in *On Keeping Providence* (ed. Barbara Doherty and Joan Coultas; Terre Haute: St. Mary of the Woods College Press, 1991), 84-101; and with Sixto J. García, "Lillies of the Field: A Hispanic Theology of Providence and Human Responsibility," in *Proceedings of the Catholic Theological Society of America* 44 (1989): 70-

90. See further: María Pilar Aquino, "Theological Method in U.S. Latino/a Theology: Toward an Intercultural Theology for the Third Millennium," in Espín and Díaz, *From the Heart of Our People*, 6-48; Fernando F. Segovia, "Two Places and No Place on Which to Stand: Mixture and Otherness in Hispanic American Theology," in *Listening. Journal of Religion and Culture* 27, no. 1 (1992): 26-40; Samuel Soliván, "The Need for a North American Hispanic Theology," in Bañuelas, *Mestizo Christianity*, 44-52; Roberto S. Goizueta, "The Significance of U.S. Hispanic Experience for Theological Method," in Goizueta, We are a People! 51-77; idem, *Caminemos con Jesus: Toward a Hispanic/Latino Theology of Accompaniment* (Maryknoll, N.Y.: Orbis, 1995); idem, "U.S. Hispanic Theology and the Challenge of Pluralism," in Deck, *Frontiers of Hispanic Theology*, 1-22; Justo L. González, *Mañana: Christian Theology from a Hispanic Perspective* (Nashville: Abingdon, 1990); idem with Catherine G. González, *Liberation Preaching: The Pulpit and the Oppressed* (Nashville: Abingdon, 1980); Orlando E. Costas, "Evangelism from the Periphery: The Universality of Galilee," in González, *Voces*, 16-23; idem, "What Belongs in a Future Ecumenical Creed? A Free Church Answer," in *An Ecumenical Confession of Faith?* (ed. Hans Küng and Jürgen Moltmann; New York: Seabury, 1979), 72-76; idem, "Predicación evangélica y teología hispana. Los parámetros del tema," in *Predicación evangélica y teología hispana* (ed. Orlando E. Costas; San Diego: Publicaciones de las Américas, 1982), 7-19; Harold J. Recinos, "Mission: A Latino Pastoral Theology," in *Apuntes* 12, no. 3 (1992): 115-26.

15. See Justo L. González, *Santa Biblia: The Bible through Hispanic Eyes* (Nashville: Abingdon, 1996); and idem, "Interpreting the Scriptures from the Hispanic Perspective," in *Engage/Social Action* 6, no. 6 (1978): 13-18. See also: Fernando F. Segovia, "Hispanic American Theology and the Bible: Effective Weapon and Faithful Ally," in Goizueta, *We Are a People!* 21-49; and Jean-Pierre Ruiz, "The Bible and U.S. Hispanic American Theological Discourse: Lessons from a Non-Innocent History," in Espín and Díaz, *From the Heart of Our People*, 100-120.

16. I have tried, unsuccessfully, to uncover a sustained reflection on *people* or *popular* during the first decade of Latina/o theology. The terms were used, and frequently, but no analyses of them appear in the literature. There are some texts on *ecclesiology* or on *church*, in those early years, but nothing on *pueblo*.

17. One recent suggestive study is Gary Riebe-Estrella's "Pueblo and Church," in Espín and Díaz, *From the Heart of Our People*, 172-88. Although *pueblo*, *church*, and *ecclesiology* are all deeply related and mutually implicated, these, nevertheless, remain distinct categories.

18. It is very relevant to emphasize that every one of the first-generation Latina/o theologians were (and still are) very much involved in pastoral work. Although not all are ordained ministers, they have always considered their pastoral work as a crucial "school" and source for their theology.

19. Perhaps, and for many obvious reasons, Catholics have dedicated more time to the study of popular expressions of faith, but Protestants have also become interested in this inescapable Latina/o religious universe. The body of literature on the theological study of popular religion is now truly remarkable and vast. Only as examples, see: Orlando O. Espín, *The Faith of the People: Theological Reflections on Popular Catholicism* (Maryknoll, N.Y.: Orbis, 1997); Roberto S. Goizueta, *Caminemos con Jesús*; Justo L. González, "Reinventing Dogmatics: A Footnote from a Reinvented Protestant," in Espín and Díaz, *From the Heart of Our People*, 217-19; Pablo A. Jiménez, "The Bible: A Hispanic Perspective," in *Teología en Conjunto: A Collaborative Hispanic Protestant Theology* (ed. José D. Rodríguez and Loida I. Martell-Otero; Louisville: Westminster John Knox, 1997), 66-79; Eldin Villafañe, *The Liberating Spirit: Toward an Hispanic American Pentecostal Social Ethic* (Grand Rapids: Eerdmans, 1993).

20. Two examples will suffice (although I am by no means saying that these two are the only theologians to rethink some of their earlier assumptions). In my 1992 article, "Tradition and Popular Religion: An Understanding of the *Sensus Fidelium*" (Deck, *Frontiers of Hispanic Theology*), I approached popular Catholicism in ways that made it methodologically difficult (for example) to ascertain the effect of sin on popular religious expressions. If the reader were to compare that text with my 1999 article, "An Exploration into the Theology of Grace and Sin" (in Espín and Díaz, *From the Heart of Our People*) it would become evident that I have more recently dealt directly with the ambivalence of Latina/o popular religious symbols and with the role of sin in and through symbols and symbol-making. Another author who has rethought some of her earlier assumptions is María Pilar Aquino; compare, for example, her earlier thoughts on culture (in her "Doing Theology from the Perspective of Women," in Goizueta, *We Are a People!*) with her more recent analyses on interculturality (in "Theological Method in U.S. Latino/a Theology," in Espín and Díaz, *From the Heart of Our People*).

21. This point, I think, is not only one of the major contributions of U.S. Latina/o theology to the wider U.S. scholarly community but also one of its distinguishing marks vis-à-vis Latin American and European American theologies.

22. *Apuntes*, published at Perkins School of Theology (Southern Methodist University), and the *Journal of Hispanic/Latino Theology*, published by the Academy of Catholic Hispanic Theologians of the United States. Both periodicals have been adamantly ecumenical from their inceptions.

23. One very important step in this direction has been the use of our research results across denominational lines. Protestants refer to publications authored by Catholics, and Catholics refer to books and articles by Protestants. Examples of this mutually enriching approach are the two recent collaborative books I have been referring to throughout this paper: Rodríguez and Martell-Otero, *Teología en Conjunto*, and Espín and Díaz, *From the Heart of Our People*. Other publications have been authored jointly by Protestants and Catholics; for example: González, *Voces*, and Fernando F. Segovia and Ada M. Isasi-Díaz, eds., *Hispanic/Latino/a Theology: Challenge and Promise* (Minneapolis: Augsburg Fortress, 1996). *Apuntes* and the *Journal of Hispanic/Latino Theology* are also examples of this movement toward an ecumenical Latina/o theology. The Hispanic Summer Program and the Hispanic Theological Initiative, through their distinct institutional means, are also important venues for this upcoming ecumenical theology.

24. There is no doubt in my mind that, among U.S. Latina theologians, María Pilar Aquino and Ada M. Isasi-Díaz have both had an important influence on our theology's increasing openness to and incorporation of critical feminist theory. There is no doubt either that these two scholars represent different approaches and schools of thought. But there are others who are making important contributions: Nancy Pineda-Madrid, Daisy Machado, Lara Medina, Loida Martell-Otero, Michelle González, Jeannette Rodríguez, and Elizabeth Conde-Frazier, among others. One very important collective work, which should be seriously read by all, is María Pilar Aquino, Daisy L. Machado, and Jeannette Rodríguez, eds., *Religion, Feminism and Justice: An Introduction to Latina Feminist Theology* (Austin: University of Texas Press, forthcoming).

25. How many Latino (male) theologians, for example, have read and been methodologically affected by the works of Ana Castillo, Gloria Anzaldúa, Oliva Espín, Adelaida del Castillo, Anna Nieto-Gómez, Cherrie Moraga, Pat Mora, or Sonia Alvarez, to name but a few important Latina thinkers? If we Latino (male) theologians expect the dominant theological academy to change and make the necessary epistemological and methodological shifts, because of what our Latina/o theology is demonstrating, doesn't intellectual honesty demand just as much of us in reference to feminist critical theory, especially as the latter is expressed by Latina thinkers?

26. On this and on what follows immediately, see Fernando F. Segovia's "Theological Education and Scholarship as Struggle: The Life of Racial/Ethnic Minorities in the Profession," in *Journal of Hispanic/Latino Theology* 2, no. 2 (1994): 5-25.

27. See similar definitions of *teología de conjunto* in Espín and Díaz, *From the Heart of Our People*, 263; and in José D. Rodríguez, "On Doing Hispanic Theology," in Rodríguez and Martell-Otero, *Teología en Conjunto*, 11-21.

28. This hope was expressed and justified by Ismael García at a national conference on "Funding Latino/a Theological Research," held in February of 2000 at the Center for the Study of Latino/a Catholicism at the University of San Diego.

29. It is impossible to list here everything that has been written by Latina/o theologians within the past twenty years and within the traditional theological disciplines. Solely as examples of these contributions, I refer the reader to the collective works I have been mentioning throughout this paper: González, *Voces*; Goizueta, *We Are a People!*; Rodríguez and Martell-Otero, *Teología de Conjunto*; Espín and Díaz, *From the Heart of Our People*; Bañuelas, *Mestizo Christianity*; and Segovia and Isasi-Díaz, *Hispanic/Latino Theology*. It is important to consult as well the thematic indexes of *Apuntes* and of the *Journal of Hispanic/Latino Theology*.

30. See Espín, *The Faith of the People*; and idem, "Development of Doctrine and Popular Catholicism," in *Crossing Borders: Mexican Religious Traditions in Twentieth-Century U.S. Catholicism* (ed. Timothy Matovina and Gary Riebe-Estrella; Ithaca, N.Y.: Cornell University Press, forthcoming).

31. Cf. González, "Reinventing Dogmatics."

32. An attempt at epistemological reflection was my "Popular Religion." A suggestive contribution, on a broader subject but with bearing on theological epistemology, is Jorge J. E. Gracia, *Hispanic/Latino Identity: A Philosophical Perspective* (Malden, Mass.: Blackwell, 2000).

33. Cf. Orlando O. Espín, "A 'Multicultural' Church? Theological Reflections from 'Below,'" in *The Multicultural Church: A New Landscape in U.S. Theologies* (ed. W. Cenkner; New York: Paulist Press, 1995), 54-71; Goizueta, *Caminemos con Jesús*; María Pilar Aquino, *Our Cry for Life* (Maryknoll, N.Y.: Orbis, 1993); Alejandro García-Rivera, *The Community of the Beautiful: A Theological Aesthetics* (Collegeville, Minn.: Liturgical Press, 1999); and Otto Maduro, *Mapas para la fiesta* (Buenos Aires: Centro Nueva Tierra, 1992). There is a growing interest, among a number of Latina/o theologians, in the philosophical work of Raúl Fornet-Betancourt; see especially his *Hacia una filosofía intercultural Latinoamericana* (San José, Costa Rica: Publicaciones del DEI, 1994) and his more recent *Interculturalidad y globalización, Ejercicios de crítica filosófica intercultural en el contexto de la globalización neoliberal* (Frankfurt: Verlag für Interkulturelle Kommunikation, 2000). Fornet-Betancourt, professor of philosophy at the University of Bremen (Germany) is very much familiar with U.S. Latina/o theology and has demonstrated a keen interest in its contributions to intercultural epistemology. His epistemological and methodological texts (all from an intercultural perspective) are worth our attention and careful consideration.

34. See notes 23 and 24 above.

35. I am thinking, for example, of the potential methodological and analytic impact of the category of "kyriarchy," proposed by Elisabeth Schüssler Fiorenza in several of her recent publications, and of Téllez's excellent critical analysis of *mestizaje* in the recent book, *¡Muera 'la Gobierna'!*

36. Several colleagues have been making this point recently. The extent and depth of these questions, and the possible means to address them, became clearer to me in conversations with two HTI doctoral awardees: Christopher Tirres and Manuel Mejido (at Harvard University and Emory University, respectively). Miguel de la Torre, a

postdoctoral HTI fellow, also made a similar point in his 1999 presentation at the American Academy of Religion convention. Tirres, Mejido, and De la Torre brought me back to my earlier study of the thought of Italian social theorist Antonio Gramsci. His work on hegemony, conscience, the historical block and ideology, and the ambivalent roles religion plays in them I still find important and pertinent to the future of the U.S. Latina/o theology.

37. As an attempt at this type of theological reflection, see my "Immigration, Territory, and Globalization: Theological Reflections," in *Journal of Hispanic/Latino Theology* 7:3 (2000): 46-59.

38. See references to two of philosopher Raúl Fornet-Betancourt's important works on interculturality in note 33 above. See also Aquino, "Theological Method." See further: Ram Adhar Mall, *Intercultural Philosophy* (Lanham, Md.: Rowman & Littlefield, 2000).

39. Besides references in preceding notes, I must mention also the extremely suggestive book by Carlos M. Pagano-Fernández, *Un modelo de filosofía intercultural: Rodolfo Kusch (1922-1979) Aproximación a la obra del pensador argentino* (Aachen, Germany: Verlag Mainz/Concordia, 1999), where the author offers a rich and persuasive reinterpretation of Kusch's thought from an intercultural perspective and that might prove useful to U.S. Latina/o theologians.

40. Again, Latino feminist theologians have been at the forefront in establishing the need for this critique of our theology (e.g., María Pilar Aquino, Ada M. Isasi-Díaz, Nancy Pineda-Madrid, Michelle González, Teresa Chávez-Sauceda, and others). Some Latino (male) theologians have also called for this critique as well (e.g., Ismael García, Samuel Solivián, Miguel de la Torre, Orlando Espín, Miguel Díaz, and others).

41. Jesús Rodríguez and Anita de Luna have begun to demonstrate some of the pastoral consequences.

42. Justo González and Daisy Machado have been at the forefront of this approach, and some younger scholars, such as Zaida Maldonado Pérez, as well as Alberto Hernández and Dennis R. Hidalgo are following their lead.

43. However, each denomination might theologically or doctrinally explain and justify these time-honored ways.

44. A recent attempt at dealing with some of these issues about tradition and "traditioning," *latinamente*, is my "Development of Doctrine and Popular Catholicism."

45. There are serious issues raised for all Christian theologies (Latina/o ones included) by the contemporary debate on whether tradition (*any* tradition!) is "invented" or "given." A very good examination of the opposing arguments, with an alternative proposal that is potentially very important to Latina/o theology's emphases on community and praxis, appears in Terrence W. Tilley's most recent book, *Inventing Catholic Tradition* (Maryknoll, N.Y.: Orbis, 2000), which, despite its seemingly denominational perspective and title, is deeply ecumenical.

10. LATINA/O CHURCH HISTORY

1. David Thelen, "Of Audiences, Borderlands, and Comparison: Toward the Internationalization of American History," *The Journal of American History* 79, no. 2 (September 1992): 432.

2. Ibid.

3. Joyce Appleby, "Recovering America's Historic Diversity: Beyond Exceptionalism," *The Journal of American History* 79, no. 2 (September 1992): 419.

4. Ibid., 420.

5. David Weber, *Myth and the History of the Hispanic Southwest* (Albuquerque: University of New Mexico Press, 1988), 157.

6. Appleby, "Recovering America's Historic Diversity," 431.

11. LEADERSHIP IN THE LATINA/O COMMUNITY

1. This brief essay stems from an invitation to share in a panel presentation at Hartford Seminary within the topic: "Leadership in the Religious Community: What Is Required Today" (2001). I will use *Hispanic* and *Latino/a* interchangeably to honor those who prefer one over the other. Although at times I may refer to the Latino/Hispanic community as one community, I want to stress the fact that our communities are not homogeneous.

2. According to a report released by the American Association of University Women (2001), Hispanic girls are dropping out of high school at a much higher rate than black or white girls. Furthermore, only 10 percent of Latinas who enter college, also the lowest rate compared to black and white females, tend to complete the four years. Reasons attributed for low dropout rates among Hispanics include Latina teen pregnancy rates that are "higher than for black or white girls; financial pressures to get a job sooner rather than later; and cultural pressures that put family needs above academic ambitions." See David Crary, "Programs Fight for Hispanic Girls," Associated Press (March 31, 2001).

3. I find it interesting that there is no indigenous word for "leader" in the Spanish language. *Líder* in Spanish is borrowed from the English *leader,* as you can very well tell from the pronunciation. This interesting and important tidbit was brought to my attention by Dr. Justo L. González.

4. See Isis Artze, "Character, Competence, Compassion, Community: 3,032 Latinos Reveal What They Value in Their Leaders," in *Hispanic Outlook for Higher Education* (May 7, 2001): 51-53.

5. Ibid., 51.

6. Ibid., 52. It should also be noted that "the study found on significant differences between Latino subgroups, between young adults and seniors, citizens or non-citizens, or between Latinos and Latinas in the qualities they deemed important for leaders to possess" (see p. 53).

7. I realize that many may have problems with the term *servant* for obvious historical reasons. However, I want to stay true to the report of the NCLL, which names "community servant" or "community servanthood" as one of the main characteristics that Latino/Hispanic participants noted was important in a leader. My aim is to explore the religious connotation of this term and its implications for our communities.

8. *Cacique* is an indigenous term (probably of Taino origin) that means "chief" of the community.

9. I am speaking now particularly from my own Latino Protestant experience.

10. In some churches, particularly the more conserving ones, this is done in their childhood when children and youth are given the responsibilities to prepare and lead worship, to testify and preach. While they are given some direction as to how to do this, they are expected to pool the resources from among themselves and to study and pray the sermon to completion. I myself experienced this in my Pentecostal upbringing.

11. Interestingly, the NCLL does not place this quality under "Community Servanthood." This oversight, as I see it, might reflect a weakness in their understanding of the community's use of the metaphor "servant."

12. The NCLL study records that Latinos rated a leadership that is intelligent, educated, and experienced high (see p. 52).

13. Eldin Villafañe does an excellent job in expressing the importance of keeping this in perspective when he refers to systemic injustices, for instance, as part of the "powers and principalities" about which Scripture warns. Any discussion of sin must take place within the framework of the "ongoing cosmic conflict between God and Satan and the restraining power of the Holy Spirit." "An Evangelical Call to a Social Spirituality" in *Seek the Peace of the City: Reflections on Urban Ministry* (Grand Rapids: Eerdmans, 1995), 12-28. The above quote is on p. 19.

14. Unfortunately, the expression also has been conveniently used to the detriment of our *líderes* when communities opt not to give the laborer her or his just rewards (Luke 10:7). This too must be acknowledged and corrected within our communities. What I want to underscore here, however, is the expression's affirmation of the notion of the leader as community servant (and this servanthood as a vocation that God honors through reward).

15. In Edwin I. Hernández, "A Proposal to Establish the Hispanic Church Research Initiative (HRRI)" (Philadelphia: Pew Charitable Trusts, 2001). Hernández was then program officer for The Pew Charitable Trusts.

16. These can include, for instance, those between denominations, churches, seminaries, colleges, high schools, and right down to grammar schools where effects of stereotyping and tracking begin to mold the minds, identities, and aspirations of our young Latina and Latino children.

17. For more on this topic see my articles, "Toward Recruiting and Retaining Latino Students and Faculty: Gauging Commitment," and "Healing an Aversion to Statistics: A Postscript," in *Perspectivas: Ocassional Papers* (Summer 2002).

13. BETWEEN BEING AND HAVING

1. The reflections that I present in this paper are more fully developed in my book *Dignidad: Ethics Through Hispanic Eyes* (Nashville: Abingdon, 1997).

2. One of the clearest classical expressions of the religious foundation of human dignity is presented by the Protestant theologian Domingo Marrero. See in particular his works *Los fundamentos de la libertad* (2nd ed.; San Juan: Talleres Gráficos Interamericanos, 1970); and *Meditaciones de la pasión* (3rd ed.; Rio Piedras: Libreria La Reforma, 1984).

3. To stress the moral and political dimension of dignity is one of the characteristics of Hispanics/Latinos/Caribbeans. Our language clearly and distinctly manifests that no contradiction exists between affirming the religious dimension and the historic dimension of dignity.

4. Two important figures in the struggle for revindication of civil rights are Dr. Martin Luther King, Jr. and César Chavez.

5. See his classical work (originally published in 1937) *The Cost of Discipleship* (New York: Simon & Schuster, 1995).

6. For a more sophisticated analysis of how attitudes of inferiority and superiority foments oppression, see the works of Paulo Freire. Among the classical theologians who have worked with this dynamic, see the work of Reinhold Niebuhr, in particular his work *Moral Man and Immoral Society* and *The Nature and Destiny of Man*.

7. This has been one of the principal contributions of the Latinoamerican liberation theology and of the political theology of Europe, in particular, the works of Johann Baptist Metz and Jürgen Moltmann

8. See the political treaty of Iris Marion Young, *Justice and the Politics of Difference* (Princeton: Princeton University Press, 1990). The work of Justo L. González provides us the biblical dimension of the distinct modes of oppression that Hispanics suffer. See *Santa Biblia: The Bible Through Hispanic Eyes* (Nashville: Abingdon, 1996).

14. BEYOND THE FRONTIER MYTH

1. Walter Benjamin, quoted in David Tracy, *Plurality and Ambiguity: Hermeneutics, Religion, Hope* (San Francisco: Harper and Row, 1987), 69.

2. W. J. Rolfe, ed., *The Complete Poetical Works of Tennyson* (Boston: Houghton Mifflin, 1898), 88-89.

3. Frederick Jackson Turner, *Rereading Frederick Jackson Turner* (New York: Henry Holt, 1994), 101. The Latin American historian Enrique Dussel argues that, as the first European to extend European civilization westward, Christopher Columbus was the first *modern* person. Modernity is defined by the need to conquer and subdue:

Columbus thus initiated modernity. . . . Because of his departure from Latin anti-Muslim Europe, the idea that the Occident was the center of history was inaugurated and came to pervade the European life world. Europe even projected its presumed centrality upon its own origins. Hence, Europeans thought either that Adam and Eve were Europeans or that their story portrayed the original myth of Europe to the exclusion of other cultures.

The Invention of the Americas: Eclipse of "the Other" and the Myth of Modernity (trans. Michael D. Barber; New York: Continuum, 1995), 32.

4. Turner, *Rereading Frederick Jackson Turner*, 32, 60.

5. Ibid., 1.

6. Turner, *Rereading Frederick Jackson Turner*, 96.

7. Ray Allen Billington, *The Genesis of the Frontier Thesis: A Study in Historical Creativity* (San Marino, Calif.: Huntington Library, 1971), 72.

8. As Justo González observes: "Even the name 'America' raises the question: What preposterous conceit allows the inhabitants of a single country to take for themselves the name of an entire hemisphere? What does this say about that country's view of those other nations who share the hemisphere with it?" *Mañana: Christian Theology from a Hispanic Perspective* (Nashville: Abingdon, 1990), 37.

9. Walter LaFeber, *Inevitable Revolutions: The United States in Central America* (New York: W. W. Norton, 1983), 300.

10. Ibid., 33.

11. Ibid., 35

12. Ibid., 36

13. Ibid., 39. The racist worldview underlying these statements is only too clear, especially when one compares U.S. attitudes toward immigration from Mexico with the very different attitudes toward immigration from Europe—at least white, Anglo-Saxon, Protestant Europe.

14. See, for example: Raúl Fernández, *The Mexican-American Border Region: Issues and Trends* (Notre Dame, Ind.: University of Notre Dame Press, 1989); Robert Lee Maril, *Living on the Edge of America: At Home on the Texas-Mexico Border* (College Station: Texas A&M University Press, 1992); Milo Kearney, *Border Cuates: A History of the U.S.-Mexican Twin Cities* (Austin, Tex.: Eakin, 1995); Federico Campbell, *Tijuana: Stories on*

the Border (Berkeley: University of California Press, 1995); Oscar J. Martínez, *Border People: Life and Society in the U.S.-Mexico Borderlands* (Tucson: University of Arizona Press, 1994); Oscar J. Martínez, ed., *U.S.-Mexico Borderlands: Historical and Contemporary Perspectives* (Wilmington, Del.: Scholarly Resources, 1996); Américo Paredes, *Folklore and Culture on the Texas-Mexican Border* (Austin: Center for Mexican American Studies, University of Texas at Austin, 1993); Gloria Anzaldúa, *Borderlands* (San Francisco: Spinsters/Aunt Lute, 1987); Ruth Behar, *Translated Woman: Crossing the Border with Esperanza's Story* (Boston: Beacon, 1993); Cruz Arcelia Tanori Villa, *La mujer migrante y el empleo* (Mexico City: Instituto Nacional de Antropología e Historia, 1989); José Manuel Valenzuela Arce, ed., *Entre la magia y la historia: tradiciones, mitos y leyendas de la frontera* (Tijuana: Programa Cultural de las Fronteras, El Colegio de la Frontera Norte, 1992); Timothy Matovina, *Tejano Religion and Ethnicity* (Austin: University of Texas Press, 1995); idem, *The Alamo Remembered: Tejano Accounts and Perspectives* (Austin: University of Texas Press, 1995).

15. For a personal account of what it means to live *in between*, see Roberto S. Goizueta, *Caminemos con Jesús: Toward a Hispanic/Latino Theology of Accompaniment* (Maryknoll, N.Y.: Orbis, 1995), ch. 1. See also the powerful account of Anzaldúa, *Borderlands*.

16. Different notions of the *border* are already embedded in the English and Spanish languages themselves: "Significantly, in English we say 'border,' and in Spanish, *frontera*. But when we translate the Spanish *frontera* back into English we can come up with either 'border' or 'frontier.' In fact, commonly used Spanish has no equivalent to the English 'frontier' as distinguished from 'border.' " Justo L. González, *Santa Biblia: The Bible Through Hispanic Eyes* (Nashville: Abingdon, 1996), 84.

17. Ibid., 85-86.

18. Ibid., 86. If one compares, for instance, the view of national borders represented by the North American Free Trade Agreement with that represented by California's Propositions 187 and 209, as well as the 1996 Welfare Reform Act denying welfare benefits to documented immigrants and their children, one receives a clear message: the United States will accord a freedom of movement to financial capital that it will not accord to mere human beings. The natural right of capital (*market* forces, the *law* of supply and demand, *free* trade) to expand into new global markets must be affirmed as absolute and inviolable, while the right of labor (i.e., human beings) to do so must be artificially restricted.

19. Johann Baptist Metz, *Faith in History and Society: Toward a Practical Fundamental Theology* (New York: Seabury, 1980), 109.

20. González, *Mañana*, 39.

21. Ibid., 40.

22. On the theological significance of the increasing physical isolation of the city from the suburb, see Goizueta, *Caminemos con Jesús*, 173-211.

23. Virgilio Elizondo, *The Future Is Mestizo: Life Where Cultures Meet* (Bloomington, Ind.: Meyer-Stone, 1988), 80. The connection between the concern for purity and the erection of borders is also observed by Charles H. Lippy, Robert Choquette, and Stafford Poole, who, citing the work of anthropologist Mary Douglas, note that "any group captured by a passion for purity must draw boundaries. It must seek diligently to distinguish between that which will promote the pursuit of holiness and that which endangers such a pursuit. It must avoid contamination at all costs, lest pollution infect and ultimately destroy true purity." *Christianity Comes to the Americas: 1492–1776* (New York: Paragon House, 1992), 268.

24. González, *Santa Biblia*, 86-87.

25. González, *Mañana*, 40.

26. Such a recognition is not, moreover, a mere utopian ideal. As anyone who has lived in or traveled to Tijuana, El Paso, or Laredo knows, the actual reality of life on the border is very different from that portrayed in the frontier myth. In towns and cities all along the Rio Grande, a truly border culture is emerging in the shadows of the southern frontier's barbed-wire fences and stone walls:

> Today, the borderlands between the U.S. and Mexico form the cradle of a new humanity. It is the meeting ground of ancient civilizations that have never met before. Old cultural borders are giving way and a new people is emerging. . . .
> . . . The borders no longer mark the end limits of a country, a civilization, or even a hemisphere, but the starting points of a new space populated by a new human group. (Elizondo, *The Future Is Mestizo*, xiv-xv)

27. This common Spanish word denoting persons who come from the United States would literally be translated as *United Statesans*. In English, of course, no such word exists; *estadounidenses* are, simply, *Americans*.

15. TOWARD A POSTCOLONIAL HOMILETIC

1. For an introduction to this debate see Joseph Natoli and Linda Hutcheon, *A Postmodern Reader* (Albany: State University of New York Press, 1993), vii-xiv.

2. Marc Augé, *Los "no lugares," espacios del anonimato: Una Antropología de la sobre-modernidad* (Barcelona: Editorial Gedisa, 1996); *Hacia una antropología de los mundos contemporáneos* (Barcelona: Editorial Gedisa, 1996).

3. For a comprehensive introduction see Bart Moore-Gilbert, *Postcolonial Theory: Contexts, Practices, Politics* (London: Verso, 1997). See also Bill Ashcroft, Gareth Griffiths, and Helen Tiffin, eds., *The Post-Colonial Studies Reader* (London: Routledge, 1995).

4. These definitions have been taken from Bill Ashcroft, Gareth Griffiths, and Helen Tiffin, *Key Concepts in Post-Colonial Studies* (London: Routledge, 1998).

5. In this section we follow Ania Loomba, *Colonialism / Postcolonialism* (London: Routledge, 1998).

6. For a full discussion of this topic, see Robert J. C. Young, *Colonial Desire: Hybridity in Theory, Culture, and Race* (London: Routledge, 1995).

7. For a comprehensive introduction to this topic see Hughes Portelli, *Gramsci y el bloque histórico* (Mexico City: Siglo Veintiuno Editores, 1973).

8. Virgilio Elizondo, *Christianity and Culture: An Introduction to Pastoral Theology and Ministry for the Bicultural Community* (San Antonio: Mexican American Cultural Center, 1975); *Galilean Journey: The Mexican-American Promise* (Maryknoll, N.Y.: Orbis, 1983); *The Future Is Mestizo: Life Where Cultures Meet* (New York: Crossroad, 1992).

9. Aimé Cesaire, *Cahiér du rétours au pays natal* (Columbus: Ohio State University, 2000).

10. Léopold Sédar Senghor, "Negritude: A Humanism of the Twentieth Century," in *Colonial Discourse and Post-Colonial Theory: A Reader* (ed. Patrick Williams and Laura Chrisman; New York: Columbia University Press, 1994).

11. Albert Memmi, *Retrato del Colonizado* (Buenos Aires: Ediciones de la Flor, 1969).

12. Frantz Fanon, *Los Condenados de la Tierra* (Mexico City: Fondo de Cultura Económica, 1963); *Black Skin, White Masks* (New York: Grove, 1967).

13. On cultural hybridization see Young, *Colonial Desire*, and Homi K. Bhabha, *The Location of Culture* (London: Routledge, 1994).

14. Fernando F. Segovia, "The Text as Other: Towards a Hispanic American Hermeneutic" in *Text and Experience: Towards a Cultural Exegesis of the Bible* (ed. Daniel Smith-Christopher; Sheffield: Sheffield Academic Press, 1995), 276-98; "Toward a Hermeneutics of the Diaspora: A Hermeneutics of Otherness and Engagement," in *Social Location and Biblical Interpretation in the United States* (ed. Fernando F. Segovia and Mary Ann Tolbert; vol. 1 of *Reading from This Place;* Minneapolis: Augsburg Fortress, 1995), 57-73; "In the World but Not of It: Exile as Locus for a Theology of the Diaspora," in *Hispanic/Latino Theology* (ed. Ada María Isasi-Díaz and Fernando F. Segovia; Minneapolis: Augsburg Fortress, 1996), 195-217.

15. Ada María Isasi-Díaz, "By the Rivers of Babylon: Exile as a Way of Life," in Segovia and Tolbert, *Reading from This Place*, 1:149-63.

16. See, for example, Leticia Guardiola, "Borderless Women and Borderless Texts: A Cultural Reading of Matthew 15:21-28," *Semeia* 78 (1997): 69-81.

17. *The Development of Christianity in the Latin Caribbean* (Grand Rapids: Eerdmans, 1969).

18. *Historia del Cristianismo* (revised in 2 vols; Miami: Unilit, 1994).

19. *Mañana: Christian Theology from a Hispanic Perspective* (Nashville: Abingdon, 1990).

20. Justo L. González, et al., *Desde el reverso: Materiales para la historia de la Iglesia* (Mexico City: Publicaciones El Faro, 1993).

21. Justo L. González, "Hispanics in the United States," *Listening* 27, no. 1 (Winter 1992): 7-16.

22. Justo L. González, *Christian Thought Revisited: Three Types of Theology* (Nashville: Abingdon, 1989).

23. Justo L. González, *Every Tribe and Nation: Theology at the Ethnic Roundtable* (Nashville: Abingdon, 1992).

24. Justo L. González, "Metamodern Aliens in Postmodern Jerusalem," in Isasi-Díaz and Segovia, *Hispanic/Latino Theology*, 340-50.

25. Ibid., 346.

26. Ibid., 347.

27. Ibid., 348.

28. Justo L. González, *Santa Biblia: The Bible Through Hispanic Eyes* (Nashville: Abingdon, 1996).

29. Justo L. González, *Hechos* (Miami, Editorial Caribe, 1992).

30. Justo L. and Catherine G. González, *Vision at Patmos: A Study of the Book of Revelation* (Nashville: Abingdon, 1978); *Revelation* (Louisville: Westminster/John Knox, 1997).

31. Justo L. González, *For the Healing of the Nations: The Book of Revelation in an Age of Cultural Conflict* (Maryknoll, N.Y.: Orbis, 1999).

32. Justo L. and Catherine G. González, *Liberation Preaching: The Bible and the Oppressed* (Nashville: Abingdon, 1980).

33. Justo L. and Catherine G. González, "The Larger Context," in *Preaching as a Social Act: Theology and Practice* (ed. Arthur Van Seters; Nashville: Abingdon, 1988).

34. Justo L. and Catherine G. González, *The Liberating Pulpit* (Nashville: Abingdon, 1994).

35. Gayatri Chakravorti Spivak, "Can the Subaltern Speak?" in Williams and Chrisman, *Colonial Discourse and Post-Colonial Theory*, 66-111.

16. DOING THEOLOGY IN SPANISH

1. David Tracy identifies the rationalistic tendencies inherent in the quest for totality found in modernism. *On Naming the Present: God, Hermeneutics, and the Church* (Maryknoll, N.Y.: Orbis, 1994), 7-22. But similar tendencies can also be identified in post-modernism as it fails to engage in ethico-political dialogue and continues to be self-absorbed in its own paradigms and philosophical language without listening to the emerging voices of the others for whom they supposedly made room. According to Tracy, postmodernity seeks the inclusion of the other, but continues to retain a theoretical-reflective paradigm defined by Western European standards. Roberto S. Goizueta points to the inherent dangers in postmodernity and its Western European modernist legacy as an inability to empower the critique of the marginalized world. *Caminemos con Jesús: Toward a Hispanic/LatinoTheology of Accompaniment* (Maryknoll, N.Y.: Orbis, 1995), 164-65.

2. The works of Alex García-Rivera, Ismael García, Roberto S. Goizueta, and Ada María Isasi-Díaz, among others, provide ample examples of Hispanic theologians and ethicists who are engaging traditional Western European models of theological scholarship in a serious and constructive manner.

3. In an effort to connect with European philosophical traditions in making this claim, let me appeal to the fallacy of misplaced concreteness as articulated by Alfred North Whitehead in *Modes of Thought* (New York: Macmillan, 1938, 1966), 18. Whitehead argues against the tendency in philosophy to abstract reductionism, mistaking the abstraction for the complexity of the concrete actuality. Other European theologians have echoed this argument. In "Theology in the Modern Age," *Concilium* 171 (1984): 33-34, Johann Baptist Metz, argues that theology has been plagued by a reductionism driven by abstract cognitive rationalism derived in part from the world of science.

4. Justo L. González, *Mañana: Christian Theology from a Hispanic Perspective* (Nashville: Abingdon, 1990), 75-87.

5. Ibid., 75, 85-87.

6. I make some preliminary arguments in this respect in my book, *Jesus Is My Uncle: Christology from a Hispanic Perspective* (Nashville: Abingdon, 1999), 16-22.

7. Ibid., 19.

8. Martin Luther advocates the need to do theology with humility, recognizing one's own limitations and the tentativeness of one's theology in the preface to the Wittenberg Edition of his German writings. *Martin Luther's Basic Theological Writings* (ed. Timothy F. Lull; Minneapolis: Augsburg Fortress, 1989), 63-68.

9. I find myself taking more of an Aristotelian stance than a Platonic one in this statement, but I would caution the reader that it is not my intent to build upon Aristotle. Rather, I find myself at a nexus of several philosophical traditions, including Whitehead's notion that speculation begins with the concrete and must return to the concrete particularity. Liberation theology, postmodern philosophies, and Tillich's understanding of the concrete-abstract dialectic also influence me.

10. Paul Tillich, in several of his writings, makes reference to how divine revelation always occurs in the concrete locus of culture. He sums it best and concisely in *Biblical Religion and the Quest for Ultimate Reality* (Chicago: University of Chicago Press, 1955), 3-5.

11. Roberto S. Goizueta makes the argument that Latin American liberation theology does not merely provide new theological content, it constitutes a new way of doing theology. *Liberation, Method, and Dialogue: Enrique Dussel and North American Theological Discourse* (Atlanta: Scholars, 1988), 23. Hence, I prefer to speak of Hispanic theological methodology as "doing" theology.

12. See Clodovis Boff's article on the methodology of liberation theologies,

"Epistemology and Method of Liberation Theology," in *Mysterium Liberationis: Fundamental Concepts of Liberation Theology* (ed. Ignacio Ellacuría and Jon Sobrino; Maryknoll, N.Y.: Orbis, 1993), 74-84.

13. González, *Mañana*, 86-87

14. Ada María Isasi-Díaz, *En la Lucha / In the Struggle: A Hispanic Women's Liberation Theology* (Minneapolis: Augsburg Fortress, 1993), 65. For further information on Harold Garfinkel's argument, see also his book, *Studies in Ethnomethodology* (Cambridge: Polity, 1984), 1-115.

15. Isasi-Díaz, *En la Lucha*, 65-67.

16. Isasi-Díaz makes the point that in *mujerista* theology, otherness and difference embrace specificity and heterogeneity, not as relativism or as a universal category but in the concrete particularity and ambiguity of life. *Mujerista Theology* (Maryknoll, N.Y.: Orbis, 1996), 81.

17. Ibid., 68-72.

18. Isasi-Díaz, *En la Lucha*, 67n11.

19. González, *Mañana*, 28-30.

20. Ibid., 28. González's actual translation for the townspeople's cry is "Fuenteovejuna, all are one." However, as I have argued in my paper, "Doing Theology as Dialogue in the Hispanic Community," *Journal of Hispanic/Latino Theology* (February 1998), that I believe that the term "all at one" is a plausible translation of the Spanish that better reflects the collaborative work of the community, without diminishing concrete individual identity by subsuming them in a singular collective.

21. González, *Mañana*, 29.

22. Ibid., 85.

23. Ibid., 29-30.

24. Ibid., 29.

25. Paul Tillich also acknowledges the communal and ecclesial nature of theology in *Systematic Theology* (Chicago: University of Chicago Press, 1951), 1:48-52.

26. For a more complete description of dialogic theology in Hispanic theology see my article, "Doing Theology as Dialogue."

27. In "Mathematics and the Good," Alfred North Whitehead explains the dynamics of a process in which the finite and the infinite exist in mutual relationship, the finite providing definition and the infinite providing the context that prevents the finite from existing in isolation. I allude to this dynamic and the hermeneutical value inherent in it as expressed by Whitehead. The infinite acquires meaning only in definition, but definition renders it finite. Yet, by participating in the infinite, the finite acquires context and a life beyond its own definition. In applying this to theology, I would say that the particular is what truly provides us with meaning and the dialogue allows the meaning to exist in a relational context that permits it to transcend beyond itself.

28. Tillich, *Systematic Theology*, 1:53-55.

17. SPIRIT WITHOUT BORDERS

1. Murray W. Dempster, Byron D. Klaus, and Douglas Petersen, eds., *The Globalization of Pentecostalism: A Religion Made to Travel* (Oxford: Regnum Books International, 1999); see also, Karla Poewe, ed., *Charismatic Christianity as a Global Culture* (Columbia: University of South Carolina Press, 1994); Walter J. Hollenweger, *Pentecostalism: Origins and Developments Worldwide* (Peabody, Mass.: Hendrickson, 1997).

2. Vinson Synan, *The Century of the Holy Spirit: 100 Years of Pentecostal and Charismatic Renewal, 1901–2001* (Nashville: Thomas Nelson, 2001), 372.

3. As quoted in Vinson Synan, *The Spirit Said 'Grow'* (Monrovia, Calif.: MARC, 1992), ii.

4. As quoted in Eldin Villafañe, *The Liberating Spirit: Toward an Hispanic American Pentecostal Social Ethic* (Grand Rapids: Eerdmans, 1993), 85.

5. André Corten and Ruth Marshall-Fratani, eds., *Between Babel and Pentecost: Transnational Pentecostalism in Africa and Latin America* (Bloomington: Indiana University Press, 2001), back cover.

6. Juan Sepúlveda, "Reflections on the Pentecostal Contribution to the Mission of the Church in Latin America," *Journal of Pentecostal Theology* 1 (1992): 97.

7. Carmelo E. Alvarez, "Panorama Histórico de los Pentecostalismos Latinoamericanos y Caribeños," in *En la Fuerza del Espíritu: Los Pentecostales en América Latina; un desafío a las iglesias históricas* (ed. Benjamín Gutiérrez; Guatemala: AIPRAL y CELEP, 1995), 37-38.

8. Villafañe, *Liberating Spirit*, 89.

9. Mark Searing, "A Theology of Urban Ministry to Reach: Eye of the Needle People in Latin America" (unpublished paper, December 2001).

10. R. Andrew Chesnut, *Born Again in Brazil: The Pentecostal Boom and the Pathogens of Poverty* (New Brunswick, N.J.: Rutgers University Press, 1997), 3.

11. Synan, *Century of the Holy Spirit*, 309.

12. Ibid., 308.

13. Christian Lalive d'Epinay, *Haven of the Masses: A Study of the Pentecostal Movement in the Churches* (London: Lutterworth, 1969).

14. Robert Mapes Anderson, *Vision of the Disinherited: The Making of American Pentecostalism* (New York: Oxford University Press, 1979).

15. Renato Pobleto and Thomas F. O'Dea, "Anomie and the 'Quest for Community': The Formation of Sects Among the Puerto Ricans of New York," *American Catholic Sociological Review* (Spring 1960).

16. Emilio Willems, *Followers of the New Faith* (Nashville: Vanderbilt University Press, 1967).

17. David Stoll, *Is Latin America Turning Protestant?* (Berkeley: University of California Press, 1990).

18. David Martin, *Tongues of Fire* (Oxford: Basil Blackwell, 1990).

19. Chesnut, *Born Again*, 6.

20. Ibid., 169-70.

21. See Luther P. Gerlach and Virginia H. Hinse, "Five Factors Crucial to the Growth and Spread of a Modern Religious Movement," *Journal for the Scientific Study of Religion* 7 (Spring 1968): 38.

22. Harvey Cox, *Fire from Heaven: The Rise of Pentecostal Spirituality and the Reshaping of Religion in the Twenty-first Century* (Reading, Mass.: Addison-Wesley, 1995), 81.

23. Ibid.

24. Ibid., 86.

25. Eldin Villafañe, " 'Salsa' Christianity: Reflections on the Latino Church in the Barrio," in *A Prayer for the City: Further Reflections on Urban Ministry* (Austin, TX: AETH, 2001), 35-51.

26. Frank Macchia, "Sighs Too Deep for Words: Towards a Theology of Glossolalia," *Journal of Pentecostal Theology* 1 (1992): 52; for an excellent scientific study on glossolalia, see H. Newton Maloney and A. Adams Lovekin, *Glossolalia: Behavioral Science Perspective on Speaking in Tongues* (New York: Oxford University Press, 1985).

27. Villafañe, *Prayer for the City*, 48-49.

28. Villafañe, *Liberating Spirit*, 129.

29. Donald W. Dayton, *Theological Roots of Pentecostalism* (Peabody, Mass.: Hendrickson, 1987).

30. Villafañe, *Liberating Spirit*, 110-32; see also, Samuel Solivan, *The Spirit, Pathos, and Liberation: Toward an Hispanic Pentecostal Theology* (Sheffield, England: Sheffield Academic Press, 1998).

31. Steven J. Land, *Pentecostal Spirituality: A Passion for the Kingdom* (Sheffield, England: Sheffield Academic Press, 1993), 113.

32. Cox, *Fire from Heaven*, 82.

33. Richard Shaull, "Salvation: A New Experience of Liberation for the Poor," in Richard Shaull and Waldo Cesar, *Pentecostalism and the Future of the Christian Churches: Promises, Limitations, Challenges* (Grand Rapids: Eerdmans, 2000), 153.

34. See Justo L. González, "Espiritualidad Política," *Apuntes* 3, no. 1 (1983): 3-9; and "Life in the Spirit" in Justo González, *Mañana: Christian Theology from a Hispanic Perspective* (Nashville: Abingdon, 1990), 157-67.

18. RELIGIOUS EDUCATION IN AN IMMIGRANT COMMUNITY

1. Mary Field Belenky, et al., *Women's Ways of Knowing: The Development of Self, Voice and Mind* (New York: Basic Books, 1986), 18.

2. Samuel Solivan, "Teología y Ministerio: Diálogo y Reflexión" (conference of the Orlando E. Costas Hispanic Program, Andover Newton Theological School, Newton, Mass., April 1995).

3. Samuel Solivan, "Sources of a Hispanic/Latino American Theology: A Pentecostal Perspective," in *Hispanic/Latino Theology: Challenge and Promise* (ed. Ada María Isasi-Díaz and Fernando F. Segovia; Minneapolis: Augsburg Fortress, 1996), 145-46.

4. Ibid., 146. This was confirmed by Brixeida Marquez, Ana Falcon, and Sandra Cruz-Serrano, three women who participated in a panel of Hispanic women in ministry at Hartford Seminary held in March 1996. For further discussion also see Loida I. Martell-Otero, "Women Doing Theology: Una Perspectiva Evangélica," *Apuntes* 14, no. 3 (Fall 1994): 67-85.

5. Elizabeth Conde-Frazier, "Hispanic Protestant Spirituality," in *Teología de Conjunto: A Collaborative Hispanic Protestant Theology* (ed. José David Rodríguez and Loida I. Martell-Otero; Louisville: Westminster John Knox, 1997), 141.

6. Jürgen Moltmann, *The Church in the Power of the Spirit* (trans. Margaret Kohl; Minneapolis: Augsburg Fortress, 1993; originally published 1977), 7.

7. Justo L. González, *The Theological Education of Hispanics* (New York: The Fund for Theological Education, 1988).

8. Ibid., 69.

9. Roberto Rodríguez, "President's Hispanic Education Commission Releases Report," *Black Issues in Higher Education* (October 1996): 6-7.

10. See José A. Caraballo, "A Certificate Program for a Hispanic Clergy and a Case Study with Projections" (DMin diss., Drew University, 1983), 99.

11. Ibid., 100.

12. For further reading on grounded theory methodology see Anselm Strauss and Juliet Corbin, *Basics of Qualitative Research: Grounded Theory Procedures and Techniques* (Newbury Park, Calif.: Sage Publications, 1990).

13. This category was named by one of the Bible institutes that participated in the study.

14. Samuel Soliván, personal interview, Newton, Mass., September 16, 1997. The following section contains insights gleaned from a conversation with Samuel Soliván about these issues.

15. Interestingly, the issue of expertise did not arise in the discussions about authority. Expertise is related to spiritual authority since it is believed that knowledge of the things of God is revealed by the Holy Spirit to those who have a relationship with the Holy Spirit (1 Cor 2:11-16). Even at the Bible institute where the pastor and director of the institute has an MDiv and is working on a DMin, this dimension of authority was not named. It is assumed, however, that the pastor of the church will gain understanding about the tradition and become able in his or her handling of the Scriptures (2 Tim 2:15). This is necessary for one to become ordained and thus related to one's authority. Perhaps because it is assumed, it was not openly named.

16. Marian Velázquez de la Cadena, Edward Gray, and John L. Iribas, *The New Revised Velázquez Spanish and English Dictionary* (Clinton, N.J.: New Win Publishing, 1985), 124. For a fuller understanding of Taino tribal organization and hierarchy see Jalil Sued-Badillo, *La Mujer Indígena y su Sociedad* (San Juan, Puerto Rico: Editorial Cultural, 1989).

17. *New Revised Velázquez Spanish and English Dictionary*, 152.

18. See Parker J. Palmer, *To Know as We Are Known: A Spirituality of Education* (San Francisco: Harper & Row, 1983), 6-10. Palmer links knowledge with compassion and love. This is in contrast with how knowledge is gained through applied empirical and analytical study where one seeks to control a body of knowledge. The knowledge is connected to being known by God and leads beyond ourselves to being in community with one another. It moves one toward love for society and the world. In his discussion about epistemology, Robert Pazmiño comments on Palmer's understanding of knowledge and relates it to Paul's description of knowledge in 1 Cor 8:1-3. See Robert W. Pazmiño, *Foundational Issues in Christian Education: An Introduction in Evangelical Perspective* (2nd ed.; Grand Rapids: Baker Books, 1997), 94.

19. Mary C. Boys, "Access to Traditions and Transformation," in *Tradition and Transformation in Religious Education* (ed. Padraic O'Hare; Birmingham: Religious Education Press, 1979), 14. Also see *Educating in Faith: Maps and Visions* (Kansas City: Sheed and Ward, 1989), 193-205; and Walter Brueggeman, *The Creative Word: Canon as a Model for Biblical Education* (Philadelphia: Fortress, 1982).

20. Boys, *Educating in Faith*, 194.

21. Ibid., 20.

22. See Samuel Soliván, "Orthopathos: Prolegomenon for a North American Hispanic Theology" (PhD diss., New York, 1993) and *The Spirit, Pathos and Liberation: Toward an Hispanic Pentecostal Theology* (Sheffield, England: Sheffield Academic Press, 1998).

23. Ibid., 91.

24. Ibid.

25. "the complaint, the scream, the pain, the clamor of the people" (Bible Institute #2, Participant #10).

26. Samuel Soliván, personal interview, January 28, 1998. I believe this is reinforced in countries where there is political repression and violence.

27. Ibid. Walter Brueggemann calls this the language of transformative imagination. He also shows how the prophets embrace the pathos. See Walter Brueggemann, *A Prophetic Imagination* (Philadelphia: Fortress, 1978). Also see chapter 3 of Walter Brueggemann, *The Creative Word: Canon as a Model for Biblical Education* (Philadelphia: Fortress, 1982).

28. Other passages are Lamentations, Job, and the Psalms.

29. Soliván, "Orthopathos," 235.

30. See Benjamin Alicea-Lugo, "Salsa y Adobo: Latino/Latina Contributions to Theological Education" *USQR* 52 (1998): 129-44.

31. See Linda Alcoff and Elizabeth Potter, eds., *Feminist Epistemologies* (New York: Routledge, 1993).

32. Orlando E. Costas, *Christ Outside the Gate: Mission Beyond Christendom* (Maryknoll, N.Y.: Orbis, 1982), 169.

33. Robert W. Pazmiño, *Latin American Journey: Insights for Christian Education in North America* (Cleveland: United Church Press, 1994), 102.

34. Ibid., 119.

19. THE MANTLE OF MENTORSHIP

1. Laurent A. Daloz, *Effective Teaching and Mentoring: Realize the Transformational Power of Adult Learning Experiences* (San Francisco: Jossey-Bass, 1986), 17.

2. Gordon F. Shea, *Mentoring: Helping Employees Reach Their Full Potential* (New York: American Management Association, 1994), 13.

3. Ibid.

4. John Carruthers, "The Principles and Practices of Mentoring," in *The Return of the Mentor* (ed. Brian J. Caldwell and Earl M. A. Carter; Washington, D.C.: Falmer Press, 1993), 9.

5. Chip R. Bell, *Managers as Mentors: Building Partnerships for Learning* (San Francisco: Berrett-Koehler, 1996), 7.

6. Shea, *Mentoring*, 13.

7. Jeffrey A. Fager, "Back to the Past: Two Instances of Mentoring in the Hebrew Bible," *International Journal of Mentoring* 2 (Winter 1988): 37.

8. Fay Head and Marilynne Miles Gray, "The Legacy of Mentor: Insights into Western History, Literature and the Media," *International Journal of Mentoring* 2 (Winter 1988): 27.

9. Fager, "Back to the Past," 35-37.

10. Jim Ryan, "Biblical Models for Mentoring," *Church Administration* (December 1995): 8.

11. Justo L. González, *Mentors as Instruments of God's Call* (Nashville: General Board of Higher Education and Ministry, The United Methodist Church, 1992), 15.

12. Francisco O. Garcia-Treto, "Naomi and Ruth: A Model for Mentors," *Apuntes* 17 (Winter 1997): 109.

13. Ibid., 109-10.

14. Ron Lee Davis, *Mentoring the Strategy of the Master* (Nashville: Thomas Nelson, 1991), 207; and Ryan, "Biblical Models for Mentoring," 10.

15. Jean-Pierre Ruiz, "Luke 1:39-56: Mary's Visit to Elizabeth as a Biblical Instance of Mentoring," *Apuntes* 17 (Winter 1997): 104.

16. González, *Mentors as Instruments of God's Call*, 35-38.

17. Efrain Agosto, "The Apostle Paul and Mentoring: Formal and Informal Approaches," *Apuntes* 18 (Spring 1998): 3-4.

18. Ibid., 10.

19. Davis, *Mentoring the Strategy of the Master*, 44-45; and Ryan, "Biblical Models for Mentoring," 9-10.

20. Davis, *Mentoring the Strategy of the Master*, 44.

21. Paul D. Stanley and J. Robert Clinton, *Connecting: The Mentoring Relationships You Need to Succeed in Life* (Colorado Springs, Colo.: NavPress Publishing, 1992), 33.

22. Ibid., 32.

23. Sondra Higgins Matthaei, "Faith-Mentoring in the Classroom," *Religious Education* 86 (Fall 1991): 540.

24. Bobb Biehl, *Mentoring: Confidence in Finding a Mentor and Becoming One* (Nashville: Broadman & Holman, 1996), 19.

25. Ibid., 22.

26. González, *Mentors as Instruments of God's Call*, 11, 12, and 25.

27. J. Ward Walker, "Mentoring in the Ministry—What's In It for Me?" *Church Administration* (December 1995): 14.

28. Joseph S. Batluck, "The Challenge of Mentoring," *Military Chaplain's Review* (Spring 1992): 15.

20. THE VOICES OF HIS STUDENTS

1. Edwin Hernández and Kenneth Davis, *Reconstructing the Sacred Tower* (Scranton, Pa.: University of Scranton Press, forthcoming).

21. HISPANIC PROTESTANT CONVERSIONS

1. Raymond F. Paloutzian, *Invitation to the Psychology of Religion* (Glenview, Ill.: Scott, Foresman, and Co., 1983), 140.

2. Lewis Rambo, *Understanding Religious Conversion* (New Haven, Conn.: Yale University Press, 1993).

22. LATINA/O THEOLOGY

1. Tim Stafford, "The New Theologians," *Christianity Today* (February 8, 1999): 31.

2. Justo L. González, *Mañana: Christian Theology from a Hispanic Perspective* (Nashville: Abingdon, 1990), 74.

3. William A. Dyrness, An Inaugural address, Pasadena, Calif., 1991.

4. González, *Mañana*, 29.

5. Ibid., 34.

6. Ibid., 29.

7. Eugene H. Peterson, *Leap Over a Wall: Earthy Spirituality for Everyday Christians* (New York: HarperCollins, 1997), 54.

8. Mouw, Richard J., *Uncommon Decency: Christian Civility in an Uncivil World* (Downers Grove, Ill.: InterVarsity, 1992), 77.

9. David Abalos, "Choosing Between the Languages of Oppression and Liberation," *Hispanic Outlook in Higher Education* 9, no. 17 (1999): 19.

10. Ibid.

11. González, *Mañana*, 79.

12. Ibid., 36.

13. Ibid., 127.

23. LIBERATIVE EDUCATIONAL PRACTICE

1. Robert W. Pazmiño, "Double Dutch: Reflections of a Hispanic North American on Multicultural Religious Education," *Apuntes* 9 (Summer 1988): 27-37.

2. Lawrence A. Cremin, *Traditions of American Education* (New York: Basic Books, 1976).

3. Bernard Bailyn, *Education in the Forming of American Society: Needs and Opportunities for Study* (New York: W. W. Norton, 1960), 45.

4. Ibid., 14.

5. Robert W. Pazmiño, *Latin American Journey: Insights for Christian Education in North America* (Cleveland: United Church Press, 1994), 117.

6. Orlando E. Costas, *Christ Outside the Gate: Mission Beyond Christendom* (Maryknoll, N.Y.: Orbis, 1982).

7. Norman G. Wilson, "Pedagogical Expectations of Hispanic Americans: Insights for Leadership Training," *Christian Education Journal* 1 NS (1997): 68-69.

8. See Stephen L. Carter, *The Culture of Disbelief: How American Law and Politics Trivialize Religious Devotion* (New York: Anchor Books, 1994).